GOVERNANCE, EQUITY, AND GLOBAL MARKETS

Governance, Equity, and Global Markets

The Annual Bank Conference on Development Economics–Europe

Edited by
JOSEPH E. STIGLITZ
PIERRE-ALAIN MUET

OXFORD
UNIVERSITY PRESS

OXFORD
UNIVERSITY PRESS

Great Clarendon Street, Oxford OX2 6DP

Oxford University Press is a department of the University of Oxford.

It furthers the University's objective of excellence in research, scholarship,
and education by publishing worldwide in
Oxford New York

Athens Auckland Bangkok Bogotá Buenos Aires Cape Town
Chennai Dar es Salaam Delhi Florence Hong Kong Istanbul Karachi
Kolkata Kuala Lumpur Madrid Melbourne Mexico City Mumbai
Nairobi Paris São Paulo Shanghai Singapore Taipei Tokyo Toronto Warsaw
with associated companies in Berlin Ibadan

Oxford is a registered trade mark of Oxford University Press
in the UK and in certain other countries

Published in the United States
by Oxford University Press Inc., New York

British Library Cataloguing in Publication Data

Data available

Library of Congress Cataloguing in Publication Data

Data available

ISBN 0–19–924155–4

1 3 5 7 9 10 8 6 4 2

Typeset by Florence Production Ltd,
Stoodleigh, Devon
Printed in Great Britain
on acid-free paper by
Biddles Ltd, Guildford and King's Lynn

Acknowledgements

Our special acknowledgements are to Jean-François Rischard (Vice-President Europe, World Bank), who took the initiative of organizing the first ABCDE–Europe Conference in Paris and who invited the French Conseil d'Analyse Économique to co-organize it with the World Bank. We also thank Boris Pleskovic (World Bank), Gilles Garcia (World Bank), Hélène de Largentaye (Secretary General of the CAE), François Bourguignon (Member of the CAE), Jean Pisani-Ferry (Adviser to the French Minister of Finance, Member of the CAE), and Laurence Tubiana (Member of the CAE), who, as members of the Scientific Committee, coordinated the conference, elaborated the programme, and worked on the proceedings. We also wish to thank Kathie Beau and Lisa Dacosta, who, as members of the CAE staff, played an important part in the publication of these proceedings.

Contents

New Thinking on Security in Labour Markets

Power and Corruption

Part Two. Equity, Public Goods, and Global Governance

Poverty

Social Insurance and Social Security Reforms

Regional Integration

Environment

List of Contributors

MICHEL AGLIETTA, Centre d'Études Prospectives et d'Informations Internationales (CEPII) and Conseil d'Analyse Économique (CAE)

ANTHONY B. ATKINSON, Nuffield College, Oxford, and CAE

ORAZIO P. ATTANASIO, University College London, Institute for Fiscal Studies, National Bureau of Economic Research (NBER), and Centre for Economic Policy Research (CEPR)

GUISEPPE BERTOLA, European University Institute, Florence, University of Turin, CEPR, and NBER

OLIVIER BLANCHARD, Massachusetts Institute for Technology (MIT) and CAE

FRANÇOIS BOURGUIGNON, World Bank, DELTA, and CAE

OLIVIER CADOT, University of Lausanna and CEPR

ALESSANDRO CIGNO, University of Florence

DANIEL COHEN, École Normale Supérieure, Centre d'Études Prospectives d'Économie Mathématique Appliquées à la Planification (CEPREMAP), CEPR, and CAE

URI DADUSH, World Bank

PAUL DE GRAUWE, University of Leuven and CEPR

JAIME DE MELO, University of Geneva, Centre d'Études et de Recherches sur le Développement International (CERDI), and CEPR

STEFAN DERCON, Catholic University of Leuven and Oxford University

JUAN J. DOLADO, University Carlos III, Madrid

DIANE ELSON, United Nations Development Fund for Women (UNIFEM) and University of Manchester

JOHN S. FLEMMING, Oxford University

OLIVIER GODARD, École Polytechnique (Econometrics Laboratory), Paris

PIERRE-HENRI GOUYON, École Polytechnique (Biology Department), Palaiseau

OLIVER HART, Harvard University

CLAUDE HENRY, École Polytechnique (Econometrics Laboratory), Paris

ANDRÁS INOTAI, Institute for World Economics, Hungarian Academy of Sciences

PIERRE JACQUEMOT, Ministry of Foreign Affairs, France

JEAN-JACQUES LAFFONT, Insitut d'Économie Industrielle (IDEI), Toulouse, and CAE

PATRICK LAGADEC, École Polytechnique (Econometrics Laboratory), Paris

JOSÉ LUIS MACHINEA, FADE, Argentina

PIERRE-ALAIN MUET, Adviser to the Prime Minister of France and Chairman of the CAE

MUSTAPHA K. NABLI, Chief Economist, World Bank

PETER NEARY, University College Dublin, École Polytechnique, Paris, and CEPR

TCHÉTCHÉ N'GUESSAN, Centre Ivoirien de Recherches Économique et Social (CIRES), Ivory Coast

STEPHEN NICKELL, Centre for Economic Performance, London School of Economics

MARCELO OLARREAGA, World Bank and CEPR

PETER R. ORSZAG, Sebago Associates Inc. and University of California, Berkeley

RAJENDRA K. PACHAURI, Tata Energy Research Institute (TERI), New Delhi

CHARLES PERRINGS, University of York

KATHARINA PISTOR, Max Plank Institute for Foreign and Comparative Private Law, Hamburg

SUSAN ROSE-ACKERMAN, Yale University

AUGUSTINE RUZINDANA, Public Accounts Committee, Kampala, Uganda

PAUL SEABRIGHT, University of Cambridge, UK

JOSEPH E. STIGLITZ, Senior Vice President and Chief Economist, World Bank

OLLI TAHVONEN, Finnish Forest Research Institute

JEAN TIROLE, IDEI, Toulouse

LAURENCE TUBIANA, Institut de Recherche Agronomique (INRA) and CAE

ANTHONY J. VENABLES, World Bank and London School of Economics

OLGA VERSHINSKAYA, Institute for Socio-Economic Studies of Population (ISEPP) and Russian Academy of Sciences (RAS), Russia

GIOVANNI L. VIOLANTE, University College London and CEPR

NORBERT WALTER, Deutsche Bank Group

Introduction

PIERRE-ALAIN MUET AND JOSEPH E. STIGLITZ

Over the last half-century, Europe has gradually built institutions for a regional economic integration. The process has been deliberate and well managed, with by and large beneficial outcomes. In this era of globalized markets, which policies and which institutions are best suited to favor development and foster social justice and equity?

This was the subject of the first European Conference on Development (ABCDE-Europe), held in Paris in June 1999 and jointly organized by the World Bank and the French Council of Economic Analysis.[1]

The conference was opened by the French Prime Minister Lionel Jospin and the President of the World Bank James D. Wolfensohn.

This book presents a selection of papers presented at the conference.

MARKETS, DEVELOPMENT, AND INSTITUTIONS

The failures of ten years of transition show that it is much more difficult than one thought to create a market economy. A story institutional infrastructure, including contract, enforcement, bankruptcy laws, and regulation of the financial system, is paramount for its good functioning. As Olivier Blanchard notes in his comment on John Flemming's paper, in a market economy, agents' decisions are based on implicit or explicit contracts. 'Explicit contracts require the existence of well-functioning laws. Implicit contracts require something like confidence or repeated relations. Take away the laws and the confidence, and the economy will come to a stop.' The collapse of the Soviet system led to a weak state unable to provide this institutional infrastructure. The situation got worse with the passage from a weak state to a 'captured' state. Organized markets have not surprisingly been able to take over and have led to the collapse of the Russian economy.

Would it have been preferable to follow the Chinese experience, to keep a strong state and to marginally introduce competition, before starting the privatization process? As Joseph Stiglitz points out, the contrasting Chinese and Russian experiences suggest that, 'if one has to choose, competition is more important than private property for the functioning of the market economy'. In other words, rather than opting for a better institutional system with a brutal transition—a big bang—towards the market economy, hoping that the institutional infrastructure somehow would develop later on, it would

---

[1] These proceedings are published more than a year after the conference. The papers naturally refer to the year 1999, when they were written.

have been better to focus more on the legal and other aspects of the institutional infrastructure to make a market economy work, not attempting to establish perfect institutions, but rather to create institutions responding to the needs of the moment by letting them evolve over time. This is also one of the topics that Mustapha Nabli develops: institutions are endogenous to the privatization process and it's necessary that they be developed as the privatization process takes place, in particular to minimize the effects of corruption.

If there is a consensus on the priority to give to the prerequisites such as institutions, contractual law, and confidence before implementing privatization, the debate remains open concerning the opposition between 'shock therapy' and 'progressive therapy'. John Flemming emphasized that many earlier interpretations of the failure of the Russian transition 'to do too much too soon' or 'to do too little too late'—the relative success of Poland seems to rather favor the second. While sharing Joseph Stiglitz's standpoint on the priority to give to institutions and their possible evolution, Olivier Blanchard considers, as does John Flemming, that there was no clear-cut path that would have given better results in Eastern Europe in a context, where, in contrast with China, confidence in the state had very quickly disappeared.

Which institutions are needed to make markets work? Oliver Hart and Jean Tirole examine the conditions that are necessary to establish efficient rules concerning bankruptcy, for the former, and to obtain an efficient regulation of competition, for the latter. After having established a typology of bankruptcy regimes, Oliver Hart comes to the conclusion that there is no unique model and that the system to be adopted must take into account the country's institutional structure and legal tradition. Proposing a 'menu of procedures' also allows the market to test them. In the long run, debtors and creditors will choose the most efficient ones. In the same way, Jean Tirole points out that no single policy can seriously promote competition. The weakness of institutions in certain developing countries, which can lead to corruption and a capturing of institutions by lobbies, sometimes requires more legal or administrative measures than those existing in European or in North American anti-trust laws.

Institutions that govern economic relations cannot be confined to legal or formal institutions. Katharina Pistor insists on the interaction between formal and informal institutions, and on the fact that institutions evolve slowly and are highly path dependent. Asian growth, for example, was founded on an institutional compromise based on tradition, networks, and confidence. Formal law was used by economic and government agents as long as it was consistent with this compromise, but it was not taken into account if it went against it. This mixed system is more flexible and sometimes more progressive than the formal legal institutions themselves.

Guiseppe Bertola focuses on the empirical implications of quantity and price rigidities (that is, respectively employment and wages) entailed by European labor-market institutions, in particular employment protection legislation. Evidence suggests that stringent employment protection legislation is associated with more stable employment paths but also with low employment creation in the long run. Stephen Nickell looks at the lessons for developing countries of the workings of the labor market in OECD economies—namely, unemployment benefit systems (which, according to him, should be time-limited and associated with a very strict work test as well as with an efficient placement system), minimum wages (which should make allowance for young workers), and labor supply reduction devices (according to the author, evidence suggests that they never work).

Asking whether state authority should be unitary or multiple is a question that is prior to economic analysis, even if Keynes considered Montesquieu as the greatest French economist. In his contribution on the separation of powers and development, Jean-Jacques Laffont analyzes the role of separation of powers in the framework of contesting informational monopolies. His conclusion is ambiguous: the reduction of costs entailed by the opportunism of regulators is greater in developing countries because of higher public spending costs and lower transaction costs of collusion. But its implementation is also more costly than in developed countries. Paul Seabright notices in his comment that microeconomic theory offers other arguments in favor of the separation of powers than the restriction of informational monopolies, such as the reduction of the risk of error when implementing public aid policies or the reduction of conflicts of interest. Conversely, splitting up regulation agencies can bring about high costs, not easily compatible with limitations in the resources of less developed countries (LDCs). Susan Rose-Ackerman also analyzes the balance that is desirable between different powers, as well as the structure of the political accountability required in order to avoid or at least reduce corruption. Besides putting in place independent controlling institutions, she advocates increasing citizens' possibilities for appealing against public authorities' decisions. Paul de Grauwe stresses that, the more independent the central bank is, the greater its accountability to democratic institutions should be. According to him, the accountability of the European Central Bank (ECB) is weak for two reasons: the absence of strong political institutions in Europe capable of exerting control over the performance of the ECB, and the vagueness of the Treaty in defining the objectives of the ECB, apart from price stability. In his discussion, Norbert Walter emphasizes that 'general accountability should not be narrowly defined as the relationship with government and parliament but as a broader concept, requiring central banks to explain their policy to the general public and to win credibility with the people'.

EQUITY, PUBLIC GOODS, AND GLOBAL GOVERNANCE

The second part of the contributions presented at this conference concerns either new approaches to more traditional subjects of development economics, or subjects that have recently appeared in the international debate, such as the precautionary principle.

Tony Atkinson and François Bourguignon's contribution concerns the definition and quantification of a world approach for poverty and inclusion. The traditional analysis opposes two measures of poverty, absolute and relative. The first approach is the poverty line applied in the 1990 World Development Report, defined as '$1 a day per person in 1985 prices'. According to this approach, more than one billion people in the world lived under the poverty line. On the other hand, according to this same definition, poverty affected only developing countries and transition countries, because this definition does not leave space for poverty problems in rich countries. In rich countries, poverty indeed concerns 'persons whose resources (material, cultural and social) are so limited as to exclude them from the minimum acceptable way of life in the Member State in which they live'. If we choose, as the European Union (EU) does, a relative poverty line, measured as a percentage of average income or spending, then poverty affected, at the end of the 1980s, 50 million Europeans for a poverty line equal to 50 percent of average income, 25 million for a poverty line of 40 percent. In their contribution, Tony Atkinson and François Bourguignon put forward a framework that unifies the measure of poverty in the developing countries and in developed countries, by combining an absolute criterion of poverty in countries of the South and a relative one in countries of the North. They thus propose a comprehensive world approach of poverty.

Stefan Dercon analyzes the respective roles of institutional and informal systems of social protection in developing countries. Public institutional systems often concern only blue and white collars in cities, who represent only a small and generally affluent proportion of the population. The author particularly emphasizes the crowding-out effects that public safety nets could have on the informal self-insurance systems. In his comment, Peter Orszag stresses that one cannot blame public safety nets for playing a significant role in crowding out private insurance, especially given the incomplete protection they provide. Moreover, public systems operate a redistribution over the whole life cycle that a self-insurance does not.

Increasing longevity in conjunction with decreasing fertility will have dramatic consequences on the financial equilibrium of pay-as-you-go pension systems over the next decades. As pointed out by Orazio Attanasio, due to the general equilibrium effects on factor prices and in particular on the rate of return to capital, these demographic changes will also strongly affect fully funded pension systems. But the lack of synchronization between demographic trends in the world constitutes an important opportunity to reduce the impact of demographic changes on pension systems. Northern capital invested in less developed regions could yield higher returns to finance the retirement of the US and European baby boomers and at the same time could help the development in Latin America and other developing regions.

How does creating a free trade area affect the distribution of activities within the area? Does it cause a tendency to convergence or divergence in income per head? Anthony Venables argues that, whereas creating a free trade area between countries with a high level of income leads to convergence, the result is opposite for a free trade area between countries with low levels of income. The analysis also suggests that, if developing countries join in a free trade area that includes countries with high levels of income, their development could be fostered, insofar as the prospect of convergence towards countries with high levels of income is enhanced. The analysis of regional integration in sub-Saharan Africa developed by Olivier Cadot, Jaime de Melo, and Marcelo Olarreaga leads however to a less pessimistic vision of the effects of regional integration between countries of the South.

András Inotai analyzes benefits and costs of EU enlargement. He emphasizes the asymmetry between the EU and the candidate countries regarding the distribution of costs and benefits. For the EU, most of the benefits due to the adjustment of the Central and East European Countries (CEECs) have already been obtained. Markets were almost fully opened up; West European companies participated in the privatization process and became market leaders in many sectors. For EU member states, benefits came first and potential costs in the form of more important transfers to the new members came at a later stage. On the other hand, East European countries are expected to finance the costs and enjoy later the benefits of a successful adjustment.

In recent years governments and citizens of industrialized countries have become increasingly aware of the health and environmental risks related to the development of the production and consumption of certain industrial and agricultural goods. Whether it be fossil fuels (the greenhouse effect), the use of tropical woods (deforestation), chemical products (pesticides), or genetically modified organisms (GMOs) the precautionary principle has led to questioning the distinctions usually made between products and processes concerning trade regulation, as shown by Olivier Godart, P.-H. Gouyon, Claude Henry, and P. Lagadec. The health and environmental protection questions introduce a 'corner' between the traditional relation associating free trade and the increase of welfare, thereby giving decisive importance to production processes, traditionally ignored by trade legislation. The precautionary principle has become today a major subject of multilateral negotiations as well as a source of conflict between developed countries and LDCs, which see it as forming the basis of a new form of protectionism.

Laurence Tubiana and Rajendra Pachauri emphasize the paradox of global governance in environment: in arriving at agreements, cooperative strategies between countries tend to prevail against non-cooperative, free rider strategies, contrary to the result anticipated by economic theory. Different factors play a role in that paradox such as the procedure and structure of negotiations as well as the interaction between negotiations. But the problems arise when compliance and observance of the rules are concerned; if there is an absence of sticks and carrots for countries, it is very difficult for the agreement to be implemented. Furthermore, there is a strong asymmetry between norms and rules that can happen to be in competition. Rules that are enforced by strong mechanisms (like trade sanctions in the WTO) prevail at the expense of rules that have no effective enforcement mechanism. In his comment, Charles Perrings looks at the creation of insurance markets and the extension of property rights on environmental goods. For him, these are essential ingredients in the self-enforcement of the agreements.

Positive externalities bred by R & D justify subsidies for research and innovation; in the same way, joint ventures related to R & D increase welfare gains for the economy. However, as shown by Peter Neary, the fact that R & D investment also improves a firm's capacities to benefit from rival companies' spillovers or from research done outside its branch leads to the result that measures improving the general level of know-how of an economy are more efficient than specific subsidies. Lastly, as in other fields of state intervention, a stable long-term environment for research and innovation policy is a condition of its efficiency.

Is gender economics just another 'dummy' variable? In her paper, Diane Elson argues that 'gender economics' should be included as a new perspective for rethinking development paradigms, which implies in particular devising new ways of coordinating market and non-market processes. The important feature that should be taken into account is the institutional dimension of gender, and not only men and women's comparative behavior.

The need for greater world coordination and regulation appears still more clearly with the development of financial crises over the last three years. The need for greater financial supervision, for more organized liberalization of capital flows, and for closer association of the private sector to the management of financial crises is widely accepted today. On the other hand, the exchange rate problem is a major aspect that still has not found a satisfactory solution. Flexibility is no doubt adapted for exchange rates between large monetary zones with strong credibility. It is less so for emerging countries and for less developed countries that do not have this credibility, while at the same time an alternative strategy of a nominal anchor to a major currency involves risks that financial crises have dramatically emphasized.

Among the numerous contributions concerning these questions, Michel Aglietta's emphasizes the common logic of the recent financial crises, which, if they have different origins (sovereign debt crises, currency crises, private-sector crises), always cause at a given stage a liquidity crisis that calls for the intervention of a lender of last resort. For the author, this role should rather be assigned to 'a network coordinating major central banks', because the IMF, as now defined, is poorly adapted to carry out this function. This perspective generated heated discussion at the conference. Uri Dadush points out in his comment that it is unlikely that a concerted action between the Federal Reserve and the European Central Bank would produce a better alternative than the current arrangements, unsatisfactory as they are.

Daniel Cohen's paper analyzes the links between financial instability and growth through the lessons drawn from African and South American experiences. The author considers low investment, political distortions, and the fluctuations of the terms of trade as the key factors explaining the African continent's weak growth. None of these variables, on the other hand, seems to explain Latin America's poor performances. The mismanagement of the exchange rate combined with the debt crises is, according to the author, the main way by which international trade damages developing economies.

CONCLUSION

The starting point of this European conference was the feeling, shared by many economists, that we had to go beyond what was called the Washington consensus. The plea for an unconditional liberalization of markets, the lack of attention paid to institutions, macroeconomic policies geared too much towards lowering inflation rates and not enough towards growth and employment, a failure to understand fully how weak financial institutions can lead to macro-economic instability as bad as large budget deficits, the failures of transition and the sometimes dramatic financial crises over the past years—all these weaknesses in the policy prescription have been brought home forcefully.

Does that mean that the conference should have come up with a new consensus? We don't think so. A consensus can be comfortable for politicians, although it limits their choice. But above all, we cannot be sure that it is useful to them. Indeed, development success stories include almost all the ingredients taught in economic textbooks: high savings, rapid capital accumulation, high level of training, strong capacity to acquire new knowledge, rapid insertion into international trade. But these ingredients alone do not ensure development, any more than putting together the best ingredients ensures great 'cuisine'. They must be rooted in the political and social reality of each nation, or, in other words, each country should adapt and combine them harmoniously. Recent crises have also illustrated the need for greater world governance, especially to manage 'public goods' such as financial stability or environmental protection. This improved world governance cannot come solely from monetary and financial authorities. It must also bring to the table employers and trade unions and must be more attuned to non-governmental organizations; above all, it must promote the information, expression, and participation of citizens.

Opening Speech

LIONEL JOSPIN

Ladies and Gentlemen.

It is a great pleasure for me to open—with you, dear Jim Wolfensohn—this first European Conference on development, organized by the World Bank and the *Conseil d'Analyse Économique*.

Over the past two years, successive shocks have hit the world economy. They have shown that world growth can be weakened and that financial stability is a common 'good' for both the developing and industrialized worlds. They also incite us—and this is the only virtue of crises—to challenge conventional wisdom and the policies sometimes based on it. Certainties become blurred, paradigms reveal their fragility. The recent crises thus make a discussion on the instruments for a better world governance even more necessary.

A pluralist and open-minded debate, bringing together economists and decision-makers from the various continents, is fruitful for an international institution's activity. The World Bank clearly understood this when, eleven years ago now, in Washington, it launched the Annual Bank Conference on Development Economics—the so-called ABCDE—in order to regularly take stock, with the scientific community, of intellectual debate on the major development issues. I'm delighted that the World Bank decided to convene, but this time in Europe, another conference of this kind.

As Prime Minister, I have myself felt the need for a body in which pluralist discussion can provide an informed background to the French government's economic choices. That's why, two years ago, I set up the Council of Economic Analysis. Through the high quality of its members' work, it has established itself as a valuable contributor to the economic debate in France.

I am pleased that the World Bank chose it as its partner for the organization, in France, of this first European Conference. I'm delighted to see the economist community gathered here this morning at the Ministry of Economy, Finance, and Industry—which I would like to thank for being our host—to discuss such fundamental issues as development, governance of the world economy, and equity.

With this in mind, I would like to emphasize three points in my speech:

- the need for a comprehensive and balanced approach to development;
- the importance of encouraging the integration of developing countries into the world economy;
- the urgent need for a genuine 'governance' of the international economy.

To be efficient, our approach to development must be balanced and comprehensive.

Development is a process that must be considered as a whole. It cannot be reduced to its economic and financial aspects alone. It must transform the society without destroying the fundamental values in which it is based. There is no such thing as a universal development model. Experience shows that a development strategy must be tailored to the history and social reality of each country. It is the quality of this transformation of society that determines the success of a development strategy, as Joseph Stiglitz described so well in a recent lecture.

The reconstruction—in less than a generation—of the European economies after the Second World War and the remarkable growth of the South-East Asian and Chinese economies over the last few decades: all these major events in economic history demonstrate that education and the collective ability to absorb new knowledge are key factors for long-term development.

The quality of economic policies, the rate of capital accumulation, and access to new technologies, through involvement in international trade, are all vitally important. Very often their positive effects go beyond those described by traditional economic analysis. But these factors do not by themselves constitute a strategy. They must take root in the social reality of nations and spread to all parts of society. A dual society in which modern sectors coexist with great poverty resulting from the destructuring of traditional societies cannot be considered truly developed. There is no real economic progress without social progress. Democracy, human rights, and good management of public affairs are basic factors in development.

So development assistance must focus on education as a long-term growth factor. It must support 'ownership' of development by national authorities. This is indeed the precise meaning of *coopération*, the French word for development assistance. It must strive to reduce inequality and concentrate its efforts on the most deprived people. It must stress respect for human rights, promote equality between men and women, and help establish the rule of law. Nor can there be sustainable development without conservation of the environment, respect for biodiversity, guarantees for the rights of future generations. These are the issues that France will focus on in its development assistance policy.

President Wolfensohn's proposal in favor of the integrated development framework contains the same global and balanced version of development.

Developing countries are not a homogenous world. Cooperation policies must thus take this diversity into account.

For emerging economies, openness to international trade and private capital flows play a role that is paramount. By contributing to the stability of the international monetary and financial system and involving these countries more closely in the elaboration of common rules and standards, we will be able to guarantee them the conditions for a balanced development. I will come back to this in a moment.

For the least advanced countries, priority must be given to satisfying basic needs: food security, health, education, the establishment or strengthening of solid institutions, protection of their natural resources. From this point of view, official development assistance plays a major role. It is necessary for the development of these countries' basic infrastructure and for ensuring the efficiency of their administrations, a key factor in the success of investment programs. The benefits for the international community will appear in the long term and they will be important: indeed, the aim is to prevent the marginalization of the poor economies, which fuels instability and political crises, organized trafficking, and the deterioration of the environment—and can even jeopardize the very survival of entire populations.

The debt burden remains, however, the major obstacle to development for these countries. In a bilateral framework, France decided to write off debts when the CFA franc was devalued and again, last year, in order to help the four countries hit by Hurricane Mitch. It was behind the initiative launched in Lyons in 1996 to help the highly indebted countries. At G7 finance ministers' meetings, Dominique Strauss-Kahn, on behalf of the French government, has put forward proposals to relieve the debt of the poorest countries. These are based on three principles:

- solidarity, which bids us give the poorest countries the most favorable treatment;
- equity, which requires a balanced sharing of the financial burden. With Japan, France is one of the countries that has contributed most to the financing of the poorest countries. This is why we have urged the G7 member states, with the OECD and Paris Club, not only to write off their residual debts, but also to make new efforts to contribute to the cost of these measures for the international financial institutions and respond directly to the developing countries' needs;
- responsibility, which mandates that these exceptional measures of support should first benefit countries that are noted for their good governance and who choose to allocate the funds released by their debts to the priority sectors for social development: education and help.

I'm delighted that the G7, at which President Chirac represented France, reached an agreement yesterday that will make it possible to implement these principles.

Every year, the amount of money France devotes to official development assistance is double the average for the developed countries. My government will maintain this effort in its now renewed policy. Through the reform of the French cooperation, which will be presented tomorrow by the Minister Delegate for Cooperation and Francophony, M. Charles Josselin, the government has definitively turned the page of relations bearing the stamp of post-colonial practices in favor of a more transparent policy, showing solidarity towards the poorest countries and satisfying their democratic aspirations.

Ladies and Gentlemen.

At the same time, we have to promote the integration of developing countries into the international trading system.

In an interdependent world, the existence of rules and institutions guaranteeing compliance with them is the best protection for the weakest economies, whose opening-up to the outside world is both necessary and risky. Therefore, this is why we must strengthen the role of the multilateral institutions and ensure better cooperation between them.

The poorest economies remain heavily based on raw materials and basic products. They are especially vulnerable to economic downturns and are suffering today from the contraction of world demand and decline in raw material prices. In world trade, they have gradually become marginalized, with their share falling from 1.5 percent in 1970 to 0.3 percent today.

In order to fight against this progressive exclusion, the developed countries must offer preferential access to their markets. The European Union (EU) has made this proposal to the least advanced countries. At the same time, it has undertaken a process of trade liberalization and enhanced cooperation with a growing number of countries. The EU is also supporting initiatives promoting the regional integration of developing economies.

The Barcelona agreements with the Mediterranean countries and the new Lomé Convention—under negotiation with the African, Caribbean, and Pacific countries—should eventually create the most extensive areas of trade and cooperation between industrialized and developing nations. Lomé 5 will thus offer an original framework for dialogue in which governments, non-governmental organizations, and private actors will exchange views on the legal rules, institutions, and the role and operation of the states, thereby giving real substance to the concept of partnership.

The opening-up of these countries is a source of new wealth and progress, but it also causes upheaval necessitating the provision of support. There needs to be a regulatory framework for the liberalization process. Regional integration agreements—without coming into conflict with the multilateral approach—are helping to build the requisite institutions.

Similarly, we must strengthen multilateral regulation of trade. Half a century after the Havana Charter, the world has established a World Trade Organization (WTO). Europe fought for its creation. And we can today work for its success. A growing number of countries want to join this organization, in which trade conflicts are dealt with through multilateral and objective procedures freely accepted by all WTO members.

Trade negotiations, just like economic globalization, affect many spheres of social life. National and regional choices in the areas of public health, environment, or public services cannot be judged solely by the yardstick of commercial rules, which were not designed to encompass such diverse spheres. Trade liberalization is 'sustainable' only if it remains consistent with each society's fundamental values. This is why other international institutions must help define rules and standards in order to establish a regulatory framework for this liberalization: in the environmental sphere, through multilateral environmental agreements; in the sphere of social standards, by strengthening the International Labor Organization; and, last but not least, in the sphere of food security.

The next round of negotiations, which will start next December at the WTO, will have to take full account of the civil society's legitimate concerns: the multilateral trade rules can and must play a decisive role in the application of standards adopted in other forums, particularly through incentives and by fully integrating the precautionary principle.

Ladies and Gentlemen.

The international financial crisis revealed the deficiencies of a world regulatory system that has not achieved, in this sphere, the level required by the degree of financial interdependence.

In order to find an answer to the deficiencies of this regulation, an in-depth reflection must be undertaken. The Minister of Economy, Finance, and Industry, M. Dominique Strauss-Kahn, will come back to this subject on Wednesday. I shall mention five main lines, which include some of the issues you will be dealing with throughout this conference:

- the functioning of financial markets;
- capital flow liberalization;
- exchange rates;
- prevention and management of crises;
- lastly, institutional reform.

Both the public and private sectors have to make major efforts to improve the functioning of the financial markets. Budgetary, monetary, and financial policies must be sufficiently clear so as to provide market actors with the basic information they need. This transparency is just as necessary for the private sector. In particular, hedge funds can present a major risk for the whole system, as the long term capital management (LTCM) affair proved. We have to pursue the efforts under way to improve the prudential supervision of banks and extend to these funds some basic rules as regards transparency and risk monitoring. We also need to make progress in tackling unlawful practices in offshore financial centers.

In the area of the liberalization of capital movements, the international community now agrees on the principle of an orderly and progressive liberalization, consistent with the state of development of national economies and particularly with their banking systems. I welcome this change, which meets a long-standing concern of France and marks a rejection of the defense of unconditional liberalization that prevailed right up until the past few years.

The crisis also highlighted the deficiency of some exchange rate systems, in a world where capital movements are very largely unrestricted. We have to learn from this. But we cannot be satisfied with a choice between two extreme approaches: unrestricted floating or rigid pegging to a major currency. Floating presents risks for emerging economies whose financial markets are too limited. Pegging exchange rates is appropriate in some circumstances, but can be costly in the long term, unless, as was the case in Europe, it is done in the perspective of a monetary union. We thus need to define quickly a balanced doctrine tailored to regional situations.

As regards crisis prevention, traditional monitoring is not enough. The International Monetary Fund (IMF), with the new preventive facility, can now intervene before a crisis erupts. This is an important change, which, combined with the recent increase in its resources, will enable it to reduce the frequency of crises. In the area of crisis management, everyone agrees today to involve more closely the private sector, but we must speed up the concrete application of this principle.

Now I come to institutional reform. This is necessary in order to give the Bretton Woods institutions greater legitimacy, representativeness, and responsibility. Today, the Ministers of Finance meet formally only twice a year to set the major guidelines. I am delighted that the IMF's 'interim committee' has ceased to be interim. But, beyond words, what matters is that it becomes, in the spirit of the French government's proposal, a real 'Council' within which the ministers collectively exercise their responsibilities. Now that the fund has existed for half a century, it is not perhaps too soon to put an end to an 'interim' period. Of course, this council must bring together all the relevant actors and so the President of the World Bank must belong to it.

Ladies and gentlemen.

Europe's role is in the background of all I have been saying. Yet, Europe, as such, is too often absent from the Bretton Woods institutions—although it is *de facto* their first shareholder.

Placed by history at the heart of the human, cultural, economic, and commercial exchanges between continents, Europe has today a special responsibility. It is already the leading contributor of official development assistance. It must now move towards a common vision so as to be able to implement better coordinated cooperation policies. Because we are combining three levels of cooperation—bilateral, European, and multi-lateral—we have to be sure that our actions on the field are both consistent and complementary.

That is why we must build a 'Europe of Development'.

Europe is already speaking with a single voice in a number of international forums, at the WTO where we are advocating a common policy, and in environmental negotiations. We must also move in this direction within the IMF and the World Bank.

Finally, since I am talking about Europe and development, how can I not mention the challenge that awaits us in the Balkans? Faced with the huge task of reconstruction in Kosovo and in its region, Europe needs to give substance to this coordination. If the Balkans are to be firmly rooted in Europe, the EU must walk in step, today at a time of peace as it did yesterday at a time of military intervention. Our common political project is to build democratic institutions without which there will not be any sustainable development.

Over half a century, Europe has been pursuing—and still is—a goal of economic integration founded on a union of nations respecting the cultural and social diversity of its population. Drawing its inspiration from this experience, it can, in the globalization era, contribute to the emergence of a better world governance. I am convinced that the discussions of this first European conference will be a major contribution to this.

Opening Speech

JAMES D. WOLFENSOHN

In listening to the remarks of Prime Minister Jospin, I am heartened to find that so much of what the World Bank Group is thinking about and working on is also on the mind of one of our principal shareholders. That is hardly surprising, however, considering that Prime Minister Jospin wrote a book on development economics some years ago. From now on, I will refer to his ideas in a footnote—and hope that, in doing that, I can leverage support from all the other prime ministers.

Prime Minister Jospin has set forth a broad framework, neatly identical to the one we are using in the Bank. So rather than repeating what he has said, let me share with you some of the concerns as we come to the end of the millennium and the beginning of the next. Let me also ask you, as you participate in the debate on these ideas over the next few days, to explore these issues and seek new insights on how we should proceed in the period ahead.

The issues before us, as Prime Minister Jospin has noted, are not just financial. Financial issues are inextricably linked to structural and social issues. While we need to have the proper macroeconomic policies in place and to address issues of growth, capital flows, and exchange rates, we also need to attend to structural and social issues. But these 'soft' concerns do not always get the same instant reaction as financial concerns because the issues are long term. Education is long term. Environment is long term. Health is long term.

It is also the case that the connections between actions taken at times of crisis and at normal times with sound macroeconomic policies are complex. Thus we may find ourselves pleading for social sensitivity at a time of crisis when, because of the financial dynamics, the first things to be cut are social programs. And so there are situations, as in Indonesia, where we are dealing successfully with one social issue—keeping children in schools—while losing out on another—children's health and nutrition. We have new data that show a worsening of child nutrition in Indonesia because adequate resources could not be found to feed and support young children. And why not? Because of the need to establish a stable framework of fiscal and monetary policy. So this tension, which is present even in normal economic and budgetary management, is heightened during times of crisis.

We also learned from this crisis that structural issues, like social issues, are crucial not only during a crisis but also during periods of transition. Even with sound fiscal and monetary policy, there will be inescapable weaknesses in the structure unless there is also good governance and a strong legal framework that protects human rights, property rights, and contracts. The judicial system too must be free of corruption, with well-trained judges whose decisions are based on law not on who pays them the most. I recently returned from Georgia, where Prime Minister Shevardnadze had confronted the power of judges, who are among the richest people in the country. With the backing of parliament, he announced that all the judges would have to pass certification examinations. The examinations were televised, and 170 of the 200 judges taking the exams failed and were replaced. This is an important precedent that offers promise not only for Georgia but for other countries as well.

The failure to deal with issues of structure can have tremendous repercussions. Witness East Asia and Russia, where the poor suffered most as a result of the weaknesses in financial system supervision. Or look what happens when you have good fiscal and monetary policy but a weak social system and then move on to privatization. There is no social underpinning to help people who are thrown out of work get through the transition. We understand now that fiscal and monetary policy can be framed only within a sound governance structure, a sound legal and judicial structure, a sound financial supervisory mechanism, and a sound social safety net.

You will understand the dilemma we are facing at the Bank as we recognize that, in all too many countries, these structures do not exist. Does it make sense to talk about fiscal and monetary policy before the proper structure is established? Can we explain the differences between formerly centrally planned economies that have done well—Poland, Hungary, the Czech Republic—and those that have not? A key difference is a structure that is undermined by rampant corruption—or no structure at all.

Our task at the Bank is to find ways to be helpful to governments in areas where the theory is clear but the practice is difficult. That applies to the linkages between a sound fiscal and monetary policy and broad-based structural reform and prioritization of social objectives.

I am troubled by this difficulty because our goals are so vital. Halving world poverty. Achieving universal primary education and improving gender equity in education. Lowering maternal and child mortality rates. Expanding access to reproductive health services. All of these are among the International Development Goals. But as I look at the numbers I am troubled. Poverty remains stubbornly high. We now have 1.2 billion people living on less than $1 a day—roughly the same number as in 1987—and nearly 3 billion people living on less than $2 a day. I am aware that income is not the full measure of poverty, but it provides an approximation of the global extent of poverty. In the next twenty-five years we will add 2 billion people to the planet. Achieving the International Development Goal of halving poverty by 2015 will be possible only with inclusive growth, only if the right combination of policies and interventions leads to sustained growth without increases in inequality.

And so, as we move into the next millennium, we face crucial questions. Do we continue to do what we are doing now, knowing that we are likely to have a bigger problem in twenty or twenty-five years? Or are there some fundamental changes that we can make in our approach to development that will bring about both quantitative and qualitative changes in the development process? One thing we are quite certain about: if we keep doing what we have been doing, we are not going to succeed.

What should we do to change trends that will not get us to our goals? Should we give greater emphasis to structure? To strengthening governance and transparency? To confronting corruption? To building a sound legal and judicial system? To installing stronger financial supervisory mechanisms? To building better social safety nets? The arguments for advancing questions of structure are quite compelling. Not, of course, in place of proper fiscal and monetary policy, but as an essential adjunct. We must also think in terms of balanced development and incorporation of the objectives set by the countries themselves, in education, health, transportation, knowledge, and others.

We would like to enter the next millennium with a better sense of priorities and balance within a broader development framework. We hope that some elements of that new framework will come out of these meetings. We need to look for ways to change the actions and the policies not only of the Bank but of the entire global development community. We can be effective only in partnership—in partnership with governments, other multilateral institutions, bilateral institutions, the private sector, and civil society.

The private sector has become crucial. Ten years ago private flows from developed to developing countries were $30 billion a year. They soared to $300 billion in 1997 then dropped down to $230 billion in 1998. Meanwhile, official institutional support has remained unchanged at about $40 billion a year. So whether you take 1998 or 1997 figures, private sector flows are six or seven times official flows.

Neither we nor the private sector has yet fully adjusted to sharing responsibility for social development in the countries in which we operate. Forty years ago the developing countries accounted for 14 percent of world GDP. Today they account for 19 percent. In another twenty-five years, they may account for as much as 30 percent of world GDP. So the growth potential in these markets is enormous, and the interest and involvement of the private sector are crucial. We need to establish ways to work together effectively.

So I would ask that in your discussions you think not only about objectives, but about methodology as well. How do we relate financial, structural, and social aspects of development? What should we do differently? How do we do all this through new partnerships with governments, multilaterals and bilaterals, private sector, and civil society? If we are to enter the next millennium with a well-founded hope of success on our major objectives rather than the certainty of success on lesser objectives, major change is essential.

I hope that you will further illuminate these issues and guide our way in the years ahead. With all the intelligence gathered together at this conference, I leave knowing that I will have an easier year ahead of me because of your insightful deliberations.

PART ONE

MARKETS, DEVELOPMENT, AND INSTITUTIONS

Transition

1

Transition: The First Ten Years

JOHN S. FLEMMING

In a conference with as broad a coverage as this, a broad brush treatment of the first decade of transition seemed appropriate. In what follows I focus in particular on selected topics from the definition and duration of the transition to the diversity of the origins and destination of the twenty-five individual countries. There are reasons for the process not being smooth and I examine relationships between reform and recovery as well as the nexus of corporate privatization, restructuring, and finance. Finally, reference is made to other welfare measures and criticisms of the reforms are addressed.

1. I was originally asked to write about 'Transition after Ten Years'. That title suggested that 'transition' was an event: the collapse of communism, perhaps to be celebrated, rather than a continuing process, possibly painful.

Transition is a process of transformation of a different order from the process of change that continually transforms any society, polity, or economy. Specifically we can imagine these processes applying to each member of two clusters of societies clearly differentiated in a number of ways: by the nature of their democracies and by the role of markets in coordinating decentralized economic activity (which itself reflects in different degrees individual initiative and private property). The role of the state in regulating economic activity and markets differs, and the allocation of social support functions between political organs (ministries, municipalities) and economic organs (enterprises) is distinct in the two groups. Transition takes place when a member of one group changes, over a number of years, in such a way as to acquire the characteristics of members of the other.

If all the members of one group embark on this process almost simultaneously, the transition concept becomes more difficult to apply. The fact that the OECD countries, if they represent the decentralized category, are changing but that there is no parallel movement of communist or centrally planned economies, because they no longer exist, means that the origin category becomes increasingly hypothetical. One might be tempted to use China as a proxy, but China too seems to be in a process of transition—in some economic respects more successful than that of the Central European and CIS states, although its destination is even less well defined.

If transition were purely economic, it might be treated in similar ways to the general questions of (per capita) GDP convergence. In particular, we have seen a sequence of countries breaking away from the pack of lower- or middle-income countries and, through a growth spurt sustained for several decades, associating themselves to a higher income grouping. Japan, Taiwan, Hong Kong, Singapore, and South Korea all fall into this category. Nor is transition only upwards. Just as social mobility involves movement in both directions, though with an upward bias as higher-status (white-collar) jobs have expanded in number relative to lower-status (blue-collar) ones, so, in relative income terms, there have been downward movements too, perhaps most strongly, and for very different reasons, by Argentina and Czechoslovakia, which were amongst the richest in per capita terms before the Second World War.

But as we have seen the transition under discussion here is about more economic dimensions than per capita GDP and has a political dimension that is as important as the economic. While at one level the political change is more discrete than the economic, and has clearly occurred in most of the former communist countries, both the extra economic dimensions and many of the political ones are represented by institutional changes that are difficult both to achieve and to measure.

2. Early estimates of the duration of transition varied from a few decades to a few generations. Taking a crude quantitative index, (per capita) GDP, and widespread modest estimates of Western economic growth, even before the extent of initial falls had been realized, I was struck by the arithmetical implication that it would take at least thirty years on average to raise a country from one-quarter to one-half of OECD levels if the transition economies grew steadily at 5 per cent per annum.

While indefinite growth at 5 per cent per annum would eventually take the transition economies past the OECD leaders, most models have convergence features that suggest that growth slows as the distance from the leaders closes (thus complete catch-up never occurs). Nevertheless, as suggested above, growth may complete a process of qualifying for membership, whether formal or not, of something like the OECD club of advanced industrial states.

I was also struck by the continuing applicability of Pushkin's description of Russia in 1830—in particular his comments on the state of transport infrastructure and associated catering arrangements—which paralleled 1990 accounts very closely. He had said that it had then been calculated that 500 years would be necessary to close the gap. I saw little reason to question the implications that a further 350 years lay ahead of them.

Some commentators drew a misleading analogy between the losers in the cold war and those of the Second World War and expected the transition economies to experience growth on the pattern of Germany and Japan in the post-war decades.

This was always a mistake. After the war the defeated nations had a dispirited populace and damaged capital stock. Making good the damage offered an abnormal rate of return if the assets were not then removed in reparations. That and other uncertainties made people cautious in consumption. Their expectations were in fact low relative to the medium-term capacity of the physical equipment (once repaired) and existing economic regime to deliver. Thus growth exceeded expectations, generating savings and fuelling further expectation-exceeding growth.

The despair of defeat proved an excellent launch pad for exceptional and sustained growth.

The situation after the collapse of communism could not have been more different. Living standards had been boosted unsustainably by cutting investment and/or by borrowing abroad. The citizens had high hopes of rapid convergence on West European living standards and would have anticipated it if they could, although their prior living standards probably exceeded that deliverable in the medium term by the physical, technological, managerial, and economic capital, including organizational structures and norms in place. Euphoria is a terrible launch pad for growth. Sustained growth becomes a possibility only after it has been converted into despair—if only briefly. Rarely are high hopes not illusory.

3. At an early stage, after the fall of communism, many attempts were made to assess the capital requirements of the transition economies, often in the context of ideas for a new Marshall Plan. Quite apart from their numerical disparity, these studies rarely assigned distinctive roles to domestic savings and investment, which contribute to national income as well as to production, and foreign capital, which contributes most directly only to the latter as the income counterpart to that contribution accrues to the foreign investor. Thus the benefit of foreign investment must come from other elements in the package such as associated technology, management, design, or marketing skills. Certainly many formerly state-owned enterprises saw their salvation in joint ventures with Western partners.

Across the whole region, many such associations have been formed, with varying degrees of success. As far as associated capital inflows are concerned, they have been concentrated, successively, at least in per capita terms, on the front-line Central European states of Hungary, Czechoslovakia, and Poland, with considerable Scandinavian money, again in per capita terms, flowing into the Baltic States. Further east, inflows have been concentrated on resource extraction projects, particularly oil in Russia and Kazakhstan.

In the CIS, however, capital flight, though even harder to measure than capital inflows, would appear to have exceeded any private capital inflow. Estimates have ranged from $10 billion to $20 billion a year, or, by now, a cumulative total of $100–200 billion. The outflows have been associated particularly with unrepatriated proceeds of exports of energy and metals, but many other routes have existed. The scale of these outflows is of the same order of magnitude as that of the international and multilateral assistance channelled through the international financial institutions.

4. Were all the countries that emerged from the Soviet empire in the same state—and did they all aspire to the same state?

The answer to this question is doubly negative. Some emerged as distinct sovereign nation states with their own currencies, and so on. Others, in the former Soviet Union, had not previously enjoyed either political sovereignty or a national currency either for substantial periods or at all recently or, even more rarely, democratically. They also differed, for instance, in their income distribution—being more egalitarian in Central Europe than in the former Soviet Union (FSU).

Their economic structure differed with private sectors of different sizes (largest in Hungary, smallest in Czechoslovakia) though all much smaller than in any OECD country. Under central planning, 'enterprise' is a misnomer and the distinction between branch ministries and production units was not always clear, but on any measure the units were few and large compared to entities in market economies. They differed in their openness to Western trade and investment, with Hungary again clearly in the lead as a result of twenty years of gradual reform as well as being geographically close to the West.

Their political situation differed in relation to minorities (Germans in Poland, Hungarians in Slovakia and in Romania, Turks in Bulgaria, Armenians in Azerbaijan, Russians in the Baltics, the Ukraine, Kazakhstan, and so on), and in their constitutional positions (that of Ukraine seems to have been a singular impediment to change). They also differed in the degree of rupture in 1990. Communist leaders stayed in power in Central Asia (except Kyrgyzstan) and in Romania (despite the violent overthrow of the Ceausescus). Fighting broke out quite soon in Azerbaijan, Georgia, Moldova, and Tajikistan (and was resolved with least damage in Moldova).

Their destinations also differed, with a clear divide between those (Poland, Hungary, Czechoslovakia, Slovenia, Baltics, Romania, Bulgaria) with clear ambitions to join the EC/EU and those content with ideas of broad market economies and broadly democratic politics (all were deemed sufficiently committed to these goals to be admitted to membership of the EBRD, though Belarus's intentions under Lukashenko are pretty dubious).

The most concrete objective of a number of transition economies is membership of the EU. Even here there is room for conceptual argument about the effective date of completion. Admission is typically phased over yet another treaty-specified transition period. Does membership occur at the beginning or the end? If the CAP does not apply fully, or if labour mobility is restricted, does that mean the entry has not yet occurred? Or is full participation in the decision-making processes the key?

Whatever the test, we do not yet have ratified accession treaties—nor will we have by the millennial deadline promised to the Poles by Chancellor Kohl. Indeed considerable scepticism is in order as to how long the process will take. The EU failed at Amsterdam to take the steps relating to its own governance universally recognized as being necessary if an enlarged Union is to be capable of governing itself. Progress on the reform of this, the CAP, and the budget, necessary before enlargement can occur, is painfully slow. Despite all the rhetoric, this goal may still be a decade off.

5. Despite the similarities of transition and convergence, the relative incomes of all the transition economies initially fell. That is, gaps that should have narrowed and vanished, on a successful transition path, in fact started by widening and are wider now than in 1990. As practised in Europe, transition from central planning to a market economy is clearly not monotonic in per capita output.

One economic consequence of the early liberalization of prices in most transition economies was a surge of inflation reflecting its intensified repression in the last days of communism as fiscal positions deteriorated for a number of reasons. These fiscal problems had led to a growing monetary overhang and put stabilization high on the agenda of the transition economies. The initial burst, which was in danger of degenerating into hyperinflation, implied that successful stabilization involved inflation too following a non-monotonic path as it first rose and then fell back to the levels characteristic of the leading industrial democracies—whose own core inflation rates have fallen sharply over the transition period.

I shall argue that the same non-monotonicity is characteristic of the institutional side of economic regulation and thus of the political economy even if not necessarily of the more specifically political institutions of democracy. Not being a political scientist, I will not venture into the area of any ideological transition. The political/electoral pendulum has swung pretty regularly in Central Europe and the Baltic States if not so clearly in Russia and among members of the CIS. The non-monotonicity in the political complexion of governments seems to be entirely appropriate in youthful democracies— especially when it can rarely be blamed for the material and institutional setbacks that have been so prevalent. On key policies, Poland, for instance, has shown remarkable consistency across governments of both left and right.

Not only did income initially fall everywhere, but regulation and compliance with the law, which may have started above Western levels, soon fell below. Why?

To take the regulatory institutions first. It is easy to see that conferring economic autonomy on entities that were previously merely cogs in a branch ministry machine, or liberating international trade that was previously reserved exclusively for state trading organizations, represents the removal of the old (central) control mechanisms without their being replaced by operative competition or regulatory bodies for commerce and finance.

Western market economies are not unregulated, and it is tempting to try to put the degree of their regulation on a scale that has at its extremes unregulated laissez-faire (0) and totalitarian central control (100). On this scale OECD countries might, on the basis of state ownership and tax ratios as well as pages of environmental and other regulations, score around 20–25 per cent, while the transition economies come from 70–90 per cent. Should we expect them to converge monotonically on 20–25 per cent as in Fig. 1, or to overshoot and eventually to converge from below, as in Fig. 2? There are two reasons for thinking that Fig. 2 offers the more plausible path. One is that already given: that the dismantling of the old control systems and the coercive arrangements behind them make the index plummet following liberalization in the wake of political discontinuities of the type we have seen in Eastern Europe (but not in China, which might follow the path in Fig. 1).

The second is that regulation in the destination states is not merely less but different in kind from that of centrally planned communism. The new style regulators have to be competent to follow the path in Fig. 1 with the grain of a market economy, not enforcing arbitrary orders by intimidation. Those trained in the latter techniques are not promising material for recruitment to the new-style regulatory bodies. Indeed, there is likely to be an awkward period when the intention to liberalize is clear, and some key steps have been taken, and yet the statute book remains replete with measures inappropriate to a market economy and an unsympathetic bureaucracy would be in a position to obstruct, or to threaten to obstruct, enterprise by invoking obsolete laws.

Although I have described this problem in general terms, it is very clear that it manifested itself very differently in Eastern Europe, on the one hand, and the CIS, on the

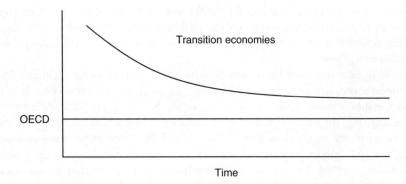

Figure 1.

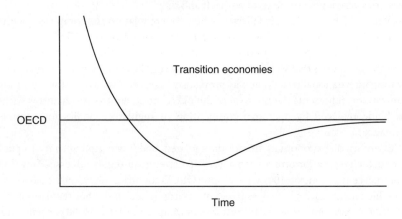

Figure 2.

other. Perhaps because the heavy-handed enforcement machinery, if it existed in the former states, was identified with the imperial Soviet power, it fell away almost immediately. The problem of such institutions and their personnel, obstructing enterprise and practical reforms and spreading the virus of corruption in the process, was much more typical of the CIS.

Nevertheless the Central and East European states have suffered from under-regulation, particularly of financial markets, even if other intrusive policies, particularly social and redistributive ones, have converged monotonically. It then depends on one's weighting of these two factors as to which path the national aggregate index is seen as following (see Fig. 3).

This regulatory non-monotonicity is not due to any legislative reversals other than the asymmetric process of liberalization and re-regulation. This is true, even though the latter process is inevitably piecemeal, uneven, and stepwise. Investors in transition economies crave a regulatory stability that it is almost impossible to deliver. Unless another country's statute book is adopted wholesale, reform in any one segment of the

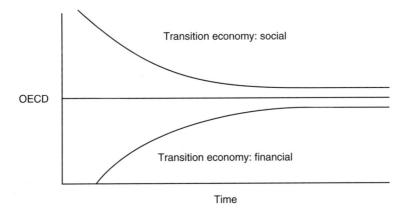

Figure 3.

law is constrained by the state of other segments. Thus progress is limited to relatively small steps and each segment has to be revisited several times before the transition is complete—and only with lesser frequency thereafter.

6. In this section I want to address two questions about the relations between inflation and growth and reform and growth respectively in the course of transition.

In Central and Eastern Europe and the Baltic States as a whole inflation peaked at 2–500 per cent per annum in 1992 and was, in general, well below 100 per cent (25–35 per cent on average) by 1994. In these countries output growth was negative in 1992, negligible in 1993, and, on average, has exceeded 3 per cent p.a. since 1994. In the CIS, inflation peaked at 2–4,000 per cent p.a. in 1993 and did not, on average, fall below 100 per cent until 1996, output growth has yet to turn positive on a weighted basis—which gives a heavy weight to Russia.

Looking at the individual countries reinforces yet again the message that very high inflation is inimical to economic growth. A large majority of countries resumed economic growth only after reducing inflation below 50 per cent, and even those such as Armenia, Belarus, Georgia, and Uzbekistan that seem to have resumed growth while inflation was high brought inflation down to 50 per cent p.a. or less shortly thereafter.

Thus the merits of liberalization and stabilization as preconditions of growth appear to be securely established. What about a reform more generally?

Table 1 ranks twenty-five transition economies by their estimated 1998 GDP relative to that of 1989. The table is headed by Poland at 118 per cent, while Georgia and Moldova come last at 35 per cent. We also show a composite 'Transition Reform Index' (TRI) based on the EBRD's tabulation of scores. Their scoring is on a four-point scale but with +s and –s, which I take to be ± 1 / 3. I also add in one-tenth of their estimates of the private-sector share in GDP (in principal this could range from 0 to 10 but in practice ranges from 3 (Tajikistan, Turkmenistan) to 8 (Hungary). The countries are also assigned to one of five regional groupings: Central and Eastern Europe (1), Baltic States (2), South-Eastern Europe (3), Caucasus (4), and Central CIS/Asia (5).

John S. Flemming

Table 1. *Reform and GDP performance*

Rank	Transition economy	(1) GDP	(1) TRI	(2) GDP	(2) TRI	(3) GDP	(3) TRI	(4) GDP	(4) TRI	(5) GDP	(5) TRI
1	Poland	118	34.5 (5)								
2	Slovenia	103	31.2 (7)								
3	Slovak Republic	100	33.8 (4)								
4	Czech Rep.	97	35.2 (2)								
5	Hungary	95	37.7 (1)								
6	Uzbekistan									88	21.5 (22)
7	Albania					87	28.2 (11)				
8	Croatia					79	29.5 (9)				
9	Romania					78	27.3 (15)				
10	Estonia			77	34.3 (3)						
11	Belarus									75	15 (24)
12	Bulgaria					66	27 (18)				
13	Lithuania			63	32.3 (6)						
14	Kazakhstan									63	27.8 (12)
15	Kyrgyz Republic									60	28.7 (10)
16	Former Yugoslav Republic of Macedonia					59	27.2 (17)				
17	Latvia			58	30.3 (8)						
18	Russia									55	27.3 (15)
19	Turkmenistan									44	13.8 (25)
20	Azerbaijan							42	22.2 (21)		
21	Tajikistan									41	17.7 (23)
22	Armenia							40	27.3 (15)		
23	Ukraine									37	24.2 (20)
24	Georgia							35	27.7 (12)		
25	Moldava					35	26.2 (19)				
	Average ranking	3	4	13	6	10	15	22	16	16	19

Notes: 1 = Central and Eastern Europe, 2 = Baltic States, 3 = South-Eastern Europe, 4 = Caucasus, 5 = Central CIS / Asia. Transition Reform Index (TRI) ranks in parentheses.

Source: EBRD Transition Report 1998.

Considering the table as a whole there is a high degree of correlation between GDP and TRI scores. Four out of five of the top GDP scores are in the top five transition scores, and vice versa, while five out of seven of the bottom GDP scores are in the last seven TRI scores, and vice versa. Yet within several of the regional groups the correlation is negligible (group 5) or strongly negative (group 4 and group 1); only in groups 2 and 3 is it at all strongly positive. The positive correlation in the population as a whole is due much more to inter-group correlation than to intra-group correlation.

As the groups are ordered roughly by distance from Western Europe, they may act as proxies for historical factors and it may be that these account for the crucial inter-group correlation. The 'other CIS' or central CIS/Asia category is both the largest and the most diverse, with 1998 GDP ranging over 37–88 per cent of 1989 levels and reform indices ranging over 14–29—but this sample also shows no correlation. If split into Belarus/ Russia/Ukraine and Central Asia respectively, there is perfect negative correlation in the first sub-group and a positive correlation in the second.

The Caucasus group is out of line in having the lowest group GDP score while having a relatively high reform score. The low GDP score is presumably due to the extent of international and civil hostilities in the region. It may also be worth commenting on other cases of extreme divergence between GDP and reform rankings. Apart from Georgia (with a difference of 12), these are Uzbekistan (16), Belarus (14), and Latvia (9). The first two have high GDP scores despite low reform scores, while Latvia, like Georgia, and, though to a lesser degree, the other Baltic States, has a low GDP score despite its high reform score.

Uzbekistan has resources, the sustainability of Belarus's GDP has been questioned, while the Baltic States may suggest that formal reform is insufficient to shake off the inheritance of participation in the FSU. More generally, the high correlation across the twenty-five countries may reflect a broader range of factors than the willingness to reform and a simple causal link from reform to GDP performance.

7. An enormous amount has been written on the question of why output declined so much in European transition economies. One set of arguments parallels the broad political ones I have already mentioned. There is a set of asymmetries that makes for immediate discontinuous negative changes not immediately offset by slower and more organic responses to positive incentives.

Thus the structure of state orders, and so on, was dismantled, presenting enterprises with a negative shock. The enterprises then took time to develop the linkages with other enterprises and their requirements that should have given rise eventually to more production better suited to users' needs.

Liberalization and convergence of product prices on world relativities meant that some enterprises found their value-added margins (the difference between the price of their material inputs and those of the products into which they transformed them) widening and others found them narrowing. The latter could contract output and employment rapidly, the former would take time to invest in extra equipment, to hire and train additional workers and to raise output. Extreme economic financial and political uncertainty in the course of transition would do little to deter contractions and much to deter the investment, broadly conceived, necessary for expansion.

A second set of arguments focuses on the macroeconomic monetary and fiscal policies adopted in the course of stabilization. Although I have spoken of contraction of output and employment, there is, in fact, across all the transition economies, little if any correlation between output falls and unemployment. The deepest falls in output are in the CIS, where unemployment has risen relatively little—although in Belarus neither output nor employment is recorded as having fallen much.

The emergence of open unemployment was limited in the CIS by the dependence of workers and their families on their employers for a wide range of social services. Enterprises were willing to keep people on, either out of social responsibility or because the cost could be made very low by paying a low minimum wage for a worker of whom little was expected.

Another source of downward bias in asymmetry relates to the problem of uncoordinated reform and liberalization in a group of countries that previously traded quite intensively with one another, even though the pattern of trade departed from that of comparative advantage at world prices. If liberalization is not complete, prices remain distorted, while people are freer than before to trade both domestically and across the new states' boundaries. Things that continue to be effectively subsidized—whether explicitly or not—are particularly likely to be exported if the neighbours do not subsidize the same items. The exporting state then has an incentive to restrict exports—and such restrictions were more widespread in the region for several years than restrictions on imports.

The importing state then suffered a deterioration in its term of trade if the goods continued to be available at all, or had to be bought on the world market, or at world market prices. This too was disruptive of output in a way that would not have affected a single reforming state or a coordinated reform undertaken by the whole COMECON area.

8. It was always clear that there was a complex nexus of privatization, restructuring, and finance. Would restructuring be better done before or after privatization? Did the answer depend on the governance structures implicit in the form of privatization? At what point should the banks be privatized? Could enterprise budget constraints be sufficiently hardened first?

It was tempting to see privatization as an end in itself to be pursued promptly, as in Czechoslovakia, and later, and differently, in Russia. But subsequent experience has validated earlier warnings that such successes might prove short lived if governance, restructuring, and competition policy were not attended to, even if, as in Poland, such attention delayed privatization. Equally remarkable in Poland's relative success has been its ability to harden budget constraints on enterprises yet to be privatized, so that its banking reforms and recapitalizations have not had to be repeated, as in Hungary.

Both the Czech voucher privatizations and Russia's variant, privileging the claims of workers and managers, have tended to entrench incumbent managements, whether as owners themselves or facing highly dispersed ownership structures. Experience there and elsewhere suggests that restructuring of enterprises is very much more effective when outsiders become involved whether directly as newly installed managers or less directly as new and sufficiently concentrated owners to exert real pressure for change on the incumbents.

One of the disappointments of transition as organized to date has been the failure of the banks to apply such pressures. In many cases they remained largely state owned even when industrial and commercial activities were apparently largely privatized. The fact that the banks retained influence as creditors or as managers of mutual funds was an important limitation to the reality of privatization. Moreover, the continuity of management in the banks then reinforced the inertia of incumbent managements in ostensibly privatized enterprises. There was even a danger that banks that had been partially privatized, or had at least been corporatized and were meant to operate as if private, would get into difficulties that would culminate in their full renationalization, even if in intention only temporary, with further qualification to the privateness of any associated companies.

Nearly every transition economy has experienced a banking crisis. In some cases these have been due largely to macroeconomic policy problems and sharp swings in real interest rates. In others they have reflected problems of regulation. There have also been widespread 'Ponzi' finance schemes outside, but affecting, banking systems in Russia, Rumania, and, most destructively, Albania. Other emerging markets, such as Portugal, have also proved vulnerable to such schemes, or scams, which are contained in fully developed market economies only by perpetual vigilance.

Russia's crisis of 1998 was by far the most dramatic. Its causes were largely macroeconomic, but inadequacy of regulation was a contributory factor. As a consequence of banking failures, the money transmission and transaction settlement systems, never adequate, became even less effective, at great cost to the Russian economy. So-called barter, however, now again very widespread, is due less to the lack of alternative transaction mechanisms than to attempts to circumvent IMF-imposed restrictions on the money supply by supplementing it by informal monies—often with the willing assistance of the authorities—including tax collectors.

9. Economic transition is not an end in itself, but is based on the view that the welfare of citizens / consumers will be higher in the destination than in the origin state. What can we say about the changes to date? Obviously there is a major benefit in terms of freedom— although the responsibilities that go with it are not always immediately welcome.

Even though part of the loss in measured GDP related to military and similar production which may not be much missed, the associated employment and status are missed by those who lost them. Unemployment is one source of the increased inequality that has occurred throughout the region during the first ten years of transition. The increase is not, however, by any means uniform, nor indeed, as mentioned above, were the starting points.

The pattern of income distribution within and between OECD and COMECON countries has shifted over the decades. In the 1980s it was possible to compare recorded earnings inequality in Czechoslovakia with that in Germany, in Poland with that in Australia, and in Russia with that in Britain, in each case inequality was much more dispersed in the latter than in the former, but less unequal than in the USA. In terms of household income, the socialist countries, along with Scandinavia and Benelux, were more equal, in terms of measured income, than the OECD norm.

During transition, individual earnings inequality, as measured by the decile ratio, rose by 25–50 per cent in Central Europe and 100–200 per cent in the CIS. These extremes are dampened in terms of household incomes where the Gini coefficient rose by 25 per cent and 100 per cent respectively. Russia, in particular, is now a very unequal society;

given also the 40 per cent fall in per capita GDP, the plight of the poor must be dire indeed.

Along with increasing inequality has gone a continued deterioration in indicators of health, particularly in the CIS, but the fact that some conditions, notably those indicative of stress, have increased even in Germany's Neue Länder, where incomes have risen and medical resources are good, suggests that it may be that the stress of transition itself, coming to terms with increased individual responsibility at a time of change and associated challenges, contributes directly to raise the incidence of some, particularly male, diseases.

10. What are the lessons after ten years of transition—or is it still too early to tell? Almost by definition, a transition may not be judged a success before it is complete—and yet we have seen that the notion of completeness may itself not be applicable to this process. Even if a country's ambition is to join the EU—and that ambition is achieved—it may still be too early to draw up a balance sheet for the transition path, which may continue to influence the economy's post-entry performance.

I started with data that suggested two conclusions: one, strongly, that macroeconomic stabilization is conducive to economic growth. This may not be related to transition at all; it certainly is not restricted to transition economies. In transition economies, as elsewhere, macroeconomic stabilization depends on the adequacy of tax-raising processes and procedures. Transition does provide a distinctive context for the transformation of revenue and expenditure systems, as personal and corporate income taxes and typically value-added taxes replace the arbitrary levies of the previous regime. Hungary had gone a long way towards putting such a system in place before 1990. It has proved much more difficult in the CIS, and particularly in Russia, whose federal structure and Yeltsin's recurrent need for political support from the regions have weakened central fiscal control.

My second, more relevant, but more qualified conclusion was that reform was conducive to economic growth (or at least its resumption in recovery). It has become fashionable, particularly since Russia's setback in 1998, to blame it on doctrinaire reformers' unquestioning pursuit of shock therapy. The critics accuse the reformers, both indigenous and imported, of neglecting the crucial stages of institution building.

This criticism seems to me to be doubly misplaced. First of all it fails to recognize the context in which many economic decisions are being taken—not in a dry dock but on the high seas. There was no economic bureaucratic or political status quo that could be put on hold while new institutions and procedures were devised. Events compelled action of some sort in the economic sphere even if not those actually taken.

Secondly, in Russia the partial reforms of the late Gorbachev period left a particularly unstable situation exceptionally open to arbitrage and more corrupt socially unproductive transactions. The reformers were less doctrinaire than conscious of the imperative of events. It is clear that their policies did not succeed, but their critics need to construct a more complete alternative if they are to establish that the mistake was to do too much too soon rather than too little too late. Poland's persistent relative success certainly points to the latter conclusion.

In the microeconomic area I still believe that the first requirement is for a set of measures that enable budget constraints to be hardened without a socially unacceptable and economically inefficient incidence of closures and unemployment. Once such measures are in place, bankruptcy, privatization, restructuring, and so on, can proceed with due attention to the needs of corporate governance, competition, and financial regulation.

The suspicion that the problems of the CIS are due to too little rather than too much reform is strengthened by the knowledge that partial reform presents profit opportunities to those well placed to grasp them, who then acquire a vested interest in maintaining reform incomplete rather than completing it—and gives them the means with which to frustrate its completion. This is the essence of the case for shock therapy—doing a lot quickly. Restating the case after ten years in which disappointments have exceeded hopes fulfilled by a wide margin may not suffice to alter the prospect of its prevailing. There is a logic, albeit perverse, to the slow progress of the CIS countries as there is to the faster alignment of the Central and East European states.

What distinguishes the CIS states is not merely the paucity and incompleteness of reforming change, but the progressive breakdown of the basic requirements of confidence in property, contract law, and the associated institutions. Until this is in place, continuing decline remains likely.

Comment on 'Transition: The First Ten Years' by John S. Flemming

OLIVIER BLANCHARD

I found John's survey very refreshing. It does not have a grand theme, but is rather a collection of insights. They are all the better because John doesn't try to mould them into one overarching structure. I find myself in agreement with most of his points. In my discussion, and for the sake of balance, I will actually take the other approach (the approach taken by Joe Stiglitz in a paper on the same theme given a few weeks back at the other ABCDE conference in Washington). I shall focus instead on the big questions and then use that structure to take up some of John's points.

There are two obvious big questions. The first one is: why did output fall by so much and for so long in some countries? That output fall came as a surprise, I think, to most of us, and we need to go back and understand it. The other question, which Joe also addressed, is: would we—we being Western economists and Western advisers—have given better and perhaps very different policy advice, given what we now know? Let me anticipate the conclusions. I find myself in large agreement with Joe in answer to the first, and in large agreement with John in answer to the second.

I. WHY DID OUTPUT FALL?

John presents a list of important events and potential causes, from the need for enormous reallocation to the collapse of COMECON, to price liberalization, to macro-policies. My sense is that these may well explain the beginning of transition but that there is some-thing much more fundamental at work. In the end, the source of the fall in output is in the very nature of transition, and that's what we have to look at.

Let me go back to some themes that were taken up in the previous session this morning. In a so-called market economy, barely an economic decision takes place without relying on either explicit or implicit contracts. Explicit contracts require the exis-tence of well-functioning laws. Implicit contracts require something like confidence or repeated relations. Take off the laws and the confidence, and the economy will come to a stop. Lenders are not going to provide external finance: they don't know whether they will get any money back. Owners are not going to trust managers. Firms are not going to get involved in complex production processes because they fear the haggling and the holding-up from suppliers and the various parties they have to deal with along the way.

In short, complex forms of economic activity will come to a near stop. The only activities that are going to remain, and maybe even grow, are the very simplest forms of economic activity, those in which you do not need external finance, where the scale is very small, and the complexity of the task is very limited.

Under central planning, there were no laws—at least not as we would define them—and there was not much confidence. But there was a very strong state. The state was able to make sure that things didn't go too wrong. A manager of a firm that needed financing would get it because the state would make sure it was coming. At the same time, the manager of the state firm knew that taking the assets and flying to the Côte d'Azur was probably not the best strategy for him to follow. But, as transition started, the state lost its legitimacy and therefore its strength. Transition countries went from a strong state to a weak state. At the same time, the institutions that are needed for markets to function—namely, confidence on the one hand and laws and institutions on the other—were not yet there. Countries found themselves with the worst of both worlds: the state was no longer able to make things happen and, at the same time, the markets were not ready to do the job. This led to the collapse of many forms of activity, especially in Russia.

There is a twist to this. Actually something worse happened: the state didn't go from strong to weak; it went from strong to weak to 'captured', and that made things worse. When the state is weak, it may be difficult to produce and make a profit, but the only thing you can do is try. When the state is captured, there is an alternative to producing—namely, use the state to extract rents from the rest of the economy, to extract subsidies instead of producing. We have seen this happening on a large scale. The state going from strong to weak to captured is of the essence in understanding why there was a collapse in output.

I see this as the main lesson of transition. Surely for transition countries; they have paid the price for learning it. But also for the other countries in the world. It is fair to say that, though most of us believed that institutions were of the essence to make markets work, we did not predict the kind of decrease in output that we have observed and therefore, by implication, the importance of institutions for the way markets work.

II. POLICY ADVICE IN RETROSPECT

Here one must distinguish between two types of criticisms of what Joe has called the Washington consensus. (I wish there was indeed such a consensus, but we all understand what Joe means when he uses the term.)

Some economists have argued that, because it takes time for institutions to be created, transition should have been slower, that the 'big-bang' strategy was a mistake. Introducing privatization, price liberalization, and other things at once, the argument goes, was just a mistake. It should have been done more slowly.

This argument, however, does not follow in any way from the previous one. If the choice had been between keeping a strong state (not only a strong state but a strong state committed to reform), on the one hand, or getting rid of the state and letting firms operate in markets without institutions, most of us would surely say: keep the state in place for a while, let the markets develop at the margins, and do it slow. And many of us see the experience of China as fitting that general description. This, however, was not the option in most East European countries. The choice was not between keeping a strong state or going the market route without all institutions in place. It was between keeping a very weak state, which had lost legitimacy and much of its control of firms anyway, or going the market route without all institutions in place. In this case, it is far from obvious which option dominates.

A more sophisticated version of the argument, which I would attribute to Joe and to others, is to say we should have been more careful in the design of the institutions. Rather than try to go for Cadillac-type institutions, we should have thought about institutions that fitted the need at the time, and let them evolve through time. I think nobody can disagree with that general proposition. It seems right, and it fits the diagnosis. The question in practice is what it actually means. To that end, I thought I would end my discussion with a discussion of what this may mean in the context of privatization. This is just one example; I could have taken bank reform, fiscal reform, and so on.

Go back to the early 1990s. The debate about privatization focused on three main options. To caricature: (1) wait and see: leave the state firms in limbo and privatize when the time is right; (2) mass privatization: do a voucher programme, give the firms to the people; (3) stakeholder privatization: see who is de facto controlling the firms, give them enough property rights, align incentives.

In retrospect, given what we know today—which is much more than we knew then—we can ask: what was the best of the three routes? I think, even today, the answer is far from obvious. Let's think of each of these options as having two dimensions: how it's going to work in the short run, and how it may evolve over time.

Start with the waiting route. At first glance, waiting would seem to satisfy the Stiglitz principle. It leaves options open, and one can wait until institutions have been put in place. But, at the same time, waiting creates an obvious conflict between the current managers of the firm and the future shareholders or owners in the future, when privatization has taken place. The incentives for the managers of the firms to steal assets are gigantic—one would expect large-scale divesting of sets. So, when privatization time comes, there may be little left to privatize. And, except in countries where the state remained relatively strong, this is indeed what has happened. Waiting does not seem like an attractive option.

Turn to mass privatization. In the short run, this creates another game, which can also be quite destructive. It is a game between the managers of the firm and the initial shareholders. Given the structure of ownership that comes out of most mass privatization plans, shareholders are in no position to prevent managers from misbehaving. So, in the short run, incentives are still strong for managers to divest assets. And, again, when this route has been followed, this is roughly what we have observed. In terms of evolution over time, the hope was that mass privatization would create a market for shares. Eventually, people who valued the firms more would be willing to pay more, so they would end up controlling managers and doing the right thing. We have learned that this may not work, or it may work very slowly. Although there may be a market for shares, the shares may in the end be concentrated in the wrong hands. My reading of the Czech Republic, while more positive than John's, still suggests that concentration in the right hands is at best a very slow process.

Turn finally to stakeholder privatization. In the short run, this would seem like a much better solution, as it eliminates the game between the stakeholders and the outside owners. Other destructive games may, however, still be at work. Very often there will be more than one stakeholder, the workers and the managers, and they may fight. Even if there is only one dominant insider group, say the workers in a country like Poland, or the managers in a country like Russia, the incentives may still not be the right ones: the manager will want to keep his job and might oppose restructuring if his job is at stake. The workers will want to keep employment at levels that are too high. This is again typically what we have observed. What will happen over time? We have learned that the hope that stakeholder privatization eventually leads to a market for shares in which some of the stakeholders sell their shares, and an outside owner arises, may not be fulfilled. In Russia, the proportion of shares in the hands of managers has typically increased, not decreased, and outside shareholders have not emerged on any relevant scale.

What conclusions should we draw? First, that which scheme satisfies Joe's injunctions is far from clear. Is it the first, because it gives flexibility of choice after? Is it the second, because it is more evolutive? Or is it the third, because it is more realistic? Second, that it is far from clear, even *ex post*, what scheme was best. If one takes the Washington consensus of the early 1990s to have been something along the lines of 'Try to do mass privatization if you can, and if, for political reasons, you can't, do stakeholder privatization', it is not clear that the advice was very wrong. In short, I like very much the direction in which Joe wants us to explore. But I end up close to John, thinking that maybe we did the best we could, given the circumstances.

To summarize: I am quite sure we enormously underestimated the size of the task involving transition, the complexity of markets, and how they work. I am also sure that there were many policy mistakes committed along the way. But it is not obvious to me that at the end of the day (or at the end of the decade) there was an obvious 'other way' of doing things, a way that would have led to a much better outcome.

2

Quis Custodiet Ipsos Custodes?⋆: Corporate Governance Failures in the Transition

JOSEPH E. STIGLITZ

I. INTRODUCTION

Two economic events have dominated the twentieth century—the socialist/communist experiment that began in the Soviet Union in 1917 and ended with the fall of the Soviet Empire just under a decade ago; and the transition of these economies to market economies during the past decade. There is widespread agreement about the lessons from the first—central planning cannot replace markets, and even market socialism cannot replace the incentives associated with capitalism—incentives to produce goods more cheaply, to produce what consumers want, and to innovate. But the lessons from the second experiment are far more ambiguous, and it is upon these that I want to focus my remarks today.

First, the facts, to say the least, are jarring. Fig. 1 compares the average growth rate of the economies in transition for the decade prior to the transition with the past decade. (With one exception, the countries have done more poorly since the transition to the market economy than before.) Indeed, the overwhelming majority of these countries have yet to reach their 1989 GDP levels. This means, on average, that these countries are worse off today than they were before the transition (Fig. 2). These results are corroborated by other indicators of well-being, such as longevity. Fig. 3 shows life spans before and after the transition. Again, the results are bleak—life expectancy in these countries has fallen on average even while world life expectancy has risen by two years.

But even bleaker are the statistics on poverty. For eighteen of the twenty-five countries for which we have data, poverty on average has increased from 4 percent to 45 percent of the population, using the $4-a-day standard, revealing the devastating changes in standards of living. Fig. 4 shows these changes in some of the most severely affected economies. Evidently, Russia and several of the other countries of Eastern Europe and the former Soviet Union (FSU) have managed to repeal one of the long standing 'laws' of economics, the trade-off between growth (efficiency) and inequality. They have

---

⋆ 'Who is to guard the guards themselves?' (Juvenal (AD 60–130), *Satires* vi. 347).

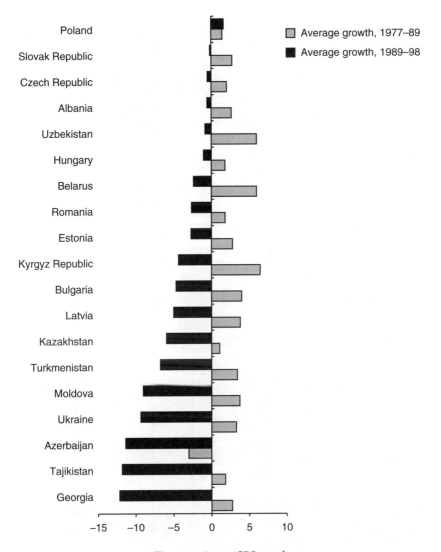

Figure 1. *Average GDP growth*

Source: Statistical Information and Management Analysis database.

managed to experience lower growth and greater inequality since the transition than before it began.

There is one marked success that I have deliberately left out of the data presented so far—China—and fortunately it is a large success, with a population greater than all of the other transition economies combined. Over the twenty-year period since its transition began, it has succeeded in growing at an average annual rate of 9.5 percent , and poverty has been brought down from 60 percent to 22 percent. Three-quarters of the increase in

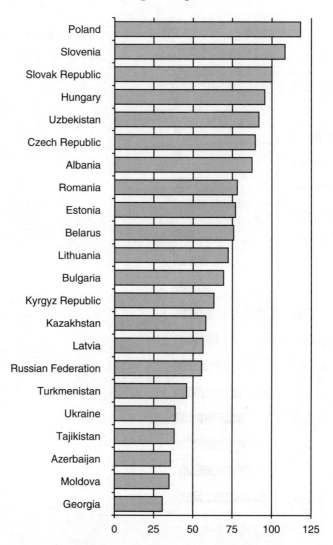

Figure 2. *Transition country GDP as percentage of 1989*
Source: Statistical Information and Management Analysis database.

incomes in low-income countries over the last decade was inside China. If the separate provinces of China were treated as separate countries—and some of them have populations of 60 million or more, larger than all but a few of the countries of Eastern Europe and the FSU—then the 20 fastest growing countries during the past two decades would be located in China (See World Bank 1997).[1] The stark contrast between China's success

[1] These statistics are not quite 'fair'—in principle, we should treat large provinces in other countries as independent data points. Were we to do so, however, the picture that would emerge would not be very different.

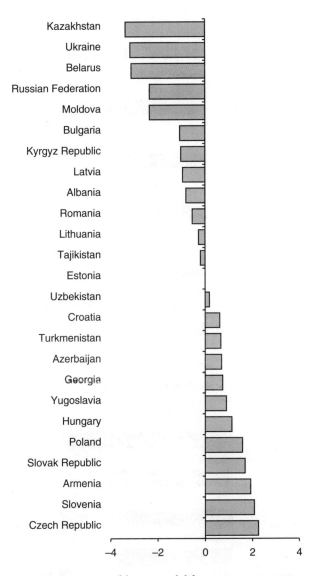

Figure 3. *Years of change in male life expectancy, 1989–1997*

and Russia's poor performance is clearly illustrated in Fig. 5, which tracks the growth of GDP in these economies during the last decade.

Not long ago, several of the economists who had played important roles in the early days of the transition expressed their optimism concerning Russia, publishing books with titles such as *How Russia Became a Market Economy* or *The Coming Boom in Russia*. The optimism was widely shared. What was surprising was the absence of data to support that optimism. Let us be clear: it is not hard for a country rich in natural resources to find

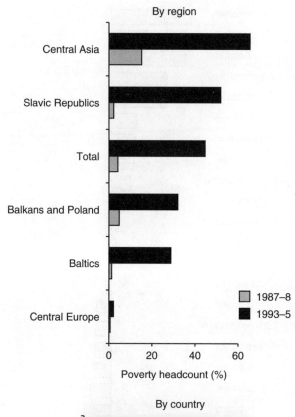

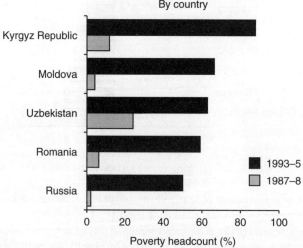

Figure 4. *Poverty headcount in transition regions*

Source: Milanovic (1998)

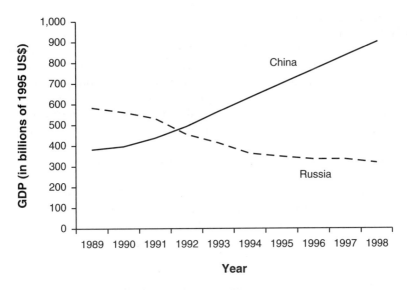

Figure 5. *Chinese and Russian GDP*

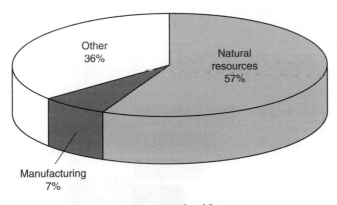

Figure 6. *1994 composition of total foreign investment*

Note: Natural resources include fuel and energy, ferrous metallurgy, non-ferrous metallurgy, logs, wood, cellulose, and paper. Manufacturing includes the chemical and petrochemical industry, machine-building and metal-processing, construction materials, and light industry.

Source: Goskomstat.

investors abroad willing to exploit those resources, especially if the price is right. Far more difficult, however, is creating an industrial or service-based economy. Fig. 6 shows the investment in natural resources and manufacturing in Russia in 1994 as a percentage of all foreign investment; in 1994, investment in manufacturing was a mere 7 percent, compared with 57 percent in natural resources. In 1997, while our data remain incomplete, preliminary statistics show the number for manufacturing to have slipped even further, to approximately 3 percent. Investment was attracted for natural resources, but not for manufacturing.

There are other seeming anomalies. The wisdom that emerged in the years immediately following the beginning of the transition was clear: 'Countries that liberalize rapidly and extensively turn around more quickly (than those who do not)' (see World Bank 1996). Countries that worked most rapidly to bring about macroeconomic adjustment and lower inflation rates were more likely to do better than those that hesitated; those that pushed rapid privatization were more likely to do better than those that went more slowly. Yet, a decade after the beginning of the transition, the league tables are markedly different from what they were a few short years ago. Among the countries of Eastern Europe, whose history, geography, and prospects are at least more similar to each other than they are to the Central Asian or Baltic states, early liberalization and overall average growth exhibit no positive relationship; if anything, they appear to have a negative correlation, as Fig. 7 shows. In fact, looking at Fig. 8, we can see that those countries that grew most quickly in the early years of transition were no more likely to grow quickly in more recent years. Recent evidence also casts doubt on the dogma of low inflation; Fig. 9 shows that, within Eastern Europe, those economies that grew the fastest were those with *higher*, not lower inflation.[2] At this juncture, then, inferences are far less clear than many asserted in 1996. Differences in initial conditions and geography imply that different countries faced different opportunities, and these differences in prospects might account for the success and/or the speed of transition (implying that any observed correlations may simply be spurious, an observation that those ready to defend the orthodox prescriptions often seemed to overlook). It is nonetheless remarkable how different the world looks today than many thought earlier on in the transition. Countries that

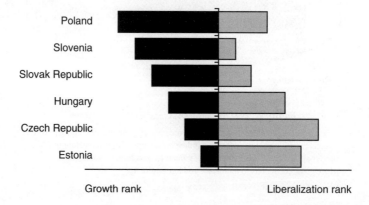

Figure 7. *Ranking of liberalization and growth in Eastern Europe*
Source: Statistical Information and Management Analysis database; World Bank (1996).

---

[2] It is important to remember that, while this may not be a statistically significant regression result, it nevertheless serves to cast serious doubt on assertions to the contrary—namely, that early liberalization and low inflation were the cornerstones of a successful transition policy.

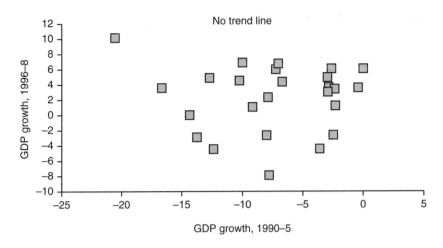

Figure 8. *Economies in transition growth, 1990–1995 versus 1996–1998*
Source: Statistical Information and Management Analysis database.

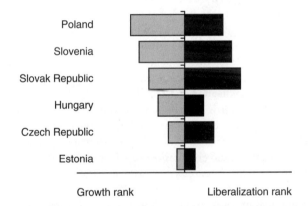

Figure 9. *Rankings of inflation and growth in Eastern Europe*
Source: EBRD (1998); Statistical Information and Management Analysis database.

were castigated a few short years ago for the slowness and incompleteness of their reforms, such as Uzbekistan and Slovenia, are performing rather well, whereas other countries heralded as models of reform, such as the Czech Republic, are now encountering difficulties.

These data are striking, and they should at least serve to undermine confidence in the previous conventional wisdom. But it should be clear that I am not presenting these as definitive results; I am simply arguing that there has perhaps been excessive and unwarranted confidence in the previous conventional wisdom—a conventional wisdom that, unfortunately, continues to unduly influence policy-makers in some circles. What is remarkable about these results is that they are not the results of any data mining—though, to be sure, they conformed in many ways to my own priors. In each case, I put forth a hypothesis, looked for standard indicators, for example, concerning corporate governance, that had been constructed by others (and had in fact been used earlier to justify the old conventional wisdom), and ran simple correlations. Whether or not coefficients are statistically significant, the results would still serve to cast doubt on the previous views, which argued for contradictory statistically and economically significant relationships.

I am confident that these results will stir up a data mining industry, providing gainful employment to Western economists, even as conventional mining grows in relative importance in Russia. Refinements are needed. As I comment later, there are inherent problems in many of the key concepts, raising questions about the corresponding indicators. Is a firm really privatized when it issues shares and the shares are owned by a public enterprise? Or when the privatization is financed by a 'soft' loan from a bank? And how do we know whether the loan is soft?

One further observation concerning interpretation of any results, and opportunities for, shall we say, further data exploration. While the large number of countries involved in the transition might suggest a wealth of variation in policies on the basis of which we could make meaningful inferences, the fact of the matter is that the countries differ enormously in their history, geography, and endowments. Not controlling for these variables throws into question any inferences. Yet, even the wealth of such relevant variables still leads to an under-identified system. Worse still, the policies pursued are, at least to some extent, endogenous, affected by the circumstances of the country. Is a country's poor performance due to the fact that it liberalized slowly, or was there some factor leading to both slow liberalization and low growth performance? The fact that some of the slow reformers have, over the long haul, done so well may convey more information about the impact of the pace of reforms on long-term growth than the observation that some country has both liberalized and grown more rapidly in the short run. This is especially the case because some of the faster reformers were in Eastern Europe—countries where the possibility of quick accession to the EU, with the access to those vast markets, provided an additional impetus for faster reforms and, perhaps, additional returns to those reforms, than might have been the case for the landlocked countries of Central Asia. That is why, in several of the figures, I have separated out those countries from the other economies in transition. Earlier studies, that failed to either recognize or take adequate account of the differential position of the different countries, failed to reflect on the endogeneity of the policy environment. In such a case, the interactions of liberalization and growth should be treated with a high degree of skepticism.

In any case, whatever results we obtain should be looked at with caution. It is only through looking at the interplay between mutually supporting pieces of theory and evidence that we can attain any degree of confidence. Data on declining GDP and increasing poverty[3] are consistent with independently arrived at statistics suggesting

---

[3] For instance, poverty data for Russia come from an independent survey. The eighth round of the Russia Longitudinal Monitoring Survey, conducted in late 1998, showed that the number of people living below the

worsening health conditions. And, as I shall argue, the observed problems are precisely those anticipated by information economics, with its emphasis on corporate governance. And this picture itself is reinforced by the reported regression results. Even the results on inflation are not inconsistent with other bits of data and theory. Inflation is traditionally a problem because it interferes with the working of the price system. But when attempts to suppress inflation are associated with a movement out of a market system and towards a heavy reliance on barter,[4] the price system works even more imperfectly. Theories of downward wage and price rigidity have contended that pushing inflation below a critical threshold actually interferes with the dynamic adjustment of the economy (see Akerlof and Yellen 1985). Clearly, the critical threshold should be higher when the required adjustments are greater. For the economies in transition, these adjustments are particularly large.

At one level, the facts speak for themselves: the transition to the market economy has not delivered what its more ardent advocates promised. To be sure, the countries have not done everything right; but no country does, and, if capitalism is so frail that it cannot survive normal human fallibility, then its virtues, at least for this world, may surely be questioned. After all, one of the longstanding criticisms of socialism was that it was too utopian. The quandary of the failure of so many experiments is particularly vexing when economic theory was so clear in its predictions: distorted prices, central planning, and attenuated incentives arising from the absence of clear property rights meant that resources were not efficiently allocated. Reducing those distortions, decentralizing decision-making, and privatizing—even if not done perfectly—should have moved countries closer to their production possibilities curve. Output should have soared—instead it plummeted.

When I put forward this argument at the ABCDE Conference in Washington a couple of months ago, there were several answers (see Stiglitz 1999). One was that output was not measured accurately. This may be true, but there are arguments suggesting that output was being overestimated (given the huge amounts of barter trade, market prices may provide an overestimate of true values of many commodities) as well as underestimated (see Gaddy and Ickes 1998 for a discussion of some of these issues).

A second argument was that such declines were to be expected, as loss-making enterprises were shut down. This kind of reasoning illustrates a level of confusion that should be embarrassing to an economist. The *relevant* losses should be calculated by looking at the value of the output relative to the opportunity cost of the resources. If a firm is making a loss (in this sense), it means that, if its inputs (the resources it uses) are redeployed to other more productive uses, output (at least correctly valued) should rise. Of course, output is not increased by moving resources from low productivity uses into idleness. The opportunity cost of such resources is zero (or the value of leisure).

poverty threshold had increased from 36% in 1996 to 39% in 1998, and the number of children less than 6 years old living below the poverty line had increased sharply from 45% to a staggering 56%.

[4] Estimates suggest that, within Russia, over 70% of transactions (by value) are now barter. There is no agreement about the reason for the growth of barter, but several of the favored explanations focus on policies striving for macro-stabilization (e.g. tax policies that use the financial system for tax collection; cash-flow constraints unmatched by expenditure constraints, which lead to arrears).

To be sure, the production possibility curves of the economies in transition are lower than they would have been had better investments been made. But that is not the issue. The point is that movement towards a market economy should lead an economy from a point interior of the production possibilities curve towards the frontier and then, as investment is allocated more efficiently, move the frontier outwards (see Fig. 10). Hence, growth *should* have been higher because of both the rapid movement towards the frontier, and the more rapid movement outward of the frontier, as investment was more efficiently allocated. That did not occur.

In my ABCDE lecture in Washington, I set forth several hypotheses attempting to explain these phenomena. At one level, there is now a growing consensus: it is far more difficult to create a market economy than was previously thought to be the case. An institutional infrastructure—including not just contract enforcement, but competition policy, bankruptcy law, and financial institutions and regulations—is required. And, although institutional infrastructure requires time to create, without it, privatization may lead more to asset stripping than wealth creation. A regression run on the effect of privatization alone on GDP growth in the transition economies revealed *no statistically significant effect* of privatization on growth (Fig. 11). If, however, the regression is run with additional data for corporate governance, for those economies receiving high scores for corporate governance and restructuring, privatization did have a positive and statistically significant effect (Fig. 12).

In my previous ABCDE lecture, I focused on several issues:

- The lack of corporate governance—combined with free capital mobility and the contractionary macroeconomic policies—made it more profitable for those who

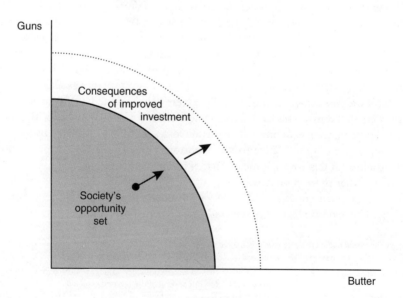

Figure 10. *Production possibilities curve*

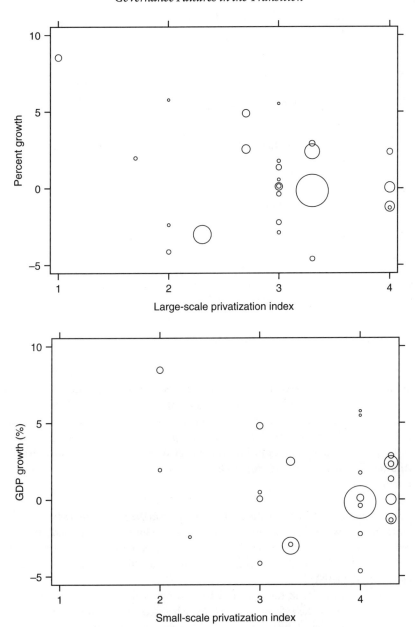

Figure 11. *Regression of GDP growth on small and large privatization and restructuring*

Note: The charts reflect the weighted (by 1989 GDP) correlation between large-scale privatization and GDP growth and small-scale privatization and GDP growth. The privatization indices are based on the 1998 EBRD *Progress in Transition* scorecard.

Weighted by 1989 GDP Source	SS	df	MS		
				Number of obs	= 25
				$F(3, 21)$	= 15.28
				Prob > F	= 0.0000
Model	177.018499	3	59.0061662	R-squared	=0.6859
Residual	81.0809533	21	3.86099778	Adj R-squared	=0.6410
Total	258.099452	24	10.7541438	Root MSE	= 1.9649

dgdp	Coef.	Std Err.	t	$P>\lvert t\rvert$	[95% Conf. Interval]	
pmean	.9013996	1.092511	0.825	0.419	−1.370602	3.173401
restruct	−3.539967	2.816531	−1.257	0.223	−9.397264	2.31733
r2	2.290305	.6654943	3.442	0.002	.9063339	3.674276
cons	−1.868984	4.358989	−0.429	0.672	−10.934	7.19603

Figure 12. *Regression of GDP growth on privatization and restructuring, with interaction effect*

Note: The dependent variable is rate of GDP growth from 1990 to 1998. 'Pmean' represents the mean of EBRD score for large-scale and small-scale privatization; 'restruct' represents governance and enterprise restructuring, as defined in the EBRD 1998 *Transition Report:* 'r2' is the interaction variable between 'pmean' and 'restruct'.

had obtained control over Russia's huge manufacturing and natural resources to divert their wealth abroad through a process of asset stripping rather than invest at home.

- While well-functioning market economies requires both competition and private property, reforms focused more on the latter than on the former, and the differential performance between China and Russia may be explained in part by these differences in emphases. Prospects for privatization—except through sales to foreigners and/or restructuring into smaller, more locally controlled units—were inherently bleak.

- Another fundamental difference between China and Russia was the former country's emphasis on enterprise and job creation, rather than an exclusive focus on restructuring existing assets.

- The destruction of social and organizational capital in the process of transition—from an admittedly weak base, and perhaps partly attributable to the speed and structure of reform—without a corresponding emphasis on the creation of new social capital, may also have played an important role in the failures in Russia and some of the other countries of the FSU.

- While all participants in the reform debate recognized the importance of political processes, many of the reform strategies were based on assumptions concerning the political dynamics for which there was neither theory or evidence. The sequence of reforms matters, in part because particular reforms lead to the creation of interest groups that can either facilitate or block subsequent reforms. Underlying some of these misguided views was a naive believe in Coasian processes—that, once property rights were appropriately assigned, efficient institutional arrangements would evolve. Such beliefs ignored both general theories that suggested that there may be inefficient institutional Nash equilibria and that evolutionary processes need not be efficient, and the problematic nature of property rights.

- Another underlying confusion had to do with the interface between macroeconomics and microeconomics. There was a widespread belief in Say's law (an idea that had been discredited three-quarters of a century ago): that somehow, if workers who were underemployed in their current jobs could only be released into open unemployment, the market would respond and create jobs for them. Price stability (low inflation) is not an end in its own, but a means to more fundamental goals, such as faster economic growth. And when pushed too far—below a critical level—not only may the costs of pushing inflation lower not be worth the benefits, but the benefits may actually be negative. Macro-stability does not, in itself, imply micro-restructuring.

In today's talk, I want to focus more narrowly on the issue of corporate governance, and touch on other issues only to the extent that they are related to this issue.

II. CORPORATE GOVERNANCE

In a lecture delivered at the end of the last century, Alfred Marshall (1897), reflecting on what had been learned during the previous century and the unsettled issues for the one to come, discussed at some length the issue that we now refer to as corporate governance. How do we ensure that the manager of the firm acts in the interests of the 'owners'—the shareholders? In nineteenth-century economics, there was simply a single owner-manager, and hence what we now call the agency problem simply did not arise. But, even by the time Marshall wrote, it was clear that there was a separation of ownership and management among many, if not most, large enterprises, that represented an ever-increasing share of GDP. There interests diverged.

Beginning in the late 1960s, I and others put this issue of corporate governance into the contexts of the problems of imperfect information and public goods.

- Owners had imperfect information concerning the opportunities facing managers and could not, by looking at outcomes, infer whether or not managers had made the right decision; indeed, imperfections of information was what necessitated the delegation of responsibility to managers.
- Managers not only knew this, but also could take actions that exacerbated the asymmetries of information, enhancing managers' discretionary authority (see Edlin and Stiglitz 1995; Shleifer and Vishny 1998).
- These problems would arise even if there was a single owner who delegated management responsibility; but, in most large companies, the diverse ownership gave rise to a public goods problem; if any shareholder works hard to improve the management of the firm, all shareholders benefit equally—management is a public good (see, e.g. Stiglitz 1982).

If managers have the means and incentives to act in their own interests, if their own interests do not perfectly coincide with that of shareholders, and if diverse ownership provides no (or inadequate) incentives for monitoring managers, then how can large firms function? If firm value maximization is the key to the success of a market economy, and if, instead, firms maximize managerial returns, then what assurance do we have of the efficiency of the market economy?[5]

There are four possible ways out of this dilemma: the first provides strong controls over the managers (the 'firm') *vis-à-vis* all shareholders, even the smallest stockholder. Actions that are viewed as depriving the small shareholder of value are grounds for legal action against the firm and its management. Management may have a high degree of personal legal liability. Only two countries have gone this route and provided sufficiently strong legal protection that diverse stock ownership systems have been sustained.

The second approach entails there being a single shareholder with a large enough stake that it pays him himself to provide managerial oversight.[6] To be sure, there is still a presumption of an undersupply of managerial oversight; but we seek not perfection—simply workable solutions, or, from the perspective of the transition, at least solutions that avoid disaster. But this raises a new agency problem—how can one be sure that the majority shareholder will not take actions that represent his interests, to the disadvantage of the minority shareholders?[7] One solution—the obvious one—is that there be no minority shareholders—a return to the classic owner-managed firm. But this approach had severe limitations—it implied that the only way that firms could expand would be through borrowing; and, though Modigliani and Miller argued that corporate financial structure didn't matter, their analysis ignored crucial issues such as bankruptcy and asymmetries of information, issues that are at the center of the problem here. I will turn to the role of banks in a minute, but, for now, I simply want to note that excessive reliance on bank/debt finance makes firms highly susceptible to fluctuations in demand and costs, significantly increasing bankruptcy probabilities, with their high transaction and managerial costs.

This brings me to the third approach—that there be strong laws to protect minority shareholders against majority shareholders. Note that these legal protections are some-what different from those discussed earlier. Actions taken in the interests of the 'firm'—the long-run viability of the enterprise, job protection of its employees—might lower all shareholder values and enhance long-run managerial incomes, but they would not be a diversion of value from minority to majority shareholders. Thus, in a sense, these protections are 'weaker' than the first protections. Here, the minority shareholders free ride on the self-interest of the large shareholders to ensure that shareholder values (as a class) are protected.

In a recent study done for the World Bank, Alex Dyck (1999) of Harvard has classified countries by the strength of their shareholder protection and by the concentration of shareholders. The hypothesis was simple: only countries with very strong legal protec-tions could support diverse ownership. Fig. 13 shows that the results confirmed the

---

[5] In fact, the conditions under which even firm value maximization leads to Pareto efficiency are highly restrictive. See Grossman and Stiglitz (1977).

[6] Note the analogy between this solution to the public goods problem and that discussed in the public goods literature concerning lighthouses (see Demsetz 1970 and Coase 1988).

[7] I first began worrying about this problem in Stiglitz (1972).

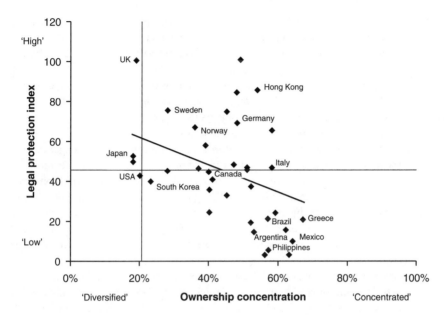

Figure 13. *Rule of law and ownership concentration*

Source: Dyck (1999).

hypothesis: no country with weak legal protections had diverse ownership. From this perspective, one can perceive the weakness of the voucher privatization scheme—as attractive as the idea of creating a people capitalism might have seemed at first blush. It attempted to occupy a position in the chart that all countries—for good reason—had previously avoided: weak legal protections combined with diverse ownership. I shall comment later about where one goes from here.

There is yet another control mechanism, which stands the theory of the firm on its head: it is not shareholders (the nominal 'owners') who really control the firm, but the banks.[8] Concepts of control and power are, perhaps by necessity, ambiguous. The shareholders have rights, but, when ownership is diverse, they must act collusively to exercise those rights; they simply lack the incentive to do so. If there is a single dominant lender, it pays him to monitor (or if there are a few lenders who interact repeatedly, so that they in effect act collusively with respect to monitoring, it pays to assign one of the group to be the lead bank, and hence the chief monitor). And if loans are short term (or if there is a succession of loans, so that the borrower must repeatedly turn to the bank), then the lender has control rights, at least in the sense that, if the borrower does not do as he wishes, he can force the repayment of the loan or force the firm into bankruptcy. Given that, under these circumstances, most firms cannot access other sources of funds, the threat of termination becomes a viable threat.[9]

---

[8] This was an idea first put forward by Berle and Means (1932), and recast, in terms of modern agency theory, by Stiglitz (1985).

[9] For a discussion of the role of threats of termination in credit markets in addressing problems of agency,

To be sure, in exercising their role as a monitor, banks are not concerned with value maximization; rather, they wish to minimize the probability of default.[10] But in monitoring against default, they at least ensure that the worst mistakes—and the worst examples of managerial theft—are avoided.

From this perspective, we can see another source of problems in the privatization strategies followed by many of the economies in transition. Banks under the former socialist system were not real banks; they were banks in name only. They were not involved in screening and monitoring; they simply allocated credit as directed by the government. In the early days of the transition, I and others warned against confusing these nominal banks with real banks, and that one of the real tasks in the transition would be to create real banks (see e.g. Stiglitz (1992). State banks, undercapitalized private banks, or private banks with an implicit guarantee of a bailout, are not, in this sense, real banks: they lack the incentive to screen and monitor on a commercial basis. Indeed, in some cases, they became a new source of soft-budget constraints; in others, they became the vehicle through which state wealth was diverted to the hands of the political cronies.

We can see, from this perspective, the difficulties facing countries seeking rapid privatization, which would or could not sell to foreigners, at least at any politically feasible price. There were, at the time, no legitimate wealth holders to buy the assets. Thus, a country could either use voucher privatization or have banks lend to someone to buy the asset. I have already discussed one of the key problems with privatization—the public good problem of management. Most of those involved in the voucher privatization were aware of this problem. (Indeed, I participated in discussions in Prague on this issue early in the 1990s.) But most thought that the voucher investment funds would take over the task of monitoring; they would aggregate interests, to the point where the public good problem was mitigated. This made sense, but the thinking needed to have gone further. But I remember asking at the time: who was going to monitor the monitors? And so it turned out: the voucher investment funds provided a vehicle for high-powered abuse (see Weiss and Nikitin 1998 for econometric analysis). The fact that the mutual funds were close ended exacerbated these problems. With open-ended funds, investors disgruntled with the performance of these funds could withdraw their money, providing an effective check on the abuses. That is why one of the recommended reforms has been to convert closed funds into open-ended funds.

There is considerable evidence concerning the magnitude and significance of these corporate governance problems. In standard theory, close-ended mutual funds should never sell at a discount (relative to the value of the underlying shares); for there is a simple strategy that would increase the market value—disband the fund and distribute the shares directly. Imperfections in the market for managers (takeovers) explain why, in advanced industrialized economies, shares and close-ended mutual funds have often sold

see Stiglitz and Weiss (1983). Indeed, the advantages of the greater 'control' associated with short-term debt may more than offset the disadvantages associated with the greater risk it imposes (on the borrower). See, e.g., Rey and Stiglitz (1993).

[10] Or, more accurately, the total expected repayment, which includes the size of the residual if the firm does go into bankruptcy.

at a discount—of up to 10 per cent. But, in the Czech Republic, discounts soared to 40 percent or more.

Moreover, standard agency theory argues that, when there is a controlling share-holder (with 20 percent or more of the shares), his interest in providing the public good of corporate oversight and management should increase the firm's market value. Empirical studies confirm these predictions. But, in the Czech Republic, controlling interests give the controller the right to strip assets, unchecked by legal restraints. Thus, it appears that often, when a single party gains control, market value plummets, reflecting the market's perception that control is more associated with asset stripping than with wealth creation.

As the companies needed cash injections to continue to operate, and as the weaknesses in the securities market made it clear that these injections could not be provided through the securities market (a telling criticism—the façade of capitalism had been created, but functioning capital markets, presumably the *sine qua non* of capitalism, did not function), they had to turn to banks. And, if banks had been real banks, then the banks themselves could have performed some of this monitoring role. But under socialism, the banks functioned largely as vehicles for state-directed credits and so had little experience with *ex ante* due diligence and *ex post* monitoring.

But the problems with the banks went deeper. First, owning the firm provided enormous option value; if the firm turned out to be greater in value than it had paid, the owner kept the difference; if it turned out to be less in value, the owner simply went bankrupt. Worse still, owning the firm provided enormous opportunities for theft. The legal structure provided enormous opportunities for diverting the wealth of the firm into the hands of the 'owner', with the owner having only limited personal liability. (In many countries, the returns per unit effort to such theft, given the weak legal structure, clearly exceeded the returns to efforts devoted at wealth creation.)

The theft-plus-option values associated with ownership meant that (in the absence of a competitive loan market) there were enormous returns associated with getting loans. The consequences were predictable—one might say almost inevitable; loans were not necessarily allocated to those who were most likely to use the assets of the firm most efficiently, but to those with political connections, and who otherwise knew best how to 'manipulate' the system.[11] If there had been *real* banks, in the sense that I defined them earlier, these abuses *might* not have occurred, or at least might not have been so prevalent. But the absence of real banks meant that there was neither the incentive nor the capacity to perform the selection and monitoring functions so important to the success of a market economy, and so vital, given the corporate governance problems associated with equity.

In short, the process of transition in general, and privatization in particular, demonstrates an old lesson of market economics—incentives matter; but it also demonstrates a key lesson that was lost on many of the so-called reformers: only under highly idealized situations do incentives result in efficient outcomes; misdirected incentives can provide incentives for asset stripping rather than wealth creation. In many of the countries in transition, that is precisely what happened.

---

[11] Even if corruption had not played an important role in the process, the heavy indebtedness (with implicit or explicit limited liability) would have distorted behavior. See Stiglitz and Weiss (1983).

I have, so far, tried to argue that there is a nexus of institutions that make capitalism work; it is not just 'private ownership', but financial institutions and legal structures, and these were deficient in the economies in transition. Privatizing without effective financial institutions and legal structures was entering into *terra incognita*—a bold experiment where already existing theory indicated strong reservations.

In fact, however, the problems were even deeper, and the predictable pitfalls more profound. I have time here but to mention two aspects. The first has to do with capital account convertibility, a subject that one might think more relevant for a discussion of macroeconomic and exchange-rate policy than for privatization. In a typical Coasian model, the mechanisms described earlier, while they clearly affected the distribution of wealth, might not have had much effect on the efficiency of the economy. After all, Coase argued that, in the absence of transaction costs, the initial wealth distribution does not matter for efficiency, so long as property rights are clear. In a closed economy, however, these new wealth holders would have had an incentive to invest their wealth in activities that yielded the highest return. Coase, of course, ignored agency costs; and those who had demonstrated the greatest ability to garner for themselves political favors were not necessarily those most suited to wealth creation, or even to selecting managers who were most suited for doing so. Hence, entrusting the country's wealth to these new 'robber barons' was not necessarily the best way of maximizing growth rates.[12] But allowing these robber barons to take their cash flows out of the country changed their opportunity sets dramatically. For now, they faced a simple calculation: were their expected returns higher if they invested their money at home or abroad (taking into account the wide-spread perception of the illegitimacy of their wealth, there might well be attempts to confiscate it, or at least to tax it at 'punitive' rates)? A robber baron advocate might argue that the real problem was not with the oligarchs, but with the governments: if only they could commit themselves to treat as legitimate wealth that which was begotten in these sometimes nefarious ways. But no democratic government can make commitments on its successors; it is through a process of social consensus that stability is maintained. But it is hard to attain such social consensus if the process of privatization (and transition more generally) does not have at least a minimal degree of legitimacy.

Making matters worse, of course, was the fact that, as each of the oligarchs decided not to risk reinvesting his or her funds in the country, it lowered the return for others doing so and provided a powerful signal to outsiders. Thus, while there might have been a Nash equilibrium in which all invested in the economy, the equilibrium that was established entailed few doing so. Capital account convertibility was thus an essential ingredient in

---

[12] Some advocates of rapid reform, while recognizing this, argued that the robber barons would have an incentive to sell their assets (in a competitive auction) to those who would best deploy the resources. The presumption was that designing such an auction was simple enough—and the robber barons had every incentive to maximize value. This did not occur, partly because they may have focused their attention on other issues—such as how they could strip value out of the firms they controlled rather than enhance market value; and partly because the very weaknesses that underlay the first round of privatization confronted the second round: who had the wealth to purchase the assets? Unless foreigners could be interested, there was no presumption that those who might have purchased in a second round (which did not occur)—those who had favored access to 'bank' loans—would have been much more efficient than those who got the assets in the first round.

the failures—in establishing the overall incentive structures leading to the disastrous outcomes described earlier.[13]

III. ALTERNATIVE THEORIES OF THE FIRM

Underlying this entire discussion are two quite contrasting theories of the firm.[14] One, a mild modification of the traditional owner-manager theory, viewed shareholders as the true owners of the firm, and the other viewed stakeholders as having clearly defined 'rights' of control and returns. Thus, 'normally,' bondholders and other lenders, workers, and local authorities have no real say in the actions of the firm. Bondholders and lenders have rights to certain flows of income. Workers have rights to be paid contractual wages. Local authorities have rights to be paid taxes due and to require conformity to general local zoning and other regulations.

But with these other potential claimants on the returns to the firm highly circumscribed, the *residual* claimant—with respect to both control and income—are the shareholders. The theory thus had a clear prediction: shareholders maximized shareholder values, presumably subject to well-defined restrictions on the claims of other claimants, and, in doing so, they maximized social efficiency. This shareholder-focused theory, when it is the clear *residual holder of control and ownership*, is usually called 'shareholder primacy' or 'shareholder sovereignty'.

There is an alternative theory (set out in my 1985 paper), which I refer to as the *multiple-principal-agent theory* and which is sometimes called the 'stakeholder theory'. In this theory, there are many stakeholders of the firm. (It is perhaps worth observing that, within the legal structure of many countries, the objective of the firm is not the maximization of share value, but a broader set of objectives that takes into account the interests of other stakeholders.) In this theory, the behavior of the firm is described as the outcome of a perhaps complicated bargaining process involving all the firm's stakeholders.

I believe this model provides a better description of the situation facing most economies in transition (and many advanced industrial economies as well). Among the important stakeholders that were ignored in the exclusively shareholder-focused theory were the local government units. Given the high (potential) levels of taxation (and the discretion to enforce or reduce those taxes) and the role of local authorities in discretionary regulation (including zoning), local authorities have control and income rights, no less than do shareholders. Similarly, workers, if they can organize and are not subjected to legal restraints, can exercise effective control rights. Metaphorically, in such a situation, ownership and control claims can exceed 100 percent—or, perhaps more

---

[13] To be sure, these disadvantages of capital account convertibility had to be offset against other concerns: the distorted incentives associated with attempts to circumvent the restrictions on convertibility. In retrospect, it is hard to believe that the distortions arising from these more traditional concerns outweighed the adverse welfare effects arising from the distortions just discussed. Capital account convertibility may also be related to the difference between corruption in Russia and in China.

[14] For an analysis that is parallel to that presented here, with an application to the problems in the Czech Republic, see Mejstrik (1999).

accurately, more than one party can exercise veto rights ('hold-up power') associated with any proposed plan and allocation of the firm's income.

We can now better see the failure of the privatization model that was pushed in the immediate aftermath of the reforms. There was a naive belief in the shareholder theory. The ownership rights of the state would be transferred to a new owner, and that owner would then act to maximize the stock-market value of the enterprise. In fact, the multiple-principal-agent model provided a better model of the firm. Transferring so-called 'ownership' from the central authority to a private owner left the other 'owners' intact. Having been left out of the new dispensation, the other stakeholders responded in non-cooperative ways (for example, predatory behavior from local officials and unproductive sullen workers), when, in fact, their full cooperation was needed to actually restructure the firms in the new environment. Many of the new shareholder owners then just turned to looting—grabbing what they could while they could.[15]

I should, at this point, say a word about China, the remarkable growth of which I referred to earlier. It did not solve the corporate governance problem perfectly (just as it would be hard to claim that the USA or any other Western government has provided a perfect solution). The great innovation of China—the source of its new enterprises and much of its growth—was the township-village enterprise. China eliminated the layered agency problems that were the source of the problem in Czech privatization, and it avoided the corporate governance problems that were the source of the difficulty in Russia.

China demonstrated that one did not have to have a perfect legal structure, with property rights perfectly clarified, in order either to attract foreign capital or to induce domestic investment.

The experience in China brings to the fore another issue that was too often forgotten in the rush to privatization—the importance of competition. Standard competitive theory emphasizes that it is only with competition (and a high degree of competition at that) that markets, private property, and the profit incentive yield efficient outcomes. To be sure, if one could have both competition and private property, one should try for both; but the contrasting experiences of China and Russia suggest that, if one has to make a choice, competition may be more important than private property, especially the form of ersatz privatizations that actually occurred. It is competition that provides the driving force for greater efficiency and lower prices. But competition is also an important part of

---

[15] Under the older shareholder 'residual theory' shareholders cannot, by definition, loot the firm: they would only be taking assets from themselves. To be sure, they might decide to decapitalize the firm, if they believed that the return to investing in the firm is sufficiently low—and that may have accounted for some of the observed behavior. (That leaves unanswered the question of why the return to capital was so low, seemingly everywhere—not every sector can have a comparative disadvantage!) But under the multiple-principal-agent model, there are multiple claimants; the shareholders try to grab what they can before other claimants do. Looting behavior, in that circumstance, may be individually rational, even if collectively irrational. The behavior may have made particular sense given the imperfections in domestic capital markets. The dominant shareholders were often older men a few years from retirement. Suppose they plow back their earnings, restructure the firm, and build up the stockholders' value. There is little or no tradition of family ownership, so they cannot pass the firm to their children. There is little or no private secondary market for firms, and even less a market for public new issues. Anticipating no other exit, the dominant shareholder may turn to a 'loot-and-liquefy' strategy to convert the big ownership block into funds for retirement elsewhere.

corporate governance: it is the absence of competition that creates rents, that so often get diverted to inefficient uses (see Commander *et al.* 1999).

IV. BANKRUPTCY

Financial turmoil—from East Asia, to Russia, and other countries in transition—has focused attention on bankruptcy and the laws that govern it. Bankruptcy rightly belongs within any discussion of corporate governance for a simple reason: bankruptcy is the means by which control rights get shifted. Bankruptcies and takeovers together can be viewed as the central ingredients in the market for management; and the rules governing bankruptcies and takeovers determine how effectively that market works—and therefore how effectively the market economy works.

Simple textbook models have been as misleading here as they have in the general theory of the firm. In the simple theory, the management team that is the most effective manager of a set of assets takes over the firm; the firm, in effect, is constantly on the auction block. Grossman and Hart (1980, 1981) long ago showed the fallacy with that theory, in the context of firms with widely dispersed owners: each shareholder, believing that a value-increasing takeover was about to occur, would retain ownership, becoming a free rider on the value-enhancing activities of the manager taking over the firm. Only if a shareholder believed that the person attempting to take over the firm would be successful in his bid, and upon success would strip the assets and reduce the market value, would he be willing to sell his shares. Thus, value-reducing takeovers would be successful. This is a dramatic example of the public good nature of management to which I referred earlier.

In fact, of course, managers of firms have within their discretion a wide range of actions that impede takeovers and increase their own bargaining power as a result, including increasing the asymmetries of information between insiders (the current management) and outsiders (not only shareholders, but those potentially taking over the firm) (Edlin and Stiglitz 1995).

If takeover mechanisms worked perfectly, of course, bankruptcies would never occur, or would at least be rare phenomena. Control, at each moment, would be exercised by those managers most able to maximize the value of those assets. If it turned out that the value of those assets (less the compensation required by the management team, which would be capped by the difference between the value of the firm under that management team and the next best management team) exceeded the claims on the assets, then those other claimants would be willing to take a write-down, in order to maximize their ongoing value—the write-down was better than what they would receive under some alternative management team. The frequency of these voluntary reorganizations and conversions of liabilities might depend on the volatility of the economy and the magnitudes of the uncertainties at the time the original contracts were entered upon; and one might have expected many such reorganizations in the aftermath of the initial privatizations. Indeed, this was one of the arguments proffered as a rationalization for an imperfect first round of privatizations. Once the market economy was in place, reorganizations of this form would occur, ultimately ensuring that each asset was 'optimally' managed.

But such arguments ignored the imperfections in the takeover mechanism, and it is these imperfections in turn that necessitate the use of bankruptcy procedures. Some thirty years ago, I turned my attention to this puzzle: under the standard paradigm, there would be unanimity about what actions would be value-maximizing, and the kinds of conflicts that appear so frequently in court disputes would never arise. At one level, the answer was easy: the standard theory assumed a complete set of prices, including prices in each state of nature and at each date, and (implicitly) there was perfect information— in the sense that there was agreement about the profits (inputs, outputs, prices, markets, and so on) in each state (this could be thought of as part of the definition of the state of nature, or at least as a consequence of assumptions concerning rationality, under-standing the nature of the equilibrium in that state). Given the obvious unreality of those assumptions, different market participants could have different judgments about the consequences of different actions, and therefore about what actions were appropriate— what actions maximized the stock-market value (or the expected utility of each participant). The conditions for unanimity are highly restrictive.

Under those circumstances, existing 'owners' might not be willing to surrender their control rights to creditors unless forced to do so. From their point of view, the presented discounted value of the income flows to equity owners might be highly positive, even though the market (reflecting the value on those income streams by the marginal outsider) believed that creditor claims exceeded the market value of the firm. In such a situation, equity owners have to be 'forced' to surrender their rights.

The traditional textbook model of bankruptcy describes a simple procedure: creditors must have their claims fully satisfied, and equity owners get the residual. If there is no residual, then the creditors take a write-down. Those with collateral get the value of the collateral. Creditors effectively seize control, choosing the management team that maxi-mizes their returns. They may choose to continue existing management, and even give the existing management an equity claim, if, by doing so, they maximize their own return.

In fact, however, matters are typically not so simple. The interests and perceptions of the various creditors may differ—there does not exist unanimity among them, just as there does not exist unanimity among shareholders. But, more importantly, courts and the legal system present important obstacles in many countries. Given the possible conflicting interests, there need to be referees to ensure that various interests are protected (according to the law) and the priorities of claims (reflecting the various contractual arrangements) are honored. But, while textbook models view courts as honest referees, they become, in many countries, especially those with weak judicial systems, active participants in the process. For instance, in many countries, the law recognizes the standing of other stakeholders, such as workers;[16] the court may rule that, to protect their interests, current management must stay in place. Or courts may demand further evidence to weigh the merits of the various claims. Any actions that maintain existing management in place—without appropriate oversight—are an invitation to asset stripping. The potential for corruption of the judicial system should be obvious.

---

[16] In a sense, in many other countries, including Germany and Japan, the law 'adopted' the model of the firm that we have called the multiple-principle-agent or multiple stakeholder model.

The problems become even more confusing when some of the debts are held in the hands of state-owned banks—the banks that lend money to political cronies in the first place. They have a double incentive: not to recognize the loss that would ensue upon bankruptcy, and to keep their political associates in power. Moreover, the owners of the firm, or their friends, can buy some of the debts, and thus become creditors. These creditors clearly have incentives conflicting with those of the 'true' creditors; but they can use their position to appeal to the courts and to block resolutions requiring unanimity or large supermajorities.

The courts themselves have played an ambiguous role in many countries. I use the term 'ambiguous' deliberately ambiguously. The consequences of their actions—to delay transfer of control to creditors—are apparent. The fact that corrupt judges may have incentives to delay resolution is also clear: so long as the firm remains under trusteeship, the court-appointed trustee has a source of income, some of which may be diverted to the judge. Even if the court is not corrupt, but relies unduly on the advice of the trustee, the resolution may be delayed. But, under the jurisprudence of many, if not most countries, the court has an obligation to look after the interests not only of the creditors, but of other stakeholders, and delay may be consistent with this broader mandate: a quick resolution in terms favorable to the creditors might lead to a shutting-down of the plant and high levels of unemployment.

In short, the economic system created in many of the countries in the beginning of the transition process was one in which incentives did play an important role—but they were incentives for asset stripping rather than wealth creation. These incentives were based on a misguided model of the theory of the firm, with residual control and income rights vested in the equity owner, where that owner was supposed to have guided the restructuring process in ways that should quickly have led to ever-increasing efficiency. A Coasian theory—in which, so long as property rights were well defined, it mattered little how they were assigned (so long as one was solely concerning with efficiency)—provided the intellectual underpinnings. In fact, the more appropriate model of the firm was a multiple-principal-agent model, in which privatization entailed the transfer of only some of the property rights. Bargaining under imperfect information does not, in general, lead to efficient outcomes; and, while repeated interactions might have (in a more static environment) eventually allowed both a reduction in the imperfections of information and a gain in efficiency, the fast-changing scene meant that market participants acted much more myopically than is required for long-term efficiency (see Farrell 1987).[17] A destructive dynamic was put into place: the deteriorating confidence in the reforms led to less investment (or perhaps, more accurately, a failure of investment to take off), in turn reinforcing the lack of confidence. The lack of confidence in the reforms undermined confidence in long-term property rights of those who had come by their wealth in ways that lacked social legitimacy. The banking system not only failed in its functions of monitoring; it was itself part of the problem. The failure of bankruptcy to protect creditors would, however, have put even well-functioning banks in a difficult position.

[17] These problems were exacerbated by the exit option offered by capital account convertibility, discussed earlier.

V. SOCIAL CAPITAL

Decision-making in the owner-manager theory of the firm and its derivatives is simple: the owner-manager takes those actions that maximize market value. To be sure, in doing so, he takes account of the impact of those decisions on others, for example, on the workers, through the wages that they will insist on in order to be willing to work for the firm. But these other parties are entirely passive: they are not actually part of the decision-making process. By contrast, in the multiple-principle-agent model (or the stakeholder model), decisions are made collectively, through an implicit or explicit bargaining process, with, in effect, various parties having veto powers. Workers, if they do not like what is being offered, can go on strike; the fact that there might be other workers willing to take the job at the offer may make little difference. The outcome of such bargaining processes may or may not be efficient. Some economies have, for instance, been characterized by frequent and long strikes, which both weaken the firm and hurt the worker.

In market economies, firms may be seen as local non-market solutions to collective action problems where transaction costs inhibit coordination by market contracts (Coase 1937). In the new post-socialist market economies, as in the established market economies, the primary example of extensive (that is, beyond the family) social cooperation in daily life is indeed found in the workplace. More broadly, recent economic literature has stressed the extent to which economic relations are not mediated through impersonal markets, and the role of *social capital* in ensuring at least a modicum of efficiency in such relationships (for a review of the extensive literature on social capital, see Woolcock 1999). A key aspect of such relationships is that they involve exchanges that do not occur at the same time, and in which there are not enforceable contracts. Rather, one person does a 'favor' for another, trusting that it will be returned at a later date. In this sense, such transactions are actually quite similar to many other market transactions, transactions that do not involve the contemporaneous exchange of two precisely defined commodities, about which there is nearly perfect information. When transactions do not occur contemporaneously, one party promises to pay (or deliver) some commodity to the other at a later date. When the properties of a commodity are not immediately transparent at the time of the transaction, the seller may make warranties concerning those properties; that again is a promise that has to be made good in the future.

There are two ways by which such contracts are enforced—through reputation mechanisms and through courts (sometimes referred to as implicit or explicit contracts). Both mechanisms are costly and imperfect. While the direct costs of legal enforcement are clear, implicit contracts, to be effective, require rents—a deviation of price from marginal cost—and this too has a social cost. The effectiveness of reputation mechanisms is attenuated when interest rates rise and when the probability of firm survival is decreased (or individual mobility is increased). The transition into a market economy is thus, in a sense, harder than the maintenance of a market economy, since initial investments in establishing reputation have to be made, at a time when reputational capital is particularly difficult to create. On the other hand, legal mechanisms were also weak in the economies in transition, particularly so since courts had no experience in being the arbiters of market economic relations. Worse still, given the immediate history of courts, there was probably little confidence in their impartiality (and even in Western countries, it has only been relatively recently, in historical terms, that they have gained a reputation for honesty).

The information requirements for, and transactions costs involved in, implicit and explicit contract enforcement are typically different, so that the two should best be thought of as complements rather than as substitutes. The problem in the economies in transition was that both enforcement mechanisms were weak: the state's legal and judicial capacities were limited, while the very process of transition—high institutional turnover, high shadow interest rates, and short-time horizons—impairs the effectiveness of implicit contracts. Thus, even if new institutions did not need to be created, the very process of transition itself would have provided impediments to the workings of a market economy.

The weakening of social capital contributed to the problems posed by inadequate systems of corporate governance. Individuals undertook actions that, if they had been detected, would have led to the 'loss of reputation' in a more stable environment, or jail sentences in an environment with better legal systems. Perhaps an alternative transitional strategy, paying more attention to the preservation of what social capital currently existed, and to the creation of new social capital, might have led to fewer abuses. We know little about how to preserve and create social capital. But this much seems clear. Breaking what is widely viewed as part of a social contract—such as not paying the elderly pensions that they believe they have earned—undermines social capital, especially if at the same time the government is transferring vast amounts of wealth to a few individuals. (Indeed, the destruction of social and organizational capital is one way of making sense of the seeming anomaly of reduced output, even as physical and human capital remains unchanged and supposed efficiency of resource allocation is increased (see Blanchard and Kremer 1997; Gaddy and Ickes 1998)). It also seems to be that case that, once dissipated, social capital—like organizational capital—is hard to reassemble. Given that what social capital exists within a firm typically exists at the plant level, there is an argument that entrepreneurial efforts that arise out of or spin off from existing enterprises may be particularly effective in post-socialist societies in preserving 'lumps' of social and organizational capital.[18]

VI. POLITICAL DYNAMICS

In the discussion so far, we have seen how politics and economics are intimately intertwined: the court systems, local authorities, state banks—all of these played a role in the failures, exacerbating or failing to address the market failures associated with corporate governance. Economists did take into account politics in their analysis of the reform process—and, indeed, it was political considerations as much as economics that provided the rationale for the reform strategy advocated by several of the reformers.

---

[18] See the township-village enterprises in China, as in Weitzman and Xu (1994), Lin *et al.* (1996), and Qian (1999).

Other social organizations that might incubate and support entrepreneurial efforts include local township governments, unions, schools, colleges, cooperatives (housing, consumer, credit, and producer co-ops), mutual aid associations, guilds, professional associations, churches, veterans' associations, clubs, and extended family groups.

Political dynamics are complicated. Reforms entail vested interests giving up their rents (what they may view as property rights). By definition, self-interested individuals never do so voluntarily. How then is reform possible? Sometimes, Pareto improvements can be found, grand bargains where all (or all major) groups are persuaded that they are better off.[19] In some cases, realignments of political powers—and changes in political perceptions—make reform possible. Political coalitions themselves are altered in the process of reform; a recognition of this may itself serve as an impediment to reform, if existing power relationships worry that changes will lead to new coalitions, with uncertain long-run implications. But often participants in the political process play chess, thinking through one, or at most a few moves ahead. With a high enough discount rate, such myopia may even be rational. Those attempting reform may play on this myopia.

In the case of the economies in transition, there were large vested interests that had much to lose by the transition to a market economy. There was a belief by some reformers that the momentum of transition was strong enough to carry forward an agenda of privatizations, over the interests of those who were acting as effective owners, but curiously that the momentum was not strong enough to overcome opposition to restructuring (Boycko *et al.* 1996). In this view then, the desired (or only feasible) sequencing was: privatize, restructure, and then regulate. With privatization would come strong economic incentives for restructuring; diseconomies of scope would lead to the disagglomerations (presumably, as it had been done in the USA in the years following each merger wave), and, once restructuring had occurred, political pressures for competition and regulation would succeed. More broadly, the privatization would set in motion a process of legal reforms that would eventually lead to efficient systems of corporate governance.

The architects of the Russian privatization were aware of the dangers of poor enforcement of property rights. Yet, because of the emphasis on politics, the reformers predicted that institutions would follow private property rather than the other way around (Shleifer and Vishny 1998: 11).

There is, to my knowledge, no theory—and scarce historical evidence—underlying this optimistic assessment of institutional evolution. Indeed, there are general results showing that the Nash equilibrium for institutions (including the interaction between markets and non-market institutions) is generally not Pareto efficient (see Arnott and Stiglitz 1991). Coase himself emphasized that transactions costs were important and that, with transactions costs and imperfect information, outcomes of bargaining processes are not in general Pareto efficient. But latter-day 'Coasians' have closed their eyes to these

---

[19] Given the magnitude of the (alleged and seeming) inefficiencies in the Soviet system, one might have thought that there was sufficient surplus to be divided by the movement to new organizational forms so that everyone could have easily been made better off. In that sense, one might have thought that the political obstacles to reform would have been smaller than in situations where the gains were smaller. There are several possible answers to this conundrum. The change in political climate may have made it difficult to compensate the old guard; but then, how was it that so many of them remained in positions of power to continue to block reforms? Perhaps the problem was that there was no way that binding commitments could be made; the reforms would set in motion a set of changes that would eventually deprive the old guard of its power; they knew it, and thus they had to block the reforms at the onset.

problems particularly in Russia, and have wagered that the secondary market redistribution of assets would work 'well enough.' It now seems that the wager was lost, and that the Russian workers and taxpayers will foot the bill.

To be fair, it is only a decade after the beginning of transition, and patience may be required. Perhaps eventually the story will develop in the way anticipated. Surely, those who advocated the reform strategies did not fully describe the vicissitudes through which the countries would go in reaching the ultimate stage. There is little evidence that they really anticipated the lack of investment in manufacturing; the flight of capital abroad; the drying-up of support for market reforms. Had they focused their analysis on economics, they might have said in defense that these adverse outcomes came from political processes that were beyond the focus of their concerns. While they might have been rightly accused of ignoring politics, at least their defense would be intelligible. But, when the strategy advocated was based not on economic analysis, but on political judgments, then such defenses seem less legitimate.

There is another political dynamic: democratic processes recognize that it is concentrations of power, economic and political, that represent the strongest threat to a viable democratic society. Reformers might have used the commitment to democratic processes to motivate a process of restructuring and devolution, breaking the power of the industrial ministries. The commitment to privatization might, itself, have weakened resistance, since the ministries' powers would, in any case, have been short-lived. In the new-founded spirit of freedom, new programs to support new enterprises might have found widespread support, and these new enterprises would themselves eventually begin to be a countervailing power to the old and established monopolies. Creating regulatory authorities over a monopoly (especially a natural monopoly) after privatization may be far harder than before. After privatization, there is a private interest seeking to maintain high prices and bar competition, and it can use its profits to further its interests. Before privatization, potential buyers do not know who will be the monopolist; there is a collective action problem—it is not in the interest of any one potential buyer to devote much energy and resources to resisting regulation. If the government is committed to privatizing, then there may be little interest in the ministry to resist such regulation—it will only affect the private sector that follows.

More broadly, I believe that, once the political process opened up those within the countries to what was going on on the outside, it was inevitable that questions would be raised: why is our standard of living lower than other countries with similar levels of education and natural resources? If market economies deliver higher growth with greater equity, the demand for market reforms will be irresistible. The problem is that those in the economies in transition look around, and those who are Bayesians —who are not totally committed to a view of the world unaffected by experience—see the dismal experiences of transition, and many are left skeptical. This is a reality that those committed to democratic market reforms will have to confront in the coming years.

VII. SHIBBOLETHS, CONFUSIONS, AND MISUNDERSTANDINGS

Looking over the experiences of the past decade, it is remarkable how confident statements made were about the appropriate paths for transition—and how quick some analysts were to come to the judgment that their predictions were correct. In fairness, while there was a wealth of experience across a multitude of countries, there were still insufficient data to come to firm conclusions: did the countries that privatized and liberalized more quickly differ in other ways—differences that might themselves have accounted for their success? Presumably, the speed of liberalization was an endogenous variable, affected by history and prospects. And the countries differed markedly in both. For the countries of Eastern Europe, the prospect of speedy accession to the European Union provided both an incentive for quick liberalization and opportunities that were far different from those of the landlocked countries deep in Central Asia. The experiences provided a Rorschach test—with different observers seeing in the data what they wanted to see. It is only over time, as applying the same lens has led to contradictory results, that analysts have been forced to face up to the facts and the ambiguities that they present.

Among these ambiguities are those concerning what is meant by privatization itself. When the UK sold the shares of one of its nationalized companies to the public, it was fairly clear that this was a privatization. But when Poland sold shares in government-controlled national investment funds on the Warsaw stock market, did that mean that all the industrial companies in the funds' portfolios had been 'privatized' (as was argued for many years)?[20] Or are the portfolio companies privatized only when they are sold off to strategic buyers or are themselves floated on the stock market (as is now being claimed)? The answer is important for an empirical analysis, because how we answer that question determines whether we view Poland as a fast or a slow privatizer. Or consider another example: if the Czech Republic uses voucher privatization, but then has state banks provide soft loans to the privatized companies, is that *real* privatization?[21] Privatization was supposed to provide hard budget constraints—yet the soft loans ensure that there are soft budget constraints. But this example presents the analyst with even deeper problems: how do we know that the loans are soft? Presumably repeated bailouts of the banks provide some evidence *ex post*. But then even so-called private banks may provide soft loans, particularly if they are undercapitalized, are gambling on redemption, and are counting on the past history of bailouts.

In a sense, as we go forward, as important as the answers are to the econometric findings, these are semantics: the lessons are the same—corporate governance matters, and prospects for privatizations that fail to adequately address corporate governance issues (whether because of failures in banking or problems on the equity side) are bleak.

The concept of restructuring presents similar ambiguities. One of the early debates was whether the government should make an attempt at restructuring or leave that to the new

---

[20] Surely our answer to that question should not be based on the government-controlled funds contracting out management to private Western investment banks—since that was done before the share floatation.

[21] Often the 'privatized' companies were substantially owned by widely-held voucher investment funds which were completely controlled by bank-owned fund management companies. Thus the banks were bailing out the companies indirectly under their own control—not exactly arm's-length due diligence.

owner after privatization. The 'first wave of wisdom' was the theory that restructuring should be left to the new owners—after all, the state had not previously shown itself very adept at restructuring. The problem with this theory was that the enterprises were seriously overstaffed with huge agglomerations of outdated and mismatched assets. The governments usually did not want to undertake mass layoffs, and would rather pass that sensitive problem on to a foreign buyer who could subsidize the workers out of his 'deeper pockets' or who could take the political heat for the mass layoffs. However, the foreign buyers hardly wanted to enter the country and take the recriminations for such politically sensitive acts (which repaired past mistakes not of their making).[22]

Another problem in the 'first wave of wisdom' was that the balance sheets were stuffed with useless assets and with 'liabilities' resulting from subsidies directed to the firm in the past. As soon as a whiff of foreign money was in the air, all those very soft loan liabilities suddenly hardened into 'legal obligations' of the enterprise to the state banks. The new buyer would, of course, have to accept the 'legal obligations' of the firm being purchased. On the asset side of the balance sheet, the assets useless to the buyer's business plan usually had no secondary market but were valued by the selling privatization agency either at cost or at the imagined 'earning potential'. Need I mention cleaning up for past environmental neglect (or hidden liabilities of the firm for the effects that emerge in the future)? Leaving aside labor problems, if the buyers accepted all the liabilities (explicit as well as hidden) and useless assets of the unrestructured firms, then most deals would have been sold for a symbolic $1. But that was politically unfeasible,[23] so the 'first wave of wisdom' generally led to the dead end of very little foreign direct investment in existing enterprises.

Restructuring theories eventually became more nuanced. It was recognized that foreign buyers did not want to be saddled with the politically sensitive tasks of cleaning up for past mistakes. It was recognized that investors wanted a 'pure play' consisting of the assets that fitted into their business plans, not the whole bundle of assets that seemed to have been randomly agglomerated in the past. It was recognized that the very uncertainty created by the mixed bag of assets and liabilities decreased the price that buyers were willing to pay. If they could not get a pure play, they might just as well go to greenfield investment, leaving the old enterprise to the junkyard (except perhaps for a few assets purchased in bankruptcy auction). It was recognized that the government had to clean up the soft loan and environmental problems on its own and could not expect foreign buyers to come in and bail everyone out. Now governments are taking more

---

[22] One anecdote is illustrative. A foreign furniture company bought a plant in a south-east European country and told the privatization agency as well as the workers that one part of the enterprise was dubious. If they could not fix it within a year's time to make a profit, they would have to shut it down. After the year, that unit had not shown much hope, so the foreign managers announced that it would be shut down. Then the police in the local town where the employment was critical occupied the plant and informed the foreign managers that they had 'broken the law' and would have to leave the country or face arrest. The foreign company then had to shut down the whole operation and demand that the national government intervene to remedy the situation. That foreign buyer probably does not support the 'leave restructuring to the buyer' theory.

[23] In fact, the political opposition in many post-socialist countries has implicitly adopted a valuation theory that says: 'Any price that a foreign buyer had actually paid was *obviously* too low, so the government may always be accused of selling out the national assets cheaply to foreigners.'

responsibility for what is called 'passive' restructuring to clean up the balance sheets and reduce the labor problems (for example, with active labor market policies and improved social safety nets)—all still without the 'active' restructuring decisions about product lines and new machinery that should be left to the buyers.

VIII. CONCLUSION

There is an old saying that one never crosses the same stream twice, and, while there is much to learn from history, and from trying to understand why things turned out differently from the way many expected, our focus needs to be on the future. Two facts stand out at this juncture: incomes and standards of living have, at best, stagnated in most countries, if not fallen; popular confidence in market processes and the optimism of transition have been eroded in many if not most of these countries. And any strategy going forward must deal with these facts.

In many of the countries, a strict interpretation of the rules of a market economy would lead quickly to government takeover of large proportions of existing assets that have been privatized in the past decade. In some countries, there are huge tax arrears; in a typical advanced industrial economy, arrears of these magnitudes would be swiftly dealt with, with government attachment of the property, to be eventually sold, with the proceeds used to pay the arrears. Moreover, in many countries, the banks are effectively bankrupt, partly because of huge arrears on the part of corporations to the banks. Again, the standard market process would be a foreclosure by the banks, and government takeover of the banks as they recapitalize them (unless the banks can find private sources of recapitalization, doubtful in most of these countries, without huge government subsidies). In a way this is good news, because there is now a second chance for government to go about the reprivatization of these assets in ways that take greater recognition of the problems of corporate governance and the other issues that I have discussed today.

But, as the process of democratic transition continues, due attention too will have to be paid to other issues that were, perhaps, given short shrift. As important as restructuring existing assets and enterprises is the creation of new ones; job creation and entrepreneurship need to be put at the center of discussions. So too must stress be placed on the other aspects of the institutional infrastructure for a market economy and a democratic society, from financial institutions to social and legal structures. The high and growing levels of corruption and perceived problems of governance are both cause and consequence of the failure of the economic transition.

The last decade of this century has been full of surprises. Few anticipated the precipitous collapse of the communist governments. After that collapse, there was a euphoria about the transition to a market economy. A decade later, those hopes have, in most cases, been dashed, replaced by a more somber realism about the difficulty of the task ahead. Yet I remain optimistic: hopefully the lessons that we can extract from the experiment, which has already extracted such a huge human toll, will stand the countries in good stead as they approach this new, and hopefully more successful phase in their democratic transition.

REFERENCES

Akerlof, G., and Yellen, J. (1985), 'A Near-Rational Model of the Business Cycle, with Wage and Price Inertia', *Quarterly Journal of Economics*, 100/5: 823–38.

Arnott, R., and Stiglitz, J. (1991), 'Moral Hazard and Non-Market Institutions: Dysfunctional Crowding-out or Peer Monitoring', *American Economic Review*, 81/1: 179–90.

Aslund, A. (1995), *How Russia Became a Market Economy* (Washington: Brookings).

Berle, A., and Means, G. (1932), *The Modern Corporation and Private Property* (New York: MacMillan).

Black, B., Kraakman, R., and Tarassova, A. (1999), 'Russian Privatization and Corporate Governance: What Went Wrong?' mimeo.

Blanchard, O., and Kremer, M. (1997), 'Disorganization', *Quarterly Journal of Economics* 112/4: 1091–126.

Boycko, M., Shleifer, A., and Vishny, R. (1996), 'Second-Best Economic Policy for a Divided Government', *European Economic Review*, 40/3–5 (Apr.), 767–74.

Coase, R. H. (1937), 'The Nature of the Firm', *Economica*, 4 (Nov.), 386–405.

——— (1988), *The Firm, the Market, and the Law* (Chicago: University of Chicago Press).

Commander, S., Dutz, M., and Stern, N. (1999), 'Restructuring in Transition Economies: Ownership, Competition and Regulation' *Proceedings of the 1999 Annual Bank Conference on Development Economics*.

Demsetz, H. (1970), 'The Private Production of Public Goods', *Journal of Law and Economics*, 13/2 (Oct.), 293–306.

Dyck, A. (1999), 'Privatization and Corporate Governance: Principles, Evidence and Future Challenges', mimeo, Harvard Business School.

Edlin, A., and Stiglitz, J. E. (1995), 'Discouraging Rivals: Managerial Rent-Seeking and Economic Inefficiencies', *American Economic Review*, 85/5 (Dec.), 1301–12.

Farrell, M. J. (1987), 'Information and the Coase Theorem', *Journal of Economic Perspectives*, 11: 113–29.

Gaddy, C., and Ickes, B. (1998), 'Beyond the Bailout: Time to Face Reality about Russia's "Virtual Economy"', *Foreign Affairs*, 77: 53–67.

Greenwald, B., and Stiglitz, J. (1986), 'Externalities in Economies with Imperfect Information and Incomplete Markets', *Quarterly Journal of Economics*, 101: 229–64.

Grossman, S., and Hart, O. (1980), 'Disclosure Laws and Takeover Bids', *Journal of Finance*, 35/2 (May), 323–34.

——— ——— (1981), 'The Allocational Role of Takeover Bids in Situations of Asymmetric Information', *Journal of Finance*, 36/2 (May), 253–70.

——— and Stiglitz, J. E. (1977), 'On Value Maximization and Alternative Objectives of the Firm', *Journal of Finance*, 32/2 (May), 389–402.

Knack, S., and Keefer, P. (1997), 'Does Social Capital Have an Economic Payoff? A Cross-Country Investigation', *Quarterly Journal of Economics*, 1251–88.

Lin, J., Yifu, F. Cai, and Li, Z. (1996), *The China Miracle: Development Strategy and Economic Reform* (Hong Kong: Chinese University Press).

Marshall, Alfred, (1897), 'The Old Generation of Economists and the New', *Quarterly Journal of Economics* (Jan.), 115–35.

Mejstrik, M. (1999), 'Privatization, Foreign Investment, and Corporate Governance: Theory and Czech Practice', Charles University Prague Working Paper, 10 Apr.

Milanovic, B. (1998), *Income, Inequality, and Poverty during the Transition from Planned to Market Economy* (Regional and Sectoral Studies; Washington: World Bank).

Qian, Yingi (1999), 'The Institutional Foundations of China's Market Transition', paper presented to 1999 Annual Bank Conference on Development Economics.

Rey, P., and Stiglitz, J. E. (1993), 'Short-Term Contracts as a Monitoring Device', NBER Working Paper 4514.

Sappington, S., and Stiglitz, J. E. (1987), 'Privatization, Information and Incentives', *Journal of Policy Analysis and Management*, 6/4: 567–82.

Shleifer, A., and Vishny, R. (1998), *The Grabbing Hand: Government Pathologies and Their Cures* (Cambridge, Mass.: Harvard University Press).

Stiglitz, J. E. (1972), 'Some Aspects of the Pure Theory of Corporate Finance: Bankruptcies and Take-Overs', *Bell Journal of Economist*, 3/2 (Autumn), 458–82.

—— (1982), 'Ownership, Control and Efficient Markets: Some Paradoxes in the Theory of Capital Markets', in K. D. Boyer and W. G. Shepherd (eds.), *Economic Regulation: Essays in Honor of James R. Nelson* (Michigan State University Press), 311–41.

—— (1985), 'Credit Markets and the Control of Capital', *Journal of Money, Banking, and Credit*, 17/2 (May), 133–52.

—— (1992), 'The Design of Financial Systems for the Newly Emerging Democracies of Eastern Europe', in C. Clague and G. C. Rausser (eds.), *The Emergence of Market Economies in Eastern Europe* (Cambridge, Mass.: Basil Blackwell), 161–84.

—— (1993), 'Some Theoretical Aspects of the Privatization: Applications to Eastern Europe', in M. Baldassarri, L. Paganetto, and E. S. Phelps (eds.), *Privatization Processes in Eastern Europe* (New York: St Martin's Press), 179–204.

—— (1994), *Whither Socialism?* (Cambridge, Mass.: MIT Press).

—— (1999), 'Whither Reform?', speech at ABCDE Conference, World Bank, Washington: For speeches in general, see http://www.worldbank.org/knowledge/chiefecon/index.htm.

—— and Edlin, A. (1995), 'Discouraging Rivals: Managerial Rent-Seeking and Economic Inefficiencies', *American Economic Review*, 85/5: 1301–12.

—— and Weiss, A. (1981), 'Credit Rationing in Markets with Imperfect Information', *American Economic Review*, 71/3 (June), 393–410.

—— —— (1983), 'Incentive Effects of Termination: Applications to the Credit and Labor Markets', *American Economic Review*, 73/5 (Dec.), 912–27.

Weiss, A., and Nikitin, G. (1998), *Performance of Czech Companies by Ownership Structure* (Washington: World Bank).

Weitzman, M., and Xu, C. (1994), 'Chinese Township-Village Enterprises as Vaguely Defined Cooperatives', *Journal of Comparative Economics*, 18: 121–45.

Wolfensohn, J. D. (1997), *Annual Meetings Address: The Challenge of Inclusion* (Hong Kong: World Bank; http://www.worldbank.org/html/extdr/am97/jdw_sp/jwsp97e.htm).

—— (1998), 'The Other Crisis: 1998 Annual Meetings Address', given at the 1998 World Bank/International Monetary Fund Annual Meetings. Internet access: http://www.worldbank.org/html/extdr/am98/jdw-sp/index.htm.

—— (1999), 'A Proposal for a Comprehensive Development Framework', a discussion draft (Washington: World Bank).

Woolcock, M. (1999), *Using Social Capital: Getting the Social Relations Right in the Theory and Practice of Economic Development* (Princeton: Princeton University Press).

World Bank (1996), *World Development Report 1996: From Plan to Market* (Washington: World Bank).

—— (1997), *China 2020: Development Challenges in the New Century* (Washington: World Bank).

Institutions and Markets

3

Privatization and Institutions in Developing and Transition Economies

MUSTAPHA K. NABLI

I. INTRODUCTION

Within the scope of factors that determine the success of privatization, there is the increasing belief among development practitioners that the institutional framework has an important role to play. In fact, some institutional factors—such as the degree of regulation, government accountability, red tape, judiciary efficiency, and corruption—are becoming increasingly recognized as critical elements that can either fasten or stand in the way of privatization.

In this paper, I develop two main ideas about privatization and institutions. The first is that the likelihood of success of privatization is directly linked to both the size of the public sector (and the scope for privatization) and the quality of institutions ('good governance'). In particular, the potential for the success of privatization is inversely related to the size of the public sector (and the scope for privatization), and positively related to the quality of institutions.

Secondly, and more importantly, institutions are endogenous to the privatization process. Failure to take this endogeneity into account in the design of the privatization program can contribute to its failure.

The paper is organized as follows. In the next section, I present findings on the relationship between privatization and institutions in a static view. Subsequently, I focus on the endogeneity of institutional capacity, by stressing the dynamic aspects of privatization and institutions.

II. PRIVATIZATION AND INSTITUTIONS: A STATIC VIEW

In this section, I consider the relationship between privatization and institutions from a static perspective. For any given country, the relationship between privatization and institutions depends on two major dimensions, which are assumed to be given at the start of the privatization process: (1) the size of the public sector, and (2) the quality of

I would like to thank Carol Gabyzon for able assistance in collecting the data, and John Nellis, Wafik Grais, and Jennifer Keller for helpful comments.

governance. There are a host of dimensions to governance quality—the accountability of the government, the efficiency of the judicial system, administrative capacity, the degree of corruption, and the degree of corporate governance. For the purpose of this paper, I have employed a corruption index as an indicator of the quality of governance.

Taking a look at initial conditions, Fig. 1 presents a scatter plot of the degree of corruption present versus the size of the public sector (SOE, as measured by the proportion of GDP produced by state-owned enterprises) in the early 1990s. I consider the corruption index component of the International Country Risk Guide (ICRG) for the year 1992,[1] which takes values ranging from 1 to 5 and is arranged such that a high value means that the country in question has 'good' institutions (that is, when countries score low on the index, it is an indication that there exists a high degree of corruption). Two points emerge from the chart: The first is that initial conditions vary a great deal in developing and transition economies, in terms of the initial size of the public sector, and the degree of corruption. The second more interesting point is that most of the developing economies fall in the lower left-hand corner—that is, the group of economies with a relatively high

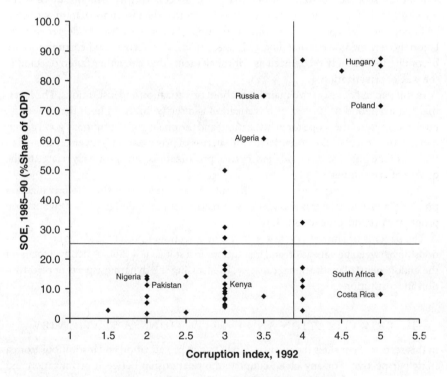

Figure 1. *Public production sector and corruption*

---

[1] The ICRG evaluates risks faced by businesses in countries around the world. The corruption index—one component of the political stability risk assessment—reflects the analysts' subjective perspectives on risk and efficiency factors, and a great deal of effort is taken to assure that the final indices are accurate and comparable across countries.

degree of corruption and a relatively small public sector. Out of the sample of about sixty countries for which there were data available on both the public sector and the corruption index, some two-thirds of the countries fall into this group. Only a handful of economies have a large public sector and a low level of corruption (less than 10 per cent). The transition economies have by and large been the economies with large public sectors, and several of them have exhibited low levels of corruption, at least in the initial stages of the privatization process in the early 1990s.

Fig. 1 suggests a distinction among four characteristic cases dependent upon the level of corruption and the size of the public sector. Fig. 2 then separates economies into four cases: (I) high degree of corruption and relatively large public sector; (II) high degree of corruption and relatively small public sector; (III) low degree of corruption and relatively large public sector; and, (IV) low degree of corruption and relatively small public sector.

A description of the cases

Case IV. This is the case where most OECD economies would fall, but only a fraction of developing economies. In this case, there is a large private sector and most of the needed institutions for a functioning private sector already exist: a well-developed financial sector, a market for managers, institutions for corporate governance, and, more generally, a wide range of market support institutions. There may be scope for improvement and strengthening of these institutions, but the main ingredients are already present. The areas of the institutional framework most likely in need of strengthening would be competition policy (and ease of entry) and development of capital markets.

Under such conditions of strong competition and market-enforcement mechanisms, privatization would lead to improved performance and gains accruing to society through the more efficient allocation of resources, improved financial performance, and innovation.

	High corruption	Low corruption
Relatively large public sector	I	III
Relatively small public sector	II	IV

Figure 2.

Unfortunately, that is often the standard view of the privatization process, without regard to the other factors necessary for privatization to result in efficiency gains, which may not be present in other situations.

Case III. These economies have a relatively large public sector, but suffer from relatively low degrees of corruption. In these cases, the countries primarily need strengthening of the institutional framework for private-sector development, involving not only increased competition and capital market development, but also improved institutions for corporate governance and their legal systems.

Case II. Into this group the bulk of the economies for which we have data fall (primarily developing economies). These economies have small public sectors accompanied by relatively high levels of corruption. There is a pre-existing private sector that operates within a weak institutional framework. The focus for this group of countries would be on strengthening institutions to control and reduce corruption.

Case I. Finally, in the economies in this group, the existing private sector is small or almost non-existent, entrepreneurship is weak, and the country suffers from a high level of corruption. In such a case, *as in many of the transition and oil exporting economies*, the challenge for the privatization process to result in improved national welfare is much greater.

Clearly, the policies and institutions required in Case IV are also needed for Case I, but they are not sufficient. The challenge is how to implement a privatization program when there is no private sector, and when the public sector is collapsing (and perhaps the institutional capacity of the public sector as well), so as to actually achieve improved efficiency with improved allocation of resources and the greatest possible social gains.

The institutional challenge involves three major tasks

1. Building the institutional base for a private sector. Institutional arrangements that are non-existent or that are very weak often include:

   - institutions for corporate governance which promote efficiency, such as those institutional arrangements protecting the rights of minority shareholders;
   - bankruptcy procedures and other mechanisms for exit, and the judiciary required for their effective implementation;
   - hard budget constraints (building on the notion above, where firms are not allowed access to government resources directly, or indirectly through state-owned banks);
   - well-developed financial institutions allowing access to external finance by firms, at arm's length from the state, and free from connected lending (with conflict of interests);
   - a minimum standard of prudential regulation and enforcement mechanisms in the capital markets.

2. Choosing methods of privatization that aim at minimizing the scope and extent of corruption and promoting efficiency, by adequately aligning rights of control with rights of cash. It is not enough to simply transfer property or ownership rights!

3. Building institutions to deal with corruption, involving:

- voice and exit mechanisms for various stakeholders;
- greater transparency;
- greater competition.

The discussion above has two major messages. First, the likelihood of successful privatization is inversely correlated to the initial size of the public sector. When the public sector is large, the required pre-existing institutions for a private sector are weak and need a greater degree of development. The likelihood that they will be developed in the time needed (preferably, prior to the privatization process) and that their development will be sufficient is much lower, and thus, so is the likelihood of success of the privatization process in general. This is a deceptively simple notion, but one that has empirical basis.

Fig. 3a charts the size of the public sector versus the success of the privatization process for our sample of economies. Success of privatization is measured by the persistence of privatization, measured by the proceeds of privatization from 1990–7 divided by the initial GDP of the economy (the average during the 1989–91 period). From that figure, when we exclude the transition economies, it is evident that, the higher is the size of the public sector, the lower is the success of privatization. With the transition economies, however, there is a spike at the right tail, simply because the size of privatization in these transition economies was extremely large.

If we take account of the fact that privatization needs to be adjusted by the relative initial size of the public sector, however, the picture is different. Instead of taking the average size of privatization relative to GDP, the privatization ratio is measured as the ratio of the proceeds from privatization as a percentage of GDP, divided by the share of the public sector in GDP (normalizing for the size of the public sector). This ratio reflects the privatization volume over the eight-year period divided by the GDP produced by the public sector in the initial period. Using this ratio as a measure of success of privatization, we observe from Fig. 3b that the likelihood of the persistence of privatization is lower the larger is the relative size of the public sector, even with the transition economies included.[2] There is a noticeably large effect in the first column, which is primarily the result of the inclusion of Argentina. The relative privatization ratio was the highest in Argentina—during the 1990s, privatization proceeds were about ten times the initial value added of the state enterprise sector. The major point, however, remains that the likelihood of success is smaller the larger is the public sector (or the smaller is the private sector).

Another result is that the likelihood of success of privatization is inversely related to the initial quality of institutions (governance). Fig. 4a and b plots the same two measures of privatization success as Fig. 3a and 3b (first, simply taking privatization proceeds over initial GDP; then normalizing for the size of the public sector) against the corruption index. It is clear that, the higher is the corruption index, the lower is the likelihood of successful privatization.

---

[2] It should be noticed that the extent of decline shown in this chart partly reflects the fact that the y-axis variable is calculated by dividing the proceeds from privatization (as in Fig. 3a) by SOE, which is the x-axis variable.

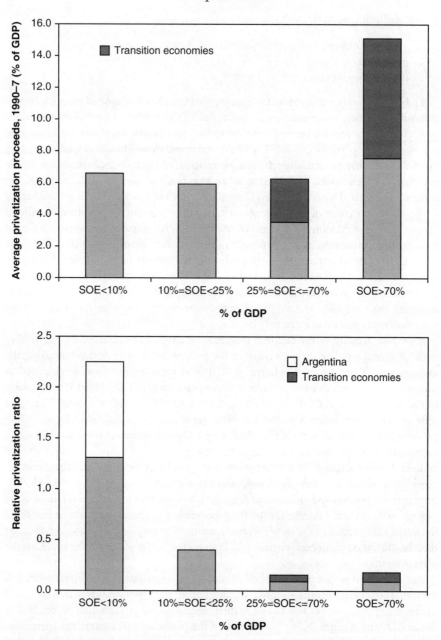

Figure 3. *Privatization and size of public production sector*

Source: Privatization proceeds: 1990–7: World Bank Privatization database, available in World Bank Statistical Information Management and Analysis System (SIMA); Public-sector share in GDP (SOE): 1985–90: World Bank SIMA, World Bank Report, 'Bureaucrats in Business', estimated figures (mostly for 1990) for transition economies from EBRD Transition Reports, 1995, 1996; corruption index; corruption index component of the ICRG.

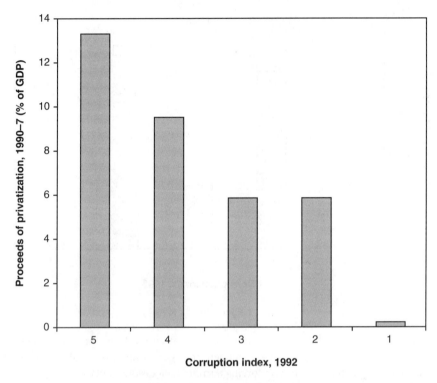

Figure 4a. *Privatization and corruption*

Source: as for Fig. 3.

III. PRIVATIZATION AND INSTITUTIONS:
A DYNAMIC VIEW

A static view of the relationship between privatization and institutions is clearly not adequate. A more dynamic view of privatization is required, for two major reasons. First, problems of sequencing arise when progress on both fronts for both building the private sector and developing institutions to deal with corruption do not proceed at the same rate. Secondly, there is a problem of endogeneity. The size of the public sector, and the quality of governance and institutions, are endogenous to the privatization process. As a clear example, the public sector progressively becomes smaller as the privatization process continues, not only because of direct privatizations, but also as the result of entry of new private enterprises (one of the desired consequences of a successful privatization program).

With regard to this issue (of the public sector and governance being endogenous to the privatization process), I would like to advance the following hypothesis: holding *other policies and institutions constant, the equilibrium (or potential) level of corruption increases with privatization.* That is to say, the process of privatization itself is likely to increase the scope for corruption. There are several reasons for this:

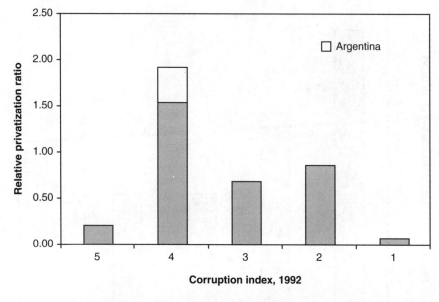

Figure 4b.

1. Privatization allows transfers of large amounts of wealth from the government to private agents, which can easily be hidden from government oversight, such as by avoiding regulations or taxes, enforcing terms of concessions, and so forth.
2. The 'social controls' on corruption are weaker as the size of the private sector increases. Wealth acquired through corruption is more easily 'explained' as originating from profits in the market economy, especially if it involves transfers from dispersed consumers.
3. There is increased scope for regulatory capture by privatized interests.
4. Increased differential in pay between the public and private sectors creates additional incentives for corruption by public officials.
5. The move from predominantly 'barter' corruption (patronage and barter exchange of favors) to 'monetized' or 'cash' corruption allows an increase in volume of this 'trade'. Under these conditions, privatization may not necessarily result in an improvement in welfare: there are potential efficiency gains from assigning property rights to private stakeholders (and assuming this is achieved successfully), but there may be losses as well in terms of income growth and efficiency associated with increased corruption. The net effect (abstracting from transfers due to corruption) may be negative.

The point is best illustrated with an example. Consider a country in Case III: a country with a relatively large public sector, but little corruption. Looking at Fig. 5, the challenge is whether the privatization process will lead the country along Path A or Path B. Path A is the path that will likely lead to welfare gains, since the process is managed in such a way that institutions are developed to minimize the corruption effects. Path B, however, is

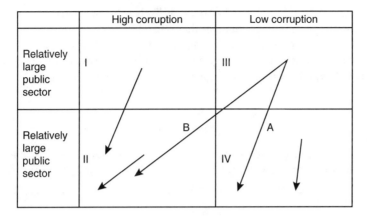

Figure 5.

likely to lead to declining welfare, and is usually characterized by insider-dominated privatization, soft budget constraints, and continued links between privatized firms, government officials, and state-owned or privatized banks.

Whether a country manages to steer itself towards Path A rather than Path B raises the issue of sequencing: is it better to move vertically from a large to a small public sector through expansion of the private sector, without privatization, and then to undertake privatization when the relative size of the public sector is smaller? The experience of China may illustrate this case. The Chinese have opted to take this more moderate approach to private-sector development, creating competition among state-owned enterprises largely without a shift to formal private ownership. Joseph Stiglitz, in fact, argues that the Chinese experience shows 'that an economy might achieve more effective growth by focusing first on competition, leaving privatization until later (see Stiglitz 1998: 2).

The problem, however, is that this strategy is not always possible, when there is a collapse of the state-owned sector and 'rampant spontaneous privatization'! Ultimately, the answer to the question depends on a central issue: whether there is the ability to build adequate administrative and government capacity that can ensure that the rule of law prevails and is reinforced and not weakened, which depends largely on the political governance structure.

If there is an adequate government capacity for policy-making and enforcement, which can build institutions, then the main issues are how to choose the privatization mechanisms that minimize the emergence of corruption, and to strengthen institutions that control corruption: regulatory bodies, voice mechanisms, exit possibilities for stake-holders, and so on. A country in Case III is more likely to be able to proceed along these lines, of course, than a country in Case IV, where the public sector is small or non-existent.

If there is little government capacity to build institutions and the political system is ineffective, postponing privatization may not be any worse than proceeding with it:

Mustapha K. Nabli

assets being transferred to private hands are as likely to be mismanaged as when they remain in state hands. In such situations the issue is not privatization anymore, but the existence of government capacity. This implies that privatization in countries in Case I, for example (high corruption and large public sector) are likely to result only in smaller public sectors, with increasing degrees of corruption and little welfare gains.

REFERENCE

Stiglitz, J. E. (1998), 'Knowledge for Development: Economic Science, Economic Policy and Economic Advice', paper given to the *Annual Bank Conference on Development Economics*, World Bank, Apr.

4

Different Approaches to Bankruptcy

OLIVER HART

I. INTRODUCTION

In the last fifteen years or so, lawyers working in law and economics and economists with an interest in legal matters have turned their attention to the topic of bankruptcy. A large amount of work has resulted, both theoretical and empirical, some of which has been concerned with the functioning of existing bankruptcy procedures and some with bankruptcy reform. Although researchers in this area have expressed different views, I believe that one can identify a consensus on certain issues—for example, the goals of bankruptcy and some of the characteristics of an efficient bankruptcy procedure. (There is probably less agreement about exactly what the best bankruptcy procedure is or how well existing systems around the world function.) In this paper, I will focus on this consensus because I believe it is useful in guiding countries with poorly developed bankruptcy procedures in efforts to improve them.[1] One point I will stress is that it is unlikely that 'one size fits all'. That is, although some bankruptcy procedures can probably be rejected as being manifestly bad, there is a class of procedures that satisfy the main criteria of efficiency. Which procedure a country chooses or should choose may then depend on other factors—for example, the country's institutional structure and legal tradition. One can also imagine a country choosing a menu of procedures and allowing firms to select among them.

It is important to recognize that bankruptcy reform should not be seen in isolation: it may be necessary to combine it with legal and other reforms—for example, the training of judges, improvements in corporate governance and the strengthening of investor rights (see LaPorta *et al.* 1998) and possibly even changes in the international financial system (see IMF 1999 and Rowart and Astigarraga 1999). I will not discuss these issues here, although they should be borne in mind in what follows.[2] Also, I will deal only with company bankruptcy and not with the bankruptcy of individuals or governments (local, state or national), even though some of the issues raised are similar.

I would like to thank Philippe Aghion, John Moore, Andrei Shleifer, Joseph Stiglitz, and, especially, Fritz Foley for helpful comments.

[1] My approach will be mainly normative: I will have very little to say about why bankruptcy laws have developed in the way they have. On this, see Berglöf and Rosenthal (1998) and Franks and Sussman (1999).

[2] Among other things, the IMF report suggests that one way to reduce financial distress might be for a firm and its bondholders to include debt renegotiation provisions in their bond contracts. This may be thought of as a private bankruptcy procedure (see below).

II. THE NEED FOR A BANKRUPTCY PROCEDURE

Firms take on debt for several reasons. Probably the most important is that they wish to commit to pay out some of their future cash flow. Whatever the reason, there will be circumstances in which a firm will be unable to pay its debts. Bankruptcy law is concerned with what happens in such situations.

In the absence of a bankruptcy law, a creditor has two main legal remedies at his disposal in countries such as the USA, the UK, and the rest of Western Europe. First, in the case of a secured loan, the creditor can seize the assets that serve as collateral for the loan. Secondly, in the case of an unsecured loan, the creditor can call on the court to sell some of the debtor's assets.

This method of debt collection runs into difficulties when there are many creditors and the debtor's assets do not cover his liabilities. Under these conditions, creditors will try to be first to recover their debts. This race by creditors may lead to the dismantlement of the firm's assets, and to a loss of value for all creditors.

Given this, it is in the collective interest of creditors that the disposition of the debtor's assets be carried out in an orderly manner, via a bankruptcy procedure.

In principle, individuals could arrange bankruptcy procedure themselves. That is, a debtor could specify as part of a debt contract what should happen in a default state. Writing such a contract may be difficult, however, given that the debtor may acquire new assets and creditors as time passes. Moreover, the empirical evidence—both the fact that firms rarely write such contracts and the fact that almost all countries have at least a primitive state-provided bankruptcy procedure—suggests that we cannot rely on this 'private' solution in practice. In other words, there seems to be a clear case for the government at least to provide an 'off-the-shelf' bankruptcy procedure—that is, one that the parties can use in the event that they do not write their own.

III. GOALS OF A BANKRUPTCY PROCEDURE

It is hard to derive an optimal bankruptcy procedure from first principles, given that economists do not at this point have a satisfactory theory of why parties cannot design their own bankruptcy procedures (that is, why contracts are incomplete). In spite of this, economic theory can guide us as to the characteristics of a good procedure.

First, there is a strong argument that a bankruptcy procedure should deliver an *ex post* efficient outcome—that is, it should maximize the total value (measured in money terms) available to be divided between the debtor, creditors, and possibly other interested parties—for example, workers. (We call this Goal 1.) Specifically, a firm should be reorganized, sold for cash as a going concern, or closed down and liquidated piecemeal according to which of these generates the greatest total value. The reasoning is that, other things being equal, more is preferred to less; in particular, if a procedure can be modified to deliver higher total value, then, given that each group receives an adequate share of this value (see the discussion of Goal 3 below), everyone will be better off.

Goal 1. Ceteris paribus, a good bankruptcy procedure should deliver an *ex post* efficient outcome.

Although Goal 1 will be readily accepted by most economists, it is worth noting that it goes against much informal thinking on the topic. It is often taken for granted that debtors will favor a pro-debtor bankruptcy procedure and creditors will favor a pro-creditor bankruptcy procedure. The informal view misses the point that, if, say, a pro-debtor bankruptcy procedure is chosen, then debtors will have to pay higher interest rates to compensate creditors in non-bankruptcy states.

The second goal concerns *ex ante* efficiency. As we have noted, probably the most important reason a firm raises funds by borrowing money rather than, say, issuing shares is to commit itself to pay out future cash flow. For such a commitment to have any force, there has to be some punishment if the commitment is not fulfilled. This punishment can take various forms. Shareholders can be punished by having their claims wiped out (see Goal 3 below). Managers can be punished by making it less likely that they can hold onto their jobs. But, without any adverse consequences at all, there is very little incentive to pay your debts.

Goal 2. A good bankruptcy procedure should preserve the bonding role of debt by penalizing managers and shareholders adequately in bankruptcy states.

Next we turn to the way value is divided among the claimants. A simple way to penalize shareholders in bankruptcy is to respect the absolute priority of claims (that is, senior creditors are paid off first, then junior creditors, and finally shareholders). Adhering to absolute priority of claims has other advantages. First, it helps to ensure that creditors receive a reasonable return in bankruptcy states, which encourages them to lend. Secondly, it means that bankruptcy and non-bankruptcy states are not treated as fundamentally different: contractual obligations entered into outside bankruptcy are respected to the full extent possible inside bankruptcy.

However, an argument can be made against absolute priority. As a number of scholars have pointed out, if shareholders receive nothing in bankruptcy, then management, acting on behalf of shareholders, will have an incentive to 'go for broke'—that is, they will do anything to avoid bankruptcy, including undertaking highly risky investment projects and delaying a bankruptcy filing. For this reason, there may be a case for reserving some portion of value in bankruptcy for shareholders.

Goal 3. A good bankruptcy procedure should preserve the absolute priority of claims, except that some portion of value should possibly be reserved for shareholders.

IV. EXISTING PROCEDURES

Although there are many different bankruptcy procedures around the world, they fall into two main categories: an asset sale (or cash auction), on the one hand, and structured bargaining, on the other hand.

Asset sale (cash auction)

The simplest bankruptcy procedure, some version of which can be found in almost all countries, consists of a sale of the firm's assets, supervised by a trustee or receiver. Often the assets are sold piecemeal; in other words, the firm is liquidated (having been closed down). Sometimes, however, the firm is sold as a going concern. Whichever occurs, the receipts from the sale are distributed among former claimants according to absolute priority (usually secured debt, then various priority claims, then unsecured debt, then subordinated debt, and finally equity); however, absolute priority is not an essential part of the procedure.

From a theoretical perspective, a cash auction has an attractive simplicity. If capital markets work well, the procedure should generate an *ex post* efficient outcome. In particular, if the firm is worth more as a going concern than liquidated, a bid to keep the firm together will dominate a set of independent bids for the parts. On the other hand, if the firm is worth more closed down, then a set of independent bids for the parts will dominate a bid for the whole.

A cash auction has another advantage. There is no haggling among the claimants about who should get what: the firm is transformed into a pile of cash, which is distributed according to absolute priority (or some other agreed-in-advance rule).

Although there is little clear-cut evidence about whether cash auctions for firms work well in practice (but see Pulvino 1998), there is plenty of indirect evidence suggesting that debtors, creditors, and society generally do not trust them. There have been discussions in many countries in the last fifteen years or so about bankruptcy reform, with new procedures being introduced in some countries, but, as far as I am aware, *all* of the discussion and changes have been in the direction of introducing a chapter 11–type structured bargaining procedure (see below); none of the movement has been in the direction of cash auctions.[3] In fact, I'm not aware of any group—management, shareholders, creditors, or workers—who is pushing for cash auctions. Thus, it seems to be a fact of life that countries are not prepared to rely on cash auctions as a bankruptcy procedure.

Structured bargaining

Because of the concern about the effectiveness of cash auctions, a number of countries have developed alternative procedures based on the notion of structured bargaining. The idea behind these procedures is that the firm's claimants are encouraged to bargain about the future of the firm—whether it should be liquidated or reorganized and how its value should be divided up—according to predetermined rules. The leading example of a structured bargaining procedure is chapter 11 of the US Bankruptcy Code; however, UK administration is based on similar ideas, as are procedures in France, Germany, and Japan.

The basic elements of chapter 11 are as follows. A stay is put on creditors' claims (that is, they are frozen: no creditor is allowed to seize or sell any of the firm's assets during the process); claim holders are grouped into classes according to the type of claim they have (secured or unsecured, senior or junior); and a judge supervises a process of bargaining among class representatives to determine a plan of action and a division of value for the

---

[3] Countries in which a chapter 11-type structured bargaining procedure has been introduced recently include Australia, Indonesia, Thailand, and Argentina.

firm. During the process, incumbent management usually runs the firm. An important part of the procedure is that a plan can be implemented if it receives approval by a suitable majority of each claimant class; unanimity is not required.

UK administration was introduced in 1986 as 'the British version of chapter 11'. An important difference between UK administration and chapter 11 is that the UK administrator (who is an insolvency practitioner) runs the firm during bankruptcy. The bankruptcy law enacted in France in 1985 is also somewhat like chapter 11. However, the court, through an administrator, has considerably more power than in the USA or the UK: it can accept a reorganization plan without the approval of creditors (or workers), provided it best ensures the maintenance of employment and the repayment of creditors.

Chapter 11 has been criticized for being time-consuming, costly, too friendly to debtors, and not respecting absolute priority. The procedure could undoubtedly be modified to deal with some of these criticisms. However, there are two fundamental problems inherent in chapter 11 and structured bargaining procedures like it. These problems arise because a structured bargaining procedure tries to make two decisions at once: what to do with the firm, and who should get what in the event of a restructuring of claims. Unfortunately, restructured firms do not have an objective value. Consequently, it is hard to know what fraction of the post-bankruptcy firm's securities each group of creditors is entitled to receive. This is true even if there is no dispute about the amount and seniority of each creditor's claim. As a result, there can be a great deal of haggling.

Perhaps even more serious, there is a danger that the wrong decision will be made concerning the firm's future. The voting mechanism is fixed in advance, which means that those people whose payoff ought not to be affected by the outcome (either because they are fully protected anyway, or because they are not entitled to anything) may end up controlling the pivotal votes.

As an example, consider a firm whose debts are approximately equal to its liquidation value. Creditors will push for a speedy liquidation (since they will be close to fully paid), while shareholders will hold out for a lengthy reorganization (since they enjoy the upside potential, but not the downside risk). Depending on the circumstances, a good firm may be terminated if creditors have the pivotal votes; or a bad firm may be kept going if shareholders have the pivotal votes.

In spite of these problems, chapter 11 has its supporters. However, it is far from clear that a country embarking on bankruptcy reform should choose chapter 11 rather than trying something new.

V. BANKRUPTCY REFORM

In this section, I will describe a class of procedures that have some of the same features as structured bargaining, but are simpler. In particular, they allow the claimants the choice to restructure the firm, but they avoid haggling about the division of the proceeds. All of these procedures involve an automatic debt-equity swap. They may or may not also include an auction for the firm's assets or a formal vote on what should happen to the firm. The merit of these procedures is that they replace *bargaining* among claimants who have different objectives with a *vote* by a homogeneous group of shareholders.

Basic procedure

When a firm goes bankrupt, its debts (most or all of them) are canceled. The former creditors become the (principal) new shareholders in the firm. A decision about the firm's future—whether it should survive as a going concern or be closed down—is made by the new shareholders. The firm then exits from bankruptcy.

There are two aspects to the procedure: the decision about whether to reorganize or liquidate the firm and the debt–equity swap. We discuss these in turn.

Decision about the firm's future

There are several ways of deciding the firm's future. We present three possibilities.

Version 1 (based on Aghion et al. 1992). The firm is put up for auction (someone—for example, a judge—supervises this). Cash or non-cash bids are allowed. In a non-cash bid, someone offers securities instead of cash. For example, incumbent management might offer the former creditors (the new shareholders) a combination of shares and debt in the post-bankruptcy firm. Thus, a non-cash bid embraces the possibility of reorganization and/or recapitalization of the firm as a going concern. The new shareholders vote on which bid to select.[4]

Version 2 (based on Aghion et al. 1995). The supervisor of the bankruptcy procedure—a trained bankruptcy practitioner (BP), say—takes over the running of the firm (he replaces the board of directors). The BP draws up a plan (or plans) for the future of the firm. The plan might be to reorganize the firm, to sell it as a going concern, or to close it down. (In fact, a plan is just like a cash or non-cash bid.) The plan is implemented as long as it receives majority approval by the new shareholders. (The BP may choose to put up more than one plan to shareholders and see which one receives greatest support.)

Version 3 (in the spirit of Bebchuk 1988). There is no formal auction or vote. Instead, the choice of what to do with the firm is determined by the new shareholders via standard corporate governance procedures. In particular, soon after the debt–equity swap, an election is held for a new board of directors. (Any staggered board provisions are eliminated.) Takeover bids are also allowed through the elimination of all anti-takeover defenses (for example, poison pills).

The versions differ according to the level of involvement by outsiders—for example, the courts—with Version 2 having the most outsider participation, and Version 3 the least. Less outsider participation comes at a cost: managers' jobs are most on the line in

---

[4] It may be efficient for incentive purposes that management retain an ownership stake in the post-bankruptcy firm. Such an ownership stake can be part of a non-cash bid.

Version 2 and least on the line in Version 3. However, all the versions put management under some pressure: that is, they go some way toward satisfying Goal 2 of Section III.

The versions also meet Goal 1. The firm's future is decided by a homogeneous group—the new shareholders—who have a strong incentive to vote for an outcome that maximizes the firm's net present value.[5]

The debt–equity swap

The other part of the scheme involves how debt is converted into equity. Again, there are several ways of doing this.

If all debt has the same priority (for example, it is unsecured), it is natural to allocate all the equity to the creditors on a pro-rata basis, possibly reserving a portion (10 percent? 20 percent?) for former shareholders.

Matters become more complicated if there is senior and junior debt. The reason is that it is not clear what fraction of the equity each group is entitled to. The leading example of senior debt in practice is secured debt. One possibility is to leave the secured debt in place, and just convert the unsecured debt into equity.[6] This turns the firm into a solvent one since the value of the firm is at least as great as the value of its physical assets (which are collateral for the secured debt).

Version A. Suppose there is a single class of unsecured creditors and some secured creditors. Then, the secured debt is left in place, and the unsecured creditors become the new shareholders (with some of the shares possibly being reserved for the old shareholders).

Version A deals quite well with secured debt, but less well with other kinds of senior debt—for example, preferred debt. Preferred debt refers to claims that society has decided should have priority over ordinary debt—for example, unpaid wages of workers and taxes owed to the government. In practice, unpaid wages are not a great burden and the post-bankruptcy firm can pay them off by new borrowing. Taxes can be much more significant, but a simple solution here is to remove the government's priority and treat taxes owed to the government as unsecured debt.[7]

Another approach to dealing with debt of different securities, including secured debt, has been suggested by Bebchuk (1988). Bebchuk proposes eliminating *all* debt, and allocating shares to the senior creditors and options to buy shares to the junior creditors and shareholders. Specifically, junior creditors are allocated options to buy equity from senior creditors by paying what these senior creditors are owed. (In effect, they buy out their claim.) Similarly, shareholders are allocated options to buy back their equity by

---

[5] To the extent that the firm is worth more as a going concern than liquidated, putting the firm's future in the hands of shareholders should also lead to the preservation of workers' jobs.

[6] To be more precise, an appraisal would be made of the collateral underlying each secured claim. If the appraised value is more than the secured creditor's debt, the debt is left in place (it is fully secured). If the appraised value is less, then only the secured part is left in place; the residual is treated as unsecured debt and is converted into equity.

[7] An even more radical approach is to eliminate the priority of secured debt too—i.e. treat *all* debt as unsecured. For a discussion of this, see Bebchuk and Fried (1996).

paying off all creditors. Note that this is a decentralized process: each option holder acts independently.

Version B. Suppose there are several classes of debt plus equity. Then the most senior class is allocated all the shares. A junior claimant (including a shareholder), owning 1 percent of his class's claims, is allocated the option to buy (up to) 1 percent of the equity from senior claimants by paying 1 percent of the total amount those senior to him are owed.

Bebchuk's scheme deals ingeniously with the general case of multiple debt classes. In effect, no junior claimant (including shareholders) can complain that he is being under-paid, since, if he thinks that those senior to him are getting more than they are owed, he can always buy them out at the face value of their debt. However, Bebchuk's scheme has the undesirable feature that junior claimants must put money in (that is, exercise their options) to get money out (to be paid). This may be a problem if junior claimants are wealth-constrained. One possible solution is for the bankruptcy procedure supervisor (a judge or BP) to create a market for the firm's options and shares, so that junior claimants can sell their options. The sale of securities in this market can also be used to pay off some creditors. For a detailed proposal along these lines, see Hart *et al.* (1997).

To sum up, we have presented two ways of carrying out the debt–equity swap, both of which are in line with Goal 3 of Section III. Combined with the three ways of deciding the firm's future, this means that we have six possible bankruptcy procedures. (Further variations on these procedures are obviously possible.) All of these procedures avoid the haggling problems that beset chapter 11.[8]

Which procedure is best? The answer probably depends on the circumstances. For example, Version 2 of deciding the firm's future, combined with Version A of the debt–equity swap, might work well in a country with trained bankruptcy specialists (for example, the UK). On the other hand, Version 3, combined with Version A, might work well in a country where the judicial system is not very developed and/or the macroeconomic environment is such that there are too many bankruptcies for the courts to handle.[9]

In fact, because it is unclear which procedure is best, a country could select a (limited) menu of schemes and let firms pick from them in advance (for example, as part of their corporate charter or debt contracts).

A final important point concerns whether the state bankruptcy procedure should be mandatory. There seems to be no compelling reason why it should be. If a firm and its creditors wish to opt out of the state system and write their own bankruptcy procedure—tailored to their own situation—why not let them do so?[10]

---

[8] These procedures also avoid the need for special 'debtor-in-possession' financing. This is because both Version A and Version B of the debt–equity swap turn the firm into a solvent one, which should be able to raise capital given a profitable investment opportunity.

[9] I am grateful to Joseph Stiglitz for this observation.

[10] An interesting example of parties writing their own procedure is Administrative Receivership in the UK. Under Administrative Receivership, an important creditor—typically a bank—contracts with the debtor to be granted what is called a 'floating charge'. This gives this creditor the right to appoint a receiver when the firm defaults. The receiver takes charge of the firm and decides whether to sell the assets piecemeal or maintain the

VI. CONCLUDING REMARKS

In conclusion, it is worth briefly touching on an important 'political economy' issue that arises in any country that is considering bankruptcy reform: the transition problem. Although we have argued that a debtor and creditors should jointly favor a more efficient bankruptcy procedure, this may not be the case in the short run, given that firms will have debts in place negotiated under a previous regime.

For example, some countries currently have pro-debtor bankruptcy laws and are thinking of making them more pro-creditor. Debtors resist the changes, because they are already paying the 'cost' of pro-debtor procedures through high interest rates. One way to deal with this problem is to leave the current procedure in place and introduce the new bankruptcy procedure as an option—that is, debtors can choose whether or not to switch to it (if they switch, they have to do so on all their debt contracts). In the short run debtors may choose not to switch. However, in the long run, as their old debts expire, they are likely to switch if the new procedure really is more efficient: they face a choice of paying high interest rates under the old procedure or low interest rates under the new procedure.

In fact, this example illustrates the desirable feature of a menu of procedures more generally. With a menu there is a 'market' test. If several procedures are available, then in the long run the efficient ones are likely to be chosen by debtors and creditors; the others will eventually be discarded.

REFERENCES

Aghion, P., Hart, O., and Moore, J. (1992), 'The Economics of Bankruptcy Reform', *Journal of Law, Economics and Organization*, 8: 523–46.

—— —— —— (1995), 'Insolvency Reform in the UK: A Revised Proposal', *Insolvency Law & Practice*, 11: 67–74.

Bebchuk, L. A. (1988), 'A New Approach to Corporate Reorganizations', *Harvard Law Review*, 101: 775–804.

—— and Fried, J. M. (1996), 'The Uneasy Case for the Priority of Secured Claims in Bankruptcy', *Yale Law Journal*, 105: 857–934.

Berglöf, E., and Rosenthal, H. (1998), 'The Political Economy of American Bankruptcy: The Evidence from Roll Call Voting, 1800–1978', paper presented at the annual meeting of the Midwest Political Science Association, Chicago.

Franks, J., and Sussman, O. (1999), 'Financial Innovations and Corporate Insolvency', mimeo, London Business School.

Hart, O., La Porta Drago, R., Lopez-de-Silanes, F., and Moore, J. (1997), 'A New Bankruptcy Procedure that Uses Multiple Auctions', *European Economic Review*, 41: 461–73.

IMF (1999): International Monetary Fund, 'Involving the Private Sector in Forestalling and Resolving Financial Crises', report prepared by the Policy Development and Review Department.

firm. As Franks and Sussman's interesting recent (1999) paper shows, Administrative Receivership is best seen as a privately negotiated contract between a debtor and its creditors. There seems no reason to interfere with such a contract.

La Porta, R., Lopez-de-Silanes, F., Shleifer, A., and Vishny, R. W. (1998), 'Law and Finance', *Journal of Political Economy*, 106: 1113–55.

Pulvino, T. (1998), 'Do Asset Fire Sales Exist? An Empirical Investigation of Commercial Aircraft Transactions', *Journal of Finance*, 53: 939–78.

Rowat, M., and Astigarraga, J. (1999), 'Latin American Insolvency Systems: A Comparative Assessment', World Bank Technical Paper No. 433.

5

The Institutional Infrastructure of Competition Policy

JEAN TIROLE

I. COMPETITION AND COMPETITION POLICY

Economists have long extolled the virtues of competition. Competition often lowers prices, enlarges product variety, and fosters innovation. It usually selects the most efficient producers. And it facilitates governance by letting claimholders benchmark their firm's performance against that of its rivals and by threatening dormant managers with marginalization and bankruptcy. To be certain, the industrial organization literature focuses (rightly so) on the many imperfections of the competitive process, and serves as a healthy reminder to ideologues that competition is at best an instrument and not a goal *per se*. This literature, however, should not be used to vindicate anti-competitive policies; it should rather be a guide for designing corrections to an otherwise beneficial competitive environment.

Industry oversight by governments has been motivated in several ways. First, in industries or segments for which competition is deemed too costly and monopolies prevail, regulation has been used to keep consumer prices low. Leaving aside regulatory incentives, three key issues have emerged: the promotion of cost efficiency and innovation and its conflict with the desire to extract the rents of regulated firms; the regulation of access to bottleneck (natural monopoly) segments to allow competition in complementary activities; and the provision of universal service (redistribution toward the needy and regional development) in a competitive world. Economists have investigated in detail the three rocks struck by industry oversight in pursuing these tasks: lack of information about technology and demand, regulatory capture by interest groups, and limited commitment ability.

In contrast, competition policy has focused on the maintenance of a favorable environment for competition by investigating mergers, prohibiting cartels and collusive agreements, and punishing abuses of dominant position.

II. A BROAD ARRAY OF COMPETITION-RELEVANT INSTITUTIONS

In the following, I will focus on two forms of government intervention impacting industry structure and behavior: regulation and antitrust. It may not be obvious to everyone that regulation impacts competition, but it does in a substantial way through various decisions: licensing, standards, line-of-business restrictions, intervention in the merger control process, and, most prominently, the choice of policies for access of competitors to bottleneck segments (local loop in telecommunications, transmission grid in electricity and gas, tracks and stations for railroads, and so forth).

Regulatory agencies and antitrust authorities are only two of the several institutional players defining the competitive environment. Strikingly enough, the other panelists' topics also bear on the development of competition.

- A proper legal enforcement of contracts, among many other benefits, facilitates entry by new players. First, in countries with poorly functioning courts, established firms bypass the legal system and procure their supplies either internally (vertical integration) or through business networks. The need to produce multiple products internally or to build reputations within a usually close-knit business network represents a barrier to entry. Proper legal enforcement facilitates entry in another way. By protecting the firm's creditors and shareholders, legal enforcement boosts its borrowing capacity. Access to capital markets is particularly crucial to younger enterprises, which cannot rely on retained earnings or on their reputation.
- Efficient and non-corrupt bankruptcy procedures also facilitate access to credit and may thereby encourage entry. They furthermore facilitate the selection process by weeding out inefficient firms more expeditiously.
- Privatization may participate to the creation of a level-playing field among firms in an industry by removing subsidies and favoritism.
- Bilateral and multilateral agreements on tariffs, international telecom settlements, standards, and so forth, obviously play an important role in creating new (foreign) entrants in a domestic industry.
- The creation of advocates for competition within and outside governments may also contribute to the awareness of the benefits of competition and to better laws and executive decisions in the matter. Consumers are too dispersed a constituency, and their natural advocate, the competition authorities, traditionally intervenes only to prevent behaviors that violate competition law. There is scope for the creation of other competition advocates who examine existing (or drafts of) laws and directives and, when needed, make the case for competition to the president, prime minister, Congress, or the public opinion. Strikingly enough, such advocates have been created in some less developed countries (for example, Mexico).

In the rest of this note, we will focus on the central debate between antitrust and regulation, but we should keep in mind that other institutional choices may bear on the corresponding tradeoffs through their impact on the feasibility of competition.

III. REGULATION VERSUS ANTITRUST

Network industries (telecommunications, electricity, postal services, railroads, and so forth) have been traditionally regulated by an industry-specific regulator. The trend, though, is toward more involvement of competition authorities in these industries. For example, the Department of Justice and US courts now intervene routinely in telecommunications matters. Sometimes, this trend is a natural consequence of the globalization of markets. A case in point is the Internet. The Internet is a truly worldwide market that, even if regulation were desirable (which is rather unclear at this stage), would have no natural regulator; competition authorities, if possible in collaboration (as was well exemplified by the DOJ–DG4 cooperation in the 1998 WorldCom–MCI merger investigation), will oversee the industry. The trend is also due in some industries to rapid technological progress, which makes standard regulatory tools inadequate (price regulation in the form of cost-of-service or price caps presumes a stable set of services to be regulated; in the telecommunications industry, for example, the set of services evolves very rapidly). The more interesting question is whether industries where regulatory oversight is still feasible will witness a demise of regulation and a move toward the New Zealand approach of abrogating regulatory institutions altogether and relying entirely on competition policy (access to bottlenecks being subjected to the essential facilities doctrine). This is a complex question, and I will attempt to provide only a few elements of reflection.

Partly because they address some of the same concerns and face the same difficulties (imperfect information, capture, limited commitment ability), antitrust enforcement and regulation share a number of features. Let us nevertheless attempt to point at some elements of departure.

Procedures and control rights. By and large, regulatory agencies have wider control rights than competition agencies and courts. Competition policy assesses the lawfulness of conducts. In contrast, regulatory agencies engage in detailed regulation of wholesale and retail prices, profit sharing, and investments, and impose lines of business restrictions. Furthermore, courts are subject to stronger consistency requirements than regulatory agencies. They must refer to the decisions of other courts and apply criteria that are uniform across industries.

To be certain, regulatory discretion is limited by procedural requirements, by statutory limits on the ability to commit in the long term, by safeguards against regulatory takings, by legal constraints on the mode of regulation (for example, price cap, rate of return, non-discriminatory and cost-based regulation of access), and by the parties' possible resort to courts. But, as a first approximation, it is fair to say that regulatory agencies have more extensive powers than antitrust enforcers.

Timing of oversight. By and large, competition policy operates *ex post* (after the fact), with the exception of merger control (in this sense, a merger task force bears strong resemblance to a regulatory agency). In contrast, regulators operate *ex ante* by defining the prices of utilities or the rules for the industry, with the exception of the *ex post* disallowance-of-investments process. The judicial process is a lengthy one, while the regulatory process can (must) be more expedient.

The difference in timing (*ex post* versus *ex ante*) has a couple of implications, First, the players in the industry perhaps face less uncertainty under regulation (this effect may be offset by the larger discretion enjoyed by regulatory agencies, as discussed earlier), since the uncertainty is partly resolved before the players take their private decisions. Secondly, antitrust enforcement benefits from the late accrual of information. That is, it may become clearer after the fact what constitutes an acceptable conduct.

Perhaps the implication of all this is that the decision rights endowed upon regulatory agencies and antitrust enforcers have a different nature. Regulators define *ex ante* a set of feasible moves for operators. Antitrust enforcers in contrast check *ex post* that anti-competitive moves in the feasible set defined by competition law were not selected.

Information intensiveness and continued relationship. Regulators often have more expertise than their antitrust counterparts, although the use of specialized courts (including patent courts) and antitrust officials tends to reduce the informational wedge between the two. This wedge has three origins. Regulatory oversight is industry-specific, antitrust enforcement is not. Regulators have long-term relationships with regulated firms, antitrust enforcers (Judge Greene for the US telecom market notwithstanding) do not. Last, regulators have larger professional staffs as well as continued procedures of data collection.

The relative shortage of data available to antitrust enforcers implies that they are usually more at ease with cases based on qualitative evidence (price discrimination, price fixing, vertical restraints, and so forth) than those based on quantitative evidence (predation, tacit collusion, access pricing, and so forth). In contrast, regulators are relatively more at ease with quantitative evidence, which they often use to set very detailed regulations, as in the case of cost-based pricing rules.

There are costs of being too well-informed, though. Too much information about profitability, for example, coupled with limited commitment power, aggravates the ratchet effect (which penalizes operators who have proved efficient or have invested). Furthermore, to the extent that expertise is partly associated with the existence of a long-term relationship between the regulator and the industry, expertise may also be correlated with a higher risk of capture by the industry.

Political independence. Although many regulatory agencies are in principle independent of the political power, they probably are less so than courts. In effect, politicians do exert some influence on the so-called independent agencies through the appropriation process and through nominations. The costs and benefits of agency independence are well known. The cost of independence is a certain lack of accountability. Its benefits are that regulators are less concerned about the electoral impact of their decisions, and therefore less biased in favor of domestic firms or powerful interest groups. And, to the extent that they include fewer political appointees, their staff may be more professional.

Our view is that, for technical matters, independence (of regulatory agencies or courts) is a virtue, even though it definitely has costs. Regulatory decisions in the telecommunications industry, for instance, are usually very technical for an outsider and their economic impact is unlikely to be understood by the public. For such decisions, the political accountability mechanism is unlikely to operate well.

Redistributive policies. Regulatory schemes have traditionally involved large cross-subsidies—for instance, between residential and business users and between city and rural customers. In contrast, antitrust authorities have no mandate to promote universal service. The regulatory trend in the matter of universal service obligations is toward more transparency. Competitively neutral mechanisms (such as Universal Service Funds) are put in place, which perform the same redistributive functions, but force regulators and politicians to be explicit about the size and incidence of these subsidies. This is a desirable evolution, which allows operators to follow business principles and forces politicians to be more accountable.

To conclude this section, I would argue that regulation and antitrust need not be inconsistent and may be complements rather than substitutes. In particular, the antitrust authorities should be the advocate of competition in situations in which regulation destroys the level playing field between incumbents and entrants. The traditional pattern has been (and probably will still often be) the capture of regulators by incumbents and a very wasteful protection against entry; but, although historically less common, the opposite pattern—an industrial policy aiming at creating entry at any cost—may also arise from capture by entrants or from the regulator's being eager to be remembered as the architect to widespread entry. Either way, competition authorities should be the watchdog and intervene to promote effective competition.

IV. JURISDICTIONAL ASPECTS AND COMPETITION AMONG AGENCIES

The multiplicity of industry overseers may reflect some complementarity. For example, competition authorities act as competition advocates in regulated industries and oversee the maintenance of a level playing field among operators. The multiplicity is often also viewed as a way of creating competition among agencies through the benchmarking of their policies.

Such regulatory competition also has clear costs: duplication of investigations by the agencies, increased costs for the private sector of dealing with multiple agencies, coordination of policies. For example, a telecommunications merger in the US may face several challenges at the federal level (Department of Justice, Federal Communications Commission) as well as challenges by each state in which the firms are active, not to mention challenges overseas. This raises the issue not only of transaction costs, but also, along the way, of the multiple concessions made by the merging parties and catering to the preferences of each overseer; multiple hurdles may discourage the process in the first place if the agencies do not coordinate.

Jurisdictional choices are also affected by the need for expertise. Regulatory and antitrust policies are becoming more and more complex technologically and economically. The scarce expertise pleads in favor of increased centralization (supranational regulators and antitrust authorities), even though this centralization reduces regulatory competition.

V. COMPETITION POLICY AND DEVELOPMENT

As usual, specificities of less developed countries (LDCs) are a matter more of degree than of nature (see Rey 1997 for a more complete discussion). Relevant characteristics of LDCs for our discussion are:

- large barriers to entry: weak credit markets, protectionist policies, poor communications infrastructure;
- weak institutions: particularly extensive capture by interest groups, corruption, poor court enforcement, lack of regulatory and antitrust expertise, stifling bureaucratic rules, and (in some countries) extensive public ownership.

In view of these various factors, no single policy will seriously promote competition. Reforms must be undertaken on several fronts. And policies must be adapted to the level of development.

The specificities of LDCs, for example, suggest a few modifications of antitrust enforcement. Incentive theory shows that threats of corruption and capture should lead to more bureaucratic, that is, less discretionary rules, and so weak institutions may plead for more *per se* rules than exist in European and Northern American antitrust laws. Mergers may have to be discouraged more often if *ex post* tacit or explicit collusion is more likely. The implications of LDC specificities for competition policy may turn out to be ambiguous as well: for instance, predation may be more of an issue in LDCs, owing to weaker credit markets, but at the same time the prosecution of predatory behavior is usually a highly discretionary exercise.

Last, it would seem that there is a strong case for many LDCs to divest themselves of part of their antitrust enforcement, for two reasons. The high potential for capture may make it desirable to put some distance between the firms and the enforcers, and the scarcity of expertise suggests some concentration of resources.

These views are, of course, tentative and more definitive conclusions must await deeper thoughts about the application of antitrust doctrine and institutions to LDCs.

REFERENCES

Aghion, P., Dewatripont, M., and Rey, P. (1995), 'Competition, Financial Discipline and Growth', mimeo.
—— —— —— (1997), 'Agency Costs, Firm Behavior and the Nature of Competition', mimeo.
Institut d'Économie Industrielle (1997), 'Network Industries and Public Service', report for the European Commission, July.
Kovacic, W. (1999) 'The Choice of Institutional Mechanisms for Applying Competition Policy to Postal Service Operators', mimeo, George Washington University Law School.
Laffont, J.-J., and Tirole, J. (1993), *A Theory of Incentives in Procurement and Regulation* (Cambridge, Mass.: MIT Press).
—— —— (1999), *Competition in Telecommunications* (Cambridge, Mass.: MIT Press).
Rey, P. (1997), 'Competition Policy and Development', mimeo, Institut d'Économie Industrielle.
Schmidt, K. (1997), 'Managerial Incentives and Product Market Competition', *Review of Economic Studies*, 64: 191–213.

6

The Evolution of Legal Institutions and Economic Regime Change

KATHARINA PISTOR

I. INTRODUCTION

Economic reforms in the former socialist countries have produced what may be called the second major law and development movement in the past forty years. In an attempt to avoid the reinvention of the wheel, legal codes from developed market economies were transplanted to these countries, or prewar enactments—often the result of earlier transplants—were revived. It was hoped that, by putting this formal legal framework in place, a viable infrastructure would be created that would promote future growth and development. However, it is now becoming apparent that the transplantation of formal law does not necessarily alter behavior—a lesson that the first law and development movement had already learned (Trubek and Galanter 1974).

The concept of law as infrastructure fails to realize that formal law is but one set of institutions that governs behavior. Where formal and informal institutions evolve over time, they tend to complement each other. In the context of a political or economic regime change, however, new formal and pre-existing informal institutions compete. Formal law may be rejected, or ignored and substituted with informal institutions that operate independently of and frequently in contradiction to the formal legal system. For formal law to be accepted and to affect behavior, a constituency is needed, whose formation and strength in turn depend on consistent policy signals and effective mechanisms for the enforcement of new formal institutions.

II. FORMAL AND INFORMAL LAW

Not only do individuals act out of their own self-interest; their behavior is also influenced by institutions—that is, by accepted standards of behavior (Coleman 1990). In the terminology of the new institutional economics, institutions are 'constraint(s) that human beings devise to shape human interaction' (North 1990: 4). By far the majority of institutions that govern our behavior are informal. They evolve through social interaction and are either internalized or enforced informally. Informal institutions govern

I would like to thank Melissa Thomas for helpful comments and suggestions.

social groups from village communities to networks and relations of the political and economic elites.

Formal law is promulgated by designated state organs. It may evolve in response to social demand. Frequently, however, formal law is designed to change social behavior or to reallocate political and economic rights. Unlike informal institutions, which are sustained only if observed by members of society, formal law may remain on the books irrespective of demand. Existing formal law is, therefore, not an indicator for its demand or use in practice.

Ideally, informal and formal law complement each other. The majority of contractual disputes in all countries are solved informally. Not even the most efficient court system could handle the amount of disputes that arise in normal business transactions. In fact, the function of formal legal institutions, such as courts, is not to settle all disputes, but to deter litigation and encourage informal dispute settlement by offering a viable threat of effective state enforcement should informal settlement fail (Shavell 1997).

The relative mix of informal and formal law differs from country to country and varies widely within a given country. Even in countries with an extensive and well-functioning legal system, such as the USA, some communities operate under a set of informal institutions that ignore the prevailing formal ones (Ellickson 1991). Some trades have opted out of the formal legal system and offer their members substitute institutions (Bernstein 1992). It should, therefore, not be surprising to find that, in many countries where formal law did not evolve, but was introduced by way of transplant, the scope of informal law is often larger.

The prevalence of informal law is not necessarily an attribute of underdevelopedness that is to be corrected by massive injection of formal law. The development process has often produced a surplus of formal law. Frequently, this has been part of a catch-up strategy in which the state sought to direct development through regulatory intervention. But even when market-based development strategies dominated, as in transition countries, formal law expanded rapidly as these countries sought to develop a market-based legal framework (Pistor 1995).

The expansion of formal law does not necessarily replace informal institutions. Frequently, the opposite is the case, as agents seek to evade state intervention and/or taxes, and therefore opt out of the formal economy. The large share that the informal sector contributes to GDP in many transition economies (Johnson *et al.* 1997) gives evidence of this process. Opting out of the formal economy often leaves no choice but to opt out of the formal legal system and to substitute it with informal rules and enforcement mechanisms (De Soto 1990). In these instances, formal and informal law operate independently of each other.

III. EFFECTS OF FORMAL LEGAL TRANSPLANTS

The history of legal transplants is long (Watson 1974) and legal transplants have been an important part of legal development in the West. Over the past two centuries, however, law was transplanted primarily from the West to other parts of the world. The experience with the new formal law varies, but it appears that the functioning of formal law often differs in transplantee countries from its functioning in origin countries. The famous gap between the law on the books and the law in action tends to be substantially larger in the former.

An important reason might be the mode of legal transplantation. Formal law was frequently introduced during colonization. Its application was sometimes limited to members of the colonizing power and was extended to the indigenous people only after a country acquired independence. In case transplantation was voluntary rather than coercive, the law on the books was little used in practice, or used in ways that differed considerably from its use in the origin countries. Contrary to expectation, the demand for this formal law did not rise automatically with the process of economic development.

Evidence for this is provided by one of the most remarkable development experiences, the East Asian Miracle. For much of the period of high-speed economic growth in East Asia since the late 1950s, the law that had much earlier been transplanted from the West[1] played only a marginal role (Pistor and Wellons 1999). The law remained on the books, but was only rarely applied. It was supplanted by negotiated bargains between governments and business elites, as well as by rulings and decrees issued by the executive, which had extensive discretionary powers. Large parts of society remained outside the realm of formal law. Private transactions were governed by customary rules, and disputes were settled out of court, frequently with the help of third-party mediators. Formal dispute settlement was available, but was often not even used as a fallback option. Sometimes a new symbiosis between informal institutions and formal legal devices was created. An example is the use of postdated checks in Taiwan as a collateral that was enforced by the state, because until 1987 bouncing a check was a criminal offense (Kaufman-Winn 1994).

The experience of Asia shows that economic development is possible even when the Weberian rational legal system plays only a subordinate role. The absence of a rational legal system is not equivalent with the absence of legal institutions. The underpinning of the growth experience in Asia was an alternative institutional arrangement (Evans 1998), which was based on custom, networks, trust, and bargains under the guidance of state agents. Formal law was used to the extent that it complemented or supported this arrangement, but was ignored by economic and government agents alike, if it ran counter to it.

One may question whether these informal arrangements are sustainable in the long term. Indeed, after the early 1980s, the prevailing institutional arrangement in the East Asian countries came increasingly under pressure. In response to growing fiscal problems and exogenous shocks (the oil crises of the 1970s), governments liberalized rules that had previously restricted imports, direct investments, and capital inflows, loosened their control over the financial sector, encouraged the development of capital markets, and launched the privatization of financial institutions and state-owned enterprises. These changes in the economic regime questioned the existing informal institutions that had previously been perceived as a source of stability, but were increasingly regarded as

---

[1] British colonies, including India, Malaysia, Singapore, and Hong Kong received British law. Japan copied extensively from German law and introduced it in Korea and Taiwan during colonial rule. Indonesia received Dutch law, and so on.

an impediment for future economic development. While many formal rules had long been on the books, a demand for them was created only with the economic regime change, which in some instances (Korea, Taiwan) was accompanied by a political regime change. This new demand exposed the weaknesses of formal rules and institutions that had long been dormant.

In the transition process of the former socialist countries, the assault on pre-existing institutions by the political and economic regime change has been even more dramatic. Only a few countries, among them Hungary and to some extent Poland, had experimented with market-based transactions and organizational principles prior to the collapse of the socialist system—the prewar experience of some transition countries with market-based systems notwithstanding. The era of reform has exposed these societies to these principles, in some cases virtually overnight. What had previously been a criminal offense and was termed 'speculation', now became accepted behavior. As a result, the subtle line between fair trade, on the one hand, and unfair competition and speculation, on the other, which is protected by formal and informal institutions in most developed market economies, has often disappeared in the 'wild East'.

IV. EVOLUTION OF INSTITUTIONS AND REGIME CHANGE

Institutions evolve slowly and are highly path dependent. Even though statutory law can be introduced swiftly, it takes time for a new law to be applied, interpreted, and fine-tuned in the process of the new law actually being used and its contents and meaning challenged in court. Only after that does the new formal law become part of the institutions that govern behavior.

Existing institutions are challenged more profoundly in the case of a political and / or economic regime change. Such a change entails the reallocation of existing control rights.[2] Examples of political regime changes include a country's independence after years of colonization, the democratization of authoritarian governments, or the extension of economic and democratic rights to previously suppressed parts of the population. Examples for economic regime change include the opening of closed economies, the change from a centrally planned economy to a market-based system, or the reallocation of control rights over economic resources through privatization or participation.

Formal law is frequently used to reallocate existing socioeconomic and political rights. The adoption of a constitution and the introduction of universal suffrage are important examples. In the economic sphere, liberalization measures, including price, trade, and capital control liberalization through changes in trade and customs regulations, but also privatization and antitrust measures, have similar effects on the existing control structure over economic resources. Whereas, in equilibrium, the primary function of formal law is to define the scope of existing rights and to offer procedures for their enforcement,[3] in the

---

[2] A regime change is only one extreme case of the emergence of new institutions, which can be best captured by a distributional theory of institutional change (see Knight 1992).

[3] To be sure, new laws, administrative decrees, and court precedents continuously reallocate existing control rights, although in more subtle fashion than is the case in a regime change.

context of a regime change, formal law is used to reallocate rights and to establish the procedure for the intended reallocation.

Those affected by the reallocation of rights are usually acutely aware of the instrumental role law plays in this process. They frequently challenge these measures by using existing informal network relations to negotiate exemptions from the application of the formal law, or simply ignore the formal law and hold on to existing control rights backed by informal institutions. Examples for the former include the exemptions from standard privatization procedures negotiated by some of the most powerful firms in several transition countries (Pistor 1997), or the continuation of policy credits in Korea well after the major banks had been privatized (Stern 1995). An example for the latter is the still low number of bankruptcy cases in transition economies after the enactment of the relevant laws, despite the fact that in these countries many and sometimes the majority of companies are technically insolvent. While the incapacity of courts and judges to handle such cases may be part of an explanation, this alone cannot explain the reluctance to trigger bankruptcy by private creditors.

These examples demonstrate that formal law alone is not sufficient to change behavior, but that it operates in the context of a particular policy regime, on the one hand, and existing informal institutions, on the other. Changing one parameter does not automatically lead to a change in the others.

The use of formal law as an instrument for reallocating political and economic rights can be called the superstructural function of law. Marx viewed law as part of the superstructure and stressed the instrumental function of law for those who happen to be in power. In this function, law is not neutral. One does not have to adopt a strictly Marxian view to see that the reallocation of control rights will be contested by those who are currently holding these rights. Who the winner will be in this contest is determined by numerous factors, including the relative power of those defending their control rights, the credibility and enforceability of the new rights, and the extent to which rights are backed by informal institutions that lend legitimacy to either existing or new control rights.

By contrast, much of the literature views law as infrastructure—as is also reflected in the title of this conference session. The idea is that formal law is neutral. It creates incentives, but is not distributional, and therefore not contested. In this view, formal law facilitates transactions between private parties by offering a set of rules off the shelf as well as formal institutions capable of enforcing contracts and property rights in case informal settlement cannot be achieved. Within a given control structure, law may in fact play this role. In the case of an economic or political regime change, however, the very process of rule-making becomes contested. It is, therefore, not surprising to observe intense competition between different parts of the government over the law-making authority in countries that experience a regime change. This struggle can usually not be contained by, and in fact often ignores, the formal division of powers prescribed by the constitution.[4] One may expect that, the more extensive the anticipated reallocation of rights, the fiercer the struggle over the right to control the process of change. A vivid

---

[4] See, however, Cooter (1996), who suggests that the division of power will promote the competition of rules and help overcome situations of normative uncertainty.

example is Russia, where the confrontation between the president and the parliament led to the October events of 1993, when the leaders of the parliament openly called for resurrection and President Yeltsin sent in the troops, and where to this day the conflict between the president and the parliament has not been resolved.

The outcome of this struggle, as well as the way it is conducted, have important implications for the reception of new formal law. It may be accepted and at least partly internalized, or rejected—that is, circumvented or substituted with alternative rules.

The implication is that changing institutions is costly. It involves not only changing the formal law, but also altering the informal institutions that have evolved over time and that are still in place. For no social system therefore is there a situation in which law could be developed 'from scratch' (Black *et al.* 1996). The transition costs may be so high as to prevent a successful regime change. Despite fundamental changes in the formal legal system, these changes may not take root. Alternatively, the introduction of formal law may lead to a competition between different sets of rules. Some may take advantage of the new formal rules, because they benefit from them. If the benefits outweigh the costs of social sanctions, they will act in accordance with the new formal rules. In the ensuing competition between different institutions, one—and hopefully the more efficient one—will prevail (Picker 1997), and a new symbiosis between formal and informal institutions will develop.

There is an important caveat to this more optimistic scenario. The period of norm competition is likely to be a period of uncertainty.[5] While the previous institutions are losing credibility with the regime change, new institutions are yet to emerge. This period of uncertainty may collapse into crisis. The often described lawlessness in many transition economies is a symptom for this. But the recent financial crisis in Asia, which was preceded by years of extensive economic and legal change, may also be interpreted along these lines.

A crisis may accelerate the process of normative adaptation, because it creates an awareness for the need for change. South Korea seems to be such an example, where proponents of extensive institutional reforms have received political support to advance their agenda and have been able to broaden the constituency for reform, although, even in this country, success of these reform efforts is not yet certain. In Russia, by contrast, the August 1998 crisis appears only to have led to a reshuffling of power among the oligarchs. Worst, a crisis situation may lead to the further deterioration of the institutional setting and give rise to outbursts of chaos and violence, as has happened periodically in Indonesia.

Which outcome prevails will depend to a great extent on specific country conditions, as well as on the choice of policy measures and the process by which the regime change is implemented. Heterogeneous, including multi-ethnic, politically divided, or economically highly unequal, societies are more prone to conflict, and this may be exacerbated by the regime change (Chua 1998). More homogeneous countries with a relatively large

---

[5] The uncertainty of a regime change is much more profound than is the case in continuous institutional change. In particular, the very status of social actors within their community, firm, network, etc. is called into question.

constituency for change and a fairly developed institutional infrastructure (for example, the countries of Central Europe and the Baltics) may risk more radical reform measures.

V. CONCLUSION

Institutions develop slowly and are largely path dependent. Formal law has often been used to introduce swift change. Where these changes reflect the political and socio-economic situation of a given country, the gap between formal and informal institutions will be relatively small and both will complement each other. Where formal law is intro-duced to promote a political and/or economic regime change, however, it openly challenges existing institutions and is, therefore, likely to be opposed by those who held extensive control rights under the previous regime.

The dynamics of legal change and the impact of formal law on economic behavior differ significantly in these two scenarios and pose different challenges for the imple-mentation and ultimately acceptance of formal rules.

Several implications follow from this analysis:

- The adoption or transplantation of formal law alone will not alter behavior. The effects of legal transplants depend on the acceptance and internalization of formal law, and this in turn is influenced by the distributional impact of the regime change, which the new formal law is designed to enforce.
- In the context of a regime change, the applicability of evolutionary, demand-led, or bottom-up concepts of legal development (Rubin 1994; Cooter 1996) is also limited. Existing informal institutions often hinder rather than further the regime change. At the same time, a regime change undermines existing informal institutions. In the ensuing vacuum, strategies to maximize short-term gains at the expense of others often prevail over longer-term strategies of mutual cooperation.
- A successful regime change requires that new constituencies emerge that support it. New constituencies may develop spontaneously, but their size and strength ulti-mately depend on their ability to effectively enforce their newly gained rights. The experience of countries that have undergone a regime change suggests that often those who had extensive control rights prior to the change were able to defend or even expand their rights in the institutional vacuum that accompanied the regime change (Aslund 1999). To avoid this entrenchment, effective legal protection of the newly created or reallocated rights *up front* is crucial.
- Policy-makers cannot always control a regime change, but they may control the pace by which their countries are exposed to such a change. The wider the gap between the existing and the new system, the less developed the legal institutions to enforce the reallocation of rights, and the more divided a society that is subjected to a regime change, the more gradual the change should be to allow for time to build new institu-tions and to form new constituencies.

REFERENCES

Aslund, A. (1999), 'Why has Russia's Economic Transformation Been so Ardous?', *Proceedings of the Annual Bank Conference on Development Economics* (Washington: World Bank).

Bernstein, L. (1992), 'Opting out of the Legal System: Extralegal Contractual Relations in the Diamond Industry', *Journal of Legal Studies*, 21/1: 115–57.

Black, B., Kraakman, R. and Hay, J. (1996), 'Corporate Law from Scratch', in R. Frydman, C. W. Gray, and A. Rapaczynski (eds.), *Corporate Governance in Eastern Europe and Russia*, ii (Budapest, London, New York: Central European University Press), 245–302.

Chua, A. L. (1998), 'Markets, Democracy and Ethnicity: Toward a New Paradigm for Law and Development', *Yale Law Journal*, 108/1: 1–107.

Coleman, J. S. (1990), *Foundations of Social Theory* (Cambridge, Mass.: Harvard University Press).

Cooter, R. D. (1996), 'The Theory of Market Modernization of Law', in M. Bruno and B. Pleskovic, *Annual World Bank Conference on Development Economics* (Washington: World Bank), 191–217.

De Soto, H. (1990), *The Other Path* (New York: Harper & Row).

Ellickson, R. C. (1991), *Order Without Law—How Neighbors Settle Disputes* (Cambridge, Mass: Harvard University Press).

Evans, P. (1998), 'Transferable Lessons? Re-Examining the Institutional Prerequisites of East Asian Economic Policies', *Journal of Development Studies. Special Issue: East Asian Development, New Perspectives*, 34/6: 66–85.

Johnson, S., Kaufmann, D., and Shleifer, A. (1997), 'The Unofficial Economy in Transition', *Brookings Papers on Economic Activity*, 2.

Kaufman-Winn, J. (1994), 'Relational Practices and the Marginalization of Law: Informal Financial Practices of Small Businesses in Taiwan', *Law and Society Review*, 28/2: 193–232.

Knight, J. (1992), *Institutions and Social Conflict* (Cambridge: Cambridge University Press).

North, D. C. (1990), *Institutions, Institutional Change, and Economic Performance. The Political Economy of Institutions and Decisions* (Cambridge: Cambridge University Press).

Pistor, K. (1995), 'Law Meets the Market: Matches and Mismatches in Transition Economies', background paper for the World Development Report 1996, World Bank.

—— (1997), 'Company Law and Corporate Governance in Russia', in J. D. Sachs and K. Pistor, *The Rule of Law and Economic Reform in Russia* (Boulder, Colo: Westview Press), 165–87.

—— and Wellons, P. (1999), *The Role of Law and Legal Institutions in Asian Economic Development* (Hong Kong: Oxford University Press).

Rubin, P. H. (1994), 'Growing a Legal System in the Post-Communist Economies', *Cornell International Law Journal*, 27: 1–47.

Shavell, S. (1997), 'The Fundamental Divergence of Social and Private Benefits of Litigation', *Journal of Legal Studies*, 26 (June), 575–612.

Stern, J. J. (1995), *Industrialization and the State: The Korean Heavy and Chemical Industry Drive* (Harvard Studies in International Development, Cambridge, Mass: Harvard Institute for International Development).

Trubek, D. M., and Galanter, M. (1974), 'Scholars in Self-Estrangement: Some Reflections on the Crisis in Law and Development Studies in the United States', *Wisconsin Law Review*, 1062–102.

Watson, A. (1974), *Legal Transplants: An Approach to Comparative Law* (Edinburgh: Scottish Academic Press; London: distributed by Chatto & Windus).

New Thinking on Security in Labour Markets

7

Cross-Sectional Wage and Employment Rigidities versus Aggregate Employment

GIUSEPPE BERTOLA

When studying real-life market outcomes and evaluating policy interventions, econo-mists like to refer to a hypothetical situation where intertemporal and insurance markets are perfect and complete. In reality, of course, laissez-faire economic interactions can hardly supply insurance against the risk of becoming or remaining unemployed, because moral hazard and adverse selection stand in the way of such potential contractual arrangements. Workers would not try as hard to avoid unemployment and find new jobs if they were covered against the negative consequences of the event, by purchasing insurance at a given market price. And workers who know their unemployment risk is particularly high would make the scheme unprofitable for insurance providers and/ or unattractive to workers with average risk. Hence, one can understand why collec-tive action would try and remedy the *ex post* inequitable or 'unfair' labour-market treat-ment of workers who, lacking insurance, became or remained unemployed despite their best efforts.

Indeed, regulation and legislation aimed at protecting workers from 'unfair' labour-market shocks have a long history (see e.g. Hepple 1986), and one that largely proceeds apace with the development of modern industrial modes of production. The Industrial Revolution led to increasingly impersonal economic interactions, and reduced the role of informal insurance arrangements at the family or village level at the same time as it concentrated economic power in the hands of employers. Thus, it is hardly surprising that national policy-making authorities (notably in Bismarck's Germany, but also in most other Continental European countries) would introduce legislation and regulation aimed at protecting workers from the health, unemployment, and old-age hazards of their trade; and it is even less surprising that workers would try and organize themselves so as to offset the bargaining power of their employers.

Provision of insurance in the presence of asymmetric information unavoidably decreases productive efficiency. Information problems, in fact, plague not only private contracts but also public intervention in both its efficiency-seeking and equity-seeking dimensions. Workers have no less incentive to decrease their job-seeking effort when covered by social rather than private insurance, and protection from 'unfair' developments unavoidably decreases the labour market's speed of adjustment. Such efficiency losses are not easily affordable for developing countries, but are not a major concern for rich and more stable societies. Hence, it is not surprising that Europe's unprecedented fast and stable growth after the Second World War led, by the late 1960s and early 1970s, to an extensive array of protective labour legislation and to equally extensive co-decision power by unions in all matters regarding the conditions of employment.

Since then, Continental European countries' employment performance has been disappointing enough to spur much interest in the labour-market implications of 'protective' legislation and regulation. As suggested by Blanchard (1998), new exogenous developments played an important role in shaping observed developments. In terms of the scheme outlined above, the oil shocks and disinflation efforts may have led to the new scenario of slower and unsteady growth, where the desirable 'fairness' benefits of European labour markets' institutional configuration were outweighed by their undesirable effects on wage and employment adjustment.

The remainder of this short note offers a brief summary of the evidence and theoretical interpretation discussed by Bertola (2000) and its references, focusing in more detail on the empirical implications of *quantity* and *price* rigidities entailed by European labour-market institutions.

As to 'quantity' rigidities, *employment protection legislation* (EPL) has a similar character in all industrialized countries (see Bertola *et al.* 2000) for a recent review). Typically, it requires that termination of individual employees be motivated and/or that workers be given reasonable notice or financial compensation in lieu of notice; and it grants workers an unrenounceable right to appeal against termination, sometimes stipulating reinstatement with back pay when the appeal is successful. As regards collective dismissals, legislation often mandates administrative procedures, involving formal negotiations with workers' organizations and with local or national authorities. Theory suggests that employers should refrain from shedding labour in downturns when firing is costly, and also refrain from hiring in upturns. Hence, more stringent EPL should be associated with smoother dynamic employment patterns, but its contrasting effects on employers' propensity to hire and fire yield an a priori ambiguous impact on average employment and wages (while, of course, unambiguously reducing the efficiency of dynamic labour reallocation in comparison to a hypothetical perfect-market environment).

Empirical work on such theoretical implications can exploit the wide variation of EPL stringency across countries, sectors, and time. Only some EPL aspects, such as the number of months' notice required for individual and collective redundancies, are readily measured quantitatively. Other aspects are more difficult to measure precisely—for example, the willingness of labour courts to entertain appeals by fired workers and the interpretation placed by judges on the notion of 'just cause' for termination. When available EPL indicators are positively correlated with each other, however, it is possible to form qualitatively unambiguous cross-country rankings of EPL, and to relate such rankings to (also qualitative) indicators of labour-market performance, in the light of theoretical implications. The evidence reviewed by Bertola (2000) and its references suggest that more stringent EPL is indeed associated to more stable aggregate employment paths.

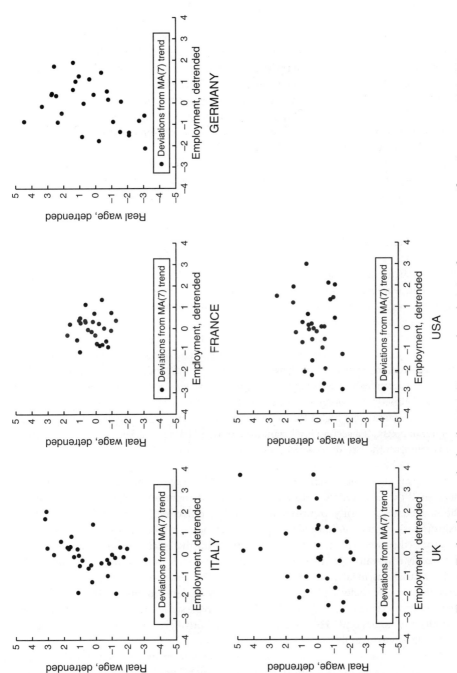

Figure 1. *Total employment and real total compensation per employee, deviations from country-specific moving averages, 1960–1996*

Notes: 1970 = 100; German data are spliced at the time of reunification for comparability.

Source: OECD Employment Outlook database; Bertola (2000: fig. 3).

The graphs in Fig. 1 show that aggregate employment fluctuations (around a simple moving average) are indeed more pronounced in countries where the qualitative EPL indicators indicate less stringency—such as the UK and, especially, the US—than in countries with a historical record of extremely stringent EPL, such as Italy. France's and Germany's relative ranking with respect to each other is somewhat less clear, but both are unambiguously ranked between Italy and the UK by existing indicators.

As to average long-run employment creation, aggregate evidence is also fairly unambiguous. The same countries that display more stringent EPL (and more stable aggregate employment paths) also display a slower trend in growth of employment, and increasing unemployment rates. Importantly, however, the diverging trend employment paths are not only associated to *speed of real wage growth*. Fig. 2 shows quite clearly that the slowdown of aggregate production since the early 1970s was accommodated in European countries by reduced employment growth and continued real-wage growth, while in the USA (and, in recent experience, in the UK as well) fast employment creation was accompanied by slow trend wage growth.

This broad empirical picture, along with the fact that wage rates are largely acyclical in all countries (as shown in Fig. 1), is readily rationalized by standard models of labour demand. As mentioned above, employment should indeed be stabilized by EPL provisions *if the wage process can be taken as given.* Cross-country evidence does indicate that aggregate wages are no more cyclical in high-EPL markets than in low-EPL markets, and the cyclical stability of aggregate employment is readily rationalized by EPL. When employment is averaged *across* aggregate cycles, theory suggests that EPL should not significantly bias it away from what would be implied by standard static labour demand models—and, to the extent that aggregate production and productivity trends are largely similar across industrialized countries, suggests that low employment creation is essentially accounted for by divergent wage trends.

To understand why high-EPL countries are also high-wage (growth) countries, it is helpful to consider a second important dimension of labour market 'rigidity'—namely, constraints on the extent to which *wages can vary across employment opportunities*. Fig. 3 shows that the same countries featuring high EPL (and stable aggregate employment) also display *highly compressed* (and relatively stable) *wage distributions*. This empirical feature, if the economic structure of industrialized countries is viewed as sufficiently homogeneous to justify comparisons, is largely reflecting institutional wage-setting constraints—such as centralized bargaining and binding minimum wages.

From a theoretical point of view, it is not surprising that relative wage variation should be heavily constrained in the same markets where EPL is most stringent. Quantitative firing restrictions, in fact, could hardly be binding if wages were completely unrestrained *over time for a given individual*: in response to the labour demand shocks that EPL is meant to protect workers from, wages could fall so as to make stable employment profitable, or to induce voluntary quits. Hence, limiting the freedom offered to employers and workers in setting wages gives force to quantity constraints.

As mentioned above, labour-market institutions such as EPL and relative-wage rigidity are meant to address important imperfections of laissez-faire market interactions. The combined policies may be rationalized by 'equal-pay-for-equal-work' principles, or

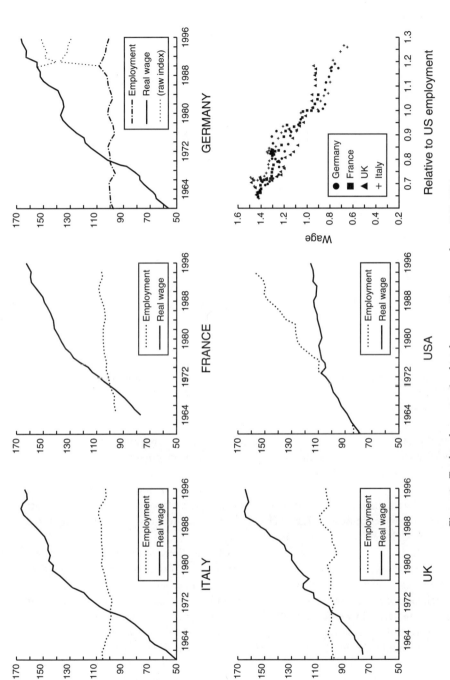

Figure 2. *Total employment and real total compensation per employee, 1960–1996*

Notes: 1970 = 100 in the country-specific panels; German raw data are plotted as a dotted line, and are spliced at the time or reunification for comparability; in the last panel, European wage and employment data are normalized by the US observation in the same year.

Source: OECD Employment Outlook database; Bertola (2000: fig. 1).

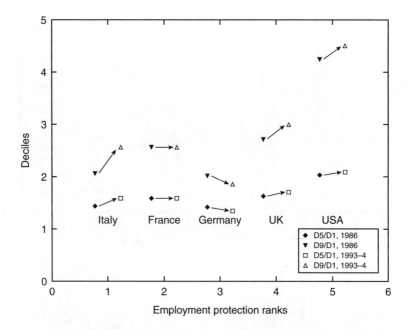

Figure 3. *Summary indicators of male earnings inequality*
Notes: The figure shows ratios of the upper limit of the 5th decile to the upper limit of the 1st decile, and of the upper limit of the 9th decile to the upper limit of the 1st decile; larger figures indicate more inequality. Country data are displayed (from left to right) in order of increasing labor market flexibility.

Source: OECD (1996: table 3).

by the belief that freely contracting parties may not be sufficiently rational or informed as correctly to evaluate the ultimate consequences of arrangements that might appear optimal at a particular moment (with, for example, detrimental effects on human-capital investments in training). The combination of wage and quantity rigidities is indeed successful if its aim is protection of workers from negative labour-market development: not only are wages compressed and stable, but also tenure lengths (as shown in Fig. 4) are clearly much longer in more rigid labour markets.

Price and quantity rigidities are, however, also associated with high real wages and unsatisfactory aggregate employment performances. To understand why, note that relative-wage constraints may also, by preventing underbidding by the unemployed, enforce monopolistic wage-setting practices by organized labour. As noted above, firing costs do not generally reduce average employment at given wages; symmetrically, EPL *per se* need not increase the bargaining power of 'insiders' relative to outsiders, since outsiders could and should in principle be able to bid down wages so as to 'buy' themselves a job. If contractual arrangements made it possible to do so, competitive pressure on equilibrium wage and employment patterns should make turnover costs next to irrelevant in wage determination in a dynamic labour demand model with

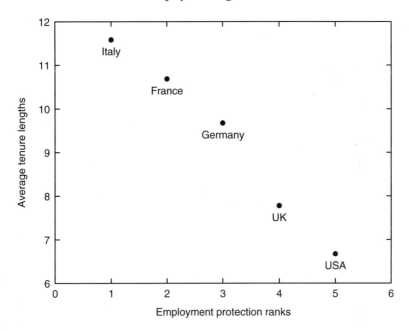

Figure 4. *Average completed tenure of existing jobs, 1995*
Notes: Country data are displayed (from left to right) in order of increasing labor market flexibility.
Source: Eurostat.

ongoing fluctuations. The combination of institutional wage compression and job security provisions is a powerful source of bargaining power, however, and their apparent association in the data with high wages and low employment is far from surprising.

This admittedly sketchy theoretical perspective offers a coherent picture of cross-comparative labour-market performances, in both their aggregate and their disaggregated aspects. Increasing dissatisfaction with the performance of rigid institutional structures should not lead one to dismiss the original motivation of collective regulatory activity in the labour market. 'Protection' from 'unfair' labour-market risk is, after all, clearly something that European workers and policy-makers are not willing to forsake easily, and political stability is further enhanced by the fact that employment rates of prime-age males (hence 'median voters') are not adversely affected by labour-market rigidity, as shown by Fig. 5, which features the same five countries considered in the other simple pieces of empirical evidence discussed here and in Bertola (2000). The negative effects of increasing and increasingly long-term unemployment (of younger, older, and female workers) on 'social cohesion' may thus have been buffered by within-family income transfers, and by old-age pension arrangements, at the same time as institutional rigidities prevented European wage inequality from increasing as much as in the unregulated American labour market.

Giuseppe Bertola

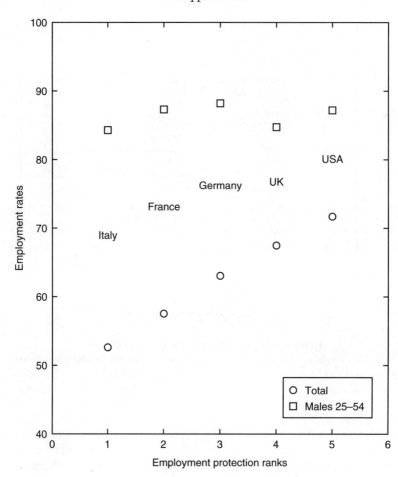

Figure 5. *Employment rates, 1990–1996 average*

Source: OECD Employment Outlook database.

However, the forces behind the latter phenomenon (whether 'skill-biased technolog-ical progress', 'globalization', or a structural shift of aggregate demand towards low-productivity service employment) clearly exert increasing stress on rigid labour-market institutions, and pose a serious challenge to European labour-market institutions—whose political stability becomes increasingly more questionable as the economies of European nation states become more closely integrated with each other and with less-developed countries. How and indeed whether this challenge might be met is a fruitful topic for discussion at the conference, and for further research.

REFERENCES

Bertola, G. (2000), 'Microeconomic Perspectives on Aggregate Labour Markets', in O. Ashenfelter and D. Card (eds.), *Handbook of Labour Economics*, iii (Amsterdam: North Holland), 2985–3028.

—— Boeri, T., and Cazes, S. (2000), 'Employment Protection in Industrialized Countries: The Case for New Indicators'. *International Labour Review*, 139/1: 57–72.

Blanchard, O. J. (1998), 'European Unemployment: Shocks and Institutions', Baffi Lecture, Banca d'Italia.

Hepple, B. A. (1986) (ed.), *The Making of Labour Law in Europe: A Comparative Study of Nine Countries up to 1945* (London: Mansell).

OECD (1996), *Employment Outlook*.

Picker, R. C. (1997), 'Simple Games in a Complex World: A Generative Approach to the Adoption of Norms', *University of Chicago Law Review*, 64: 1225–1349.

Comment on 'Cross-Sectional Wage and Employment Rigidities versus Aggregate Employment' by Guiseppe Bertola

JOSÉ LUIS MACHINEA

I would like to start by saying that the topic of debate is a very interesting one, both from the theoretical and the applied perspective. Even though I should say I am not a labor economist, I find the issue extremely relevant, timely, and, in particular, I found Professor Bertola's presentation very interesting.

Professor Bertola started his presentation reminding us that it is hardly surprising that national policy-making authorities would introduce legislation and regulation aimed at protecting workers from the health, unemployment, and old-age hazards of their trade; and it is even less surprising that workers would try and organize themselves so as to offset the bargaining power of their employers. I agree. As a policy-maker, I believe that one of our great challenges is to arrange institutions that provide assistance to those facing difficulties without damaging incentives.

Job security provisions, however, are often held responsible for the poor employment performance of European economies. It is also often mentioned among the main culprits of the high unemployment rates Europe faces. Professor Bertola's argument does not directly support this view, which is consistent with his previous work, but now he argues that job security plays a more important role in explaining poor employment performance than the one considered in some previous work. Of course, his argument is far from trivial.

Bertola (1990) clearly shows that firing costs stabilize employment in downturns but also lead employers to refrain from hiring in upturns for a constant or any other cyclical wage pattern. Since employment protection has contrasting effects on employers' propensity to hire and fire, its net effect on the long-run employment is ambiguous. He presents simulations in which the net effect is negligible.

In his presentation, Bertola shows us empirical evidence that indicates that high firing costs are associated with low employment variability. He also shows us that wages are not very cyclical and that developed countries face the same output volatility. Thus, he still argues that employment protection alone cannot explain the dismal employment performance of many European countries.

Professor Bertola also shows that the countries in which employment rates decreased are the ones where we observe high wage growth. He also points out that countries with high employment protection are those that present high wage compression—that is, cross-sectional wages are relatively more compressed. Finally, he states that the combination of institutional wage compression and job security provisions is a powerful source of insider power and concludes that their association in the data with high wages and low employment is far from surprising.

I would like to emphasize this point, which is Professor Bertola's central point today, before I make some comments. He is not saying, for the case, that high employment protection would generate high unemployment rates. His argument is that job security is binding only when it is complemented with wage restraint. Thus, it is the combination of both wage compression and job security that generates both high wages growth and high unemployment.

It seems to me that this argument has been discussed in the recent literature. Of course, as I said before, I am not a labor economist so I am only speculating. Some labor economists have speculated that employment growth in the USA has been possible only because of the job flexibility that allowed the real wages of less-skilled workers to decline in the face of persistent negative demand shocks. In Western Europe, on the other hand, institutional factors, such as union wage setting, employment protection, and generous unemployment benefits, are thought to have prevented real wage declines among less-skilled workers and held down job growth.

Why do I think these two arguments are related? Because I suppose that the way in which high wage growth is implied by cross-sectional wage compression is by avoiding unskilled workers' wages to decline (at least in relative terms, which will suffice for this matter). Institutional factors in many countries, it is supposed, serve to raise pay at the bottom end of the wage distribution and generate pay compression.

However, there is some consensus in the literature that the numbers reveal that the relative demand for skilled workers has outstripped the relative supply by far more in the UK and the USA than in any other developed country. This seems to mostly answer why wage differential widened so much more in the UK and the USA than in other countries without recourse to any special arguments about unions, minimum wages, and relative wage inflexibility (see, among others, Nickell and Layard 2000). Naturally, Professor Bertola knows all that better than me and, in his chapter in the *Handbook of Labour Economics* (Bertola 2000), he points out that the evidence also suggests that wage inequality patterns are similar when individual characteristics are controlled for. This means that in the UK and the USA there is more within-group inequality than in other European countries. Nevertheless, he also recognizes that such international comparisons are influenced by different degrees of labor-force heterogeneity.

Additionally, this literature also concludes that the demand shifts against the less skilled has not contributed substantially to the large increase in unemployment in the European countries where unemployment increased (see, among others, Card *et al.* 1996, Nickell and Bell 1996, and Manacorda and Petrongolo 1999). This is quite relevant. Remember that what we want to see is that wage compression implies greater wage growth. Demand shifted against the less-skilled labor and, if the above argument holds, we should find that the change in labor demand has contributed substantially to the increase in unemployment.

Some other factors may explain the increase in unemployment and, thus, the increase in real wages. A combination of adverse shocks with generous unemployment benefits is likely to have played an important role. Still, I should say that Professor Bertola's argument is very interesting and it may be part of the story. We certainly need more research in this area, because the measurement of the impact of employment protection is what really matters to do cost-benefit analysis.

REFERENCES

Bentolila, S., and Bertola, G. (1990), 'Firing Costs and Labor Demand: How Bad Is Eurosclerosis?', *Review of Economic Studies*, 57: 381–402.

Bertola, G. (1990), 'Job Security, Employment and Wages', *European Economic Review*, 34/4: 851–86.

—— (2000), 'Microeconomic Perspectives on Aggregate Labour Markets', in O. Ashenfelter, and D. Card (eds.), *Handbook of Labour Economics*, iii (Amsterdam: North Holland), 2985–3028.

Card, D., Kramarz, F., and Lemieux, T. (1996), 'Changes in the Relative Structure of Wages and Employment: A Comparison of the United States, Canada and France', NBER, Working Paper 5487.

Manacorda, M., and Petrongolo, B. (1999), 'Skill Mismatch and Unemployment in OECD Countries', *Economica*, 66: 181–207.

Nickell, S. and Bell, B. (1996), 'Changes in the Distribution of Wages and Unemployment in OECD Countries', *American Economic Review*, 86/2.

—— and Layard, R. (2000), 'Institutions and the Labour Market', in O. Ashenfelter, and D. Card (eds.), *Handbook of Labour Economics*, iii (Amsterdam: North Holland).

8

Institutions and the Workings of the Labour Market

STEPHEN NICKELL

I. INTRODUCTION

Across the OECD economies there is a wide variety of labour-market institutions, some of which have changed significantly over time. Consequently we have a fair bit of information as to what works and what does not work, both with regard to employment or unemployment, and with regard to productivity. My purpose here is to summarize what we think we know and indicate the lessons that might be learned by the non-OECD world. Much of the evidence is taken from Nickell (1997) and Nickell and Layard (2000), where a vastly fuller discussion may be found. So we shall not burden this note with lots of references. Turning to the specific issues we discuss, these are (1) benefit systems, (2) unions and minimum wages, (3) labour standards and employment protection, (4) labour taxes, and (5) labour supply reduction. In the next section, we consider each of these in turn and then, in the final section, we look at the lessons for developing countries.

II. LABOUR MARKET INSTITUTIONS: THE EVIDENCE

Unemployment benefit systems. The positive impact of a high benefit replacement ratio on unemployment is well documented. Another important feature of the benefit system is duration of entitlement. Long-term benefits generate long-term unemployment. The impact of a relatively generous benefit system can be offset by suitable active methods to push the unemployed back to work. These include devoting resources to make unemployed individuals both willing and able to take up employment. Such policies work particularly well when allied to a relatively short duration of benefit entitlement, a strictly operated work test, and an efficient placement system. In particular, they can reduce long-term unemployment while alleviating the distress that might be caused by simply discontinuing benefits without offering active assistance towards a job.

Unions and minimum wages. Because unions increase wage pressure, they will, *ceteris paribus*, raise unemployment. And the more workers they cover, the higher the impact.

Furthermore, the evidence also suggests that, on balance, they have a negative impact on productivity. However, several things can nullify these negative features of trade unionism. First, if unions behave in a cooperative fashion rather than an adversarial manner, none of these bad effects need apply. Secondly, such cooperative behaviour is more likely if either the economy develops corporatist institutions within which trade unionism can be absorbed and/or product market competition in the economy is so intense that unions are forced into a conciliatory stance. It is probably no coincidence that corporatist institutions generally survive best in small open economies in which a good part of the economy is subject to international competition.

Turning to minimum wages, the overall evidence suggests that low minimum wages for adult employees probably have little impact on employment while serving to ensure that employers do not pay absurdly low wages. The only serious problems seem to arise when the minimum wage makes no allowance for young workers, particularly when there are high payroll taxes that cannot be shifted onto the workers because of the minimum wage. A lower minimum for the young seems to get around this problem.

Labour standards and employment protection. When studying labour-market regulation, it is important to distinguish between rules that simply add to labour costs, such as mandatory sick pay, and rules that raise the costs of employment adjustment, such as employment protection legislation. Starting with the former, the limited evidence that exists suggests that mandates and regulations are fully compensated by downward wage adjustments and have only a small effect overall. However, having strict employment protection rules for so-called 'permanent' employees while employing the rest on short-term contracts may raise apparent employment flexibility but typically has little impact on employment. This is mainly because the permanent employees, with their buffer of temporary workers, have such strong bargaining power in wage negotiations. Finally, job security appears, if anything, to have a positive impact on productivity growth.

Labour taxes. The major impact of labour taxes operates via the total tax wedge between product and consumption wages—namely, the sum of payroll, income, and consumption tax rates. There is strong evidence that changes in the tax mix have little effect on unemployment, although relatively high personal income tax rates seem to have a negative impact on growth. The effect of the overall tax wedge is subject to some degree of uncertainty, with large variations from one study to another. In my judgement, the impact on employment is small but significant—say a 1 per cent fall in unemployment requires a 5–10 percentage point fall in the tax wedge. The effect on growth rates is even harder to discern, in part because, in the OECD, the countries that are furthest behind tend to be converging fastest and to have the lowest taxes. Tax effects are much attenuated when convergence is taken into account.

Labour supply reduction. This simply refers to the innumerable schemes that have been introduced in the OECD countries whose effect is to lower the size of the labour force in order to reduce unemployment. Since wage pressure is influenced equally by a 1 per cent rise in employment for a given labour force or a 1 per cent fall in the labour force at given employment, any scheme to reduce the labour force will, in the long run, leave unemployment unchanged, but lower both employment and output (see Layard *et al.* 1991: 504 for the evidence). Since the scheme will typically require a rise in taxes, the final outcome is even worse. Yet governments, under pressure to do something about unemployment, continue to find such schemes irresistible, despite all the evidence that they never work.

III. LABOUR MARKET INSTITUTIONS: THE LESSONS

Before listing the specific lessons following from the above, it is worth noting that it is not worth introducing rules and regulations of any kind if the resources are not available to enforce them in a proper fashion. Rules that are not enforced are a waste of time and regulations that are enforced corruptly will typically have a negative impact. From Section II, the following points stand out:

1. If an unemployment benefit system is introduced ensure (*a*) benefits are time limited, (*b*) there is a very strict work test, (*c*) the government job placement service is located in the same place as the benefit office.
2. The government should not have a monopoly on job placement.
3. Ensure that laws governing trade unions encourage responsiveness to the wishes of the entire membership—secret ballots for all officials, for strikes, and so on. Union power should be derived from the membership, not from political position.
4. Do not have extension laws whereby wages agreed in union firms are extended to non-union firms.
5. Encourage openness and product market competition.
6. Minimum wage rules should always set lower levels for young people.
7. Bear in mind that, unless they improve productivity, labour-market regulations will either lower wages or cost jobs, typically the former. Ask the question, are workers really better off with lower wages and regulations rather than with higher wages and no regulations?
8. Don't combine very strict employment protection laws for permanent employees with encouragement to hire workers on fixed-term contracts. Better to make employment protection less strict.
9. Never introduce a scheme to reduce labour supply.

REFERENCES

Layard, R., Nickell, S., and Jackman, R. (1991), *Unemployment: Macroeconomic Performance and the Labour Market* (Oxford: Oxford University Press).

Nickell, S. (1997), 'Labour Market Flexibility and Unemployment: Europe versus North America', *Journal of Economic Perspectives* (Summer), 55–74.

—— and Layard, R. (2000), 'Labour Market Institutions and Economic Performance', in O. Ashenfelter, and D. Card (eds.), *Handbook of Labor Economics*, iii (Amsterdam: North Holland).

Comment on 'Institutions and the Workings of the Labour Market' by Stephen Nickell

JUAN J. DOLADO

It is a great pleasure to be able to discuss Professor Nickell's contribution to this conference. The chosen topic is a timely and important one. Moreover, given the importance of the author's contributions to the debate on the role of labour-market institutions in determining the workings of the economy, I tend to share most of his conclusions. There are, however, two topics that are hardly covered in the paper and where I would like to place some more emphasis. They are: (1) the political feasibility of reforms in democratic societies, and (2) the reasons why piecemeal reforms might have little success in reducing unemployment.

In the sequel, I will take these points in turn.

First, the work on the 'political economy' of labour-market reforms, following Alogoskoufis *et al.* (1996) and Saint-Paul (1996), argues that reforms that could reduce unemployment substantially may be blocked by different political majorities. For example, according to the well-known 'insider–outsider' theory, that majority may be formed by employed workers. This is so since the interest of this group centres upon maximizing take-home pay, and therefore might oppose those policies that fight unemployment by lowering wage pressure.

Further, useful labour-market policies are also likely to be blocked if they happen to affect a very heterogeneous group of people, such as, for instance, employers and skilled and unemployed workers. This grouping includes both the richest and the poorest people in society. They may have common interests on the need of improving the workings of the labour market but very different views on all other policy issues, ranging from the redistribution of taxes/transfers to other social policies. Thus, the fact that people choose between competing policy packages rather than on single issues makes it difficult to implement labour-market reforms, unless they are approved in a referendum.

Next, there is the issue of uncertainty about who will gain and who will lose from reforms. Consider the following simple example of this problem. Suppose that society is formed by three groups (A, B, and C) of equal size, and that the proposed reform is one where Group A loses 6 from the reform, Group B gains 4, and Group C gains 10. Thus, the aggregate gain is 8 and efficiency requires that the reform is implemented. Now, consider the case where, owing to uncertainty about the final fortune of each worker, members of Groups A and B expect to end up in the other group with a 50 per cent probability. Then, the expected gain from the reform for workers in both groups is −1 (= 0.5((4–6)) and the reform will be blocked by a two-thirds majority. Hence, uncertainty about who benefits and who loses will lead to a bias in favour of the status quo. This uncertainty problem also underlies the explanation of the difficulties that are faced in practice when trying to establish a set of compensating interpersonal transfers to make everybody better off, enabling the winners to 'buy-out' the losers. Take, for illustrative purposes, the existence of a minimum wage, disregarding any monopsony problems. If it is set above the competitive level, it will raise the unskilled wage and reduce the demand for unskilled labour. If skilled and unskilled labour are cooperant factors on production, then the demand for skilled labour will fall as well. Thus, the minimum wage redistributes income from skilled to unskilled labour, at the cost of creating unemployment. So, elimination of the minimum wage would be favoured by skilled and unemployed and only opposed by the unskilled employed. However, in the absence of an *ex ante* system of taxes and transfers, it turns out to be impossible to improve everybody's welfare by eliminating the minimum wage.

Secondly, I would like to stress the work on 'policy complementaries', following the work of Coe and Snower (1997), which argues that, since rigidities reinforce each other, policies in isolation tend to be much less effective than where taken in conjunction with other policy measures enhancing the right workings of labour markets. As an illustration of such a phenomenon, take the case of reform on fixed-term contracts that took place in Spain, one of the countries with the most rigid labour market in OECD at the time, in 1984 (see Bentolila and Dolado 1994). Given the impossibility of lowering severance payments, which were high for all workers, the government introduced a two-tier reform that entitled employers to hire new workers under temporary contracts, with low firing costs, whereas the existing workers with permanent jobs and high job protection were entitled to keep their rights. Since 'insiders' dominated the wage bargaining under the existing industrial relations, they pushed for higher wage pressure under the expectation that those workers who would lose their jobs would be those with temporary contracts. This turned out to be the case and unemployment rose again. Another illustrative example could be the introduction of part-time jobs in countries where trading hours are strongly regulated in shops or the abolition of a minimum wage in countries where there may be poverty traps. In all those cases, identification of the right combination of policies turns out to be a necessary requirement for success.

REFERENCES

Alogoskoufis, G., Bean, C., Bertola, G., Cohen, D., Dolado, J., and Saint-Paul, G. (1996), *Unemployment: Choices for Europe* (Monitoring European Integration 5; London: CEPR).

Bentolila S., and Dolado, J. (1994), 'Labour Flexibility and Wages Lessons from Spain', *Economic Policy*, 18: 53–100.

Coe, D., and Snower, D. (1997), 'Policy Complementaries: The Case for Fundamental Reform',
    IMF Staff Papers, 44: 1–35.
Saint-Paul, G. (1996), 'Exploring the Political Economy of Labour Market Institutions', *Economic
    Policy*, 23: 265–300.

Power and Corruption

9

Separation of Powers and Development

JEAN-JACQUES LAFFONT

I. INTRODUCTION

It is well recognized now that the design of proper institutions is the key to development. Among the characteristics of governmental institutions, separation of powers stands as a shining cornerstone of democracy. Article 16 of the French Declaration of the Rights of Man of 1789 goes as far as saying: 'A society in which the guarantee of rights is not assured, nor the separation of powers provided for, has no constitution.' Indeed, since Montesquieu (1748), separation of powers is explicitly recognized as vital: 'Tout serait perdu si le même homme, ou le même corps des principaux et des nobles, ou du peuple, exerçaient les trois pouvoirs: celui de faire des lois, celui d'exécuter des résolutions publiques, et celui de juger les crimes ou les différends des particuliers' (p. 589).

Hamilton and Madison in the *Federalist Papers* (Madison *et al.* 1788) referred to Montesquieu as 'the oracle who is always consulted and cited on this subject'. They put these principles into practice for the American Constitution within a broader view of checks and balances.

Separation of powers is valuable, but not easy to implement because it is costly, because it affects the transaction costs of collusion, and because the 'separated' powers may collude. The cost-benefit analysis of separation of powers depends on the characteristics of the country. In this paper, we are asking how the net value of separation of powers is affected by the level of development. More specifically, and more modestly, we will consider the regulation of an industry and we will ask how the value of duplicating regulation changes as various parameters characterizing the level of development vary.

It is only recently that economists have started modeling the value of separation of powers.

A first reason for duplicating regulation agencies is yardstick competition. Using the correlation of the signals obtained by these agencies enables the principal to extract in a costless way their information rent. This idea was modeled by Shleifer (1985) in the case of perfect correlation and Crémer and McLean (1988) in the case of an arbitrary degree of non-zero correlation.

A second reason for separation of powers is to act as a device against regulatory capture. This general idea has been known for a while by political scientists (Wilson 1980; Moe 1986; Mueller 1997). The public-choice school has emphasized the fact that institutional rules may be designed to discourage rent-seeking behavior. Rose-Ackerman (1978) and Congleton (1984) have argued that increasing the number of individuals who must be bribed before getting a permit may be optimal. Laffont and Martimort (1999) have provided a modeling of this idea that must be distinguished from yardstick competition, which is a pure informational competition.

A third reason reported in Moe (1986) is that separation of powers may be beneficial when intertemporal commitment is limited. It may act as an indirect way to commit. Agency models have been developed recently to capture this idea (Olsen and Torsvick 1993; Tirole 1994; Martimort 1995).

In this note, we model separation of powers as an imperfect tool for yardstick competition under the threat of regulatory capture.

II. THE MODEL

We consider a Baron-Myerson (1982) regulation model in which the marginal cost of the regulated firm can take two values, a low level ($\underline{\theta}$) corresponding to a good type firm and a high level ($\overline{\theta}$) to a bad type firm. The social welfare maximizer (SWM) who is uninformed about this marginal cost wishes to maximize expected social welfare. The good produced by the regulated monopoly is a public good and there is a cost of public fund λ. Because the marginal cost is private information of the firm, the SWM must give up an information rent to the firm when it is a good type. To mitigate this cost, the SWM delegates the task of supervising the firm to regulators. A regulator observes a signal correlated with the marginal cost. This enables the SWF to decrease the information rent. More precisely, a regulator discovers in a verifiable way the true value of the marginal cost with some probability, when it is the low value.

Two supervision technologies are available, corresponding to two signals that are themselves correlated. One can either give the two technologies to a single regulator or use two regulators, each one associated with one technology.

Regulators are risk neutral and face a limited liability constraint, which implies that their payments must be non-negative.

When a regulator transmits his signal to the SWM, the firm loses its information rent. The regulator has the discretion of hiding the signal he has observed and therefore there is a risk of capture. Following Laffont and Tirole (1993), we know that collusion-proof regulation requires a payment to the regulator when he reports the signal that the firm has a low cost, which is greater than the stake of collusion (which is here proportional to the size of the asymmetric information (the difference of marginal costs $\Delta\theta$) discounted by the inverse of the transaction cost of collusion κ).

III. THE ANALYSIS

First, we characterize, with one regulator, the optimal collusion-proof regulation.

Four parameters can be used to determine the level of development. One can argue that a less developed country will have a higher cost of public funds (λ), lower transaction costs of collusion (higher κ), greater asymmetric information, and less efficient technologies ($\Delta\theta$ higher with a higher $\overline{\theta}$) and a less efficient supervision technology. We obtain that all these parameters have the same effect on the power of incentives in the optimal collusion-proof mechanism.

Proposition 1. *Optimal collusion-proof regulation should be less high-powered in less developed countries.*

Similarly, if we characterize optimal collusion-proof regulation with two regulators, we have:

Proposition 2. *Separation of powers saves on incentive payments for regulators and produces a higher-powered optimal regulation.*

We can then study how the gain from separation varies with the parameters characterizing development.

Proposition 3. *The gain from separation of powers increases with κ, $\bar{\theta}$, λ.*

So we conclude that separation of powers is more valuable in developing countries (note, however, that the gain from separation increases with the quality of supervision).

But three factors limit the value of separation of powers. First, there is the possibility that the regulators collude and coordinate their collusive behavior, which is greater in less developed countries. There is the mere cost of an additional regulator, which is higher in a developing country with a higher cost of public funds, and, if we believe that the transaction costs of collusion decrease when the regulator is more specialized, this weakening effect is higher for countries with a low transaction cost of collusion. We obtain:

Proposition 4. *The implementation of separation of powers is more costly in developing countries.*

This last result is important to moderate the enthusiasm of recent development economics, which (rightly) sees institution building as the key to development. Even though improvements in institutions are even more valuable in developing countries than developed ones, it is unfortunately more difficult to implement them in such countries.

IV. CONCLUSION

We have shown that the institution of separation of powers that can be useful to mitigate the costs created by the opportunism of regulators is even more valuable in developing countries. This is because these countries suffer from high costs of public funds (due to inefficient tax systems), from low transaction costs of collusion (due to poor auditing and monitoring), and from less efficient technologies. However, the implementation of this institution is more difficult and more costly for the same reasons, leaving us with an ambiguous overall net result if the various weaknesses of these countries are not addressed simultaneously.

We believe that this type of result is quite general,[1] and more research is needed to go beyond the indeterminacy stressed in this paper.

---

[1] Laffont (2000) argues similarly that competition policy is also more useful in developing countries but more difficult to implement.

REFERENCES

Baron, D., and Myerson, R. (1982), 'Regulating a Monopoly with Unknown Cost', *Econometrica*, 50: 911–30.

Congleton, R. (1984), 'Committees and Rent-Seeking Effort', *Journal of Public Economics*, 25: 197–209.

Crémer, J., and McLean, R. (1988), 'Full Extraction of the Surplus in Bayesian and Dominant Strategy Auctions', *Econometrica*, 56: 1247–58.

Laffont, J. J. (2000), 'Competition, Information and Development', in *World Bank Annual, ABCDE Conference* (Washington).

—— and Meleu, M. (1997), 'Reciprocal Supervision, Collusion and Organization Design', *The Scandinavian Journal of Economics*, 99: 519–40.

—— and Martimort, D. (1999), 'Separation of Powers against Collusive Behavior', *Rand Journal of Economics*, 30: 232–62.

—— and Tirole, J. J. (1993), A Theory of Incentives for Procurement and Regulation (Cambridge, Mass.: MIT Press).

Madison, J., Hamilton, A., and Jay, J. (1788), *The Federalist Papers* (Penguin Classics Edition; Harmondsworth Penguin Books, 1987).

Martimort, D. (1995), 'Multiprincipals Regulatory Charter as a Safeguard against Opportunism', mimeo, Institut National de la Recherche Agronomique, Toulouse).

Moe, T. (1986), 'Interests, Institutions, and Positive Theory: The Policies of the NLRB', *Studies of American Political Department*.

Montesquieu, Charles de Secondat, Baron de (1748), 'De l'esprit des lois', in *Ceuvres Complètes* (Paris: Éditions du Seml, 1964).

Mueller, D. (1997), *Constitutional Democracy* (Oxford: Oxford University Press).

Olsen T., and Torsvick, G. (1993), 'The Ratchet Effect in Common Agency: Implication for Regulation and Privatization', *Journal of Law, Economic and Organization*, 9: 136–58.

Rose-Ackerman, S. (1978), *Corruption: A Study in Political Economy* (New York: Academic Press).

Shleifer, A. (1985), 'A Theory of Yardstick Competition', *Rand Journal of Economics*, 16: 319–327.

Tirole J. (1994), 'The Internal Organization of the Government', *Oxford Economic Papers*, 46: 1–29.

Wilson, J. (1980), 'The Politics of Regulation', in J. Wilson (ed.), *The Politics of Regulation*.

Comment on 'Separation of Powers and Development' by Jean-Jacques Laffont

PAUL SEABRIGHT

Whether state authority should be unitary or multiple has been explicitly debated with vigour since the eighteenth century, but on some interpretations at least has a pedigree stretching back to the ancient Greeks. It would be mischievous to suggest that the question whether the optimum degree of separation is related to the level of a country's development has any relation to ancient debates over the suitability of Greek and Roman institutions for barbarian races. But one can at least say that the sensitivity of institutional performance to the underlying economic and social context has long been recognized. In the modern microeconomic literature on institutional separation there are at least four distinct strands of argument bearing on these questions. I want to suggest that Laffont's paper is, in one sense, more specialized than it claims to be, since it represents only one of these four strands of argument. But, in another sense, it is also too modest in its presentation, for it makes a more general and powerful claim than is apparent from its rather particular interpretation in terms of a regulated industry.

From the literature on the microeconomics of incentives under asymmetric information one can discern four main rationales for the separation of powers:

- diminishing the risk of error in the application of public policy;
- contesting monopolies of information;
- restraining regulatory hold-up problems;
- reducing confusions of function and conflicts of interest.

Arguments of the first kind (see Sah and Stiglitz 1986) are compatible with the presence of a perfectly benevolent state, but the others all to some degree appeal to the idea that the state's functionaries need to be given incentives to behave in the interests of its citizens. For the technically minded, the second category of argument appeals to pure adverse selection, the third to failures of commitment, while the fourth involves both.

The Laffont paper is an example of the second kind of argument. A single regulator benefits from having a monopoly of information about the regulated firm. The presence of a second regulator contests this monopoly. Note that this is different from saying that the second regulator provides more information (though this may be true as well). The additional information provided by the second regulator is smaller if the signals observed by the two are correlated. When they are perfectly correlated, the second regulator brings no new information at all, but instead he acts to prevent the first from exploiting what would otherwise be a monopoly. Indeed, the second regulator's ability to do so is enhanced by correlation in the signals, in exactly the same way that a second firm's ability to constrain the market power of a first is enhanced the greater is the substitutability between the two firms' products.

How is this argument affected by the special circumstances of poor countries? As a general rule, the benefit to society of having more competitors in a particular market is decreasing in the number of competitors that already exist (if this were not so, anti-trust policy would be no harder on monopolies than on any other type of market structure). In poor countries, information is more often monopolized (because of high communication costs), and therefore competition in access to information is more valuable.

However, we also know from simple microeconomics that the incentives for any given number of participants in a market to collude are also decreasing in the number of competitors in the market as a whole. For two of us to collude is much more attractive to us if there is no independent third party to challenge our cartel. So in poor countries the incentives for collusion are likewise high. To the extent that separation of powers contests informational monopolies, both its benefits and its attendant collusive risks are likely to be particularly high in poor countries. The Laffont argument is powerful and quite general, and does not depend at all on the particular circumstances of the model in which it is embedded.

Nevertheless, separation of powers is not just about contesting informational monopolies. Let me sketch briefly some issues that arise under the third and fourth kinds of argument. Hold-up problems arise because the state's officers may underperform certain 'essential' functions (such as issuing licences) in order to receive rents. If achieved in the right way (as in the institution of judicial review), the separation of powers can challenge the 'essentiality' of functions performed by any one bureaucrat. But, in the wrong circumstances, the separation of powers may also *increase* the potential for hold-up (for instance, when multiple approval is required for the issuing of a licence, and every bureaucrat has a veto).

What about the fourth set of issues, the reduction of confusions of function and conflicts of interest? Here are some questions that help to determine the extent to which the separation of powers may help (a fuller treatment can be found in Seabright 1999):

1. Can a regulatory task be separated into natural components? Some examples:

- In telecoms regulation, two reasonable but distinct subgoals may be to:
  - (*a*) increase the number of installed lines;
  - (*b*) improve service quality.
- In tax collection, the state may need to:
  - (*c*) improve fiscal receipts;
  - (*d*) minimize the economic distortions caused by the tax system.
- In the criminal justice system, it is important to:
  - (*e*) increase arrest and/or conviction rates;
  - (*f*) reduce the rate of wrongful arrests and convictions.

2. Are the components *offsetting* or *reinforcing*? That is, does the performance of one make it harder to perform the other? If so, the tasks should be entrusted to different individuals (or agencies), since otherwise one component may be ignored in favour of the other. In the examples given, the components are clearly offsetting for both tax collection and criminal justice: reducing economic distortions requires not simply loading all of the burden onto those from whom taxes can be most easily extorted, while arrest and conviction rates would be easy to raise if considerations of justice were of no consequence. For telecommunications, the answer is more subtle. If the constraint on the number of installed lines comes from the demand side, then improving service quality will help to encourage additional demand. If (as in many poor countries) the constraint comes from the supply side, improvements to service quality may well slow down the rate at which new lines can be installed.

3. Do the components require: *skill*—which is easier to monitor—or *judgement*—which is harder to monitor?

   As Holmstrom and Milgrom (1991) have shown, requiring the same agent to perform two tasks may involve a diversion of effort away from the task which is relatively easy to monitor and towards the task that is harder to monitor.

4. Finally, are the talents and resources required for the different tasks significantly correlated? If so the duplication of regulatory tasks by different individuals or agencies may involve unnecessarily high costs.

These observations give only a hint of some of the issues that arise in thinking about the separation of powers in a different context from the contesting of informational monopolies studied by Laffont. They also provide a rich set of questions for further investigation.

REFERENCES

Holmstrom, B., and Milgrom, P. (1991), 'Multi-Task Principal-Agent Analyses: Incentive Contracts, Asset Ownership and Job Design', *Journal of Law, Economics and Organization*, 7: 24–52.

Sah, R., and, Stiglitz, J. E. (1986), 'The Architecture of Economic Systems: Hierarchies and Polyarchies', *American Economic Review*, 76: 716–27.

Seabright, P. (1999), 'Skill versus Judgment and the Architecture of Organizations', *European Economic Review*, 44/4.6: 856–68.

10

Bureaucratic Corruption and Political Accountability

SUSAN ROSE-ACKERMAN

Bureaucracies need to be accountable to the public. Their technical decisions and policy judgments should be open to public scrutiny. People and groups need to know what government is doing and have avenues for making complaints and holding officials responsible for their actions. An accountable bureaucracy is not only more democratically legitimate; it is also less prone to corruption and insider influence. In this note I discuss the legal and political constraints on the implementation of statutes, consider the role of judicial review, and highlight ways to achieve openness and public participation.

I. ACCOUNTABLE IMPLEMENTATION

Legislators often voluntarily draft statutes that limit their own control over implementation. The statutes leave the development of precise standards to government agencies, but may include detailed procedural requirements (Moe 1990; Rose-Ackernman 1992: 33–96). The traditional justifications for delegation combine a belief in the expertise of executive agencies with the claim that legislators should not be making individual personnel and procurement choices or deciding enforcement priorities. Thus regulation-writing is delegated because the legislature is not competent to carry out this essentially legislative task, and purely executive or adjudicatory functions are not appropriate for the legislature under separation of powers principles.

Some American scholars, however, argue that delegation is instead a response to uncertainty about who will control the legislature in the future. Worried that opponents will gain control, interest groups in the USA push for laws that specify detailed procedural and substantive standards. According to this view, parliamentary systems are superior because they are not subject to the same pressures. Laws, once passed, are easy to repeal when another regime comes to power. Thus public agencies will be less encumbered by externally imposed rules and the bureaucratic system will be more simple, coherent, and rational (Moe 1990; Moe and Caldwell 1994).

These claims in favor of parliamentary systems seem overblown. Whatever the explanations for constrained delegation in the USA, the results are not uniformly bad. Since

This paper is derived from Rose-Ackerman (1999: ch. 9).

rules issued by agencies under enabling statutes have the force of law, the process by which they are produced requires accountability. Otherwise the processes may be honestly or corruptly influenced for the benefit of powerful groups. Whether one focuses on executive branch accountability to the public or on the avoidance of corrupt payoffs, the procedural constraints of the American Administrative Procedures Act seem valuable. Under the American act, agencies must give notice of their intent to issue a regulation, accept testimony from a broad range of individuals and groups, and issue a statement of reasons along with the final rule. The rule can be challenged in court if proper procedures are not followed or if the end result is inconsistent with the underlying statute. This process has been criticized as time-consuming and cumbersome, but inconvenience is the price of limitations on the arbitrary power of an executive (Rose-Ackerman 1995a).

By way of contrast, Germany's parliamentary system imposes fewer controls on executive branch rule-making. German rule-making procedures are much less transparent than American ones and have been criticized for being too open to industry influence. Payoffs do not seem to be a problem, but excess influence may be (Rose-Ackerman 1995a). The UK seems to have a less procedurally constrained administrative process than does Germany. This could imply a more rational administrative process, but there seems no good, logical reason why that should be the result. If interest groups want influence, they can get it in a much more opaque and potentially corrupt manner under the procedurally unconstrained UK system. An administrative law system that is beholden to the current legislative majority and lacks procedural safeguards seems prone to the ongoing influence of narrow groups. Thus, from the point of view of constraining rent-seeking by politicians and narrow groups, the weak administrative law constraints produced by parliamentary governments create serious accountability problems.

Other problems can arise in political systems with weak legislative branches. Critics of Latin American governments argue that most have overly powerful executives (Mainwaring and Shugart 1997). As a consequence, incentives for rent-seeking and corruption are high within the executive branch. The president has extensive decree power, may control a secret financial account that can be used to reward supporters, and is less subject to popular control while in office. Furthermore, the judiciary is generally less independent in practice and, until recently, has seldom effectively constrained the executive (Del Granado 1995: 19–20; Manzetti and Blake 1996). Some Asian countries exhibit a similar pattern. For example, in Thailand, the executive in the past controlled and limited legislative activity so that it could rule by degree (Pasuk and Sungsidh 1994). Executive rule has been accompanied by close business-government relations (Hewison 1993; Anek 1994: 208–11). China is an extreme case, where some courts have held that only the National People's Congress, not the courts, can decide on the legality of administrative rules. Chinese judges are not independent—their budgets and the terms of their appointments are controlled by governments at all levels (Bing 1994: 6–7, 17–18).

Administrative law reform ought to be a part of governance reform strategies. The background conditions that determine rule-making in the executive branch should be examined to assure adequate participation and transparency. The public needs avenues for appeal to the judiciary if the government has not followed its own procedures or has acted lawlessly. The goal is to make corrupt deals harder to hide by forcing review of the process and the substantive outcome. A review process aimed at achieving good substantive policy and democratic accountability can indirectly fight corruption. Even a country with a weak legislature or a unitary parliamentary system could limit the opportunities for corruption and other types of influence by adopting more transparent administrative processes.

II. THE JUDICIARY

Bureaucratic accountability is facilitated by judicial review of administrative action. However, countries with a weak and corrupt judiciary will obviously be reluctant to give judges additional powers. A corrupt judiciary is costly for democracy, because it cannot credibly play the role of watchdog of constitutional values or monitor the honesty of the other branches of government (Fuke 1989: 226; Bing 1994: 5–8). Many countries have poorly functioning courts and legal systems.[1] Corruption is a response to underlying problems in the administration of justice, but the existence of widespread payoffs makes reform difficult.

If major investment deals involve the state as purchaser, privatizer, or provider of a concession, an independent court system is a necessary guarantor of impartiality to outside investors. If the prestige and competence of the judiciary can be established, their independence from the political branches should be assured. Obviously, independence is not valuable if judges are not viewed with respect, but even respected and independent judges can produce rulings that undercut reform. For example, in Brazil, the Supreme Court delayed major privatizations as it reviewed challenges to the sale (*Financial Times*, 1998*a*, *b*). In the Philippines, the Supreme Court overturned a contract to privatize a hotel and declared unconstitutional a law deregulating the oil industry (*Financial Times*, 1997*d*, *e*). Even in Argentina, where compliant judges made no objection to President Menem's first round of economic reforms, a 1997 decision struck down a presidential decree offering a concession on the country's airports (*Financial Times*, 1997*b*). Although these rulings are inconvenient for reformers, they are the cost of an independent judiciary that can also take on cases of malfeasance by high-level officials.

In some situations the problem is not the independence of the judiciary *per se*, but the unreformed character of the underlying laws and constitutional principles it must interpret. If an independent judiciary enforces laws that are biased in favor of the regulated industry, reform will be difficult without a change in underlying legal standards. For example, in the Philippines, oversight of the banking industry in the 1980s was hampered by lawsuits brought by banks against both regulatory agencies and the public officials themselves. As one banker admitted, lawsuits were a way 'of preventing officials from implementing the regulations. You intimidate the bureaucracy' (quoted by Hutchcroft 1998: 202).

---

[1] A survey of businesses in Latin America indicated that the judicial system was among the top ten most significant constraints to private-sector development (Dakolias 1996: 3). On the problems facing judicial reformers in Venezuela, see Lawyers' Committee for Human Rights and the Venezuelan Program for Human Rights Education and Action (1996: 41–80).

Although an honest government administration will be difficult to establish if the judiciary is venal, nevertheless an *honest* judiciary sometimes can help maintain a corrupt system. Suppose that private individuals and firms engage in secret corrupt deals with public officials. Private actors are willing to make payoffs because they are confident that the procurement contracts, concessions, and privatization deals they obtain will be upheld by the honest, impartial judicial system. Suppose, as in the USA, that the public prosecutor is part of the executive branch of government, not a part of the judiciary. If the government, outside of the judiciary, is organized to facilitate corruption, the private firms are confident that they will not be prosecuted. Even if a scandal does develop, only public officials may suffer politically. This may deter some public officials, but it does not constrain private individuals.

The best example of a corruption-friendly polity comes from the early years of the American Republic. A corrupt land sale approved by the legislature of Georgia in the early 1800s was upheld by the US Supreme Court in the case of *Fletcher* v. *Peck*. The Court was unmoved by the fact that all but one of the legislators had been bribed. When the scandal was revealed, the entire legislature lost office in the next election, but the Court held that the contract was a legal obligation of the state of Georgia (Magrath 1966). What better way to encourage payoffs than a legal system that upholds public contracts no matter what the underlying corrupt deals?

The case of *Fletcher* v. *Peck* is a warning that establishing an honest independent judiciary is not sufficient if corruption is commonplace. Deeper reforms in the political system are necessary. Judicial independence, however, does seem a valuable, if elusive, concept. In the USA life tenure and limits on congressional ability to reduce salaries help maintain the independence of the federal judiciary, but many countries have independent judiciaries without these constraints. In the USA the appointments' process is politicized with presidential appointment followed by Senate confirmation. At the state and local level, some judges are elected. In some countries, appointments to the Constitutional Court are more firmly controlled by the legal profession and, in others, special committees make the choices. In most countries with a civil-law tradition, the judges in the lower courts are essentially career bureaucrats who choose a judicial career on leaving law school. The judiciary is, however, generally recruited and organized separately from the rest of the civil service to maintain its independence. Thus, there does not appear to be a single blueprint available for developing countries. Nevertheless —however it is accomplished—skeptical politicians would do well to support an independent judiciary as a necessary step in creating a credible state commitment to the rule of law.

III. OPENNESS AND ACCOUNTABILITY

The public can be an important check on the arbitrary exercise of power by government. This check can only operate, however, if the government provides information on its actions. Citizens must then have a convenient means of lodging complaints and must be protected against possible reprisals. Finally, government officials must find it in their interest to respond to complaints. There are two basic routes for public pressure—

collective complaints by groups of citizens concerning general failures of government, and objections raised by particular individuals against their own treatment at the hands of public authorities. Both collective and individual routes can help spur the reform of governmental structures.

Information and auditing

A precondition for either type of complaint is information. Government must tell citizens what it is doing by publishing consolidated budgets, revenue collections, statutes and rules, and the proceedings of legislative bodies. Such practices are standard in developed countries, but many developing countries are seriously deficient.[2] Former colonies often use systems originally imposed by the colonizer that may or may not fit local conditions. Financial data should be audited and published by independent authorities such as the General Accounting Office (GAO) in the USA or the Audit Commission in the UK. The GAO monitors the federal executive branch but reports directly to Congress. It resolves contracting disputes, settles the accounts of the US government, resolves claims of or against the USA, gathers information for Congress, and makes recommendations to it (Tiefer 1983; Abikoff 1987). The UK Audit Commission audits both local governments and the National Health Service and reports to the national government (UK Audit Commission 1993, 1994). Both institutions are independent of the government agencies they audit—a necessary condition for credibility.

The legislature can play an important role in reviewing the spending of the executive. In presidential systems, congressional committees, aided as in the USA by the GAO, can provide continuing oversight. In parliamentary systems on the Westminster model, Public Accounts Committees (PACs), often headed by a leading opposition Member of Parliament, perform a similar function (Chester 1981: 218–19, 370). In the UK, for example, the PAC issued a report in 1994 arguing that serious failures in administrative and financial systems existed that had led to money being spent wastefully or improperly (Doig 1996: 174). In contrast, the PAC in Kenya, like the parliament itself, has been politically divided and unable to operate as a strong counterweight to the executive (Kibwana *et al.* 1996: 76, 92–93, 157–8).

In both the USA and in Westminster democracies, the involvement of opposition politicians in oversight means that the review will have a political cast. The input may be in the form of accounting documents, but the debate will be influenced by political factors. This is as it should be in a well-functioning democracy, but it is hardly an unbiased way of uncovering malfeasance. If violations of the criminal law are uncovered, there must also be an unbiased prosecutorial and judicial system available to pursue the allegations.

In many countries outside review is hampered because unaudited, secret funds are available to the chief executive and to top ministers. These funds are an invitation to corruption throughout the world.[3] For example, in Brazil, when President Collor's impeachment was before the Congress, observers worried that his allies were seeking to

---

[2] An overview of public expenditure management systems is in Premchand (1993).
[3] In Venezuela, President Carlos Andrés Pérez resigned amid charges that he had misused $17 million in funds from such a secret account (Little and Herrera 1996: 268).

use secret government funds to bribe the members to obtain a favorable verdict (Geddes and Ribeiro Neto 1992).

Sometimes governments collect a good deal of information on their own operations but do not routinely make it public. In such cases, statutes that give citizens a right to gain access to this information can be an important precondition for effective public oversight. The Freedom of Information Act in the USA serves this function, and the EU has a directive requiring member states to pass such laws with respect to environmental information.[4] These laws permit citizens to obtain government information without demonstrating a need to know. They may request the information as members of the public without showing that their own personal situation will be affected. Exceptions protect privacy, internal memorandums, and the integrity of ongoing prosecutions. But a Freedom of Information Act has little value if government does not gather much information. Many countries must first put information systems in order, provide for the publication of the most important documents, and assure public access to other unpublished material.

Publicizing problems and making complaints

Even a government that keeps good records and makes them available to the public may operate with impunity if no one bothers to analyze the available information—or if analysts are afraid to raise their voices. If the aim is to pressure government to act in the public interest, the role of both the media and organized groups is important. In all cases there is the problem of fear. If government officials or their unofficial allies intimidate and harass those who speak out, formal structures of accountability will be meaningless.

The media. The media can facilitate public discussion if they are privately owned and free to criticize the government without fear of reprisal. Nominal press freedom will be insufficient if most of the media are associated with political parties. For example, in Italy, corruption only became big news as the Italian press became increasingly independent from the political system (Gigilioli 1996: 386). Government can also keep the press in line through advertising, printing contracts, and payments to journalists. Mexican newspapers, for example, have been controlled through these methods. Another subtle form of control is to overlook underpayment of taxes by editors and media companies, retaining the possibility of prosecution as a threat.[5]

In many countries, restrictive libel laws give special protections to public officials (Tucker 1994; Pope 1996: 129–141; Vick and Macpherson 1997: 647). This is just the reverse of what is needed. Politicians and other public figures should be harder to libel than private citizens, not easier. They should not be immune from facing charges of

---

[4] The US Law is 5 USC §552. The EU Directive is 90/313/EEC, 1990 OJ (L 158) 56–8. See also Rose-Ackerman (1995a: 113–15).

[5] *The Times* (1991) discusses the resignation of a newspaper editor after pressure was put on his paper through the cancellation of government advertising and printing contracts. *Financial Times* (1993) discusses these practices, but claims that some newspapers have retained their independence.

corruption, and allegations of libel should be handled as civil not criminal matters. In this, at least, the USA provides an outstanding example with a law that makes it more difficult to libel public figures than private individuals and that treats libel as a civil offense. Those in the public eye have assumed the risk of public scrutiny and have access to the media to rebut accusations. In a similar vein, participants in political debate in Germany relinquish some of the protections of defamation law, and the Netherlands has a public figure defense. Threats of lawsuits operate as a serious deterrent elsewhere. The UK has no public figure defense. Some claim that its libel law deters critical reporting of issues affecting the public interest. An especially clear example of the chilling effect of a strong libel law is Singapore, where top politicians have been active in suing both the media and political opponents (*Far Eastern Economic Review* 1997; *Financial Times* 1997a, c). In Latin America, libel is frequently prosecuted as a criminal instead of a civil action (*New York Times*, 23 Nov.).

Citizen complaints. Even in a country with permissive libel laws, a free media with good access to government information is not likely to be a sufficient check. The media may focus on lurid scandals and may have no real interest in reforms that would reduce the flow of corruption stories. Individuals and groups must push for change. Individuals face a familiar free-rider problem. Information may be available, but no one may have an incentive to look at it. The scandals uncovered by investigative journalists may provoke outrage, but no action.

Laws that make it easy to establish private associations and non-profit corporations will help. This will facilitate the creation of watchdog groups like Transparency International, a Berlin-based non-profit organization focused on corruption, with national chapters in more than forty countries (*Transparency International* 1998). Some governments, worried that non-governmental organizations (NGOs) will be used for monitoring purposes, however, limit such groups or make it very costly for them to organize. Formal legal constraints may be high, and members may be subject to surveillance and harassment. Another problem is cooptation. Some non-profit organizations administer development programs for the poor. Their financing may be provided by the state or by aid funds administered by the state. Thus, their very existence depends upon cooperation with public authorities. As a consequence, they may be reluctant to criticize officials openly (Bratton 1989: 578–9). To avoid such tensions, an NGO that takes on an anti-corruption mandate should avoid participation in service delivery.

Non-profit organizations can also usefully carry out and publish public opinion surveys that reveal public attitudes toward government services. Pioneering work of this sort has been carried out by the Public Affairs Centre in Bangalore, India (Paul 1995; Mohn 1997). One Report Card Study focused on the delivery of urban services to slum dwellers in five cities. Although the incidence of reported bribery varied across the cities, it was common overall. Across service areas, the higher the prevalence of corruption, the lower the capacity or willingness of public-service agencies to solve clients' problems. The World Bank has also sponsored several surveys that provide useful models. Such surveys are a way of isolating the impact of corruption on the poor, who may otherwise have few ways of registering complaints.

In countries with an honest and independent judicial system, another possibility arises for the indirect control of corruption. Private individuals and groups can be given the right to bring suits to force compliance with tax and regulatory laws. In the USA, the federal bribery statute does not incorporate a private right of action (*Ray* v. *Proxmire*, 581 F.2d 998 (1978), but most US environmental statutes include explicit provisions for citizen suits that permit private plaintiffs to sue dischargers to require compliance with the law. If the suit is successful, the plaintiffs obtain discharger compliance with the rule; they do not obtain damages (Rose-Ackerman 1995b: 319). Under the most familiar version, private individuals and public interest groups sue those who violate Environmental Protection Agency rules or orders. The US statutes frequently facilitate such suits by requiring regulated firms to supply data on their own pollution discharges and by paying the legal fees of successful or 'substantially prevailing' plaintiffs.

In India, this idea extends beyond the environmental area. Citizens affected by illegal or oppressive government actions can bring Public Interest Actions to vindicate the collective rights of the public. Plaintiffs need not show a direct specific injury (Agarwala 1996: 174–84). The Indian Supreme Court has endorsed an expansive right of standing for ordinary citizens, arguing that: 'public spirited citizens having faith in rule of law are rendering great social and legal service by espousing causes of public nature. They cannot be ignored or overlooked on technical or conservative yardsticks . . .' (*Bangaire Medical Trust* v. *Mudappa*, 1991 AIR 1902 (SC) (India). Some citizen actions have played a role in pushing the courts to force the government to pursue corruption allegations against top officials.

Outside of the USA the losing party in a lawsuit commonly pays the legal fees of both sides. The American innovation is one-sided fee shifting—private plaintiffs who bring citizen suits against the government or polluters are compensated for their legal fees if they win but are not required to pay their opponents' fees if they lose. Enforcement cases have clear external benefits for all who gain from more honest government. One-sided fee shifting gives public interest groups an incentive to focus on the most worthy cases. It forces firms that gain from paying bribes to pay most of the cost of enforcing the law against them. Because accusations of corruption and malfeasance can be motivated by revenge, the law might include a provision that shifts all legal fees onto the plaintiff for suits found to be harassing or vindictive—so long as the courts can be relied upon to apply the rule sparingly.

In countries with weak courts and ineffective governments, reform efforts can be frustrating. A group knows that government is working poorly, can document its failure, and speaks out in protest. The media report the group's complaints, and they are the source of widespread public debate. But the government may not react. Even if the government does not actively intimidate its critics, it may stonewall until the protest groups have exhausted their energy and resources. An anti-corruption organization can do little without some cooperation from the country's political leadership. Here corruption may be an easier issue for citizens to tackle than other controversial topics such as land reform or labor rights. Nevertheless, serious anti-corruption efforts may require a realignment of the relationship between ordinary people and the state. Citizens may be rightly afraid that complaining will only make things worse for them personally. Greater popular voice may challenge deep-seated views about the prerogatives of rulers.

IV. CONCLUSIONS

Corruption can be controlled indirectly by limits on political power. I have considered two broad types of limits. The first are government structures that create veto points and independent sources of political, administrative, and judicial power. They limit corruption by making it less profitable for both officials and bribe payers. The second gives people and groups a way to complain about government and the poor services it may provide. The government supplies information about its actions, the media and the public can voice complaints, and private organizations and individuals can push for public accountability. The first type of limit is most compatible with democratic government structures, but even autocrats will sometimes favor checks on their own power as a way of creating popular legitimacy. The second type, which increases openness, leaves government vulnerable to popular discontent. Thus many regimes, even nominally democratic ones, may view such policies with suspicion. They are, nevertheless, an essential check on corruption and self-dealing that can arise if officials are insulated from popular oversight.

REFERENCES

Abikoff, K. T. (1987), 'The Role of the Comptroller General in Light of Bowsher v. Synar', *Columbia Law Review*, 87: 1539–62.

Agarwala, B. R. (1996), *Our Judiciary*, 2nd edn. (India: National Book Trust).

Anek, L. (1994), 'From Clientelism to Partnership: Business–Government Relations in Thailand', in A. Macintyre (ed.), *Business and Government in Industrializing Asia* (Ithaca, NY: Cornell University Press), 195–215.

Bing, S. (1994), 'Assessing China's System of Judicial Review of Administrative Actions', *China Law Review*, 8: 1–20.

Bratton, M. (1989), 'The Politics of Government –NGO Relations in Africa', *World Development*, 17: 569–87.

Chester, N. (1981), *The English Administrative System, 1780–1870* (Oxford: Oxford University Press).

Dakolias, M. (1996), *The Judicial Sector in Latin America and the Caribbean: Elements of Reform* (World Bank Technical Paper No. 319, Washington: World Bank).

Del Granado, J. J. (1995), *Legis Imperium* (La Paz: Fondo Editorial de la Universidad Iberoamericana).

Doig, A. (1996), 'Politics and Public Sector Ethics: The Impact of Change in the United Kingdom', in W. Little and E. Posada-Carbó (eds.), *Political Corruption in Europe and Latin America* (New York: St. Martin's Press), 173–92.

Far Eastern Economic Review (1997), 'Throwing the Book: PAP Launches Legal Barrage against Opposition Leaders', 6 Mar.

Financial Times (1993), 'Survey of Mexico', 10 Nov.

—— (1997a), 'Singapore Leaders Awarded $5.6 m in Libel Damages', 30 May.

—— (1997b), 'Argentine Sell-Off Frozen', 16 Sept.

—— (1997c), 'Singapore Leader Wins Libel Case', 30 Sept.

—— (1997d), 'Oil Ruling Puts Philippine IMF Position in Doubt', 7 Nov.

—— (1997e), 'Philippine Sell-Off Setback', 3 Dec.

—— (1998a), 'Lawsuits Threaten Telebrás Sale', 27 July.

—— (1998b), 'Injuction Threatens Telebrás Sale', 29 July.

Fuke, T. (1989), 'Remedies in Japanese Administrative Law', *Civil Justice Quarterly*, 8: 226–35.

Geddes, B., and Ribeiro Neto, A. (1992), 'Institutional Sources of Corruption in Brazil', *Third World Quarterly*, 13: 641–61.

Giglioli, P. P. (1996), 'Political Corruption and the Media: The Tangentopoli Affair', *International Social Science Journal*, 48: 381–94.

Hewison, K. (1993), 'Of Regimes, States, and Pluralities: Thai Politics Enters the 1990s', in K. Hewison, R. Robison, and G. Rodan (eds.), *Southeast Asia in the 1990s: Authoritarianism, Democracy, and Capitalism* (St. Leonards, Australia: Allen & Unwin), 161–89.

Hutchcroft, P. D. (1998), *Booty Capitalism: The Politics of Banking in the Philippines* (Ithaca, NY: Cornell University Press).

Kibwana, K., Wanjala, S., and Okech-Owiti (1996), *The Anatomy of Corruption in Kenya*. (Nairobi, Kenya: Center for Law and Research International (Clarion)).

Lawyers' Committee for Human Rights and the Venezuelan Program for Human Rights Education and Action (1996), *Halfway to Reform: The World Bank and the Venezuelan Justice System* (New York: Lawyers' Committee for Human Rights, Aug.).

Little, W., and Herrera, A. (1996), 'Political Corruption in Venezuela', in W. Little and E. Posada-Carbó (eds.), *Political Corruption in Europe and Latin America* (New York: St Martin's Press), 267–86.

Magrath, C. P. (1966), *Yazoo: Law and Politics in the New Republic: The Case of* Fletcher v. Peck. (Providence, RI: Brown University Press).

Mainwaring, S., and Shugart, M. S. (1997) (eds.), *Presidentialism and Democracy in Latin America* (Cambridge: Cambridge University Press).

Manzetti, L., and Blake, C. (1996), 'Market Reforms and Corruption in Latin America: New Means for Old Ways', *Review of International Political Economy*, 3: 662–97.

Moe, T. (1990), 'The Politics of Structural Choice: Towards a Theory of Public Bureaucracy', in O. Williamson (ed.), *Organization Theory: From Chester Barnard to the Present and Beyond* (New York: Oxford University Press), 116–53.

—— and Caldwell, M. (1994), 'The Institutional Foundations of Democratic Government: A Comparison of Presidential and Parliamentary Systems', *Journal of Institutional and Theoretical Economics*, 150: 171–95.

Mohn, C. (1997), 'Speedy Services in India', *TI Newsletter*, Mar., p. 3.

Monroe, K. R. (1996), *The Heart of Altruism* (Princeton: Princeton University Press).

New York Times (1996), 'Is Mexico's Press Free, or Just Taking Liberties?', 23 Nov.

Pasuk, P., and Sungsidh, P. (1994), *Corruption and Democracy in Thailand* (Bangkok: Political Economy Centre, Faculty of Economics, Chulalongkorn University).

Paul, S. (1995), 'Evaluating Public Services: A Case Study on Bangalore, India', *New Directions for Evaluation* (American Evaluation Association, Washington), 67 (Fall).

Pope, J. (1996) (ed.), *National Integrity Systems: The TI Source Book* (Berlin: Transparency International).

Premchand, A. (1993), *Public Expenditure Management* (Washington: International Monetary Fund).

Rose-Ackerman, S. (1992), *Rethinking the Progressive Agenda: The Reform of the American Regulatory State* (New York: Free Press).

—— (1995a), *Controlling Environmental Policy: The Limits of Public Law in the United States and Germany* (New Haven: Yale University Press).

—— (1995b), 'Public Law versus Private Law in Environmental Regulation: European Union Proposals in the Light of United States Experience', *Review of European Community & International Environmental Law*, 4: 312–20.

Rose-Ackerman, S (1999), *Corruption and Government: Cases, Consequences and Reform* (Cambridge: Cambridge University Press).

Singh, G. (1997), 'Understanding Political Corruption in Contemporary Indian Politics', *Political Studies*, 45: 626–38.

Tiefer, C. (1983), 'The Constitutionality of Independent Officers as Checks on Abuses of Executive Power', *Boston University Law Review*, 63: 59–103.

The Times (1991), 'It Happened in Monterrey', 29 Nov.

Transparency International (1998), *Combating Corruption: Are Lasting Solutions Emerging?* (TI Annual Report, Berlin: Transparency International).

Tucker, L. (1994), 'Censorship and Corruption: Government Self-Protection through Control of the Media', in Duc V. Trang (ed.), *Corruption and Democracy: Political Institutions, Processes and Corruption in Transition States in East-Central Europe and in the Former Soviet Union* (Budapest: Institute for Constitutional and Legislative Policy), 185–89.

UK Audit Commission (1993), *Protecting the Public Purse: Probity in the Public Sector: Combating Fraud and Corruption in Local Government* (London: HMSO).

—— (1994), *Protecting the Public Purse 2: Ensuring Probity in the NHS* (London: HMSO).

Vick, D. W., and Macpherson, L. (1997), 'An Opportunity Lost: The United Kingdom's Failed Reform of Defamation Law', *Federal Communications Law Journal*, 49: 621–53.

Comment on 'Bureaucratic Corruption and Political Accountability' by Susan Rose-Ackerman

AUGUSTINE RUZINDANA

> Civilisation is not by any means an easy thing to attain to. There are only two ways
> by which man can reach it. One is by being cultured, the other by being corrupt.
> Country people have no opportunity of being either, so they stagnate.'
>
> (Oscar Wilde, *The Picture of Dorian Gray*)

After twenty-five years of violent civil war, instability, economic decline, and massive corruption, Uganda has been steadily moving towards renewed economic growth and greater democracy. Elections for the president have been held and the first real parliament was elected in June 1996 The press is free and civil society is growing stronger day by day. A sweeping programme of public-sector reform has been underway for some time and other reforms in the economy and politics are taking place facilitated by the popular mandate the government enjoys. Strong overall growth rates and good macro-performance have been registered, although widespread extreme poverty, social imbalances, and worsening rural problems persist.

Since coming to power in 1986, the government has identified corruption as one of the evils inherited from the past and a key obstacle to progress and good governance in Uganda. As a result, a number of anti-corruption measures have been taken and several institutions are involved in the fight against corruption. Fighting corruption has been seen as part of the democratization process.

I. THE INSPECTOR GENERAL OF GOVERNMENT

The Inspector General of Government (IGG) was established in 1986 to combat corruption and abuse of office. Article 225 of the Constitution sets out the mandate of the IGG as 'the elimination of corruption' and the promotion of 'good governance' in Uganda. The IGG Statute passed in 1988 gives the IGG wide powers to investigate, arrest, prosecute, inspect premises, and examine documents in the pursuit of his functions. Another function of the IGG is to supervise the Leadership Code, which requires specific leaders to declare their income, assets, and liabilities and to explain how they acquired them.

II. PARLIAMENT

The Parliament of Uganda has an oversight duty to require political leaders and officials to account for their decisions and actions. This can be done individually by an MP asking a question or through committees. In the area of financial accountability, the Public Accounts Committee (PAC) reviews and acts upon the report of the Auditor General. After decades of inactivity, this committee has now been active for some time. Public hearings are held, in the presence of the press, with departments and persons reported on. Collaboration with the CID of the police ensures that, where a crime is established to have been committed, then immediate follow-up by the police is possible. Other committees are also active in their areas of competence. In addition to focusing on financial accountability, parliament also focuses on the purposes of government expenditure. As a result, a number of agencies in government have been investigated and decisions of government awarding contracts have been challenged. Parliament has also passed laws giving power to the police, prosecutors, and courts to deal with corruption.

The Constitution includes another provision to promote greater integrity within public service and political offices. Parliament is empowered to review the backgrounds and qualifications of individuals seeking or being considered for political office or senior positions in the civil service. Some presidential nominations have been rejected. In addition, parliament can censure ministers, and already two have been censured successfully and some others have been reshuffled at the instance of parliament.

III. AUDITOR GENERAL

The Auditor General conducts regular audits of government operations. In recent years, the increased frequency of these audits has helped to identify poor accounting practices that encourage corruption. The Constitution gives power to the Auditor General to audit all accounts of government, including making value for money audits. The Auditor General's annual reports to parliament have regularly documented corruption, waste, and mismanagement. The PAC reviews and then enforces the findings of the Auditor General.

In addition to the work of the Auditor General, the inspectorate system in the civil service conducts regular checks within various departments to ascertain whether funds are being used for the purposes intended.

IV. REFORM MEASURES THAT HAVE HELPED TO CURB CORRUPTION

A series of macro-economic reforms are gradually eliminating numerous distortions that encourage corruption. Reforms have involved the elimination of monopolies and abolishing quota systems and import monopoly rights on certain products. Export monopolies in traditional commodities (coffee, tea, cotton) have been abolished and export procedures have been simplified. A new investment code encourages investment by foreign and local investors.

Removal of price controls, elimination of marketing boards, and deregulation of foreign exchange markets have helped to liberalize the economy. The *privatization* of public enterprises has helped reduce state control over the economy. However, divestiture and privatization can be exploited by corrupt individuals. Such processes can also be manipulated so that select groups benefit or receive preferential access. It is, therefore, important to address broader governance issues early on in the process of both political and economic reform.

V. DECENTRALIZATION

Decentralization is important in the fight against corruption because public-sector decision-making had largely been conducted in secret, through highly decentralized institutions, and with little accountability. Now government administration, resources, and delivery of services have been decentralized in order to ensure greater public accountability and reduce corruption.

VI. ROLE OF THE PRESS

The press is crucial in fighting corruption and in providing the public with information regarding the public-sector reforms as well as corruption and the measures being taken against it. However, a free press being new, professionalism is low and sometimes reporters and editors succumb to bribery and replace reporting with libel and defamation. To improve professional journalism the Inspector General of Government, together with the Danish International Development Agency (DANIDA), the Economic Development Institute (EDI) of the World Bank, and Transparency International, have organized workshops to train journalists in investigative techniques and about 400–500 journalists have gone through these workshops.

VII. WHY IS THERE THIS CONCERN WITH INTEGRITY AND ACCOUNTABILITY?

Some time last month, I addressed ministers of the Government of Uganda and their permanent secretaries on the issue of corruption and good governance. When we came to question time, a perturbed minister asked me why ministers are generally perceived by the public to be very corrupt when, in his view, ministers have no opportunity to misappropriate public funds. He said that permanent secretaries and other civil servants are the ones who manage public funds and, therefore, they have the best opportunity to be corrupt, but not ministers.

This clearly poses the question of the relationship between bureaucratic corruption and the responsibility of the political leadership. Is it possible for bureaucratic corruption to occur without the connivance of the political leadership? The immediate answer that comes to mind is that it is not possible. Indeed, corruption cannot occur without the connivance, even if passive, of the political leadership. Whereas it is true that there are certain forms of corruption open to the bureaucracy and others open to political leaders, neither of these sectors of public officials can be corrupt without the implicit sanction of the other.

The second issue raised by the minister's question relates to what is perceived as corruption by the public. The public in Uganda lumps together corruption, waste, and mismanagement. All of them are classified as corruption. So anyone involved in misman-agement of public assets or wasteful expenditure, and this includes the personnel of the donor community, is considered corrupt. Indeed, both bureaucratic and political corrup-tion are rampant. The bureaucracy in Uganda, in spite of the improvements of the last several years, remains an uncontrolled and unaccountable centre of power. The political leadership for the first several years was relatively corrupt free. But, with the introduc-tion of elections, the need for funds changed the situation for the worse.

Therefore, the democratization process has an impact on the increase of some forms of corruption. Election campaigns must be financed. Therefore, contributions are made to leading politicians and their political organizations to finance election activities. Kickbacks for contracts, current and future, are exacted from businessmen who expect government contracts in return. In an environment where there are no clear regulations governing campaign-funding, the temptation to invest in politicians and their organiza-tions is high. Similarly, extortion and bribery have been noticed to rise during elections. In fact, quite a number of senior officials in departments where bribery and extortion are common (customs, income tax, and immigration) contested the last elections and, as expected, they seemed to be well founded.

For some time now, popular demand for democratic reforms that would facilitate the curbing of corruption has been consistently heard everywhere in Africa. This has happened because the growing capacity of civil society in Africa has enabled it to hold public officials accountable for their actions and also to demand that public institutions fulfil their functions and responsibilities. Thus, every passing day, the press, in response to popular feelings, chronicles cases of corruption by civil servants and political leaders. Therefore, action should be taken to support and strengthen the capacity and confidence of the ordinary citizen and civil society organizations to enable them more effectively to hold public officials and institutions accountable.

VIII. WHICH GOVERNMENT FUNCTIONS ARE MORE PRONE TO CORRUPTION?

Where corruption has become endemic, it is found in almost all aspects of life. Endemic corruption implies a breakdown of the rule of law, and a loss of state legitimacy. People come to rely on connections and favours instead of formal political, social, and economic rules, and illegitimate use of state resources becomes acceptable.

However, public procurement is particularly a problematic area, given the range of actions it encompasses and the significant sums of money involved. For example, procurement of military hardware and arms; government provision of energy, transport, and communications infrastructure; government involvement in the issuing of licences or concessions for exploitation of resources such as minerals, forests, oil, and gas; taxa-tion, customs, and the issuance of permits and licences.

Political corruption is linked to the access to and control of power and the way in which such power is exercised. The most prevalent types of political corruption centre on campaign finance, the award of government contracts on the basis of political support or affiliation, donations to political campaigns in the expectation of later benefits in the form of appointments, or access and appointments, to high office on the basis of patronage. Political corruption reinforces and encourages other forms of corruption and also erodes confidence in the institution of government.

IX. EXAMPLES THAT SHOW THE RANGE AND DIMENSION OF THE CORRUPTION PROBLEM

- In Uganda, investigations revealed that thousands of 'ghost' workers were paid regularly as existing workers of government. A similar situation was found in Guinea, where 11,000 'ghost' workers were discovered in a civil-service census.
- In Uganda, the sale of expired supplies of drugs and vaccines is quite common. Similarly, in Cameroon, adulteration of official drugs was discovered, while the real drugs were sold on the black market and the adulterated supplies passed into the official health-care system.
- In many African countries, investigations of road construction and other infrastructures have revealed that project costs increased between 100 and 350 per cent. In addition, the quality of work is generally poor, thus generating heavy maintenance costs.
- In various countries in Africa, incidences of sale of expired goods and medicine unfit for human consumption and in violation of safety standards have been uncovered.
- In various countries in Africa, customs and tax revenue amounting to 10 per cent or more of GDP are lost because of corruption.
- Wildlife in Uganda was decimated between 1970 and 1985 as a result of collusion between officials, the military, poachers, and international dealers. Elsewhere in Africa, corruption has encouraged the trade in endangered species.

X. CONCLUSION

Uganda and many countries are at various stages on the road to democracy and good governance. Over the long term, political and economic reforms create a situation in which the occurrence of corruption should become more difficult. However, in the short term, corruption can increase because of the uncertainty that political and economic transition creates. Those who are threatened by a reform can try to maximize their gains while they are in a position to do so. Moreover, as the old methods of control break down but new ones are not yet institutionalized, the opportunities for corruption can increase. Also those who could not previously benefit from corruption may take advantage of new-found opportunities to do so. Additionally, corruption can become more apparent with reform, in that the resulting greater freedom, accorded to the press and civil-society organizations, brings hitherto hidden corrupt practices to light.

Bureaucratic corruption and political corruption generally overlap, mainly because those who become corrupt rarely confine themselves to one type of corruption. As long as corruption pays and the risks of getting caught are low and the penalties for both giver and taker are also low, then corruption remains uncontrollable. Laws and controls prove insufficient when systems to implement them are weak or do not exist at all. Combating and controlling corruption must, therefore, begin with designing better systems. In the final analysis, the best way of controlling corruption is through making government business open to public control. This is not easy, even in the more and better established democratic systems.

11

Independence and Accountability of Central Banks

PAUL DE GRAUWE

I. THE DESIGN OF THE EUROPEAN CENTRAL BANK: THE MAASTRICHT TREATY

In the post-war period, two models of central banking have evolved. One can be called the *Anglo-French model*, the other the *German model*. These two models differ from each other on two counts. One has to do with the objectives a central bank should pursue, the other is related to the institutional design of the central bank.

The Objectives of the Central Bank. In the Anglo-French model, the central bank pursues different objectives—for example, price stability, stabilization of the business cycle, the maintenance of high employment, and possibly others too. In this model, price stability is only one of the objectives and does not receive any privileged treatment. This is very different in the German model, where price stability is considered to be the primary objective of the central bank. And, although the central bank can pursue other objectives, this is always conditioned on the requirement that their pursuit does not endanger price stability.

The Institutional Design of the Central Bank. The Anglo-French model is characterized by the fact that the central bank is politically dependent—that is, the monetary policy decisions are subject to the approval of the government (or of the minister of finances). Thus, in this model, the decision to raise or to lower the interest rate is taken by the minister of finance.

Things are very different in the German model, where the guiding principle is political independence. Decisions about the interest rate are taken by the central bank without interference of political authorities. This principle is enshrined in the statutes of the central bank and jealously guarded by the central bank authorities.[1]

When the European countries negotiated the Maastricht Treaty, a choice between these two models had to be made. It can now be said that the Anglo-French model was

---

[1] In the German model, there is some ambiguity about who is responsible for the exchange-rate policy, the central bank or the government. We return to this issue at a later stage.

discarded as a guide for the design of the European Central Bank (ECB), and that the German model prevailed. This is made clear by analysing the statutes of the ECB, which are enshrined in the Maastricht Treaty. In fact, the language used by the drafters of the statutes of the ECB is tougher on inflation and political independence than the statutes of the Bundesbank (see De Grauwe 1997 for an analysis).

The success of the German model of central banking is an intriguing phenomenon. After all, when the EU countries negotiated the Maastricht Treaty, the Anglo-Saxon model of central banking prevailed in almost all the EU member states. Why then was this model rejected in favour of the German one? Two reasons can be identified. One has to do with an intellectual development—that is, the 'monetarist counter-revolution'; the other with the strategic position of Germany in the process towards European Monetary Union (EMU).

The basic insights of the monetarist counter-revolution are well known. Monetary authorities cannot systematically lower the unemployment rate below its natural level. They can only lower unemployment temporarily. If they target the unemployment rate below the natural one, they will do this at a price—that is, they will create a systematic inflation bias. The only way to lower unemployment permanently is by lowering the natural unemployment rate. This can only be achieved by 'structural policies'—that is, by introducing more flexibility in the labour market and by lowering labour taxes. Conversely, the central bank must only occupy itself with what it can control—that is, the price level.

This monetarist view also led to a new view about the nature of the relations between the central bank and the government. Since the pressures to follow expansionary mone-tary policies aimed at stimulating the economy typically come from politicians who pursue short-term electoral gains, the central bank should be protected from these polit-ical pressures by making it independent.

These theoretical prescriptions were given a strong empirical backing by a series of econometric studies that appeared during the 1980s and early 1990s. These demonstrate that countries in which central banks were politically independent had managed their economies better. These countries had maintained lower inflation on average without experiencing costs in terms of higher unemployment or lower economic growth (see Cukierman 1992; Alesina and Summers 1993; Eijffinger and Schaling 1993).

It is no exaggeration to state that, since the 1980s, the monetarist paradigm has become the prevailing one, especially among central bankers. In annual reports and countless speeches of central bank officials, the monetarist analysis and prescriptions have become the dominant intellectual framework.

It is no surprise, therefore, that, when the central bankers drafted the Delors Report (which provided the intellectual framework for the Treaty), they were willing to take the Bundesbank as their model. By stressing price stability as the primary objective and polit-ical independence as the instrument to achieve this objective, the Bundesbank appeared as the living embodiment of the new monetarist paradigm.

The second reason why the Bundesbank was taken as the role model for the ECB has to do with the particular strategic position of Germany during the run-up towards mone-tary union. The German authorities faced the risk of having to accept higher inflation when they entered monetary union. In order to reduce this risk, they insisted on creating a central bank that would be even more 'hard-nosed' about inflation than they were themselves. Put differently, in order to accept EMU, the German monetary authorities insisted on having an ECB that gave an even higher weight to price stability than the Bundesbank did. There is no doubt that the German monetary authorities succeeded in achieving this objective. This victory was greatly facilitated by the fact that most central bankers had been converted to monetarism.

II. INDEPENDENCE AND DELEGATION OF POWER

The enthusiasm with which central bank independence has been embraced in the EU is fascinating. It certainly testifies that economic ideas can be very powerful in shaping institutions. What has been lacking in this process towards making central banks independent, however, is an analysis of the political conditions that are necessary to make independence sustainable in the long run.

In order to develop such an analysis it is good to start from the basic idea that, in a democracy, citizens delegate power to politicians. The politicians exert this power until they face the electorate again. Thus, the delegation of power to the politicians has two stages. The first one starts when the politicians are vested with power. During this stage they exert this power independently from the electorate. The second stage is the accountability stage, when the electorate evaluates and sanctions the record of the politician.

Much of what politicians do is to further delegate power to specialized institutions. This secondary delegation must have the same two stages. In the first stage, the politician delegates power to the institution in the form of a contract in which the objectives and the means to achieve the objectives are specified. In the second stage, the politician evaluates the performance of the institution. The first stage can be called the stage in which some form of independence is granted; the second one is the stage in which control is exerted (accountability). These two stages are inextricably linked. The politician, who is accountable to the electorate, cannot afford to delegate power to an institution (make it independent) unless he can also exert control over that institution.

The more the politician delegates power, the better the control must be organized about how this power is used. If there is little delegation, there is little need for control. Thus, (applying these principles to the central bank), if the government decides about the interest rate, then there is no need to have explicit accountability of the central bank. If, however, the government delegates a lot of power to the central bank, there is a corresponding need to have a lot of accountability. The reason is that the government maintains its full accountability towards the voter, and therefore cannot afford to delegate power without maintaining control over the use of this power. Thus, independence and accountability are part of the same process of delegation.

These ideas are given a graphical interpretation in Fig. 1. We represent the degree of independence granted to the central bank on the vertical axis. On the horizontal axis, we set out the degree of accountability of the central bank. The upward sloping line represents the optimal combinations of independence and accountability from the politician's point of view. The more independence he grants, the more risk he takes and therefore the more he wants to hedge his risks by organizing a system of control over the performance of the central bank.

In Fig. 1, the empirical evidence about the degree of independence of three central banks—the Federal Reserve (Fed.), the Bundesbank, and the ECB—is used. This evidence is based on Cukierman (1992) and a recent update by Bini Smaghi and Gros (1999). Using several indicators of independence (for example, Who sets the targets? Who formulates the policy? What are the limitations on lending to governments? What is the length of the terms of office?, and so on), Bini Smaghi and Gros conclude that the ECB is the most independent central bank, followed by the Bundesbank and the Fed.

Can it also be concluded that the ECB has the strongest degree of accountability? This does not seem to be the case. On the contrary, the evidence suggests that the degree of accountability of the ECB is less well developed, at least compared to the Fed. (see Buiter 1999 on this issue). Although the presidents of both central banks have to appear regularly before the parliament, the implications are very different. When the Chairman of the Fed. appears before Congress, he faces an institution that can change the statutes of the Fed. by a simple majority. He therefore cannot afford systematically to disregard the opinions of the congressmen. When the President of the ECB appears before the European Parliament, he faces an institution that has no power whatsoever to change the statutes of the ECB. These can be changed only by changing the Treaty. As a result, the balance of power is very much tilted in favour of the ECB.

In addition, the Fed. is required to publish the minutes of the meetings together with the voting record. No such constraints are imposed on the ECB. On the contrary, the Treaty (Article 10.4 of the statutes) forbids the publication of the minutes and the votes.

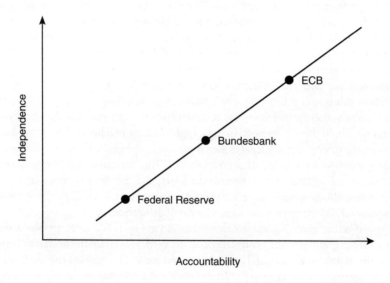

Figure 1. *Optimal relation between independence and accountability*

Thus, the ECB is an institution that was granted a lot of independence compared to the other major central banks, while the degree of accountability it is subjected to appears to be weaker than in these central banks. This goes against the theory developed here stressing that accountability should be increased with the degree of independence.

III. HOW TO DELEGATE POWER: THE DESIGN OF CONTRACTS

Delegation of power implies the writing of a contract in which the objectives to be pursued are defined, together with the method to achieve these objectives.

A crucial issue is the precision with which the objectives are described.[2] If objectives are left vague, it will be difficult to monitor the behaviour of the central bank. Accountability will be weak. The more precise the objectives are defined, the easier is the monitoring.

How does the ECB compare here with other central banks?

As pointed out earlier, the Maastricht Treaty has singled out price stability as the primary objective of the ECB. At the same time, the Treaty mandates the ECB to support the general economic policies of the EU, provided this does not interfere with price stability. Two issues arise here. First, the concept of price stability has not been given a precise content in the Treaty. This has made it possible for the ECB to fill the void and to define this concept itself. Thus, in a sense, the ECB has itself filled out the fine print of the contract it has with the politicians.

Secondly, the other objectives the ECB should pursue (provided price stability is guaranteed) have been left very vague in the Treaty—so vague that it is unclear what these other objectives are. This state of affairs has made it possible for the ECB to develop its own interpretation of the objectives it should pursue. This interpretation has been made public in the ECB's *Monetary Policy Strategy* (ECB 1999). Something remarkable has happened. Given the vagueness of the Treaty about the other objectives besides price stability, the ECB has interpreted this to mean that it has to pursue only price stability. All reference to other objectives has been dropped. As a result, the ECB has drastically restricted the domain of responsibilities about which it can be called accountable.[3] If the ECB's interpretation of the Treaty is left unchallenged, the ECB will be able to claim that its only responsibility is inflation, and that it cannot be made responsible for business-cycle developments and movements in employment. This strategy, if successful, will make the ECB accountable only for its performance in the area of inflation.

The contrast with other central banks is big. The Fed., for example, has been made responsible by law for movements in employment. There is no way it could decide on its

---

[2] There are other issues—e.g. how detailed the contract should be, or how to design the right incentives for the agent. We do not discuss these issues here (see Walsh 1998).

[3] This interpretation is increasingly communicated to the outside world. In a recent speech, Issing (1999) wrote: 'The democratic act of granting independence to central banks is closely related to the recognition that monetary policy can and should be held responsible for the single objective of price stability.' Note Issing's use of the word 'single' in contrast to the Treaty's use of the word 'primary' objective. The former implies that there is only price stability to be concerned about, while the latter implies that there are also other objectives to worry about.

own that the employment objective is none of its business, the way the ECB has done. As a result, the area of responsibilities about which the Fed. is accountable is much broader than the ECB's.

To summarize, the accountability of the ECB is weak for two reasons. First, there is an absence of strong political institutions in Europe capable of exerting control over the performance of the ECB. Secondly, as a result of the Treaty's vagueness in defining the objectives of the ECB (apart from price stability), the ECB has effectively restricted its area of responsibility to inflation, so that it will be accountable only for its inflation performance.

This state of affairs creates a long-term problem for the political support of the ECB. Modern central banks have a wider responsibility than just price stability. Their responsibility extends to macroeconomic stability in general—that is, reducing business-cycle fluctuations, avoiding deflation, and maintaining financial stability. It is difficult to see how European politicians will continue to support an institution to which great power has been delegated and over which they have so little control. Conflicts between the ECB and the European governments will arise when the ECB is perceived to do too little to avoid recessions and escalating unemployment.

The ECB could do a lot to diffuse these conflicts. First, in order to compensate for the lack of formal accountability, it could enhance informal accountability. This could be achieved by greater transparency. Given its high degree of independence, the ECB should in fact be more transparent than other central banks. It is unclear whether it is willing to do this for the moment. Secondly, the ECB should broaden its area of responsibility and recognize that there are objectives other than price stability. Whether the ECB would be willing to move in this direction remains an open question.

REFERENCES

Alesina, A., and Summers, L. (1993), 'Central Bank Independence and Macroeconomic Performance', *Journal of Money Credit and Banking*, 25/2 (May), 151–62.

Bini Smaghi, L., and Gros, D. (1999), 'Open Issues in European Central Banking', unpublished manuscript.

Buiter, W. (1999), *Alice in Euroland* (CEPR Policy Paper, No. 1; London: CEPR).

Cukierman, A. (1992), *Central Bank Strategy, Credibility and Independence: Theory and Evidence* (Cambridge, Mass.: MIT Press).

De Grauwe, P. (1997), *The Economics of Monetary Integration* (Oxford: Oxford University Press).

ECB (1999), European Central Bank, *Monthly Report* (Frankfurt, Jan.).

Eijffinger, S., and Schaling, E. (1993), 'Central Bank Independence in Twelve Industrial Countries', *Banca Nazionale del Lavoro Quarterly Review*, 184. (Mar), 39–83.

Issing, O. (1999), 'The Euro—a Stable Currency for Europa', speech delivered at the SUERF Conference, Athens, Greece, 9 June.

Walsh, C. (1998), *Monetary Theory and Policy* (Cambridge, Mass.: MIT Press).

Comment on 'Independence and Accountability of Central Banks' by Paul de Grauwe

NORBERT WALTER

These days support of democratic accountability is a matter of political correctness. To favour concepts of decision-making, on the basis of expertise and rational analysis instead, is considered old-fashioned. Talk of transparency rules the day.

Before addressing more specific points of Paul de Grauwe's paper, please allow me a few general remarks on the optimal relationship between institutions and society and some words—plus a few facts—on what constitutes the 'German central bank model', which, according to the mainstream view, is the very basis of the ECB.

Karl Kraus, an Austrian liberal and master of satire, once said about his relationship with the public at large: 'Our relations are excellent. The general public does not comprehend what I say, and I do not formulate what they would prefer to hear!'

Accountability can be interpreted as accountability to the government and parliament or to the general public. But who is the general public? It consists of many different players, including academia, the man in the street, business and—with growing importance—the media.

A concept of partnership, which builds trust and which can help the public to understand the course and motives of monetary management, might be a better principle for a central bank in order to 'win over the public', instead of just aiming at accountability. Such a partnership, which establishes credibility of monetary policy, and which secures clear constitutional support for the institution's independence, is also much more comprehensive than mere accountability.

This kind of credibility would be further enforced if the targets explicitly given to, and fulfilled by, the central bank are of critical importance to the people. Price stability, certainly, is such a target. The ECB can and must be held accountable for reaching its price stability target of under 2 per cent inflation. The fact that it has received its authority through politicians does not automatically imply that it is accountable to the politicians on a daily basis and thus exposed to the fashion of the day in politics. Therefore, I strongly support the view that the ECB should not be required to publish its minutes and voting records. In fact, I am very appreciative of the 'constitutional' support of the statutes of the ECB. That means that the statutes cannot be changed except by unanimous agreement of all the member states' parliaments. Having this form of indirect rather than direct democracy has the potential to stabilize democratic systems rather than put them at risk.

Is the ECB's degree of accountability weaker than, for example, that of the Fed.? A lack of accountability in a substantive meaning might emerge only if the target of price stability were not achieved. Only then could the ECB's accountability appear to be weak. So far, the ECB has shown considerable strength. Besides fulfilling the price-stability target, the ECB has—by cutting the interest rate in April 1999—also acted responsibly with respect to other targets—for example, the promotion of economic growth. At that time, this was quite compatible with its main objective of maintaining price stability, since deflation was a more probable risk than inflation. In a formal sense, the account-ability of the ECB is no less explicit than that of the Fed. The ECB president informs the European Parliament and, in the press conferences after the ECB meetings, very clear explanations of the ECB's actions and assessments are provided. Other publications and speeches by ECB staff add further to the transparency of actions and assessments of the ECB.

Since the 'German model' is seen in quite a number of circles as the 'culprit' for the specific design of the ECB, a few words on the experience with German monetary policy might be appropriate.

Political accountability in the narrow sense has been practised in Germany for almost the first half of this century. The central bank was under constant domination of the ministers of finances. This became especially clear during both world wars, when the aim of monetary policy was shifted from price stability to 'war finance'. Back then, German monetary policy was steered entirely by elected politicians.

After the Second World War and the second currency reform in fifty years, which had wiped out financial wealth almost completely, there was a strong desire for an institu-tional change in monetary policy in Germany. In practice, however, it was the USA that told Germany what type of monetary system to adopt. US advisers gave the clear direc-tive to adopt the Fed. model—thus, any talk of a German (European) versus an Anglo-Saxon model lacks historical foundation. However, the wording of the Fed.'s and the ECB's statutes is different. For example, the Fed.'s constitution not only specifies the target of 'price stability' but also mentions 'employment' as a second target. This does not constitute different philosophies or actual orientations of the two institutions but simply relates to the fact that the US law dates back to times when the negatively sloped Phillips curve was the prevailing theory, while this was no longer a mainstream concept when the ECB was founded.

Ever since its inception, maintaining price stability has been the Bundesbank's main goal. Keeping inflation under control leads—in the opinion of both the public and the Bundesbank—to long-term growth and social stability. It supports the weakest members of society, who would suffer most from inflation. This is what the German public had to learn the hard way several times this century! This is why the Bundesbank has earned so much credibility and support from the German public. The Bundesbank's policy has become a success story, not only for the Germans.

The first part of Paul de Grauwe's paper reflects very much the same view. Thus, his praise of independence for central banks. It goes without saying that institutions that are independent of democratically elected branches of power have to be extremely account-able. This applies to central banks as well as to constitutional courts. However, the second part of Paul de Grauwe's paper contains quite a surprise, since his interpretations of the Fed.'s role and behaviour and his criticism of the ECB—lack of accountability and transparency—seem to me to be at odds with the factual policies of central banks over the last two to three decades.

The Fed. is not the US job-creation machine, just as the Bundesbank was not to blame for the rise in unemployment in Germany, as the much better employment record of the Netherlands shows (the Dutch central bank has not done anything but follow Bundesbank policy). Accountable central banks have to admit that lags of monetary policy are long and variable and that good forecasting is systematically rare. Thus, a 'trend orientation' of monetary policy is the best available option. Certainly, Paul de Grauwe's view that central banks have to support the stability of the financial sector must be respected. While the ECB is of course the lender of last (Euroland) liquidity, it is very obvious that the ECB is not the lender of last resort. This role rests with the EU national governments (and the taxpayers in the final analysis). Until there is a United States of Europe, there will be little chance to change this assignment. Even the role of the decisive supervisory authority does not (yet) belong to the ECB, but to widely diverging sets of EU national authorities. While this is far from ideal, it is clear that the ECB shares accountability for the health of the financial sector with quite a few other players.

Therefore, I do not share Paul de Grauwe's request for a broadening of the set of targets for the ECB. This does not mean that the ECB cannot be improved. Announcing a more precise inflation target (1 5 per cent for the HICP instead of a vague 'under 2 per cent') would give markets a better guidance. Similarly, giving up the reference value for monetary expansion, until a stable demand-for-money function has been established, would be another improvement on the ECB's mission statement.

However, in general, accountability should be defined not narrowly as the relation-ship with government and parliament but as a broader concept, requiring central banks to explain their policy to the general public and to win credibility with the people.

PART TWO

EQUITY, PUBLIC GOODS, AND GLOBAL GOVERNANCE

Poverty

12

Poverty and Inclusion from a World Perspective

ANTHONY B. ATKINSON AND FRANÇOIS BOURGUIGNON

This paper adopts a world approach to the definition of economic poverty and exclusion, seeking to provide a framework that unifies the measurement of poverty in developing and developed countries. Defining poverty as inadequate command over resources, it relates the poverty standard to more fundamental concerns in terms of capabilities, which in turn are connected to inclusion in a particular society. Implementation of this approach means that we have to confront the tension between absolute definitions of poverty, such as $1 a day, and the relativity adopted in many OECD countries. We consider two possible resolutions of this tension. The first sees a hierarchy of capabilities, with absolute poverty having lexicographic priority. The second consists of making relative and absolute poverty two dimensions of the capability space to be evaluated jointly through an aggregate index.

I. INTRODUCTION: A WORLD PERSPECTIVE

'Poverty' and 'Inclusion' are terms that are used in many different ways and we are not alone in seeking to provide clarification as to their meaning. The particular focus of the present paper is that it seeks to adopt a world perspective. We take it as axiomatic that such a world viewpoint must embrace an approach to the measurement of poverty in which all citizens of the world enter with equal standing. National boundaries have no intrinsic status: it is a world, rather than an international, approach. In other words, any measure must be 'globally inclusive'. The adoption of a world perspective is not, we appreciate, uncontroversial, but neither is it new. Rothschild (1999) has shown how eighteenth-century thinkers gave a lot of consideration to the implications of shrinking distances. She points out how Adam Smith, in *The Theory of Moral Sentiments*, discussed the moral relationships between people in different parts of the world, with his well-known example of a hypothetical Chinese earthquake. He argues that conscience 'calls to us . . . that we are but one of the multitude, in no respects better than any other in it' (1976 edn.: 235). Rothschild quotes René de Chateaubriand asking in 1841, 'What would a universal society be like which would have no particular country, which would be neither French nor English . . . nor Chinese, nor American, or rather would be all of these societies at the same time?' (quoted in Rothschild 1999: 1). In his 1841 writing, Chateaubriand goes on to address the issue we are concerned with in this paper, saying that, 'The too great disproportion of conditions and fortunes could be sustained as long as it was hidden; but as soon as this disproportion has been generally noticed, the death blow has been dealt' (quoted in Rothschild 1999: 2). The resulting tensions are ones with which the world is still grappling. However, in this paper, we take the straightforward view that the World Bank, the International Monetary Fund, the International Labour Office, and other such bodies would find difficult any position other than global inclusion.

We are, therefore, concerned with poverty worldwide, embracing developing and developed countries.[1] What this implies is more open to question; and the paper addresses the conceptual problems of designing and implementing a measure of global poverty. The first section sets out the way in which we conceive of poverty in this paper, in terms of inadequate command over economic resources. Such a definition is both too general and too limited. Moreover, it is an intermediate objective that needs to be related to more fundamental concerns, which we take here to be capabilities in the sense of Sen (e.g., 1983). This approach is closely attuned to the concept of poverty as exclusion from participation in a particular society. Implementation of this conceptual approach, the subject of the second section, means that we have to confront the tension between 'absolute' definitions, such as the $1 a day (or $2 a day) standard applied in many World Bank studies, and the thoroughgoing relativity adopted in many OECD countries when measuring poverty. We consider in the third and fourth sections two possible resolutions of this tension. The conclusions are summarized in the final part of the paper.

II. THE CONCEPTS OF POVERTY AND INCLUSION

In this section, we address some of the conceptual issues that are relevant to the central subject of the paper.

Poverty and command over resources

The term 'poverty' is often used in a very general sense, as in 'the poverty of nations'. The World Development Reports on Poverty rightly interpret their brief widely. Here, however, we limit the term to 'inadequacy of command over economic resources'. People are poor when their command over resources falls short of an agreed standard, and the severity of their poverty depends on the extent of that shortfall. In adopting this definition, we are not making any claim for its superiority; we are simply stating the way in which this paper should be interpreted.

In choosing this definition, we are aware that it is too limited. Many legitimate concerns are excluded. People may not be classified as poor in terms of command over resources but may be illiterate or racked by untreated disease. Economic resources are not the sole ones that are relevant, and may well not be the most important. The variables discussed in this paper are not the only ones that should enter any social evaluation,

---

[1] In this respect, we differ from Lipton and Ravallion (1995), who provide a thorough survey of the issues, but whose 'global' poverty measure is confined to developing countries.

and we support those who have sought to extend the scope of analysis beyond income or consumption. At the same time, we insist that economic resources *are* part of the picture. We are concerned whether person i, or household i, has resources y_i, which are below the specified poverty line, z, and the determination of z is a central issue in the economics of poverty.

Command over resources is not the same as *use of* resources. We have deliberately referred to 'command' in order to concentrate on those resources over which the individual has control. A person may benefit from publicly provided goods and services; he or she may receive benefits by virtue of employment. These benefits undoubtedly affect the level of economic welfare, and their prevalence affects the weight that we attach to individual command over resources. Income poverty is less significant in a society where housing is provided by the state at low rents, where education and health care are free, and where public transport is subsidized. Cutbacks in public provision increase the salience of low incomes, but are not here equated with a reduction in money incomes.

Command over resources is, therefore, a limited concept. It may also be regarded as too broad, in that it does not distinguish between different uses of resources. Following the distinction between general and specific egalitarianism (Tobin 1970), we may distinguish between a general lack of resources and a specific lack. Lack of food is a clear example where it is the consumption of a specific good j, x_j, with which we are concerned, not the general capacity to buy goods. Specific shortages, such as those of food or housing, are very important, but are not the concerns about which we are writing here.

Capabilities

Resources are a means to an end, and the elimination of resource poverty is an intermediate objective. For the purposes of this paper, we take the ultimate objective to be the ensuring of capabilities, in the sense that the target level of resources is sufficient to allow people to achieve a specified set of functionings. For instance, the capability of feeding one's family requires the input of resources (food, fuel, and so on) and of time. A person who is physically disabled may depend on others to supply the time, so that the resources have to encompass the ability to secure that time. The level of resources required is, therefore, higher for a disabled person. To take a second example, the capability of entering the labour market requires goods, such as appropriate clothing, in addition to time. The goods required to compete for jobs are influenced by those available to others in the same labour market. A century ago in Britain one might have needed a bicycle; today one might need a mobile phone.

Specification of the underlying capabilities provides a basis for specifying the needed level of resources. It is not taken to mean that we should require people actually to *possess* the goods in question. Poverty is not being defined by the absence of a mobile phone; rather it is that the level of resources should permit the purchase of a phone, if that is deemed necessary to compete in the labour market. The procedure being examined here can therefore be summarized as follows: we are asking whether a person's resources, y_i, which are broadly cash income plus home production, are greater or less than the poverty line z, which varies with the characteristics of the person or household.[2] The poverty line is determined by the value of goods required for a specified level of capabilities. There is a vector of capability levels, **c**, and a matrix **A** which converts these capability levels into goods requirements, so that the value at prices given by the vector **p** is

$$z = \mathbf{p} \mathbf{A} \mathbf{c} \tag{1}$$

It is important to stress that the matrix **A**, relating capabilities to goods, depends on the particular society. In this way, as Sen (1983) has emphasized, an absolute level of capabilities, **c**, may translate into a set of goods requirements that is relative to the standard of living of a particular country. It should also be stressed that restating the choice of z in this way does not eliminate the difficulties of determining the poverty level: it pushes the problem one stage back to the determination of the specified level of capabilities. We return to the central problem of implementation below.

Inclusion and participation

Social inclusion is a more recent entrant into political vocabulary but, like poverty, it has acquired a variety of meanings. Our aim here is not to elucidate its different interpretations, but to see how it contributes to understanding the issues already evoked.

In one sense, the notion of inclusion has already formed part of our discussion. The capability approach is close to the concept of poverty based on participation in customary social activities. Such ideas of participation have been developed in the work of Townsend (1979), and the broad notion is embodied in the European Council of Ministers' definition of poverty as 'persons whose resources (material, cultural and social) are so limited as to exclude them from the minimum acceptable way of life in the Member State in which they live' (Council Decision, 19 Dec. 1984).

The European definition has been implemented by taking a poverty criterion of 50 per cent of average income, although the choice of this percentage—or indeed of a proportionate measure—is justified only by its transparency and political acceptability. What the capability approach offers is a way of providing a firmer foundation in theoretical terms. This has been explored in Atkinson (1995), where the capability of being included in the labour market is assumed to depend on the input of a specified, indivisible commodity (such as a means of transport). The price of this input is determined by a supplier with monopoly power, and the resulting price depends on the willingness to pay of other members of the society. A person in one society may have the capacity to take part in the labour market, but in another be excluded because the existence of people with greater resources leads the monopoly supplier to price the good out of his or her reach. Depending on the form of the distribution, rising living standards may increase the income necessary to ensure the specified capacity.

It should be noted that we are here using capabilities as a means of identifying the standard to be applied when judging the adequacy of resources; we are not asking directly

---

[2] There are other important issues, such as the definition of the unit, and the weighting of units, which are not discussed here (see Atkinson 1998).

about those capabilities, as in studies of deprivation, such as Nolan and Whelan (1996), or in the non-income components of the Human Development Index.

III. IMPLEMENTATION OF GLOBAL POVERTY MEASURES

It may be helpful to begin with two concrete ways in which the measurement of poverty has been implemented.

Two approaches

The first approach is that of the $1-a-day poverty line applied in the 1990 World Development Report ($1 a day per person in 1985 prices, adjusted for purchasing power).[3] This standard was applied to all developing countries and in 1985 more than 1 billion people were below this line. The second implementation of poverty measurement is that applied in the European Union (EU), taking as a poverty line 50 per cent of mean expenditure or income. The results of this approach indicate that some 50 million were living below this EU poverty line in the late 1980s (see Atkinson 1998). Taking the lower poverty cut-off of 40 per cent of the mean leads to a figure of 25 million. These numbers are small in relation to 1 billion, but still of considerable significance in a European context. This relative approach adopted in Europe contrasts with the official poverty line in the USA, which started from the US Department of Agriculture's 'economy food plan' for households of different composition, and set out with the intention to adjust the poverty line solely in relation to prices. Nonetheless, there were expected to be periodic adjustments for rising real incomes. Lampman (1971: 53), for example, argued that the poverty line should be 'a goal unique to this generation. That goal should be achieved before 1980, at which time the next generation will have set new economic and social goals'. These new goals would, it is assumed, reflect rising average living standards. Such a relative poverty line has been applied to the USA in, for example, the study of poverty in developed countries by Smeeding (1997).

These two approaches to the measurement of poverty are not aligned. According to the $1-a-day approach in the 1990 World Development Report, there are no poor people in OECD countries and the problem of world poverty is a problem of developing and transition countries. This may be a reasonable perspective, but it leaves no space for genuine concerns about poverty in rich countries. On the other hand, the EU approach applies a poverty standard that is at once both much higher in rich countries and lower than $1 a day in poor countries. To apply a purely relative poverty standard seems to tilt the balance too far in the opposite direction. Certainly a globally inclusive approach needs more in the way of justification for treating a particular level of resources in one country as meriting more concern than the same level of resources in another country.

The EU approach is an example of using *national* poverty lines. Ravallion, Datt, and van de Walle (1991) have carried out an interesting study of national poverty lines, and

---

[3] They also applied the lower line of $275 per year per person, which was broadly the poverty line applied in India. See Ravallion *et al.* (1991) for discussion of the underlying methods and data.

their data for thirty-three countries are shown in Fig. 1. Ravallion (1998) fitted the logarithm of the poverty line to a quadratic in the logarithm of mean consumption. An alternative description of the data in Fig. 1 would set the poverty line as constant in purchasing power, π, until this is equal to a fraction, λ, of mean income or consumption, μ. On a simple diagram, as in Fig. 1, this generates a kinked line, with slope first zero and then λ. Such a representation has a clearer logic; it avoids problems when mean consumption rises, causing the poverty line eventually to become inoperative; and, judged by eye, values of $\pi = \$30$ a month in 1985 prices and $\lambda = 0.37$ provide a reasonable fit to the data (the fitted points are shown by crosses). The kink is at a level of mean consumption (some $85 a month in 1985 purchasing power), close to that for Morocco.

Implications of the two approaches

The two approaches identified at the start of this section may therefore be seen as corresponding to the two segments of the dashed lines in Fig. 1. It is a formalization of the statement in the 1990 World Development Report that a 'poverty line can be thought of as comprising two elements: the expenditure necessary to buy a minimum standard of nutrition and other basic necessities and a further amount that varies from country to country, reflecting the cost of participating in the everyday life of society' (World Bank 1990: 26). In the report, the Bank applies the second poverty line 'when discussing poverty within countries' and the first when discussing global poverty and making cross-country comparisons. Such a two-level procedure is understandable, but it avoids the crucial question as to what happens if we seek to combine them, so that the two standards

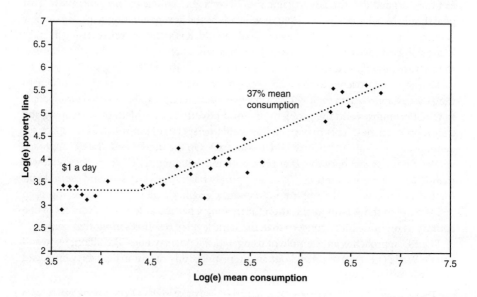

Figure 1. *Poverty lines across countries*

'cohabit'. It assumes that the two kinds of analysis can proceed in parallel without being brought into conjunction.

The implications can be set out formally in a simplified model where we have two regions: the North and the South. They differ in their resources (referred to as 'income'). Poverty is measured according to a measure of the Foster–Greer–Thorbecke (1984) kind, and we allow for the possibility of different poverty lines, z_N in the North and z_S in the South. World poverty is then

$$1 / (1 + \alpha) \sum_N \{(1 - y_i/z_N)^{1+\alpha}\} + 1/(1 + \alpha) \sum_S \{(1 - y_i/z_S)^{1+\alpha}\} \qquad (2)$$

where we consider non-negative values of the 'poverty-aversion' parameter α, $\alpha = 0$ corresponding to the poverty gap. Both summations in (2) are taken over individuals whose income falls below z_N and z_S respectively. The marginal valuation of income, for y_i below both poverty lines, is[4]

$$(1 - y_i/z_N)^\alpha / z_N \text{ and } (1 - y_i/z_S)^\alpha / z_S \qquad (3)$$

The marginal valuation is different where $z_N > z_S$. Where poverty is measured by the poverty gap, then the marginal valuation is higher at any income in the region with the lower poverty line. On the other hand, where α is greater than zero, the marginal valuation can be lower in the South. For example, where $\alpha = 1$ (poverty is measured by the square of the relative poverty gap), it may be seen by differentiating (3) with respect to z that an increase in the poverty standard raises the marginal valuation of an extra dollar where incomes are more than 50 per cent of the poverty line. We have then to ask why a marginal dollar going to a person with a given income should be valued more highly if he or she is in the North than in the South.

World versus international approaches

At this point, we should address the difference between a world approach and an international approach to poverty measurement. It could be argued that the existence of the international agencies presupposes that all member countries be taken into account, but that this is consistent with nation states being treated as entities, as in the two-level approach just outlined. In our view, however, the country in which one lives has no *intrinsic* claim on our attention; a case has to be made for different treatment. In support of this view, we would point to the implications of changing national boundaries or the formation of supranational communities, such as the EU.[5] These developments may affect our evaluation of global poverty, but we need to know on what basis a different poverty standard is being applied.

---

[4] Where z_N is a function of mean income, then the marginal valuations in the North are interdependent: the value of a marginal $1 to person i, where $y_i < z_N$, is an increasing function of y_j where $j \neq i$. This generalized interdependence is different from the case where the evaluation of income y_i depends on specific income levels (e.g. those of people close to i in the distribution).

[5] The implications of adopting a Europe-wide approach are discussed in Atkinson (1990, 1998).

IV. A HIERARCHY OF CAPABILITIES

How can we bring together the two approaches described above in terms of the concepts of poverty and inclusion? The answer explored in this section is to suppose that there is a hierarchy of two levels of capability. The first capability concerns physical survival, and requires a bundle of goods that is broadly fixed in absolute terms—such as nutrients or shelter. These have priority. A second capability concerns social functioning and requires a basket of goods that depends on the mean level of income.

On this basis, we have two (or more) measures of poverty. The first applies an absolute standard, such as $1 a day, and measured poverty is largely found in developing countries. The second applies a relative measure, identifying those who are below the relative poverty line applicable to their country. Surviving in a society requires first the physical satisfaction of basic needs for an absolute amount π and then the satisfaction of some socially defined minimum consumption standards summarized by a proportion of the mean income in a country, $\lambda\mu$. We have, therefore, both absolute and relative poverty measures, with a lexicographic relationship between them. Physical survival has priority, and this is the first criterion by which policy should be evaluated, but relative poverty legitimately comes next on our list of concerns.

If we are willing to work with multiple numbers, then this approach represents an obvious way forward. There remains, however, the problem of providing a justification for the hierarchy of capabilities. For a critic it may appear too much like working back from the answer to the question.

Economic structure. There are a number of ways in which we might seek to provide a deeper justification. Here we simply sketch one approach that links the functioning of households to the rest of the economy, or more specifically the labour market, building on the link between resources and the capability to work referred to in Section II.

The working of the labour market provides the main explanation of poverty and social exclusion in developed countries (although one should not lose sight of exclusion from the consumption of some goods or of exclusion operating in the capital market). Things may be different in developing countries, where access to the formal labour market is in any case more limited and the availability of productive resources (land, physical and human capital) and demographic characteristics like family size appear as stronger determinants of relative poverty. Because of this, it may be reasonable to posit that at low levels of development the main requirement for capability to work is nutritional. A fixed bundle of goods may be the appropriate basis for the poverty line. On the other hand, as the economy industrializes, and the formal labour market becomes more important, so the goods requirements begin to depend on average living standards. The nature of work changes, and with it the appropriate poverty line in terms of resources.

This approach might be taken to apply at an individual level, but this is not the interpretation made here. Rather, we see it as a metaphor, explaining why a societal property —the poverty standard—should evolve with the development of the economy.

V. POVERTY AND INCLUSION IN A TWO-DIMENSIONAL FRAMEWORK

A second rationalization of the two approaches is to regard absolute and relative poverty as distinct dimensions in the space of capabilities. Drawing on previous work on multi-dimensional poverty measurement (see Anand and Sen 1997; Bourguignon and Chakravarty 1998), it is then possible to provide an alternative justification for the general world poverty measure (2) above and also to generalize it in an interesting manner.

Suppose that, at any level of development, the simultaneous satisfaction of both physical basic needs and socially defined minimum consumption standards is necessary. Any individual whose resources fell short of either one of these two limits would then be considered as poor. In the space of capabilities, one dimension would thus correspond to functioning satisfactorily in purely physical terms and the other to functioning satis-factorily in social terms. The first dimension would be represented by some absolute poverty line—$1 a day—whereas the second one would be measured by a relative poverty line indicating how a given individual compares with other people in the country where he or she lives.

In this two-dimension space of capabilities, poor individuals are those who fall short of at least one of the two poverty lines. Of course, it will be the case in poor countries that some proportion of the population falls short of both poverty lines—see Fig. 2, where people are located according to their own income (vertical axis) and the mean income of the country in which they live (horizontal axis). People can be in four different situations: poor on both accounts (area BOPD), poor in absolute but not relative terms (area OAP), poor in relative but not absolute terms (open triangle PCD), and not poor (remainder). The point P is where the relative poverty line $\lambda\mu$ cuts the absolute level π, or broadly a mean income per head of $3 a day (in 1985 purchasing power, if λ is taken to be around 1/3). Countries with a mean below this may be referred to as 'poorer' and countries

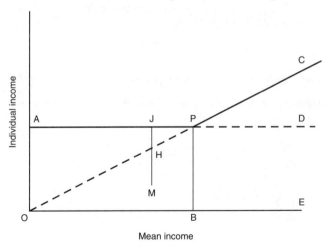

Figure 2. *Combining absolute and relative poverty lines*

above this as 'richer'. However, these definitions must be taken in relative terms, since we saw above that the switching income B corresponded to a country at the development level of Morocco.

This approach is a headcount version of equation (2). It involves in effect adding to those identified by the $1-a-day absolute poverty line those in richer countries with incomes below, say, 33 per cent of the mean. On the basis of the figures for developed countries given by Smeeding (1997: table 2) for those below 40 per cent of the *median*, we may estimate that this means adding some 60 million, plus those in middle-income and transition countries.

If it is felt that this procedure gives too much weight to richer countries (even though the number added is likely to be much smaller than 1 billion), then we could weight the number added by a factor, β, less than 1. The same weighting may be relevant if we consider a second objection, which is that simple addition takes no account of the multiple deprivation of those who are below both lines. Somebody at M in Fig. 2 suffers an absolute deprivation measured by MJ and a relative deprivation measured by MH. This multiplicity would be allowed for in a 'double-counting' measure which added to those below the $1-a-day line β times those below the relative line. More generally, with a measure of the Foster–Greer–Thorbecke (1984) type, we could add the weighted poverty shortfalls in the two dimensions for those who fell below both poverty lines. World poverty would appear as the sum of three distinct terms: (*a*) poverty among those people in all countries below *both* the absolute poverty line, π, and the relative poverty line in their country, $\lambda\mu$ (BOPD in Fig. 2); (*b*) poverty among people (in poorer countries) below the absolute but above their relative poverty line (OAP); (*c*) poverty among people (in richer countries) below their relative poverty line $\lambda\mu_N$ but above the absolute line (DPC).

The formulation just described assumes that less relative poverty may compensate more absolute poverty on a fixed trade-off. Following Bourguignon and Chakravarty (1998), we may allow for less than perfect substitutability in the 'double-counting' measure, introducing the additional parameter θ (greater than unity)[6] for the possible substitutability between the two dimensions of poverty. A general measure of poverty is then the sum over all individuals i of:

$$1 / (1+\alpha)[\{\max[0,(1 - y_i/\pi)]^{1+\alpha}\}^\theta + \beta.\{\max[0,(1 - y_i/\lambda\mu)]^{1+\alpha}\}^\theta]^{1/\theta}. \tag{4}$$

World poverty is then given by the sum of three terms corresponding to the situations (a)–(c) identified above.

$$\frac{1}{1+\alpha} \cdot \sum_{y<\text{Min}(\pi,\lambda.\mu)}\left[\left(1 - \frac{y_i}{\pi}\right)^{(1+\alpha).\theta} + \beta\left(1 - \frac{y_i}{\lambda.\mu}\right)^{(1+\alpha).\theta}\right]^{\frac{1}{\theta}}$$

$$+ \frac{1}{1+\alpha} \cdot \sum_{\lambda.\mu<y<\pi}\left(1 - \frac{y_i}{\pi}\right)^{1+\alpha} + \frac{\beta}{1+\alpha} \cdot \sum_{\pi<y<\lambda.\mu}\left(1 - \frac{y_i}{\lambda.\mu}\right)^{1+\alpha}. \tag{5}$$

---

[6] This approach is proposed at an aggregate level (i.e. with society characteristics such as literacy rates) by Anand and Sen (1997).

One important consequence of adopting this measure, or the simpler 'double-counting' measure, is that the evaluation of world poverty is sensitive to changing inequality within developing countries. If the mean income of a poorer country increases without any change in absolute poverty (a person below the absolute poverty line moves to the right in Fig. 2), expression (4) will record an increase in world poverty. The β parameter can be taken to represent the extent to which national governments and international agencies may want to allow for this factor in the evaluation of anti-poverty policies. The θ parameter is meant to control for the extent of double counting of absolute and relative poverty. Double counting or perfect substitutability between absolute and relative poverty occurs when $\theta = 1$. On the contrary, when $\theta \to \infty$ it may be seen that what matters is the poverty dimension that yields the largest shortfall—after weighting the shortfall with respect to the relative poverty line by β. In the case where $\beta = 1$, (5) is then identical to (2).

Fig. 3 illustrates the possible implications of the preceding argument in favour of world inclusive poverty measures. It is based on observed PPP corrected GDP per capita figures for 122 countries as given for 1997 in the 1998 World Development Report and on hypothetical distributions within countries. GDP per capita data for 1980 and 1990 are obtained using the growth rates available in the same source. In each country it was assumed that the distribution of income was lognormal with a mean equal to the mean GDP per capita and some hypothetical variance for the logarithm of income. This variance was supposed to be constant over time. Three values were used depending on whether a country was known to be strongly inegalitarian—as for many Latin American countries—strongly egalitarian, or in the middle. Practically, however, the results would be similar if the same variance were used for all countries. For the ease of computation the lognormal distribution was approximated by a set of 20 vintiles of individuals

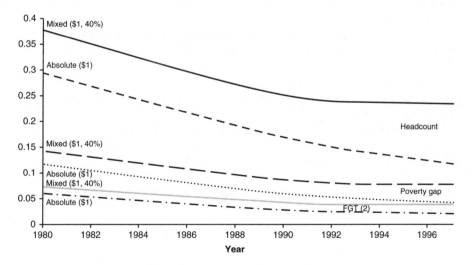

Figure 3. *Hypothetical evolution of world poverty with absolute or mixed definition of (extreme) poverty, 1980–1997*

assumed to have identical incomes. Computing the world distribution of income and poverty measures could then be done easily by manipulating these 122*20 supposedly homogeneous groups of individuals.[7]

Poverty measures were then computed on the basis of this hypothetical evolution of the world distribution of income between 1980 and 1997. The physical poverty limit of $1 a day at 1985 PPP prices was taken to be equivalent to a little less than an annual income of $750 at 1997 prices. There are two types of correction behind this figure. On one hand, prices have increased between 1985 and 1997. On the other hand, the income figures in our hypothetical distribution are based on GDP per capita whereas consumption expenditures would be more appropriate to measure poverty. The $750 1997 figure thus includes a correction for switching from consumption to GDP. The relative poverty limit is taken to be 40 per cent of the mean income—that is, GDP per capita—in each country.

Fig. 3 shows the evolution of world poverty when measured in absolute terms or when measured by combining both absolute and relative poverty as in (2) above—this is denoted 'mixed' in Fig. 3.[8] In both cases the figure shows the evolution of poverty head-count, and the FGT measures with $\alpha = 0$ (poverty gap) and $\alpha = 1$– denoted FGT(2).

The interesting feature in Fig. 3 is that, under the very crude and arbitrary assumptions used here, the evolution of poverty appears to be different depending on whether one uses the 'absolute' or the 'mixed' definition. With the absolute definition, poverty falls throughout the period at a rate that slightly slows down in the 1990s. With the 'mixed' definition there is a very clear inflexion in the evolution of world poverty after 1990. All curves almost flatten out after this date.

The reason for that difference is simple and has probably not very much to do with the very crude assumptions made to represent the distribution of income within countries. It simply happens that many countries are close to the switching point P of Fig. 2 during the period under analysis. Before 1990 most of them are below that income level and income growth thus corresponds to a drop of both 'absolute' and 'mixed' poverty. After 1990, however, many countries are above P. Income growth keeps driving absolute poverty down, but this is no longer the case for 'mixed' poverty. This is because the 'relative poverty' component has become much more important and can fall only with some equalizing of the distribution of income, a possibility that is ruled out by the assumptions behind this exercise.

Of course, these calculations are essentially illustrative of the theoretical argument in this paper. Making a serious application of the various concepts developed here to the world distribution of income is a task that goes much beyond the present paper. It is nevertheless interesting that the elementary calculation reported here leads to different conclusions when using the various definitions of world poverty discussed in this paper.

---

[7] This type of methodology has actually been used with real distribution data on deciles or vintiles by Atkinson (1996) in Europe and by Berry *et al.* (1983) for the world distribution. Milanovic (1999) uses a much richer information on national distributions to estimate the world distribution of income and its evolution.

[8] Attempts with expression (5) led to results similar to those obtained with (2).

VI. CONCLUSIONS

This paper may appear to the reader to be ending in complexity, but its concern is a straightforward one: how to provide a framework that unifies the measurement of poverty in developing and developed countries. It attempts to reconcile the use of absolute poverty lines in the South with relative poverty lines in the North, so as to be able to define poverty on a world-inclusive basis. It is a *world* and not just an *international* approach.

Our first line of reasoning is to recognize a hierarchy—or lexicographic order—in the field of poverty. Poverty is first defined on an absolute basis as referring to people whose income is insufficient to cover physical basic needs. When this is achieved, poverty is then defined on a relative basis as referring to people whose income does not allow them to function properly in their social environment, and in particular to be employed in the formal labour market. A second line of reasoning consists of making relative and absolute poverty two dimensions of the capability space to be evaluated jointly through some aggregate index. Such a view leads to defining poverty in developing countries as some combination of the absolute and relative poverty concepts. It may modify substantially the evaluation of both national and world poverty and the way they may change owing to the effects of economic growth. Our discussion has been purely theoretical, but there is clearly a need for an ambitious empirical project, building on the foundations laid by Ravallion, Datt, and van de Walle (1991) and Chen, Datt, and Ravallion (1994), examining the quantitative implications of the different approaches described in this paper.

REFERENCES

Anand, S., and Sen, A. (1997), 'Concepts of Human Development and Poverty: A Multidimensional Perspective', *Human Development Papers* (New York: United Nations Development Program).

Atkinson, A. B. (1990), 'Poverty, Statistics and Progress in Europe', *Analyzing Poverty in the European Community* (Eurostat News Special Edition, 1–1990, Luxembourg).

—— (1995), 'Capabilities, Exclusion, and the Supply of Goods', in K. Basu, P. Pattanaik, and K. Suzumura (eds.), *Choice, Welfare, and Development* (Oxford: Oxford University Press).

—— (1996), 'Income Distribution in Europe and the United States', *Oxford Review of Economic Policy*, 12 / 1: 15–28.

—— (1998), *Poverty in Europe* (Oxford: Blackwell).

Berry, A., Bourguignon, F., and Morrisson, C. (1983), 'Changes in the World Distribution of Income between 1950 and 1977', *Economic Journal*, 93 / 37: 331–50.

Bourguignon, F., and Chakravarty S. R. (1998), 'The Measurement of Multidimensional Poverty', DELTA Document 98–12.

Chen, S., Datt, G., and Ravallion, M. (1994), 'Is Poverty Increasing in the Developing World?', *Review of Income and Wealth*, 40 / 4: 359–76.

Foster, J. E., Greer, J., and Thorbecke, E. (1984), 'A Class of Decomposable Poverty Measures', *Econometrica*, 52: 761–66.

Lampman, R. J. (1971), *Ends and Means of Reducing Income Poverty* (Chicago: Markham).

Lipton, M., and Ravallion, M. (1995), 'Poverty and Policy', in J. Behrman, and T. N. Srinivasan (eds.), *Handbook of Development Economics*, vol. IIIB (Amsterdam: Elsevier).

Milanovic, B. (1999), 'True World Income Distribution: 1988 and 1993: First Calculation Based on Household Surveys Alone', mimeo, World Bank.

Nolan, B., and Whelan, C. T. (1996), *Resources, Deprivation, and Poverty* (Oxford: Oxford University Press).

Ravallion, M. (1998), 'Poverty Lines in Theory and Practice', World Bank Living Standards Measurement Study Working Paper No. 133, Washington.

—— Datt, G., and van de Walle, D. (1991), 'Quantifying Absolute Poverty in the Developing World', *Review of Income and Wealth*, 37/4: 345–61.

Rothschild, E. (1999), 'Globalisation and Democracy in Historical Perspective', Centre for History and Economics, Cambridge.

Sen, A. K. (1983), 'Poor, Relatively Speaking', *Oxford Economic Papers*, 35: 153–69.

Smeeding, T. (1997), 'Poverty in Developed Countries: The Evidence from the Luxembourg Income Study', *Human Development Papers* (New York: United Nations Development Program).

Smith, A. (1976 edn.), *The Theory of Moral Sentiments* (Indianapolis: Liberty Classics).

Tobin, J. (1970), 'On Limiting the Domain of Inequality', *Journal of Law and Economics*, 13: 263–77.

Townsend, P. B. (1979), *Poverty in the United Kingdom* (London: Allen Lane).

World Bank (1990), *World Development Report* (Oxford: Oxford University Press).

Social Insurance and Social Security Reforms

Social Insurance and Social Security Reform

13

Safety Nets, Savings, and Informal Social Security Systems in Crisis-Prone Economies

STEFAN DERCON

In the developing world or in transition economies, large economic fluctuations, climatic shocks, and natural disasters demand further development of support systems during crises. In this paper, we discuss the role played by self-insurance (via savings) in the presence of informal social security systems. We argue that better functioning asset markets and more attractive savings instruments for the poor could make self-insurance much more effective. Finally, publicly provided safety nets should take into account their crowding-out effects on informal risk-sharing or self-insurance. We argue that minimizing crowding-out may be difficult with standard safety nets such as targeted employment schemes. Asset market support to encourage group-based savings schemes may provide a useful alternative.

I. INTRODUCTION

- *Social security systems in LDCs exclude the majority of population, dependent on agriculture or informal sector self-employment.*

Most formal social security systems in developing countries focus on urban white- or blue-collar workers, who constitute only a small but relatively well-off proportion of the population. They tend to be provided with pension schemes, health insurance, and sometimes even unemployment benefits. However, most of the population remains excluded from these schemes.

- *Rural and urban households face substantial idiosyncratic and common risk, resulting in high income-variability.*

The need for safety nets in most of Africa, Asia, or Latin America is therefore in the first instance for systems that provide purchasing power during crises for rural households dependent on agriculture (as smallholder or casual wage labour) or self-employment activities, or for urban self-employed households. The issue is not, for

This paper presents some of the issues discussed in 'Income Risk, Coping Strategies and Safety Nets', which was written as a background paper for the 2000–1 World Development Report on Poverty.

Table 1. *Shocks faced by rural households in Ethiopia*

Events causing of hardship	Percentage of households reporting hardship episode in last 20 years
Harvest failure (drought, flooding, frost, etc.)	78
Policy (taxation, forced labour, ban on migration, etc.)	42
Labour problems (illness, deaths)	40
Oxen problems (diseases, deaths)	39
Other livestock (diseases, deaths)	35
Land problems (villagization, land reform)	17
Assets losses (fire, loss)	16
War	7
Crime/banditry (theft, violence)	3

Source: own calculations based on Ethiopian Rural Panel Data Survey (1994–7).

example, unemployment benefit provisions to wage workers, or pension systems. Climatic risks, economic fluctuations, but also a large number of idiosyncratic shocks, make these households very vulnerable to serious hardship. For example, Table 1 gives details of shocks causing serious hardship to rural households in Ethiopia in the last twenty years. A large number of shocks are reported. Not surprisingly for Ethiopia, climatic events are the most common cause of shocks, but large numbers of households suffer from other common or idiosyncratic shocks related to economic policy, labour, or livestock. Many other studies have reported large variability of income related to risks of various forms (e.g. Townsend 1994, Udry 1994). At the same time, formal insurance and credit markets remain underdeveloped.

- *Households in risky environments have developed sophisticated* (ex ante) *risk-management and* (ex post) *risk-coping strategies, including self-insurance via savings and informal insurance mechanisms. However, despite these strategies, high vulnerability remains and safety nets are required.*

Households do not just undergo the consequences of high risk, despite missing credit or insurance markets. Livelihood systems have developed that focus on long-term survival and well-being. One can distinguish risk management from risk-coping strategies. The first attempts to affect *ex ante* the riskiness of the income process. Examples are income diversification, by activities with low positive covariance, taking up low-risk activities even at the cost of low return, and so on. In practice, this implies that households are usually involved in a variety of activities, including farm and off-farm activities, use seasonal migration to diversify, and so on (Morduch 1991; Alderman and Paxson 1994).

Risk-coping strategies involve self-insurance (through precautionary savings) and informal group-based risk-sharing. Households can self-insure themselves, by building up assets in 'good' years, to deplete these stocks in 'bad' years. Alternatively, informal arrangements can develop between members of a group or village to support each other in case of hardship. These mechanisms are often observed operating within extended families, ethnic groups, neighbourhood groups, and professional networks. In this paper we will mainly focus on these risk-coping strategies.

Despite these strategies high vulnerability remains. Questions about the development of social security systems via safety nets remain, especially in dealing with common shocks. Initiatives to develop safety nets should take into account existing risk-coping strategies. In Section II, we discuss the relationship between self-insurance and asset market imperfections. In Section III, we introduce informal risk-sharing mechanisms and the link with savings. Each section presents some policy conclusions for the analysis.

II. SELF-INSURANCE AND ASSET MARKET IMPERFECTIONS

- *Deaton's model provides a useful description of the advantages of self-insurance. Policy conclusions may be limited.*

Deaton (1991) sets out clearly the benefits of self-insurance via savings when credit markets are imperfect. However, it is not easy to draw policy conclusions from this work, except for developing credit and insurance markets, which, as is well known, face inherent problems not easily addressed by interventions (Besley 1994). In many ways the results follow largely from the impatience of households: if only they were patient, they would build up sufficient assets to cope with future stress.

- *In practice, assets are risky, not safe. The covariance of asset values and income that are due to common shocks makes self-insurance a far less useful strategy.*

Deaton's model assumes that savings can occur in a safe form with a positive rate of return. In practice, this may not be possible. The lack of integration of asset markets and difficulties that face the poor in obtaining access to the better (internationally traded) assets and securities means that the portfolio of assets available to the poor is far from ideal. When a common negative shock occurs, incomes are low and returns to different assets are also low—often even negative. As a consequence, just when assets are needed, net stocks could be low as well. For example, if assets are kept in the form of livestock (as they are commonly throughout most of the developing world), then during a drought not only are crop incomes low, but some livestock may die as well and fertility will be low. The consequence is a smaller herd or even loss of all livestock, just when it is needed as part of the self-insurance scheme. Similarly, stock-market returns may be low when crisis hits an economy—as recent experience in Asia has shown. To the extent that some of these stocks are kept for precautionary motives, similar effects occur.

Another form of risk related to assets is related not so much to the return *per se*, but to the terms of trade of assets relative to consumption. If a negative common shock occurs, households would like to sell some of their assets. However, if everybody wants to sell their assets, asset prices will collapse and the consumption that can be purchased with the sale of assets will be lower. Similarly, when a positive shock occurs, all will want to buy assets for future protection, but then prices will be pushed up. In all, self-insurance becomes far more expensive as a strategy.

There is a lot of evidence, albeit some of it anecdotal, that this is indeed common occurrence. During the famine in Ethiopia in 1984–5, terms of trade between livestock and food collapsed—relative food prices became three times higher than usual, reducing the purchasing power of assets by two-thirds. In recent times, house prices in Indonesia and other Asian economies have collapsed after a boom during the early 1990s. Note that the same occurs during positive shocks. Bevan *et al.* (1991) reported on the construction boom taking place during the coffee boom in the mid-1970s in Kenya: prices for construction materials and other durables increased considerably. Households tried to put some of their positive windfalls into more assets, but their choice set was strongly restricted owing to the macroeconomic policies.

- *We can quantify the consequences of risky assets, covariate with incomes, using simulations.*

Using a simple model and some simulations, we can illustrate some of the problems arising from asset market imperfections in this context. Let the household maximize a standard intertemporally separable utility function v. Instantaneous utility u is defined over consumption c and strictly concave. Let δ be the rate of time preference. So at t, the household maximizes

$$u_t = E_t \left[\sum_{\tau=t}^{T} (1 + \delta)^{t-\tau} v(c_\tau) \right] \tag{1}$$

Let y_t be risky income and A_t, the stock of assets. Assets have a risky return r_t. However, we also introduce the complication that assets are kept in another form than consumption units. With consumption prices as the *numéraire*, transforming consumption into assets is at a price p_t per unit of the asset. We can think of p_t as the terms of trade or the exchange rate between the asset and consumption, or equivalently, a measure of the purchasing power of assets at t. See above for some examples where this may be relevant.

The asset equation linking period t and $t + 1$ can be written as

$$P_{t+1}A_{t+1} = \frac{p_{t+1}}{p_t} (p_t A_t + y_t - c_t)(1 + r_{t+1}). \tag{2}$$

We introduce credit constraints in a simple way, stating that assets can never be non-negative, or

$$A_t \geq 0, \forall t \tag{3}$$

Restricting c_t, y_t, p_t and $(1 + r_t)$ to non-negative values only, we can write the optimal decision rule for consumption and savings between t and $t + 1$ as:

$$v'(c_t) = \max \left[v'(p_t A_t + y_t), E_t \left[\frac{p_{t+1}}{p_t} \frac{(1 + r_{t+1})}{(1 + \delta)} v'(c_{t+1}) \right] \right]. \tag{4}$$

Households will consume and not save until intertemporally, appropriately discounted and valued expected marginal utility is equated to current marginal utility (second term on the right-hand side); however, if liquidity constraints bind, then the first term will be higher, so that all assets and income are used for consumption. Equation (4) is standard, except for the relative prices of assets. Note that, in this formulation, the path of prices (p_{t+1}/p_t) is relevant for evaluating expected future utility relative to current marginal utility, while only r_{t+1} matters, not r_t. This allows us to consider different ways risk can enter into asset values over time.

Further analytical results on the consequences of risk in asset values are not obviously obtained. Using (4), we can, however, conduct some numerical simulations using different assumptions about risk. Details are in Dercon (1999). These simulations first calculate the risk premium, which we define as the consumption the household is willing to give up in the first year to obtain the optimal path of consumption without liquidity constraints (that is, with perfect credit and insurance markets). Obviously, access to savings instruments, however imperfect, would result in a lower (residual) risk premium. The success of self-insurance can be measured by the reduction in the risk premium via savings and assets.

The results of the numerical simulations using these assumptions are given in Table 2. In each period, there is a draw of income and, if applicable, of the terms of trade of assets and of the rate of return. On the basis of this information and assets carried over from the last period, the household will decide its optimal consumption and asset

Table 2. *Risk premiums with imperfect assets under liquidity constraints*

Case	Correlation coefficient between the asset and income risk process (ρ)	Risk premium as a percentage of the mean of the income process y^a	One minus the risk premium, as a percentage of risk premium of the benchmark[b]
Benchmark: Income risk, $y_t = c_t$ (no assets)	n.a.	19.8	0.0
Case 1: Safe asset	None	6.4	67.6
Case 2: Covariate risk in Asset returns	−0.5	5.7	71.3
	0	7.0	64.7
	0.5	8.2	58.5
	1	9.4	52.5
Case 3: Covariate terms of Trade risk	−0.5	−0.7	103.7
	0	9.9	49.9
	0.5	16.7	15.7
	1	19.8	0.1

Notes:
[a] The amount the household is willing to give up in the first period to get rid of all uncertainty.
[b] The percentage of the risk premium that is recovered by savings – i.e. the value in column (3) divided by 19.8%. Simulations using equation (4) (backward solution) with logarithmic utility, $T = 20$, $\delta = 0.05$, with (approximately) normally distributed income risk: income has mean 100 and a coefficient of variation of 0.20. With a safe asset, the return is 5%. The risk in assets is always assumed to be with a coefficient of variation of 0.20. We allow different forms of covariance with income with different correlation coefficients ρ. Details are in Dercon (1999).

holding. The algorithm uses the optimal programme, based on the backward solution of condition (4).

The results show the consequences of risk in assets and covariance with income. First, comparing the benchmark with the case of a safe asset, we notice that two-thirds of the risk premium is recovered through self-insurance. However, if we introduce risk in the returns to assets, then this risk premium goes up, unless income and asset returns are negatively correlated. Negative correlation ($\rho_{yr} < 0$) simply means that whenever one wants to sell assets to smooth consumption owing to a bad income draw, asset returns happen to be higher, so they are obviously more attractive and useful. Positive covariance gradually reduces the effectiveness of the asset as a buffer for consumption. When income and asset returns are perfectly correlated ($\rho_{yr} = 1$), the risk premium has increased by almost half. Self-insurance is still useful—the risk premium is still less than half that in the benchmark.

The situation changes when the risk is in the terms of trade or exchange rate between assets and consumption or income. Recall that positive covariance means pricey assets whenever income is high (and households want to buy), and very low exchange rates when income is low (and households want to sell). It is clear that terms-of-trade risk reduces the ability to smooth consumption via self-insurance. Even without covariate income and asset prices, this source of risk is very costly, increasing the risk premium by half relative to the case of a safe asset: the non-zero probability that you may need to sell cheap and buy at high prices is causing this. Also, with a positive covariance between income and the asset terms of trade, self-insurance quickly loses its attractiveness—even with a correlation coefficient ρ_{py} of 0.5, very little benefit can be obtained from savings in this form. Although these are results based on numerical solutions, the difference between risk in the returns to assets and in the terms of trade of assets is intrinsic, and not just dependent on the numerical example used. The latter case, with positive covariance, not only results in a bad draw for low asset values when you would want to sell them (this is also the case when there is a bad draw in asset returns). Also, when income is high, windfall income is transformed into assets only at a high price, when terms-of-trade risk is present (which is not the case when we have risk in asset returns). In other words, the current asset terms of trade affect the effectiveness of transforming income into assets.

There is some evidence of household behaviour consistent with these predictions. During the 1984–5 famine, households in Ethiopia were observed rather to cut their consumption to dangerously low levels rather than sell their assets, when asset terms of trade had totally collapsed. This is consistent with the model described above: the return in terms of consumption of keeping onto their assets is very high, since at present very little consumption can be obtained.

- *Policies that influence asset market risks could be beneficial to households attempting to deal with shocks. Policies could include providing more attractive and diversified savings instruments. Micro-finance initiatives should put savings for self-insurance on the agenda. Macroeconomic stability during income downturns would also allow self-insurance to function better.*

Providing households access to a larger set of better and less risky assets should avoid some of these problems. Integrating asset markets with the wider economy could avoid much of the often-observed covariate movements in asset prices and incomes. For example, if in rural Africa or India, holding other assets, such as low-cost financial savings via post-office accounts, and so on, could be facilitated, then communities could use alternatives to animals to store wealth. Introducing a focus on savings for self-insurance in the booming number of initiatives related to micro-finance operations could be of help.

The terms-of-trade risk between assets and consumption is of particular concern. This has partly to do with macroeconomic stability. For example, terms-of-trade declines often coincide with consumer price increases relative to asset prices (for example, in the famines in Bangladesh in 1974, and in Ethiopia in 1985). Low inflation and exchange-rate stability could reduce these large shocks in relative prices when incomes are low. Policies that limit the macroeconomic effects of common shocks would contribute as well.

III. SELF-INSURANCE, INFORMAL RISK-SHARING, AND SAFETY NETS

- *There has been increasing interest in the empirical analysis of informal risk-sharing and theoretical modelling on the sustainability and consequences of these arrangements.*

Beyond self-insurance, households use a variety of informal risk-sharing arrangements to cope with the consequences of risk. Typically, they involve a system of mutual assistance between family networks or communities. In recent years, research into the extent of risk-sharing obtained by these institutions has boomed. Some of this literature has had a clear empirical emphasis. Central questions addressed have been whether there is any empirical evidence of complete risk-sharing both in communities in developing countries and in a wide variety of settings, including the USA, and how (partial or complete) risk-sharing is obtained. The tests have generally found that complete risk-sharing has to be rejected, including in the USA, in communities in India, in extended families in the Panel Study on Income Dynamics, or even within nuclear households in Ethiopia (Cochrane 1991; Mace 1991; Townsend 1994; Hayashi *et al.* 1996; Dercon and Krishnan 2000). Nevertheless, there is evidence of partial risk-sharing via transfer behaviour in different countries or state-contingent ('quasi')-credit (Udry 1994; Lund and Fafchamps 1997).

- *Risk-sharing can be viewed as the cross-sectional equivalent of consumption smoothing over time.*

The existence of full risk-sharing implies that all group resources are effectively pooled, although the theory is agnostic about who gets what share of the joint resources. Risk-sharing implies that any unpredicted event is covered by a state-contingent transfer from other members in the group. From this it should be obvious that the group can insure against idiosyncratic shocks, not common shocks. It would then be tempting to suggest that other means should be used to insure against common shocks—savings or public safety nets should be developed to cope with these risks. However, the consequences of these alternatives should be well understood.

- *Without enforcement problems, better savings opportunities, and a public safety net providing transfer when common shocks occur, could improve welfare without crowding out the informal insurance arrangement. A transfer-based safety net is, however, likely to crowd out private (precautionary) savings.*

Suppose that full risk-sharing is always feasible for the group. The easiest assumption to justify this is that, besides full information, strong social norms exist that punish deviations, so that it is never better to renege on the agreement to share risks. If saving is possible, then households would have incentives to build up assets to cope with hardship. However, if they know that they are locked into a risk-sharing arrangement, then assets will be built up to cope only with common shocks, since the risk-sharing agreement would continue to handle idiosyncratic shocks. Effectively, this would be equivalent to building up assets at the group level for self-insurance of the group to cope with common shocks. The corollary, the implications for savings when a group enters into a risk-sharing agreement, would be to reduce precautionary savings, since idiosyncratic shocks could now be insured via other means.

The introduction of a public safety net based on transfer, and activated when a common shock occurs, has similar effects. If it deals only with common shocks, then the risk-sharing arrangement would not be crowded out, but function for idiosyncratic shocks. If savings are possible, then the introduction of a public safety net would reduce precautionary savings, since overall risk has been reduced, which by definition means lower precautionary savings (Deaton 1991). Private savings would be crowded out. These savings are generally kept in liquid form and are not very suitable as a basis for credit multiplication. However, if one worries about this crowding-out effect, then improving savings opportunities may be superior in some circumstances to a transfer-based public safety net.

Finally, if a public safety net is also available for dealing with idiosyncratic shocks, then some displacement of the informal insurance system is likely, especially if the safety net provides net transfers into the community (rather than an actuarially fair insurance system).

- *Informal insurance arrangements are likely to have to be self-enforcing, imposing sustainability constraints. Circumstances in which risk-sharing arrangements may be sustained are,* inter alia: *a low discount rate of the future, high frequency of interactions, situations in which idiosyncratic shocks are more frequent relative to other shocks.*

Enforcement through norms alone is unlikely to be sufficient. In recent years, formal models of informal insurance arrangements have clarified the conditions in which agreements could be sustained (Coate and Ravallion 1993; Thomas and Worrall 1994; Ligon *et al.* 1997). The models rely on specifying an enforceability (or sustainability) constraint in each state, in which individuals must find it in their interest to remain in the scheme, rather than going it alone. Punishment for reneging on the agreement is exclusion from the scheme in the future. These models systematically find that risk-sharing arrangements can be sustained if individuals discount future returns at a low rate, so that any future benefits matter in deciding whether to enter or to remain in the scheme. Also, they rely on a large number of shocks and interactions; idiosyncratic shocks can be insured, or, in general, shocks in which a large number of members are not affected by a shock relative to the number of members affected.

- *Evaluating the effects of alternative coping mechanisms such as via savings, or policy interventions such as providing better savings instruments or a public safety net, needs to take into account their effect on incentives to sustain the agreement rather than to go it alone. It is possible that opportunities for precautionary savings or a public safety net would actually be welfare reducing and displace the informal insurance arrangement by more than one to one.*

The standard models do not allow for self-insurance. Introducing the possibility of savings in the model provides better insurance to individuals to cope with common shocks. However, it will also affect the outcome when leaving the arrangement, since self-insurance can reduce the consequences of both idiosyncratic and common shocks (and, as was shown in Section II, rather substantial insurance could be obtained in this way). Ligon *et al.* (1998) have shown that it may then not be optimal to sustain the agreement and the risk-sharing arrangement may break down. Indeed, it can be shown that fewer agreements would be sustained. Unless the welfare effect of having access to savings increases beyond the loss from the breakdown of the arrangement, welfare would be lower after the introduction of savings. Self-insurance via private savings could crowd out the informal insurance scheme by more than one to one—that is, more is lost than gained.

This principle of the possible ambiguous consequences of alternative insurance opportunities on the informal insurance arrangements and on welfare is more general, if the alternatives result in improving an individual's outcome when reneging on the agreement—that is, the enforceability constraints are affected. In that case, more than one-to-one crowding-out of the informal arrangement could occur and overall welfare could be reduced (although this is not necessarily so). In particular, Attanasio and Rios-Rull (1999) consider the consequences of introducing a safety net to deal with common shocks. Since the insurance of some part of the total risk faced by households improves the households' autarky position, it is possible that more than one-to-one crowding-out occurs and total welfare is reduced by the safety net.

- *Any policy intervention that improves an individual's position outside a private group-based informal risk-sharing arrangement may provide incentives to break down the informal arrangement. Targeted interventions that target only some members of communities or groups could be particularly counterproductive.*

Policy interventions, such as a public safety net, are presented with a dilemma. If informal arrangements are present, then any outside intervention that provides an alternative source of insurance may displace the existing informal arrangements. The reason is again that the individual's outside option—part of the enforceability constraint—is likely to be affected.

Currently, many safety-net interventions are targeted: particular groups—for example, women or landless workers—tend to be targeted by schemes. Public-works employment schemes are set up for able-bodied people; direct transfers target the ill and infirm, and so on. Targeted intervention has become part of the standard safety-net package supported by international donors, including, for example, in the current crisis in Indonesia or in the recurrent local famine situations in parts of Africa. Note that they may affect current informal systems, since they affect the enforceability constraint by changing the outside options available to members. If one is concerned about sustaining informal (traditional) insurance systems, more attention should be paid to understand the existing mechanisms.

To avoid these problems, schemes that target groups rather than individuals—for example, employment schemes for the group or the whole community involved in an informal scheme, may be more appropriate. This, of course, requires detailed information about the informal schemes operating (Attanasio and Rios-Rull 1999). If the scheme deals only with common and not idiosyncratic shocks, none of the crowding-out or welfare effects should apply. Of course, this presents substantial design and information problems.

- *Group-based savings schemes could provide a useful alternative or complement if one is concerned about crowding out. The possibly negative welfare effects can be avoided.*

An alternative could be to encourage and support groups involved in informal insurance arrangements to develop group-based self-insurance mechanisms. Indeed, the standard distinction that individual-based self-insurance can deal best with common shocks, while informal arrangements are suitable for idiosyncratic shocks, is misleading. Groups have incentives to self-insure as well, especially if there are economies of scale in asset holdings (for example, transactions costs, opportunities for risk-pooling of assets, and so on). Groups could build up assets in good years, to deplete in bad years for the benefit of its members, using transfer rules and mechanisms parallel to the risk-sharing arrangement for idiosyncratic shocks.

If individuals can benefit from the savings only when part of the group, then the negative incentive effects, working via the enforceability constraints of the agreement, would not exist. Groups could then extend their brief to deal, to the extent possible, with common shocks as well.

Policy interventions could provide incentives for this type of behaviour. Better savings instruments, access to banking, but also macroeconomic stability would assist this process. One could also endeavour to include a more important savings-for-insurance element in group-based credit programmes, a current favourite in donor interventions.

- *Whether the crowding-out and potential negative welfare effects of interventions on informal insurance mechanisms are significant is an empirical question. If common shocks are dominant and if groups and communities rather than just individuals are targeted, these effects are likely to be less.*

Ultimately, more empirical research should shed light on the very groups and institutions engaging in informal arrangements, their functioning and role and their potential for expansion. Also, we need more work on whether and how these informal arrangements are affected by interventions and whether alternative schemes can be designed. It is likely that interventions should especially be cautious in contexts conducive to these private informal institutions—for instance, where tightly-knit groups are affected by substantial idiosyncratic shocks. In a context where common shocks are dominant and where groups or communities can be targeted, the interventions are more likely to be beneficial in net terms.

REFERENCES

Alderman, H., and Paxson, C. (1994), 'Do the Poor Insure? A Synthesis of the Literature on Risk and Consumption in Developing Countries', *International Economics Association Moscow*, 4.

Attanasio, O., and Rios-Rull, J. (1999), 'Consumption Smoothing and Extended Families: The Role of Government-Sponsored Insurance', mimeo, University of Pennsylvania.

Besley, T. (1994), 'Savings, Credit and Insurance', in J. Behrman, and T. N. Srinivasan (eds.), *Handbook of Development Economics*, iii, A (Amsterdam: North Holland Press).

Bevan, D., Collier, P., and Gunning, J. W. (1991), *Peasants and Governments* (Oxford: Oxford University Press).

Coate, S., and Ravallion, M. (1993), 'Reciprocity without Commitment: Characterisation and Performance of Informal Insurance Arrangements', *Journal of Development Economics*, 40: 1–24.

Cochrane, J. (1991), 'A Simple Test of Consumption Insurance', *Journal of Political Economy*, 99: 957–76.

Cox, D., and Jimenez, E. (1992), 'Social Security and Private Transfers in Developing Countries: The Case of Peru', *World Bank Economic Review*, 6/1: 115–69.

Deaton, A. (1991), 'Savings and Liquidity Constraints', *Econometrica*, 59/5: 1221–48.

Dercon, S. (1999), 'Income Risk, Coping Strategies and Safety Nets', background paper for the World Development Report 2000–1.

—— and Krishnan, P. (2000), 'In Sickness and in Health: Risk-Sharing within Households in Ethiopia', *Journal of Political Economy*, 108/4: 688–727.

Fafchamps, M. (1996), 'Risk-Sharing, Quasi-Credit and the Enforcement of Informal Contracts', mimeo, Standford University.

Hayashi, F., Altonji, J., and Kotlikoff, L. (1996), 'Risk-Sharing between and within Families', *Econometrica*, 64/2: 261–94.

Ligon, E., Thomas, J., and Worrall, T. (1997), 'Mutual Insurance with Limited Commitment: Theory and Evidence from Village Economies', mimeo.

—— —— —— (1998), 'Mutual Insurance, Individual Savings and Limited Commitment', mimeo.

Lund, S., and Fafchamps, M. (1997), 'Risk-Sharing Networks in Rural Philippines', mimeo.

Mace, B. (1991), 'Full Insurance in the Presence of Aggregate Uncertainty', *Journal of Political Economy*, 99/5: 928–56.

Morduch, J. (1991), 'Risk, Production and Saving: Theory and Evidence from Indian Households', manuscript, Harvard University.

Morduch, J. (1997), 'Between the Market and State: Can Informal Insurance Patch the Safety Net?', mimeo.

Rosenzweig, M., and Wolpin, K. (1993), 'Credit Market Constraints, Consumption Smoothing, and the Accumulation of Durable Production Assets in Low-Income Countries: Investment in Bullocks in India', *Journal of Political Economy*, 101/2: 223–44.

Thomas, J., and Worrall, T. (1994), 'Informal Insurance Arrangements in Village Economies', mimeo, University of Warwick.

Townsend, R. M. (1994), 'Risk and Insurance in Village India', *Econometrica*, 62/3: 539–91.
Udry, C. (1994), 'Risk and Insurance in a Rural Credit Market: An Empirical Investigation of Northern Nigeria', *Review of Economic Studies*, 61/3: 495–526.

Comment on 'Safety Nets, Savings and Informal Social Security Systems in Crisis-Prone Economies' by Stefan Dercon

PETER R. ORSZAG

Stefan Dercon's paper serves an extremely useful function: it emphasizes the potential crowding-out effects that could result from public safety nets, especially in developing economies. Its basic theme reminds me of the answer the woman gave when asked why her 20-year-old son was carried from the car to the apartment by the family's chauffeur. 'Of course he can walk,' she said, 'but thank God he doesn't have to' (Stein 1986: 13).

Worrying about crowding out and unintentional adverse effects is clearly wise in making public policy. But Stefan seems to go beyond that, to argue that the crowding-out effect is so potent that it may dominate any direct beneficial effects of the safety net. Unfortunately, the paper leaves to future work most of the crucial empirical evidence needed to support that conclusion. In effect, it argues that the 20-year-old son would be much better off without the chauffeur—but without telling us for sure whether the son can indeed walk, or how far away the car is from the apartment.

I. EMPIRICAL ISSUES

One natural question with regard to the paper's fundamental argument arises from its discussion of coverage under public safety nets. The paper trenchantly emphasizes that public safety nets in many developing economies effectively cover only urban wage workers, who represent a small percentage of the overall population. Yet, if the public safety net does not cover the rural and small business sectors that comprise the majority of the labor force, how could it significantly crowd out self-insurance and group insurance for a substantial share of workers? In effect, we can criticize the public safety net for crowding out private insurance in a significant way, or we can criticize it for woefully incomplete coverage, but in most cases it has to be one or the other.

To be sure, the paper does cite one study about the degree of crowding-out in Peru. But it is difficult to evaluate the magnitude involved there—'private transfers from the young to the old in Peru would have been nearly 20 percent higher' without social security payments. My interpretation of that statement—which could be interpreted in several ways—is that the 20 percent figure represents the crowd-out factor: that is, private transfers decline by 0.2 sol for every one sol increase in social security transfers. If so, the degree of crowd-out is non-trivial but perhaps not overwhelming. In other words, that amount of crowding-out seems unlikely to be so large as to tip the balance in evaluating whether a public safety net is a net social benefit or cost. The study was cited to show the crucial importance of crowding-out. A tentative conclusion (in the absence of additional data) may therefore be that the issue should be taken into account in evaluating and designing public social insurance programs—but it does not seem powerful enough to require a fundamental shift in our underlying views about public safety nets.

As another example of where more empirical grounding would be helpful, the paper uses numerical simulations to show that the covariances between income and asset returns, and between income and the terms of trade between asset prices and consumption, significantly affect the potential welfare benefits from self-insuring against negative income shocks. Calibrating the various alternative simulations to some real-world data—admittedly an extremely difficult task—would have been extremely helpful to readers in evaluating the empirical relevance of much of the discussion. Interestingly, the paper notes that positive covariances may be more prevalent than commonly thought, which would attenuate the benefits of self-insurance. But that does not seem to affect the overall tone of the paper, which remains quite enthusiastic—at least to this reader— about the benefits of self-insurance.

II. THE PURPOSE OF PUBLIC SAFETY NETS

The calculations in the paper do not compare self-insurance to a public safety net, which would also obviously be capable of providing insurance against negative income shocks. That raises the next point: the lack of clarity with regard to what public safety nets are intended to provide.

In particular, the paper does not distinguish between high-frequency and low-frequency insurance—or, equivalently, between short-term insurance and long-term redistribution. Many public social insurance programs have two objectives: to provide insurance against short-term shocks, and also to provide protection against bad lifetime outcomes. In the USA, for example, the progressivity of the social security system provides some protection against low lifetime earnings—a type of risk that by definition cannot be insured against through self-insurance. Similarly, the Earned Income Tax Credit—another component of the social safety net in the USA—is not primarily a short-term smoothing device. Rather, it is intended to accomplish longer-term redistribution toward poor working families.

Lifetime redistribution can be achieved through group insurance—an alternative form of insurance discussed by the paper—but only if the group remains cohesive. And, even in that case, the lifetime redistribution by definition can occur only within the group, not across groups. The paper notes that group insurance cannot provide protection against shocks that hit the entire group. But the time horizon being considered is not clear in that discussion. In other words, the issue is not just that the group cannot insure against short-term shocks that hit all its members, but also that it cannot insure its members collectively against lifetime shocks that hit them all.

In evaluating crowd-out and the net benefits of public safety nets, we need to be careful about what time horizon and precisely what risks we are considering. Are we worried only about intertemporal smoothing, or do we wish to accomplish some lifetime redistribution through the social safety net? Should such redistribution be left only to the tax system? If not, then a public safety net may be beneficial even if it engenders some crowding-out of private insurance.

III. DYNAMIC CONSISTENCY AND PRIVATE INSURANCE SCHEMES

The fact that public safety nets often attempt to provide lifetime insurance in addition to short-term insurance raises another important issue that is not addressed in the paper: the potential dynamic consistency problem in relying solely on self-insurance or even group-insurance schemes. Assume for a moment that governments scale back public safety nets and emphasize that self-insurance and group-insurance schemes are to be assigned a much more prominent role. Will society and the political system be willing to allow individuals and groups to bear the consequences, regardless of what they may be? What happens when a self-insurance account is depleted?

Fundamentally, how far can we push the self-insurance and group-insurance systems? If governments are inevitably going to intervene to rescue those in extreme poverty, how important is the resultant moral hazard risk within the self-insurance and group-insurance systems?

If one deals with the moral hazard problem by making self-insurance mandatory, then the issues take on a somewhat different nature. In that case, we would need to be comparing different methods for the state to provide mandatory insurance: either providing a safety net directly, or mandating that individuals provide it for themselves. The tradeoffs involved in that choice—involving issues such as differential administrative costs and the differential ability to spread risks across groups and even generations —are being actively examined in debates over individual retirement accounts versus public pension systems in countries across the globe.

IV. ADMINISTRATIVE COSTS, FINANCIAL LITERACY, AND REGULATORY CHALLENGES

The paper advocates expanding the use of financial assets for self-insurance. But for very small financial accounts, the administrative costs could be overwhelming—especially if the covariance between income and asset returns were reduced by allowing access to foreign markets, and sophisticated financial instruments were allowed. A focus on directing more activity into financial assets is unlikely to prove beneficial without devoting attention to the difficult task of providing low-cost accounts.

Another challenge is investor education. In the USA, the level of understanding about financial markets is relatively low for much of the population. For example, according to the US Securities and Exchange Commission, half of all Americans do not know the difference between a stock and a bond—and only 12 percent know the difference between a load and a no-load mutual fund. In the agricultural and informal sectors in developing economies that are the subject of the immediate discussion, we need to pay careful attention to investor education to ensure that the potential benefits of insurance are not eroded by poor investment decisions.

The high share of agricultural and informal workers in the developing economies that are the focus of this paper would also raise substantial regulatory challenges for enforcing and policing a mandatory system of self- or group-insurance. In economies with weak government institutions, the public safety net is often corrupted, incomplete, or ineffective. But how, one wonders, does the government that is so ineffective in providing a safety net suddenly become effective in regulating individual accounts? And the experience of the UK with individual retirement accounts is not encouraging (see Murthi *et al.* 1999). It has been consumed recently by the so-called mis-selling scandal, in which high-pressure sales tactics were used to persuade members of good pension schemes to switch into unsuitable individual accounts. Providers are now being forced to pay compensation. If that type of scandal can happen in the UK, there is no reason that it could not also happen in countries with weaker governments. A weak government is unlikely to create and enforce a strong regulatory system—and, without such a system, fraud is a serious concern (see further Orszag and Stiglitz 1999).

V. OTHER ISSUES

Two final issues deserve mention. The first is to what degree paternalistic concerns are a legitimate cause for government intervention. The high discount rate cited by the paper is at least suggestive of potential problems with a self-insurance scheme: in a sense, if the discount rate is too 'high,' individuals will 'under-insure' because they do not value the future 'enough'. All the capital market reforms and other steps called for in the paper are not going to change that fundamental fact. Perhaps the high discount rate is rational, and the degree of insurance is optimal even if it appears low to us. But perhaps not. The large literature on hyperbolic discounting and other forms of imperfect rationality should give some additional pause to those who put zero weight on paternalism.

The second issue is why self-insurance and group-insurance schemes would or would not be preferable to public safety nets. In other words, to control for the degree of insurance provided, assume the crowd-out is 100 percent. How do we feel about that situation? Is social welfare higher, lower, or unaffected if the insurance is provided through a public safety net, or a system of self-insurance and group insurance? An exclusive focus on crowd-out would implicitly suggest a view that social welfare would be unaffected. Yet the correct answer presumably involves a set of interesting but difficult issues—including the incentive effects, potential macroeconomic effects, and externalities of the different approaches—not fully explored here. For example, Joseph Stiglitz, Dennis Snower, Michael Orszag, and I examined the incentive effects from self-insurance (individual accounts) and public defined benefit systems for both retirement and unemployment insurance (Orszag *et al.* 1999). The results were much more complicated than the oft-repeated but not necessarily correct response that self-insurance provides stronger incentives. Similarly, are there positive externalities to group insurance in terms of the relationships created and the market experience acquired? Fundamentally, for any degree of crowd-out, how worried should we be about it?

VI. CONCLUSION

In summary, Stefan's paper raises a series of important issues with regard to why we have public safety nets, as well as highlighting the potential negative side effects that arise from them. Stefan seems somewhat less enthusiastic than I am about the potential for reforming, rather than eviscerating, public safety nets. But the questions he poses are healthy ones for us to be debating.

REFERENCES

Murthi, M., Orszag, J. M., and Orszag, P. R. (1999), 'The Charge Ratio on Individual Accounts: Lessons from the UK', Birkbeck College Working Paper 99–2, University of London, Mar.

Orszag, P. R., and Stiglitz, J. E. (1999), 'Rethinking Pension Reform: Ten Myths about Social Security Systems', paper presented at the conference on 'New Ideas about Old Age Security', World Bank, Sept.

Orszag, J. M., Orszag, P. R., Snower, D., and Stiglitz, J. E. (1999), 'The Impact of Individual Accounts: Piecemeal versus Comprehensive Approaches', paper presented at the Annual Bank Conference on Development Economics, World Bank, Apr.

Stein, H. (1986), *Washington Bedtime Stories: The Politics of Money and Jobs* (New York: Free Press).

14

Pension Reform and Demographic Trends: Is Funding the Solution?

ORAZIO P. ATTANASIO AND GIOVANNI L. VIOLANTE

I. INTRODUCTION

The issue of pension reform has recently received a considerable amount of attention both in developed countries and in developing ones. In most developed countries, the debate was stimulated by the fact that the current demographic trends, which project a dramatic increase in dependency ratios in the next 20–40 years, make the unfunded pay-as-you-go (PAYG) systems, that are in place in most of these countries, simply unsustainable. Some countries in Latin America, on the other hand, have pioneered the move towards pension systems that are funded and private. Chile was the first country to go into that direction, followed in recent years by several countries, including Mexico, Colombia, and Argentina. The issue of the future liabilities of pension benefits is also being discussed in other large countries, such as Brazil.

The economic debate[1] of the last decade has made clear the dramatic implications that current and future demographic trends have for unfunded PAYG systems and for the transition from such a system to a funded and possibly private one. It has become obvious that the progressive ageing of the population in many parts of the world, associated with decreasing fertility and increasing longevity, will make it very difficult to maintain PAYG systems with the current level of benefits and contributions. In the USA the Social Security Fund, which will soon run a current deficit and will be exhausted, according to the most current projections, before 2030, has stimulated a vigorous debate among US academic and policy makers alike. In European countries, such as Germany, France, and Italy, the problem is even more serious, at least if one measures it in terms of size of unfunded liabilities implied by the current system.

The possible solutions to the problem are many. They vary from more or less radical changes to the parameters of the current systems (such as the level of contributions, the level of benefits, the age of retirement, and so on) to more radical changes involving funding, at least in part, the pension system. The issues at stake are also many, ranging from the different properties of funded versus unfunded systems, private versus public

---

[1] The literature on pension reform and demographic trends is now too voluminous to be exhaustively cited here. Some interesting papers can be found in the volumes edited by Arnold *et al.* (1998) and Feldstein (1998).

systems, defined benefits versus defined contributions, and so on. The properties of each system, in terms of inter- and intra-generational risk-sharing and redistribution, administrative costs, efficiency, and implied distortions, have also been studied in conjunction with the problems of the transition from the systems currently in place to the new one. These problems are particularly obvious when one discusses the possibility of moving from an unfunded to a funded system. However, two important aspects of the problems associated with the ageing of the population and its implication for the design and reform of social security systems have been only marginally discussed, if not completely neglected.[2]

First, the same demographic trends that make the PAYG system unsustainable are bound to have important and possibly dramatic implications for the welfare of a relatively 'large' generation followed by a relatively smaller one, even in situations in which the pension system is fully funded and possibly private. The reason for this is the general equilibrium effects on factor prices and, in particular, on the rate of return to capital. In a situation in which the capital–labour ratio is relatively high, the return on capital is bound to be low. As a consequence, the consumption that can be sustained by the 'large' generation when it retires might be small. This could be complicated even further if such a generation has to pay, at least in part, the cost of the transition from an unfunded to a funded scheme.

Secondly, very little has been said about the fact that demographic trends across the world are not synchronized. While in Latin America fertility rates have dropped quite dramatically in the last ten years or so, they are still well above those observed in developed countries. At the same time, longevity has increased in both regions, but it is still considerably lower in Latin America. The important consequence of this lack of synchronization is the fact that dependency ratios are projected to be much larger for the USA and Europe than in Latin America. We argue that these differences in population structure among different regions of the world could constitute an important opportunity to reduce the impact that the dramatic demographic changes of the last few decades have created.

As different regions of the world age at different speed, this creates the potential of large production factor flows that could benefit substantially both regions. If the capital–labour ratio is high (relative to the rest of the world) in a given region because of the prevailing demographic structure of the population, there will be incentives for capital to move out and labour to move in to exploit return differentials. In what follows we will focus mainly on the issue of capital mobility: other papers, such as Storesletten (1999), have looked at the possibility that labour migration could alleviate some of the problems faced by the US social security system. Northern capital invested in less developed regions could yield returns that cannot be obtained at home and, in doing so,

[2] An important exception is the recent paper by Brook (1999). Abel (1999) considers a general equilibrium model as we do, but by using an AK specification for the production function effectively takes the rate of return as given. DeNardi *et al.* (1998) consider a general equilibrium model but focus more on the different properties of various reform proposals than on the general equilibrium effects of the current demographic trends on factor prices. Huggett and Ventura (1997) and Miles and Timmerman (1999) also consider a general equilibrium model. Their focus, however, is also different from ours.

finance the retirement of the US and European baby boomers. At the same time, this process could help the process of development in Latin America and other developing regions.

The main aims of this paper are two. First, we would like to quantify the effect that, in the absence of production factors flows, the current demographic trends have on the welfare of a generation that is larger in size than both its predecessors and its offspring. The obvious example of such a generation is that of the US and European baby boomers. (Our simulations will be calibrated to the numbers of the baby boomers and their adjacent cohorts.) However, it should be remembered that this type of problem will be faced by other regions in the future.

In order to quantify the importance of these effects we use an overlapping generation model à la Auerbach and Kotlikoff (1987) in which all retirement saving is funded and private. The model is very stylized, especially in terms of the assets available to each generation to transfer resources to the future. Such a model, however, is calibrated using the current and predicted demographic trends and some of the most important features of developed economies and is very useful to drive home our first important point.

Secondly, we want to stress the potential of different and unsynchronized demographic trends and differences in existing capital stocks for the solution of the social security reform problem. As mentioned above, this problem is of immediate relevance in the USA and Europe, but could become of extreme importance for other regions as well. Furthermore, if the solution to the low welfare of the retired baby boomers is to be found in the difference between demographic trends across different regions, such a solution could be relevant for these other regions as well in so far as the related capital inflows foster development and growth in these regions.

The disparities in level of development between the USA and Europe, on the one hand, and developing countries, on the other, in principle increase the likelihood that the effects we discuss are important. In other words, if the returns to capital depend negatively on capital–labour ratios, both the differences in (future) demographic trends and differences in the existing levels of capital stock will point to flows of capital (and possibly labour) to arbitrage out rate of return and wage differentials. These considerations, however, are attenuated by the fact that the stock of human capital is much smaller in the developing world than in the USA and Europe.

The rest of this paper is organized as follows. In the next section we present the basic demographic factors that motivate the worries discussed in this paper. In the following we present a simple overlapping generation model that we calibrated using, among other facts, the demographic projections illustrated above. We simulate the model to quantify the effects of the demographic trends on factor prices and welfare. The final section concludes with a discussion of the opportunity created by differential demographic trends and with a list of possible development for future research.

II. THE MAIN DEMOGRAPHIC TRENDS, 1950–2050

As mentioned above, the main fact behind the worries about the sustainability of the PAYG systems in the USA and Europe originates from the progressive ageing of the population. This phenomenon is caused by an increase in longevity and by a massive decline in fertility rates. While, especially for fertility, the decline is different in different developed countries,[3] the overall trend is quite similar in these countries. On the other hand, in other regions of the world the trends are not the same. To illustrate these facts and give an idea of their magnitude we use the UN demographic projections for several countries. From this data-set we construct fertility rates, life expectancy, total population, and dependency ratios for two wide regions. We form the first by aggregating the USA and all the European countries. We form the second, instead, by aggregating all the Latin American countries. We focus on Latin America because, even though the region has undergone a massive reduction in fertility, the basic demographic facts are still quite different.

In Fig. 1, we plot fertility rates for the two regions from 1950 to 2050. Two things are worth noting. First, for the North, the baby boom of the early 1950s is followed by a substantial decline. Secondly, in Latin America, we witness a massive decline in fertility that drops from around 6 in the early 1950s to 3 now. However, even with this large drop, fertility rates are still higher in Latin America than in Europe. In Fig. 2, we plot life expectancy in the two regions. The increase for both regions is quite marked. We also notice a slow convergence of Latin America towards the levels of the North.

In Fig. 3, we plot the total population in the two regions. Notice that, while the total population in the 'North' is still larger than that in Latin America, the difference between the two regions declines and Latin America is projected to become more populous than the USA and Europe combined in the near future.

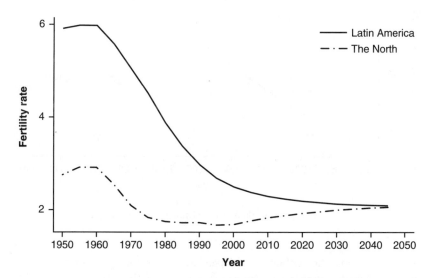

Figure 1. *Fertility rates, the North and Latin America, 1950–2050*

---

3 Interestingly, the largest decline in fertility has occurred in southern European countries such as Spain and Italy, where fertility rates are now below 1.2 and therefore much below reproductive levels.

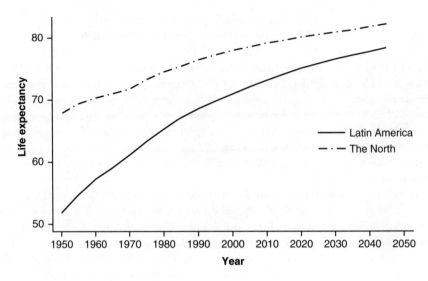

Figure 2. *Life expectancy, the North and Latin America, 1950–2050*

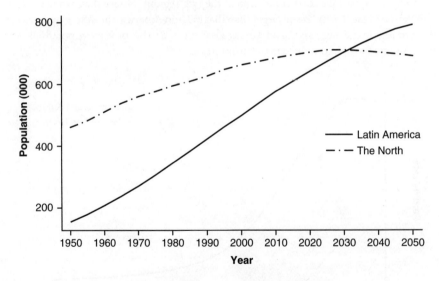

Figure 3. *Population, the North and Latin America, 1950–2050*

In Fig. 4, we plot a first definition of dependency ratios for the two regions. This is obtained dividing the number of adults over the age of 65 and half the number of children aged 0–14 by the number of working age individuals (aged 15–64). Notice that, while this definition of dependency ratio is already increasing for the 'North', it is still declining for Latin America.

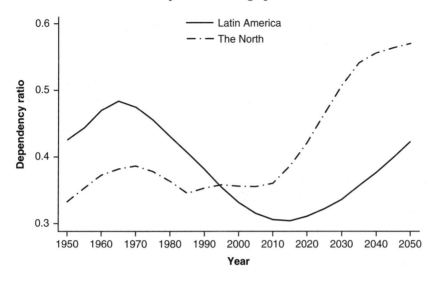

Figure 4. *Dependency ratio, including children, the North and Latin America, 1950–2050*

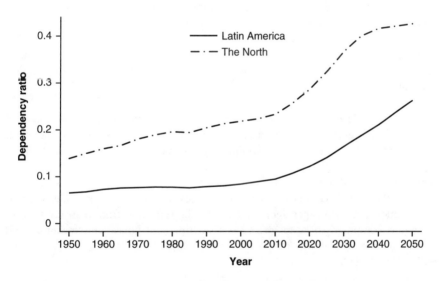

Figure 5. *Dependency ratio, excluding children, the North and Latin America, 1950–2050*

Finally, in Fig. 5, we plot an alternative definition of dependency ratios that excludes from the denominator the children. While this definition is increasing for both regions, the level of this variable is still much higher in the 'North'. Moreover, the difference between the two regions is projected to increase in the next few years.

III. AN OVERLAPPING GENERATION MODEL TO EVALUATE THE EFFECTS OF DEMOGRAPHIC TRENDS

To quantify the general equilibrium effects we construct a simple overlapping generation model of the type pioneered by Auerbach and Kotlikoff (1987). In particular we make the following assumptions. More details on the model specification can be found in Attanasio and Violante (1999). Here we list the main building blocks of our model.

Demographics. People live at most for twenty periods. We calibrate a period to be about five years. People enter the model in Period 3 of their life. In each period they can have some children. Fertility and mortality rates are calibrated with UN data from the 'North' so to match the dynamics of fertility, life expectancy, and population. We calibrate the initial steady state to match the age population shares of the 1950s and the final one to match the projections for 2050. We assume that in the early 1950s the initial steady state is disturbed by a (gradual) reduction in fertility and a (gradual) increase in life expectancy. We assume that, while the change comes as a surprise, the pattern of adjustment (the initial increase and subsequent decrease in fertility) is fully anticipated.

Consumer behaviour. Households supply inelastically their labour and consume. They are endowed with efficiency units that roughly match earning profiles in the USA. Efficiency units go to zero after 'retirement' age. They can only save using the capital stock. Returns to capital constitute their only income after retirement. Consumers maximize expected utility and discount the future at a certain rate that varies with mortality probabilities.

Firm behaviour. Firms maximize profit in a competitive environment and are endowed with a Cobb Douglas production function. They hire the two factors of production (labour and capital). There is no uncertainty in production.

Equilibrium. The steady state equilibrium is a situation in which consumers and firms optimize, the capital market clears, and factor prices are constant. This implies also that consumption per capita (per age) is constant. The transition from a steady state to another is computed so as to guarantee that firms and households maximize and intertemporal budget constraints hold. Details on the techniques are given in Attanasio and Violante (1999).

In Figs. 6, 7, and 8, we show how the model behaves as a reaction to the demographic shock. The four panels of Fig. 6 report the pattern of some demographic variables. In particular, we plot fertility rates, life expectancy, average age of population, and dependency ratios in the simulated economy. The demographic trends of our model are chosen so that these figures match closely those we report above for the 'North'.

In the four panels of Fig. 7, we plot the behaviour of some important macro-variables: saving rates, efficiency units of labour, growth rates in wages, and interest rates. While these graphs are discussed in detail in Attanasio and Violante (1999), here we want to

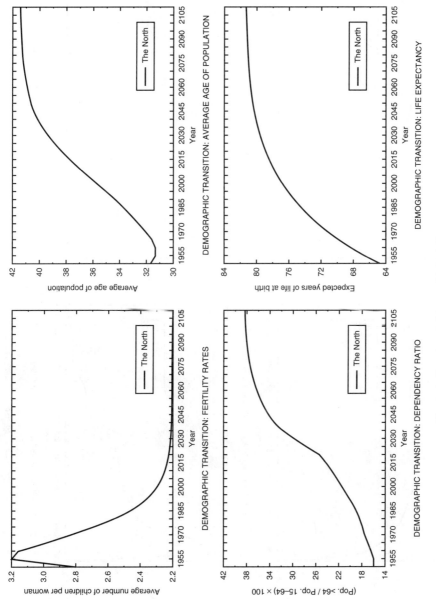

Figure 6. *Reactions to demographic variables, 1955–2105*

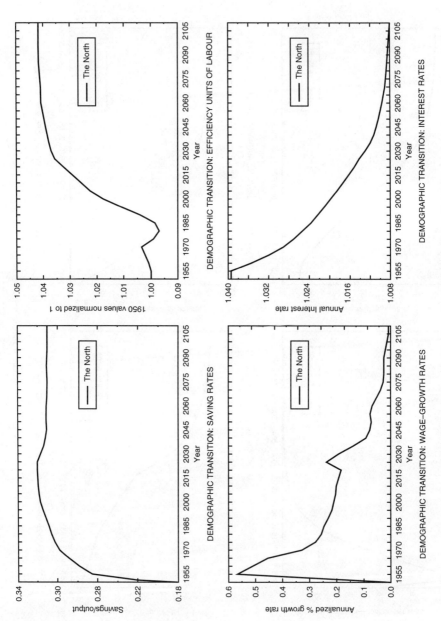

Figure 7. *Reactions to demographic macro-variables, 1955–2105*

stress the dynamics of the rate of return to capital, which declines dramatically from the initial steady state to the new one. The decline starts during the transition.

The effects that changes in the equilibrium variables have on the welfare of various generations are described in Fig. 8. Here we plot a measure of compensating variation designed to quantify the welfare loss of the generations born around and after the demographic transition. We measure it as the percentage increase in lifetime consumption to be given to a generation born in a given year to make it as well-off as those born before the demographic transition. Notice that, as we are abstracting from growth in our model, this is a legitimate exercise.

From the figure it is apparent that the baby boomers are those who lose most. Moreover, the welfare loss is quite sizeable, reaching almost 8 per cent of consumption. Notice that this result is derived in a model without social security. Moreover, the effect is likely to provide a lower bound on the welfare cost of the demographic changes because we are assuming that the demographic trends, after the initial shock in the early 1950s, are fully anticipated, so that the baby boomers can adjust to it. Nonetheless, the movements in factor prices are very negative for these generations.

IV. OPEN ECONOMY

In the simulations reported above we maintained the assumption of a closed economy. As discussed in the introduction, the possibility of considering several regions simultaneously is attractive because the current demographic trends, and the level of development, are not perfectly synchronized in the world. In particular, as we saw above, there are regions with much lower dependency ratios (and with a widening difference). Even if

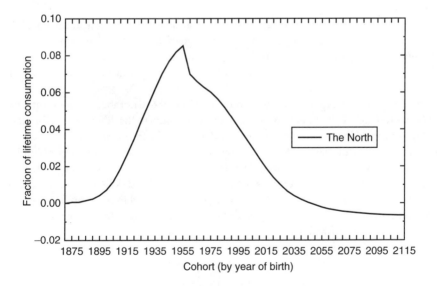

Figure 8. *Demographic transition: Welfare loss by cohort, 1875–2105*

one ignores the possibility of migration flows because of political issues, it is obvious that there is a potential for attenuating the effects described and quantified in the previous section with capital flows. In the presence of well-functioning capital markets, investment will flow to regions where the capital labour ratio is lower (and return higher) to equalize equilibrium rates of returns. If one assumes that in the very long run the demographic trends in the various regions will converge, the differences in the current trends can be used to attenuate the cost to the baby-boom generation and to spread across many generations. Attanasio and Violante (1999) show that the effect of considering two open economies with the demographic trends of the North and Latin America is that of 'lowering' and 'spreading' the welfare cost depicted in Fig. 8.

V. EXTENSIONS AND CONCLUSIONS

While the exercise we discussed provides some useful pieces of information, it misses at least two important issues. First, our model, in its current form, ignores any kind of risk, which instead is an important factor in evaluating the trade-offs between funded and unfunded schemes. Should one conclude that a move towards a funded scheme is indeed desirable, most developed economies will have to go through a transition from an unfunded to a funded system. This transition might be costly and might have an effect on the ability to exploit the opportunities afforded by the differences in demographic trends. Secondly, even in the presence of large differences in capital stocks, we currently observe relatively small capital flows. Obviously this paper cannot hope to explain why such flows are so small. However, in evaluating the impact that the difference in demographic trends might have, we want to take into account the possibility that capital flows might take time to build up. Moreover, several risk factors, including political and default risks, should be taken into account.

The issue of impediments to capital flows is particularly important. If the potential from fully mobile capital is large, both in terms of guaranteeing large enough returns for US and European investors and to develop Latin American societies and economies, there will be strong incentives to put in place the right type of institutions that could guarantee the orderly flow of capital.

Finally, in concluding this note, we would like to point to a number of important areas of future research. In particular, we want to draw attention to the differences in the stock of human capital in the two regions we consider and to the importance of the process of human capital accumulation. Moreover, and related to the issue of the stock of human capital, we would also like to consider the possibility of specialization in the production of commodities with different intensities of human capital and skilled labour in the two regions. Finally, while the focus of the paper are the USA and Europe, on the one side, and Latin America, on the other, similar arguments could be applied to other developing regions, such as Africa and Asia.

REFERENCES

Abel, A. (1999), 'The Social Security Trust Fund, the Riskless Interest Rate, and Capital Accumulation', NBER Working Paper 6991.

Arnold, R. D., Graetz, M. J., and Munnell, A. H. (1998) (eds.), *Framing the Social Security Debate* (Washington: National Academy of Social Insurance).

Attanasio, O. P., and Violante, G. L. (1999), 'Demographic Transition and International Capital Flows', mimeo, UCL.

Auerbach, A. J., and Kotlikoff, L. J. (1987), *Dynamic Fiscal Policy* (Cambridge: Cambridge University Press).

Brook, R. (1999), 'Asset Market Effects of Changes in the Age Distribution', mimeo, IMF.

DeNardi, M., Ýmrohoroðlu, S., and Sargent, T. (1998), 'Projected US Demographics and Social Security', Working Paper, University of Chicago.

Feldstein, M. (1998) (ed.), *Privatizing Social Security* (Chicago: Chicago University Press, NBER).

Huggett, M., and Ventura, A. (1997), 'The Distribution Effects of Social Security', mimeo, ITAM.

Miles, D., and Timmermann, A. (1999), 'Risk-Sharing and Transition Costs in the Reform of Pension Systems in Europe', *Economic Policy*, 29.

Storeseletten, K. (1999), 'Sustaining Fiscal Policy through Immigration', *Journal of Political Economy*.

Comment on 'Pension Reform and Demographic Trends: Is Funding the Solution?' by Orazio P. Attanasio and Giovanni L. Violante

ALESSANDRO CIGNO

Much has been made, in recent years, of the fact that pay-as-you-go (PAYG) pension systems are vulnerable to demographic fluctuations, in particular that fertility decline tends to raise the ratio of pensioners to tax-payers, and thus the level of the contribution that the latter have to make in order to secure any given pension level. Professor Attanasio makes the valuable point that, as fertility decline raises also the capital–labour ratio, and consequently depresses the return to capital, present demographic trends have undesirable effects not only on PAYG, but also on fully funded pension systems. The latter, therefore, are as vulnerable to demographics as the former. Since the transition from PAYG to full funding is costly, the move, Attanasio argues, is not advisable.

The argument is strictly true only so long as demographic events and economic growth are entirely exogenous. There is evidence (e.g. Cigno and Rosati 1996), however, that social security coverage discourages fertility and raises aggregate household saving. What affects household saving negatively is not social security *per se*, but the deficit in the social security account (the difference between pensions paid out and contributions levied). On the one hand, therefore, social security tends to reduce the number of future contributors; on the other, if it does not create deficits, it stimulates the growth of real per capita income. It is not possible to say, a priori, whether the tax base on which social security contributions are levied is eroded or enhanced by the existence of a non-deficit-making mandatory pension system. Some considerations can be made, however.

In economies like those of Europe, where social security coverage has already reached its physiological limits, demographic forecasts based on the extrapolation of past trends may be unduly pessimistic. Indeed, in some countries (for example, Italy), premature retirements have pushed pension coverage, intended as the ratio of old-age pensions paid out to number of persons of pensionable age, well over 100 per cent. Simply stopping early retirement schemes (motivated, in the past, by labour-market considerations) could thus slow down and ultimately reverse the downward trend of fertility. By removing a major source of imbalance in the social security account, such a move might also counter the negative effect of the reduction in coverage on the level of household saving. Cigno, Rosati, and Balestrino (1997) simulated the effects of reducing social security coverage to 100 per cent, and reducing deficits to zero, in Great Britain, Hungary, and Italy. They show that, in steady state, the policy would raise complete fertility by between three (in Britain and Italy) and six (in Hungary) children per hundred women. The net effect on household saving would be to add between two (in Britain) and four (in Italy) percentage points to the household saving rate.

The finding that social security may be good for growth runs counter to the theoretical prediction of life-cycle theory, and conflicts with the well-known finding of Feldstein (1980), that pension coverage discourages household saving. However, life-cycle theory is based on the assumption that individual asset formation is the only alternative to social security for a person wanting to provide for old age. That is why life-cycle theory predicts that social security contributions reduce voluntary saving euro for euro. If we relax that assumption, and allow for the possibility that middle-aged individuals provide for old age, at least partly, by engaging in intertemporal trade with their children, it can then be shown analytically (see Cigno 1993) that the demand for children (the vehicle for intertemporal trade) responds negatively, while aggregate household saving may respond positively, to the public provision of pension coverage. Within the same theoretical framework, it can also be shown that aggregate household saving responds negatively to social security deficits. The Feldstein estimates, not too robust on their own grounds (see e.g. Graham 1987), may be vitiated by the treatment of the age structure (hence, of fertility) as exogenous, and by the failure to control for social security deficits.

REFERENCES

Cigno, A. (1993), 'Intergenerational Transfers without Altruism: Family, Market and State', *European Journal of Political Economy*, 9: 505–18.

—— and Rosati, F. C. (1996), 'Jointly Determined Saving and Fertility Behaviour: Theory and Estimates for Germany, Italy, UK and USA', *European Economic Review*, 40: 1561–89.

—— —— and Balestrino, A. (1997), 'Pension Impact on Fertility and Household Saving: A Comparative Study of Britain, Hungary and Italy', in M. Augusztinovics (ed.), *Pension Systems and Reforms: Britain, Hungary, Italy, Poland, Sweden* (European Commission's ACE Programme, Research Project, 95–2139–R).

Feldstein, M. (1980), 'International Differences in Social Security and Saving', *Journal of Public Economics*, 14: 225–44.

Graham, J. W. (1987), 'International Differences in Saving Rates and the Life Cycle Hypothesis', *European Economic Review*, 31: 1509–29.

Regional Integration

15

Regional Integration Agreements:
A Force for Convergence or Divergence?

ANTHONY J. VENABLES

We examine the way in which the benefits—and costs—of a free trade area (FTA) are divided between member countries. Outcomes depend on the comparative advantage of member countries, relative to each other and relative to the rest of the world. We find that free trade agreements between low-income countries tend to lead to divergence of member country incomes, while agreements between high-income countries will cause convergence. These comparative advantage induced changes may be amplified by agglomeration effects. Our results suggest that developing countries are likely to be better served by 'north–south' than by 'south–south' free trade agreements.

I. INTRODUCTION

How does the formation of an FTA or customs union affect the distribution of activity within the area? Are the gains (or losses) divided between members, or do some gain while others lose? Do the real incomes of member countries tend to converge or diverge? The standard theory of economic integration (from Viner 1950 onwards) tells us that the effects of membership are ambiguous, but gives little guidance on the answers to these questions.[1]

In this paper we use two strands of research to address these questions. The first involves identifying underlying characteristics of economies that make them more or less prone to trade creation or trade diversion. In particular, we look at the comparative advantage of member countries, relative to each other and relative to the rest of the world, and show how this provides a basis for predicting who gains and who loses. Typically the country in the FTA that has comparative advantage most different from the world average is most at risk from trade diversion. Thus, if a group of low-income countries form an FTA, there will be a tendency for the lowest-income members to suffer real income loss owing to trade diversion. In contrast, if an FTA contains a high-income country (relative to other members and to the world average), then lower-income members are likely to converge with the high-income partner.

Thanks to M. Schiff and participants in the ABCDE Conference for helpful comments.

[1] There is a large literature on sufficient conditions, typically in terms of changes in endogenous variables. For a survey, see Baldwin and Venables (1995).

The second strand of research analyses the importance of agglomeration forces, which tend to lead to the spatial clustering of activities. We argue that the tendency for these forces to lead to large concentrations of economic activity will be more pronounced in FTAs amongst low-income countries than for those containing high-income countries. This will be a further force for divergence of income levels in developing country FTAs.

Taking these arguments together, our main conclusions are that there are economic reasons for thinking that an FTA between developing countries might lead to divergence of their income levels, with the richer countries benefiting at the expense of the poorer. However, FTAs that contain high-income members are more likely to lead to convergence rather than divergence of income levels. There is, therefore, a case for developing countries to forge trade links with high-income countries.

Our analytical arguments about the effects of FTAs are consistent with at least some experiences of convergence and divergence within FTAs. The experience of the European Union (EU) is one of considerable convergence of per capita income levels of member countries. The historical record from 1947 (when the BeNeLux Customs Union was created), through 1957 (the creation of the EEC), 1968 (when internal tariffs were finally eliminated), to the early 1980s is studied by Ben-David (1993). He finds that per capita income differences narrowed more or less steadily, falling by about two-thirds over the period, mainly owing to more rapid growth of the lower-income countries.[2] The most interesting features of the more recent experience are the strong performance of Ireland, Spain, and Portugal, which have made substantial progress in closing the gap with richer members of the EU. Whereas in the mid-1980s these countries' per capita incomes were, respectively, 61, 49, and 27 per cent of the income of the large EU countries,[3] by the late 1990s, the numbers had risen to 91, 67, and 38 per cent.

The experience of a number of developing country FTAs paints a very different picture, and suggests some instances at least in which integration has promoted divergence. Perhaps the best-documented example of this is the concentration of manufacturing in the old East African Common Market. Uganda and Tanzania contended that all the gains of the East African Common Market were going to Kenya, which in the 1960s steadily enhanced its position as the industrial centre of the Common Market, producing more than 70 per cent of the manufactures and exporting a growing percentage of them to its two relatively less developed partners. The Common Market collapsed in 1977 as it failed to satisfy the poorer members that they were getting a fair share of the gains. More recent examples include the concentration of industry, commerce, and services in and around Guatemala City and San Salvador in the Central American Common Market, and Abidjan and Dakar in the Economic Community of West Africa. Guatemala and El Salvador now account for over 80 per cent of manufacturing value added in the Central American Common Market, up from 68 per cent in 1980. And, in the Economic Community of West Africa, the combined share of the Côte d'Ivoire and Senegal in manufacturing value added has risen from 55 per cent in 1972 to 71 per cent in 1997.

---

[2] Differences measured by the standard deviation across countries of log per capita incomes.
[3] We use the average of France, Germany, Italy, and the UK.

The remainder of the paper is structured as follows. In the next section we develop the relationship between trade diversion and the comparative advantage of members of an FTA. We do this by developing some simple examples and by drawing on more technical material from Venables (2000). Section III discusses the agglomeration arguments, and Section IV concludes.

III. TRADE CREATION AND TRADE DIVERSION

Internal and external comparative advantage

The classic analysis of the real income effects of membership in an FTA is that of Viner (1950), who established the ideas of trade creation and trade diversion. Membership in an FTA changes the sources from which products are supplied to member country markets, increasing supply from the partner countries as these receive preferential treatment, but possibly also reducing supply from domestic production and from the rest of the world. To the extent that overall supply is increased and lower-cost imports from the partner country replace higher-cost (previously protected) domestic production, we expect the welfare gains of *trade creation*. However, to the extent that increased imports from partner countries displace lower-cost imports from the rest of the world (a possibility that arises because of the preferential treatment of partner imports), then the country experiences the welfare loss of *trade diversion*.

To link these forces to the characteristics of member countries we need to look at the comparative advantage of these countries relative to each other and relative to the rest of the world. Let us start by thinking through an example of two developing economies that both have a comparative disadvantage in manufactures relative to the rest of the world, but the disadvantage is less for one of them than the other. Kenya and Uganda can serve as examples. Their comparative disadvantage in manufactures could come from many alternative sources—technological, geographical, or institutional differences—but let us suppose that it is because of low endowments of human capital: Kenya has little human capital per worker relative to the world average, and Uganda has even less. The initial position is one in which both Kenya and Uganda have some manufacturing (which we suppose is human-capital intensive), serving local consumers and surviving because of high tariff protection.

What happens if these two countries form an FTA? Since Kenya has a comparative advantage in manufacturing (relative to Uganda, but not relative to the rest of the world), it will draw manufacturing production out of Uganda, so consumers in both countries will be supplied with manufactures from Kenya. This moves Kenya's production structure further away from its comparative advantage (relative to the world at large), while moving Uganda's closer. What are the effects of this on real income? Surprisingly, Kenya will gain from the relocation, and Uganda may lose (and will certainly do less well than Kenya). The reason is that Uganda is suffering trade diversion—some manufactures that were previously imported from the rest of the world are now imported from Kenya. But, for Kenya, there are gains from being able to supply manufactures to the Ugandan market, protected from competition with the rest of the world.

This argument focuses just on manufactures. Are there not forces cutting in the opposite direction for other sectors, such as agriculture, offsetting the argument? Just as Kenya expands its manufacturing production and exports, so Uganda expands its agriculture. However, given the initial comparative advantage of these countries, they are both exporting agriculture to the rest of the world, so trade diversion does not arise.

This simple example makes the point that it is possible to relate the distribution of the gains and losses to the comparative advantage of member countries—compared to each other and to the rest of the world. And, in this example, the country with the comparative advantage most different from the rest of the world is the loser (Uganda). Intuitively, a country suffers a lot of trade diversion if its partner has a comparative advantage that comes between it and the rest of the world.

A Ricardian example

A rigorous argument—albeit for a very special case—is made on Fig. 1. There are two goods, X and Y, and three countries, a large rest of the world (Country 0), and two small countries (1 and 2). The figure has on the axes quantities of Goods X and Y, and we assume (for simplicity) that consumption of the goods takes place in fixed proportions, along the consumption line illustrated. The world price of Good Y in terms of X is p_0.

Production possibilities for Countries 1 and 2 are illustrated by the solid lines XY_1 and XY_2. The levels of these lines are unimportant, so they are all constructed to go through

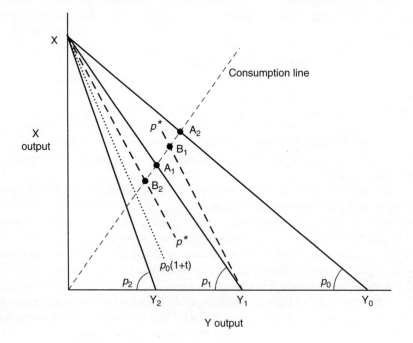

Figure 1. *Preferential liberalization*

the same point X on the vertical axis, and we also draw a world price line (XY_0) through this point. The slopes of the lines do matter, since they measure the rate of transformation between goods. The figure is constructed such that Country 1 has comparative advantage in good Y relative to Country 2, but not relative to world prices, p_0. Country 2 has a comparative advantage in Good X relative to both Country 1 and the rest of the world. (These comparative advantages can be seen by comparing Y_1 with Y_0 and Y_2.)

In the initial situation all countries have a tariff at *ad valorem* rate t on all imports. What is the pattern of trade? Imports of Good Y from the rest of the world will have price $p_0(1 + t)$, which is the slope of the dotted line. At these prices Country 2 specializes in Good X and imports Good Y. Its internal price ratio is therefore $p_0(1 + t)$, and its consumption is point A_2; although internal decisions are governed by price ratio $p_0(1 + t)$ the terms of trade are p_0 and government revenue is being earned, this financing consumption at A_2. In contrast, Country 1 does not trade. Given the tariff rate on imports of Y, it is cheaper to produce them domestically than import them; and it does not pay to export them, since it would receive only p_0 per unit, not $p_0(1 + t)$. Its price is p_1, between p_0 and $p_0(1 + t)$, and, since it is not trading, its consumption is at point A_1.

Now, consider the effects of an FTA between Countries 1 and 2. Since trade between Countries 1 and 2 is tariff free, they will have the same price ratio, and this will be somewhere between the initial prices in the two countries (that is, between $p_0(1 + t)$ and p_1). It is illustrated by price ratio $p^\star$, the slope of the heavy dashed lines.[4] At this price ratio Country 1 specializes in Good Y and Country 2 in Good X; they trade with each other (and not with the rest of the world), and consume at points B_1 and B_2. We see that Country 1 gains (consumption goes from A_1 to B_1) and Country 2 loses (consumption goes from A_2 to B_2) from formation of the FTA.

There are several messages from this figure. First, Country 1 experiences trade creation; it is able to exploit its comparative advantage (relative to Country 2) and reap some gains from trade that it was not getting in the original position. These gains arise despite the fact that Country 1's production structure has moved in the opposite direction from the way it would have had it gone under full free trade. In contrast, Country 2 suffers trade diversion; its production structure has not changed, but it is now getting its imports of Y at price $p^\star$, which is less than the private cost of importing from the rest of the world, $p_0(1 + t)$, but greater than the social cost, p_0.

Secondly, the losing country—Country 2—is the one with comparative advantage most different from that of the rest of the world. The intuition is as we saw in our Kenya–Uganda example above. The outlier has little scope for trade creation—it was trading in the initial situation. However, freeing up trade with a country with comparative advantage between it and the rest of the world is exactly the sort of circumstance in which trade diversion is likely. The general argument here is that countries with comparative advantage closer to the world average do better in an FTA than do countries with more extreme comparative advantage. Interposing the 'intermediate' country between the 'extreme' one and the rest of the world distorts the extreme country's trade, causing it to switch import supplier. But the intermediate country does not experience this switch

---

[4] This price is determined by the equality of supply and demand within the customs union.

in supply; its trade with the 'extreme' country and its trade with the rest of the world are less close substitutes, and therefore less vulnerable to trade diversion.

Results from a model

A more general analysis of these issues requires a model in which (unlike the Ricardian model of the preceding subsection) countries do not completely specialize and all countries trade both within the FTA and externally. Such a model is developed and analysed in Venables (2000), and here we just illustrate some of the main points from it. The model is a generalization of a Heckscher–Ohlin trade model, and assumes that all countries have the same technology and have different endowments of two factors, which we refer to as skilled and unskilled labour, S and U. There are three countries, one of which—the rest of the world—is large, and is endowed with equal quantities of these two factors.[5] Countries 1 and 2 may have factor endowments different from each other and from the rest of the world, and these differences are the basis of their comparative advantage.

Each country can produce three goods. One is a non-tradeable, and uses S and U symmetrically (so has isoquants symmetric around the 45° line). The other two are tradeable, and use S and U in different proportions. Each of these goods is differentiated by location of production—an Armington assumption. We impose this primarily for computational convenience, and set the amount of product differentiation at a minimal level—the elasticity of substitution between products from different locations is 50 in the examples that follow. Also, for ease of interpretation, we impose symmetry between the two tradeable products, assuming that they take the same share in consumption, and that the factor intensity of one industry is the reciprocal of that in the other industry.

The model is constructed such that prices in the rest of the world are unity, and this we take to be the world price ratio, held constant in all experiments. In the initial equilibrium all of the imports of Countries 1 and 2 face the same tariff rate, regardless of source or commodity type. The internal price ratios and trade patterns of Countries 1 and 2 reflect these tariffs and each country's factor abundance. The experiment we study is the removal of the tariff between Countries 1 and 2; we want to see how outcomes depend on the endowments of the two countries, relative to each other and to the rest of the world.

Results are illustrated on Fig. 2, the axes of which give the Country 1 and 2 factor endowments, expressed as deviations from unity. Thus, point 0 on the horizontal axis corresponds to a point where $S_2 = U_2 = 1$, giving Country 2 the same endowment ratio as the rest of the world. To the right of this, Country 2 becomes S abundant and U scarce. As S_2 is increased, so we reduce U_2 to hold their sum constant; thus, at point $\Delta S_2 = 0.4$ we also have $\Delta U_2 = -0.4$, so the endowment levels are $S_2 = 1.4$, $U_2 = 0.6$. Similarly on the vertical axis; Country 1 is S abundant (relative to the world) above point 0 and U abundant below. While comparison of countries' endowments with those of the rest of the world is done with reference to the 0 points on each axis, comparison of Country 1 with

---

[5] This fixes the units of measurement for the two factors.

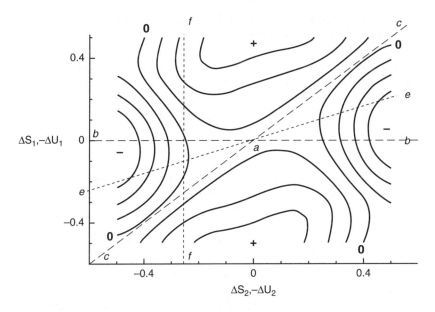

Figure 2. *Country 2 welfare change contours*

Country 2 is done with reference to the 45° line (labelled *cc*). Above this line Country 1 is S abundant relative to Country 2, while below the line it is U abundant.

The contour lines on the figure are the Country 2 welfare changes caused by formation of the FTA with Country 1.[6] The lines marked 00 are the zero contour, and the plus and minus signs indicate regions of Country 2's gain and loss from FTA formation. The welfare surface forms a saddle, with very small gains occurring along the 45° line, on which the countries have the same relative endowments.[7]

The figure illustrates, first, that the gains from union between Countries 1 and 2 are largest for a country with relative factor endowment close to that of the rest of the world. Thus, the highest levels of welfare change for Country 2 arise when the Country 2 endowment ratio is the same as the rest of the world's, $\Delta S_2 = -\Delta U_2 = 0$. And, secondly, the gains for this country are largest if the country with which it forms the FTA has a relatively extreme endowment, well away (in either direction) from that of the rest of the world (that is, at the top and bottom of the figure).

The reason is as we have argued previously. If a country has endowment like that of the rest of the world, there is little scope for trade diversion; it is doing little trade with the rest of the world in the initial situation, so the potential amount of trade that can be diverted is small. Forming an FTA with a country with a very different endowment maximizes the scope for trade creation.

---

[6] Welfare is measured as the utility of a single representative consumer.
[7] The welfare gain on line *cc* arises only because of the Armington assumption and the small amount of product differentiation we have introduced.

The converse of this is that countries with 'extreme' endowments, well away from that of the rest of the world, are most likely to suffer a welfare loss. Thus, if S_2 is very low (or high), Country 2 is likely to experience welfare loss, particularly if its partner is like the rest of the world (ΔS_1 close to zero). In the two triangle-shaped regions marked *cab*, both countries' endowment ratios are on the same side of the world ratio, but Country 2's is further away than Country 1's. Inspection of the figure indicates that these are regions in which Country 2 is relatively likely to experience welfare loss.

Convergence and divergence

We can now address the question, does FTA membership promote convergence or divergence of members' real incomes? Let us suppose that Country 2's endowment is always more extreme than Country 1's, and do an experiment in which we vary their difference from the world average. The precise experiment is to vary endowments along the line *ee* in Fig. 2. At all points on this line Country 2 is more extreme than Country 1, but the two countries vary from being U abundant relative to the world to being S abundant.

Fig. 3 gives the welfare effects of FTA formation for this set of endowments. Country 2 always does worse than Country 1 (except at point 0, where they have the same endowments as the rest of the world, and both experience the same gain from forming a union). As 1 and 2 become more different from the world average, so 2 does even worse—relatively and absolutely—and 1 does better; essentially, as comparative advantage differences open up, so welfare changes are magnified.

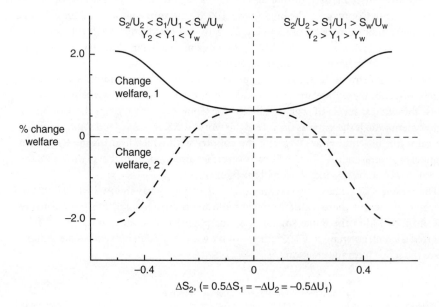

Figure 3. *Welfare change along line ee*

The welfare *changes* from forming the FTA that are reported on Figs. 2 and 3 can also be related to underlying welfare *levels*. It will generally be the case that initial welfare levels depend on factor endowments—so, for example, per capita income is higher the more physical or human capital there is per worker. Let us suppose then that economies that have higher endowments of S relative to U have, initially, higher per capita income levels.[8] Starting at a point on the left of Fig. 3, this means that Country 2 has little S relative to U, and a low initial income, relative both to Country 1 and to the rest of the world (as summarized at the top of the figure, where Y_i denotes real income, and subscript W denotes the rest of the world). Formation of the FTA therefore reduces the welfare of the low-income country (2), and raises welfare in the higher-income country (1). But now select a point to the right of point 0, at which Country 2 is initially relatively well endowed with S and has relatively high income: it is now the relatively high-income country (2) that loses and the lower-income country (1) that gains.

What this shows is that FTAs between low-income countries will cause divergence of real income, with the low-income (extreme endowment) country losing. FTAs between high-income countries will cause convergence, with the high-income (extreme endowment) country losing.

We have already discussed a hypothetical example of the low income case, with our Uganda–Kenya FTA. The high-income analogue might be, say France and Portugal. If France is relatively S abundant (so higher income), then it would be better off importing its U intensive products from the rest of the world than from Portugal—which has a comparative advantage in such products relative to France but not relative to the rest of the world, the FTA causes France trade diversion. But for Portugal the FTA results in an increase in imports of S-intensive products from France and the price of these in S-abundant France is less than the world price. Thus in this high-income FTA it is the high-income country that suffers trade diversion, and the low-income one that experiences trade creation.

North-south agreements

The preceding subsection looked at a case in which both members of the FTA are on the same side of the world average. What if the two countries are on different sides—a 'north-south' FTA? To explore this let us fix the endowment of Country 2 and show how the effects of FTA membership depend on the endowment of its partner. In terms of Fig. 2, the comparisons we make are along line *ff*, with Country 2 endowment fixed at a moderately U abundant level ($\Delta S_2 = -0.25$), and Country 1's varying from U abundant to S abundant. The welfare changes from FTA formation for this set of endowments are illustrated on Fig 4, with Country 1's factor abundance varying along the horizontal axis.

What type of partner is best for Country 2 (assumed moderately U abundant)? From Fig. 4 we see that it does well with either a very U-abundant or a very S-abundant partner. What it wants to avoid is a partner that is close to the world average.

[8] Factor endowments are both inputs to production and sources of household income. Once an ownership structure of factors is specified, changes in the ratio of S to U will generally change household income. Providing such a change is monotonic, the argument of the text goes through.

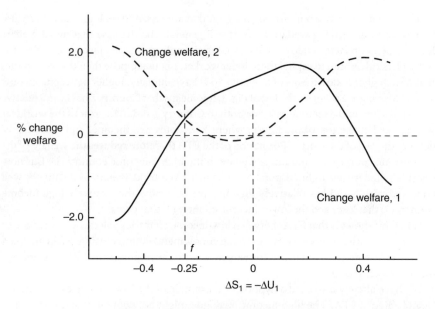

Figure 4. *Welfare change along line ff:* $\Delta S_2 = -0.25$

The logic behind avoiding a country similar to the world average (for example, in the interval between f and 0) is as we have described before. Country 2 has little scope for trade creation, but maximum scope for trade diversion, as its partner comes between it and the rest of the world.

The benefits from picking a country with even higher U abundance (to the left of f, where $\Delta S_1 < \Delta S_2 = -0.25$) is also as we have seen. Country 2 has trade creation, since its partner has comparative advantage quite different from the rest of the world. However, in this 'south–south' agreement Country 2's gain is associated with a much worse outcome for the partner country.

The 'north–south' agreement ($\Delta S_1 > 0$), by contrast, offers gains for Country 2 and for the partner. They both benefit from liberalizing trade with a partner country that has a very different factor endowment. Both countries' production structures move towards production of the good intensive in the factor with which they are abundantly endowed. This factor abundance is now relative to each other *and* relative to the rest of the world, and it is this that creates the mutual benefits.

Increasing the S abundance of the partner country (1) brings increasing gains for Country 2.[9] However, Country 1's welfare change turns down beyond some point, eventually becoming a loss. The intuition is that, once Country 1 becomes extremely S abundant, then the FTA as a whole is S abundant relative to the rest of the world. At the margin, Country 1 would then do better expanding trade with the rest of the world than within the FTA.

---

[9] Until quite extreme levels, at which point countries have moved to the edge of their cones of diversification.

Pulling this together, we see a strong case for 'north–south' integration schemes. If Country 2 links with another U abundant country ($\Delta S_1 < 0$ on Fig. 4), then it may gain or lose, and any gains it makes usually come at a cost to its partner, so at least one of the 'southern' countries is losing. But if it joins an FTA with an S-abundant country ($\Delta S_1 > 0$), then Country 2 gains—as may its partner also.

III. AGGLOMERATION AND CUMULATIVE CAUSATION

Comparative advantage is not the only force that drives relocation of activity in an FTA. As economic centres start to develop, so 'cumulative causation' mechanisms come into effect, leading to the spatial clustering (or agglomeration) of economic activity, and extending the advantage of locations that have a head start.[10]

Spatial clustering of economic activities is all pervasive. Cities exist because businesses, workers, and consumers benefit from being in close proximity. Particular types of activity are frequently clustered, the most spectacular examples being the electronics industries of Silicon Valley, cinema in Hollywood, and the concentration of banking activities in the world's financial districts. Clustering also occurs in many manufacturing industries—for example, US automobile manufacturing in the Detroit area, or industries such as medical equipment, printing machinery, and others studied by Porter (1990).

We can analyse clustering by thinking of it as the outcome of a balance between 'centripetal' forces, encouraging firms to locate close to each other, and 'centrifugal' forces, encouraging them to spread out. We want to ask whether membership of an FTA changes this balance, promoting concentration—or deconcentration—of activities. Let us start by outlining the main centripetal and centrifugal forces.

The centripetal forces are usually classified in three groups (Marshall 1920). The first are knowledge spillovers, or other beneficial technological externalities that make it attractive for firms to locate close to each other—in Marshall's phrase, 'the mysteries of the trade become no mysteries, but are, as it were, in the air . . . ' The second are various labour-market pooling effects, which encourage firms to locate where they can benefit from readily available labour skills—perhaps by attracting skilled labour away from existing firms. The third centripetal force arises from 'linkages' between buyers and sellers. Firms will, other things being equal, want to locate where their customers are, and customers will want to locate close to their suppliers. These linkages are simply the 'backwards' (demand) and 'forwards' (supply) linkages of Hirschman (1958). They create a positive interdependence between the location decisions of different firms, and this can give rise to a process of cumulative causation, creating agglomerations of activity.[11]

These centripetal or agglomeration forces can operate at quite an aggregate level, or can be much more narrowly focused. For example, aggregate demand creates a backwards linkage, drawing firms from all sectors into locations with large markets. Some agglomeration forces affect broad classes of business activity—providing basic industrial

---

[10] This section is based on Puga and Venables (1998) and Fujita *et al.* (1999).

[11] This argument works only if there are increasing returns to scale in production. (If not, firms can put small plants in many different locations.) For formal analysis, see Fujita *et al.* (1999).

labour skills, or access to business services such as finance and telecommunications. In contrast, other forces are more spatially focused. Knowledge spillovers affecting particular technologies, or the availability of highly specialized inputs, might operate at the level of a narrowly defined industry. In this case the forces work for clustering of the narrowly defined sector, rather than for clustering of manufacturing as a whole.

Pulling in the opposite direction are 'centrifugal forces', encouraging the dispersion of activity. These include congestion, pollution, or other externalities that might be associated with concentrations of economic activity. Competition for immobile factors will deter agglomeration, as the price of land and perhaps also labour is bid up in centres of activity. In addition, there is demand from consumers who are located outside the centres of activity; dispersed consumers will encourage dispersion of producers, particularly if trade barriers or transport costs are high.

How might the balance between centripetal and centrifugal forces be upset by membership of an FTA? Can membership cause, or amplify, the clustering of economic activity, and if so might it widen income differentials between partner countries?

By reducing trade barriers, membership in an FTA makes it easier to supply consumers (or customers more generally) from a few locations. This suggests that the balance of forces may be tipped in favour of agglomeration, although the ensuing relocation of industry could develop in several different ways.

One possibility is that particular sectors become more spatially concentrated, and this is likely if the centripetal forces act at a quite narrow, sectoral level. For example, industries in the USA are much more spatially concentrated than in Europe (even controlling for the distribution of population and manufacturing as a whole), suggesting that regional integration in Europe could cause agglomeration at the sectoral level (for example, Germany gets engineering, the UK financial services, and so on). The possibility that this might happen is generating some concern in Europe, although evidence for it is so far rather weak. If it does happen, it will create considerable adjustment costs— as the industrial structure of different locations changes—but aggregate benefits, as there are real efficiency gains from spatial concentration. This sectoral agglomeration need not be associated with increases in inequalities in intra Regional Integration Agreements; each country or region may attract activity in some sectors.

An alternative possibility is that, instead of relatively small sectors each clustering in different locations, manufacturing as a whole comes to cluster in a few locations, deindustrializing the less-favoured regions. In this case, it is likely to lead to divergence of the income levels of members of the FTA. Under what circumstances might this be the outcome? It will be relatively more likely to occur if manufacturing as a whole is a small share of the economy. This is because fitting the whole of manufacturing in one (or a few) locations is then less likely to press up against factor supply constraints and lead to rising prices of immobile factors (such as land). It will be more likely if linkages are broad, across many sectors, rather than narrowly sector specific. This in turn is more likely in early stages of development, where a country's basic industrial infrastructure—transport, telecommunications, access to financial markets and other business services—is thinly developed and unevenly spread. And it will be more likely to occur with preferential trade liberalization—an FTA—than with general import liberalization. This is because an FTA is inherently more inward looking, strengthening linkages between firms in the FTA, so increasing one of the centripetal forces.

These arguments suggest that there is possibility that FTA membership could lead to agglomeration. For industrialized countries this is more likely at the sectoral level, in which case it need not lead to divergence of per capita income levels. But for countries with less-developed industrial sectors, it is more likely to occur at the level of industry as a whole, in which case it will foster income divergence.

We expect that these agglomeration forces will interact with the comparative advantage arguments we made in the preceding section. In south–south FTAs they are likely to be reinforcing. For example, as Nairobi, Abidjan, and Dakar have attracted manufacturing, so they have started to develop business networks and the linkages that tend to lock manufacturing into the location. The process might be further accelerated by the propensity of foreign direct investment to cluster in relatively few locations. Agglomeration then accentuates the comparative advantage forces for divergence. In 'north–south' FTAs that span a wide range of factor endowment ratios, the forces may pull in opposite directions. For example, firms choosing locations in Europe may want the agglomeration benefits of locating in France, but factor price differences create an incentive for them to locate in Portugal.

IV. CONCLUDING COMMENTS

The analysis contained in this paper has not covered all the forces that might drive convergence or divergence of income levels between member countries of an FTA, and in 'north–south' FTAs in particular additional forces for convergence are likely to operate. For example, a country may be able to use the agreement as a commitment mechanism to lock in economic reforms. This seems to have happened in Mexico with NAFTA, and in the agreements between the EU and East European economies. An FTA may also promote technology transfer from the high-income country to lower-income members. Although the mechanisms of technology transfer are not fully understood, an important body of work argues that it is promoted by trade flows. For example, Coe and Helpman (1995) and Coe, Helpman, and Hoffmaister (1997) construct an index of total knowledge capital in each industrial country, and assume that trading partners get access to a country's stock of knowledge in proportion to their imports from that country. They find that access to foreign knowledge is a statistically significant determinant of the rate of total factor productivity across OECD and developing countries.[12] Thus an FTA might promote technology transfer via its effect on trade. Similarly, FTAs typically promote foreign direct investment, another likely source of technology transfer. These considerations probably reinforce the argument that a 'north–south' FTA may promote convergence of income levels.

---

[12] The conclusion has been challenged because the paper assumes, rather than tests, that imports from industrial countries provide the correct weights with which to combine stocks of foreign knowledge. Keller (1998) has suggested that the results are little better than would be obtained from relating total factor productivity to a random weighting of foreign knowledge stocks.

What we have shown in this paper is that the distribution of the benefits of an FTA can be linked directly to the comparative advantage of member countries—comparative advantage relative to each other and to the rest of the world. This leads to the strong result that FTAs between low-income countries will tend to cause divergence of their income levels, whereas FTAs between high-income levels will lead to convergence. We have argued that agglomeration forces might amplify divergence forces in FTAs between low-income countries. The analysis suggests that developing countries are likely to gain more from FTAs with high-income countries, where there are better prospects for convergence with the other—high-income—members.

REFERENCES

Baldwin, R., and Venables, A. J. (1995), 'Regional Economic Integration', in G. Grossman and K. Rogoff (eds.), *Handbook of International Economics*, iii (Amsterdam: North Holland).

Ben-David, D. (1993), 'Equalizing Exchange: Trade Liberalization and Income Convergence', *Quarterly Journal of Economics*, 108: 653–79.

Coe, D. T., and Helpman, E. (1995), 'International R & D Spillovers', *European Economic Review*, 39: 859–87.

—— —— and Hoffmaister, A. (1997), 'North–South R & D Spillovers', *Economic Journal*, 107: 134–49.

Frankel, J. (1995), *Regional Trading Blocs in the World Economic System* (Washington: IEE).

Fujita, M., Krugman, P., and Venables, A. J. (1999), 'The Spatial Economy: Cities, Regions and International Trade' (Cambridge, Mass.: MIT Press).

Hirschman, A. (1958), *The Strategy of Economic Development* (New Haven: Yale University Press).

Keller, W. (1998), 'Are International R & D Spillovers Trade-Related? Analyzing Spillovers among Randomly Matched Partners', *European Economic Review*, 42: 1469–81.

Marshall, A. (1920), *Principles of Economics*, 8th edn. (London: Macmillan).

Porter, M. E. (1990), *The Competitive Advantage of Nations* (New York: Macmillan).

Puga, D., and Venables, A. J. (1998), 'Trading Arrangements and Industrial Development', *World Bank Economic Review*, 12: 221–49.

Venables, A. J. (2000), 'Winners and Losers from Regional Integration Agreements', Discussion Paper, Centre for Economic Policy Research, London.

Viner, J. (1950), *The Customs Union Issue* (New York: Carnegie Endowment for International Peace).

16

Asymmetric Regionalism in Sub-Saharan Africa: Where Do We Stand?

OLIVIER CADOT, JAIME DE MELO,
AND MARCELO OLARREAGA

The paper reviews the likely economic effects of the Regional Economic Partnership Agreements (REPAs) proposed by the European Union (EU) to the ACP (African, Caribbean, Pacific) countries to succeed to the Lomé IV agreements. We argue that, in spite of some likely positive effects because of reciprocity and the North–South partnership, the pronounced asymmetries among the southern partners will lead to strong redistributive and marginalization effects that will require compensations that are likely to be costly to implement. It is also pointed out that efforts at regional cooperation agreements would avoid some of the shortcomings associated with the proposed discriminatory trade preferences that would accompany the proposed REPAs. And, if the REPAs are negotiated, they should be accompanied by compensatory transfers from the European Union (EU) for tax revenues losses attributable to the agreements.

The recent growth in Regional Integration Agreements (RIAs) has been numerically dominated by the EU's activities. Among these are the European agreements with countries of Eastern Europe, the renewal of RIAs with Mediterranean countries, and, currently, the European Commission's proposal to put EU–ACP trade relations on a reciprocal basis for those ACP (Africa, Caribbean, Pacific) countries wishing to enter into a Regional Economic Partnership Agreement (REPA) with the EU. This proposal for cooperation (to become Lomé V if it is carried out) is to replace Lomé IV.[1] While it is recognized that this proposal is part of the EU's 'foreign policy', it is also understood that 'one of the key objectives of the EU's development cooperation under the Maastricht Treaty is the smooth and gradual integration of developing countries into the world

We thank participants for useful comments. Any views are the authors' and should not be attributed to any of their respective affiliations.

[1] Granting preferential access has been a cornerstone of the EC/EU's approach in its relations with its former colonies, but so far there has been no reciprocity, and the beneficiaries were not requested to enter in RIAs among themselves. Instead of the proposed Lomé V route to be discussed here, the EU could have opted either for: (1) an extension of the GSP to non-ACP developing countries, perhaps including differential preferences according to per capita income; (2) bring down most favoured nation tariffs to Lomé levels, requesting in exchange that other OECD members also reduce tariffs in sectors of interest to ACP exporters. Stevens et al. (1998) explore the first option, and Winters (1998) gives convincing arguments in support of the second alternative.

economy. It is widely recognized that regional integration forms an essential part of the strategy for achieving this' (Kennes 1998: 26).[2]

These 'new' elements in the Lomé V approach to cooperation are: (1) reciprocity in the trade relations between the EU and the ACP countries—an element that was supposed to be present in their trade relations early on, but was abandoned; (2) encouragement of prior RIAs among the countries that would enter REPAs—for example, the West African Monetary Union (WAMU) and Ghana would be encouraged to form an FTA (and there would be encouragement for all ACP countries to join the WTO); (3) a preferential trading arrangement (with about 80–90 percent of bilateral trade between the EU and REPAs abolished over a ten-year period (2005–2015)) with REPA members allowed to 'backload' their reforms, postponing the main tariff reductions till the end of the period.

This paper takes a critical look at these new elements from the point of view of the ACP countries, whose alternatives, as members of the WTO, are essentially a reliance on non-discriminatory trade policies based on a combination of unilateral and multilateral trade liberalization. It draws on recent work evaluating the regional approach to trade (and other) policies at the theoretical and empirical levels. Finding new approaches to trade policy in sub-Saharan Africa (SSA) is arguably urgent, as a compelling case can be made that the poor performance of SSA countries is partly due to their poor trade performance: falling market shares in world markets and higher than average tariff and non-tariff protection than comparable countries.[3] Also, previous attempts at regionalism, by and large, failed, both in terms of their ambitious objectives and in terms of their accomplishments.

In spite of being able to draw on recent work,[4] much of what follows relies on a priori reasoning, and tenuous comparisons with experience elsewhere. It is mostly guesswork, both because it is difficult to judge the likely effects of these proposals, and because it is hard to foresee what the ACP countries would do in the alternative of no REPA. Section I looks at some of the implications of the asymmetries within the proposed regional groupings and Section II at the credibility arguments of north–south agreements. Section III argues that the focus on preferential agreements should not detract from the potentially large (and non-controversial) gains to be had from other forms of non-discriminatory cooperation.

---

[2] Grilli (1993) is the authoritative source on the EU's approach to relations with the ACP countries. Sapir (1998) reviews the dimensions of EU regionalism and Solignac Lecomte (1999) provides a broader perspective, taking into account the diplomatic aspects of reciprocity in the REPAs.

[3] Over the period 1962–4 to 1991–3, the SSA share of world exports declined by $11 billion per year. Wang and Winters (1998) show that this is due to a general loss of competitiveness, as the share of OECD imports of the 'newer' SSA exports fell from 9.4% to 6.3%. At the same time, the average tariffs in SSA were 26% compared with 17% for other developing countries and non-tariff barrier (NTB) coverage ratios were 34% compared with 18%. For arguments as to why trade reform is difficult in Africa, see Rodrik (1998).

[4] Foroutan (1993) gives a thorough review of the reasons for failure of previous attempts at regional integration in SSA. Oyejide (1996), Wang and Winters (1998), Winters (1998), and World Bank (1999) provide more recent evaluations.

I. ASYMMETRIES, TRANSFERS AND COMPENSATIONS, AND MARGINALIZATION.

Pronounced asymmetries between countries, the small size of each proposed regional bloc, and the structure of their foreign trade and of their tariff structure suggest predictions on the likely economic effects of the proposed two-stage regional approach to integration in world markets.[5]

Consider the first stage, where countries are to form regional FTAs prior to joining REPAs. The standard Vinerian analysis of preferential trading arrangements suggests that the potential for trade creation of these regional FTAs is low, as these countries have very similar patterns of trade, importing and exporting similar goods. These characteristics imply a very substitutable pattern of trade, which raises concerns of relatively large trade diverting effects of these FTAs. Michaely's (1996) trade complementarity index indicates that NAFTA and the EU-15 members have a within-members complementarity index twelve times larger than SSA countries, and MERCOSUR three times larger.[6]

Moreover, compared to other developing countries with FTAs, tariff levels and dispersions are high in SSA (averages followed by coefficients of variation in parentheses): SSA (19.6 percent; 0.73); Latin America (11.6 percent; 0.56). Usually, the large country in each grouping is the more industrialized, with the higher tariff and perhaps the sole producer.[7] So, unless there is simultaneously across-the-board trade liberalization with the rest of the world, there will be a large income transfer in terms of forgone tariff revenue to the dominating country in the group.

By and large, the second stage in which the REPAs will be implemented provide one-way market access for EU exporters in ACP markets. Indeed, ACP countries pretty much have zero-duty market access into the EU for manufactures and non-sensitive agricultural products, sensitive agricultural products being, at this stage, excluded from the REPAs. Currently, post-Uruguay round average tariffs for developing countries exporters are 4.5 percent for industrial goods and 1.5 percent for non-agricultural primaries (Finger *et al.* 1996), so that market access gains will be negligible. Such an outcome is all the more likely now that the EU has RIAs with all but seven countries in the world (see Sapir 1998: table 1), so that any preferential market access is likely to get translated into lower prices for EU consumers than into accrued rents for ACP producers. Finally, if the REPAs are indeed to substitute rest-of-the-world imports with EU imports, the loss in government revenue could be substantial and unevenly distributed (see below).

[5] There is a considerable literature on the trade-diversion and trade-creation aspects of RIAs. See e.g., Anderson and Blackhurst (1993), de Melo and Panagariya (1993), and Bhagwati and Panagariya (1996). The discussion here draws on these sources and on CERDI (1998) and Winters (1998).

[6] The Michaely trade complementarity index between country i and country j is given by $C_{ij} = 100 - \Sigma_k(|m_{ik} - x_{jk}|)/2$, where x_{jk} is the share of good k in total exports of country j and m_{ik} is the share of good k in all imports of country i. It reflects the low share of intra-regional trade in SSA of 12% (5% for oil exporters and 16.5 for non-oil exporters) as the region exports 80% of its production to OECD countries (Yeats 1998a), 51% to the EU, and 24% to NAFTA), which again raises questions regarding the potential benefits of intra-regional preferential trade agreements.

[7] For example, in the WAMU, the Côte d'Ivoire had higher tariffs in 1997 than other members for all broad categories of goods (region-wide averages after the semi-colon). Producer goods (15.1; 7.8); intermediates (19.5; 10.5); consumer goods (29.6; 18.1) CERDI 1998: table 3.

Transfers and compensation. Strong asymmetry in size is a particularity of most SSA RIAs: Kenya dominates the East African Community (EAC), the Côte d'Ivoire the WAMU, Cameroon the Central African Customs Union (CEMAC), South Africa the South African Development Cooperation (SADC), and Egypt the proposed Common Market for Eastern and Southern Africa (COMESA).[8] In each grouping, there is a 'hegemon' whose presence brings the following remarks.

First, the hegemon is likely to be far from the world efficient suppliers (with the exception perhaps of South Africa). In each SSA grouping, government revenue from trade taxes is usually around 30 percent of government revenue, but up to 50 percent (or 7.3 percent of GDP) for the WAMU in 1995. How much revenue would be transferred from the poorest to the richest? In the case of the EAC, Yeats (1998*b*) estimates that the full implementation of an FTA for the EAC would result in an 8–10 percent decline in customs collection for Uganda and a 5–6 percent percent decline for Tanzania. Given the dependence of SSA governments on trade taxes, the transfers alluded to above could become quickly politically (or budgetarily) unsustainable, unless the hegemon also reduces substantially its protection against the outside world.[9]

Secondly, in the case of a customs union (as is under way for the WAMU), one can, in principle at least, avoid transfers to the richest economy if the Common External Tariff (CET) is set at the level of the country with the lowest tariff. Then, there will be no incentives for inefficient producers to increase their production and sell it in the more protected markets within the FTA. As shown by Richardson (1995), this outcome may occur endogenously if governments are conscious of the income transfers related to preferential trade, as in a non-cooperative framework there will be Bertrand-type competition leading to a 'race to the bottom' via competition for tariff revenues. In an extension of Richardson's analysis, Cadot *et al.* (1999) show such an outcome is likely to happen endogenously only when countries are of relatively similar size (that is, when every member can inundate other members' markets). If countries vary in size (as is the case in SSA), they show that these forces are not at play, as the large members may actually have incentives to increase their tariff.

Thirdly, given the poorly developed fiscal systems and the estimated size of the revenue loss, increases in VAT rates would be too large to be implementable. So, unless the EU comes up with compensation, it will be a challenge to find ways of reaching fiscal balance without introducing distortionary compensation, as was the case in the previous preferential trading arrangements (PTAs) in SSA (see Foroutan 1993).

Fourthly, in the case of franc zone countries, in spite of the relatively high degree of policy coordination in the franc zone, which has prevented large deviation in trade policies in the region, differences in structure are likely to require different patterns of

---

[8] One would be tempted to speak of 'hegemonic' RIAs though, so far, this is only relevant in the case of the South African Customs Union (SACU). Interestingly, this is a typical 'North-South' RIA whose experience has relevance in an assessment of the REPAs. Rodrik (1998) argues that Botswana's superior economic performance is largely due to her having delegated her trade policy formulation to South Africa.

[9] The sustainability of MERCOSUR is largely due to such an approach of simultaneous opening to the outside world: Brazil reduced its tariffs from 80% in 1986 to 12% in 1995, Argentina from 41 to 11%, Uruguay from 36 to 11% and Paraguay from 20 to 9%.

adjustments, which will be more difficult to achieve without use of the exchange rate as they belong to a monetary union.[10]

Marginalization. Among the causes of failure of the first wave of south–south regionalism was the inability to agree on the location of industry investment. The new wave of RIAs has moved away from central planning and views regional integration as a way to promote investment, win capital inflows, and affect industry location. Foreign direct investment (FDI) from outside countries could increase as a result of the two-stage regional strategy proposed by the EU, though the 'hub-and-spoke' approach to regionalism followed by the EU biases investment towards the hub rather than towards the spokes. First, regional FTAs would give duty-free access to a larger market, which raises the return on investment.[11] Secondly, the reciprocity of the REPAs could bring multinationals to redirect investment to SSA, as the environment would be perceived as sufficiently stable and predictable to bring multinationals to set up export platforms.[12]

Marginalization of the periphery would also be predicted by 'economic geography' models that suggest that reciprocal liberalization will draw industry into the country with the larger market and away from the smaller countries as centripetal forces operating through demand and cost linkages will dominate centrifugal forces.[13] Such effects are not universal though (for example, Portugal and Spain in their accession to the EU), but are likely to be less pronounced in unilateral or multilateral trade liberalization. Thus RIAs in SSA can be expected to lead to further divergence among asymmetric countries and to deindustrialization of the smaller countries. For example, FDI flows into the MERCOSUR have favored Argentina and Brazil.

In SSA, the tensions created by industry agglomeration have already been important during the first wave of RIAs in the 1950s and 1960s. For example, the EAC collapsed in 1977 as it failed to satisfy the poorer members that they were getting a fair share of the gains. Similar tensions are building in the community again and are likely to develop in all the region groupings in SSA where the dominating economy in the region will reap most of the benefits from the RIAs, yet be unable to compensate the losing partners both because of lack of institutions and political will (strife and political tensions are widespread in that part of the world).

[10] If the experience of integration among unequal partners elsewhere applies, in the case of the MERCOSUR, sectors with significant trade creation will be exempted, the convergence to the CET will be slower than scheduled (in the WAMU it is scheduled for 2000), and the CET will represent the preferences of the member country that has the greatest production in the sector.

[11] Excluding Egypt and South Africa, the combined GDP of SSA countries barely exceeded that of Belgium in 1995. With such small markets, unit production costs could fall substantially because of unexploited economies of scale.

[12] Following the creation of NAFTA, FDI to Mexico increased substantially ($4.3 billion in 1991 to $11 billion in 1994). Likewise, FDI inflow into the EU expanded from ECU 10 billion in 1984 to ECU 63 billion in 1989. One would expect the REPA effect to dominate as the evidence of south–south RIAs on investment and growth shows negligible effects (see Brada and Mendez 1988; de Melo *et al.* 1993).

[13] Centripetal forces include: knowledge spillovers or other beneficial technological externalities; labor-market pooling effects; linkages between buyers and sellers as firms will want to locate close to buyers. Centrifugal forces include: congestion, pollution, or other externalities associated with concentrations of economic activity; competition for immobile factors whose prices are bid up by agglomeration; demand coming from dispersed consumers.

II. WHICH EXTERNAL ANCHOR?

Because of recidivism in the past and because of changes in government policies, it has been argued that north–south RIAs in SSA could increase credibility. Collier and Gunning (1995) argue that for a number of factors, including the heavy conditionality on aid disbursement, SSA countries face time-consistency problems, which explain why so many reforms in the past have been reversed. A north–south RIA along the proposed lines would help solve this problem and serve as a signaling device in a world of asymmetric information.

Fernandez and Portes (1998) develop the arguments why such benefits from RIAs are not as readily available within the multilateral framework of the WTO. Winters (1998) sees merits to this argument, though he notes that credibility is not an independent characteristic of RIAs (a beneficial RIA is more credible than one that is not beneficial) and also that there are other means of signaling and winning credibility, as, for instance, in binding trade policy with the WTO. Here it is instructive that SSA governments have generally bound their tariffs at several multiples of the rates currently applied.[14] The opportunity to signal tough-mindedness has not been taken.

Because the EU is a large market accounting for close to half of ACP trade for some regions, one could argue that the insurance motive of market access in case of a trade war is relevant. Equally relevant is the motive to avoid the major partners' contingent protection: safeguards and anti-dumping duties. Winters believes that the EU will not be willing to give up the right to exercise anti-dumping duties against its partners.

Rewards and punishments. While the WTO is not likely to be a good means of achieving enforcement and avoiding recidivism, it is not clear that the EU will be any better, especially in its dealings with former colonies. If Mexico raised its tariffs following the 1994 crisis, it is hard to see how the EU will be able to oppose similar behavior by ACP countries, especially if tariffs are raised against third countries, which is an available option given the very high rates at which tariffs are bound. One could imagine that ACP countries would not dare raise tariffs on EU products, so they would end up raising tariffs to the outside world, but even more so to get the same revenue increase with the well-known deleterious effects on welfare, since the costs of protection increase with the square of the tariff level.

For the extra-credibility gains to be had from anchoring to the EU rather to the WTO, the negotiations should yield a fairly stringent set of rewards and punishments. Take as an example the WAMU which is setting up a customs union by 2000 and is engaged in talks for a REPA to be carried out over the period 2005–17 with much backloading (over 50 percent of the reductions for sensitive products starting in 2013).

CERDI (1998) estimates revenue effects for each country in the region by aggregating separate estimates for each individual product in a standard partial equilibrium demand and supply simulation analysis. The novel aspect of their estimates is the econometric

---

[14] CERDI (1998: table 8.1) reports the following rates (average tariffs followed by maximum bindings in brackets with a semi-colon separating agriculture and industry: Benin (6.1 [119]; 6.9 [69]); Côte d'Ivoire (17.5 [221]; 14.7 [260]); Senegal (26.5 [180]; 30.1 [180]).

estimation of the relationship between exemption rates and tariff levels, which is subsequently built into analysis (thereby lowering revenue loss estimates by about one-half).[15]

Based on the CET rates agreed in July 1998 (consumer goods (9.8 percent); intermediates (10.9 per cent); capital goods (6.9 percent)), the WAMU should have a customs union by 2000 with fairly low and uniform tariffs close to the levels of the low-protection country, much as was suggested above. Though the estimates reveal much variance across countries, for the WAMU as a whole, the annual loss of moving to the lower CET level is estimated at 0.23 percent of annual WAMU GDP. And moving to the REPA by 2017 would give an extra annual loss of 0.59 percent on an annual basis. Given the small GDP of the region ($33 billion in 1997), compensating for government losses during transition to the REPA would require only $19.5 billion on an annual basis from the EU. It seems that the EU should be able to come up with an incentive scheme, conditional on performance, that would compensate for government revenue loss during the transition. Such a proposal would also have the added advantage of helping reveal the 'true type' of ACP countries at the negotiating table.

III. A GREATER ROLE FOR REGIONAL COOPERATION

Africa has set up over 200 regional cooperation schemes in the last thirty years, most of them involving preferential trading arrangements that are discriminatory. However, there are two other types of non-discriminatory arrangements that merit attention in SSA, even though asymmetries in country sizes, interests, and the general lack of institutional development in the region make them hard to implement. The first is cooperative arrangements (for example, the sharing of training costs, and of projects with economics of scale such as infrastructure or power-sharing); the second is cooperation in the management of a common resource that generates externalities in its use and where property rights are uncertain (for example, river basins). The second type of arrangement is more difficult to achieve, not only because, like the first, it must be self-enforcing,[16] but also because agreement on property rights must be reached. Following are two examples taken from World Bank (1999) and de Melo (1998).

The Southern African Power Pool (SAPP). Inaugurated in 1995, the SAPP represents an interesting case of cooperation in the power sector. Power exchange in the southern part of Africa first arose because of the distribution of power sources in the region: a large reserve of low-cost hydroelectricity in the northern part (especially the Inga Reservoir), large reserves of cheap coal in South Africa, and the Kariba dam (on the border between Zambia and Zimbabwe), which being in the middle of the regional system can play the 'buffer' role.

---

[15] The results are similar to those in Pritchett and Sethi (1994): exemptions are an increasing function of the height of the tariff, and in some cases of the variance of variance.

[16] Self-enforcement is necessary because, in contrast to agreements that internalize intranational externalities, international externalities cannot be enforced by a third party so that the agreements must include the mechanisms that by themselves can sustain a cooperative agreement. It is for this reason that, usually, only a few of the parties concerned participate and that the Pareto frontier is not reached in these agreements.

The benefits of the pool include reductions or postponements in new requirements for generating capacity and reserves, reductions in fuel costs, and more efficient use of hydroelectricity. A South African Development Cooperation (SADC) electric power study conducted in 1990–2 estimated a saving of 20 percent in costs over 1995–2010 amounting to $785 million (estimates would be larger if the Democratic Republic of Congo and South Africa, who are members, had been included in the study).

The agreements incorporate the SADC Treaty, the SADC Dispute Resolution Tribunal, the SADC energy ministers, and the Technical and Administrative Unit. The energy ministers are responsible for resolving the major policy issues in the SAPP, and the Technical and Administrative Unit for seeking funding according to recommendations of the executive committee. Three factors played a key part in the development of the regional agreement: the availability of complementary power sources, an active regional organization for economic cooperation, and the political will to support increased regional energy trade. The SADC served as a focal point for the promotion of regional integration facilitating investments in the needed interconnection projects.

Costs of non-cooperation along the Nile. The ten Nile riparians could gain much annually if the current annual allocation of 84 billion cubic meters (BCM) of water to Egypt and Sudan under a 1959 treaty was renegotiated. It is estimated that, if Blue Nile reservoirs were developed, there would be an increase in the annual long-term water yield of between 4 and 5 BCM annually. This is because along the Blue Nile evaporation rates are 50 percent of those downstream and reservoirs in mountainous terrain use lower surface-to-volume ratios. Likewise elimination of the antiquated Jebel Auria reservoir on the White Nile (that serves mostly for hydropower) would yield a reduction in evaporation loss of 2.8 BCM. Rough-and-ready calculations suggest that a better allocation of water among Blue Nile riparians could raise their annual growth rate by between 0.5 and 1 percentage point per annum.

Reaching an agreement is proving very difficult, because the unidirectional nature of upstream-downstream externalities makes it necessary to look for multi-good cooperation (for example, water and hydropower) as a way of concretizing this positive-sum gain. But introducing side issues may help in the case of a high degree of externalities, as this provides the necessary rewards for cooperation, and the punishment for defection requires a more elaborate institutional framework that is currently absent (though it could emerge in the development of COMESA, which could also help build trust).

These two examples, and there are others, show that there are sizeable gains to be obtained from regional cooperation in SSA. If the case can be made that regional integration on a preferential basis can be good politics as increased trade builds security,[17] it also points out that the institutional framework needs to be there (which can come from

---

[17] Using a standard Vinerian model in which security enters the utility function and is positively related to the volume of trade with neighboring countries, Schiff and Winters (1998) show that giving preferences to a neighbor raises welfare as it diminishes fear and the potential for conflict. They also cite evidence that the propensity for less conflict among democratic countries comes from a causality in which it is trade that reduces conflict rather than the opposite.

institutions developed in the course of PTAs, as in the case of the SADC). Two remarks are pertinent here: first, the proposed REPAs can help develop institutions that resemble those developed in the EU (as has been the case in the Europe agreements in certain areas). Secondly, there is a high opportunity cost to negotiations, especially in the human-capital scarce SSA countries. Since the gains from non-discriminatory cooperation are likely to be sizeable, scarce human capital should not be distracted to negotiating cumbersome, costly, and time-consuming necessary details that are part of every FTA (such as rules of origin).

REFERENCES

Anderson, K., and Blackhurst, R. (1993) (eds.), *Regional Integration and the World Trading System* (New York: Wheatsheaf).

Bhagwati, J., and Panagariya, A. (1996) (eds.), *Free Trade Areas or Free Trade?: The Economics of Preferential Trading Agreements* (Washington: AEI Press).

Blomstron, M., and Kokko, A. (1998), 'Regional Integration: A Conceptual Framework. Three Cases', Policy Research Working Paper, No. 1750, World Bank.

Brada, J., and Mendez, J. (1988), 'An Estimate of the Dynamic Effects of Economic Integration', *Review of Economics and Statistics*, 163–68.

Cadot, O., and de Melo, J. (1995), 'The Europe Agreements and EU–LDC Relations: The Case of France', in A. Kuvenhoyven, O. Memedovic, and N. Van der Windt (eds.), *Transition in Central and Eastern Europe: Implications for EU–LDC Relations* (Amsterdam: Kluwer Academic Publishers), 10–41.

—— ——and Olarreaga, M. (1999), 'Regional Integration and Lobbying for Tariffs against Non-Members', *International Economic Review*, 40: 635–58.

CERDI (1998), 'Étude de l'impact économique de l'introduction de la réciprocité dans les relations commerciales entre l'Union européenne et les pays de l'UEMOA et le Ghana.' Université d'Auvergne.

Collier, P., and Gunning, J. W. (1995), 'Trade Policy and Regional Integration: Implications for the Relations between Europe and Africa', *World Economy*, 18: 387–410.

—— Guillaumont, P., Guillaumont, S., and Gunning, J. W. (1997), 'The Future of Lomé: Europe's Role', *World Economy*, 20: 285–86.

de Melo, J. (1998), 'Regional Economic Integration in the Nile Basin', mimeo, World Bank.

—— Montenegro, C., and Panagariya, A. (1993), 'L'Intégration régionale, hier et aujourd'hui', *Revue d'économie du développement*, 7–49.

—— and Panagariya, A. (1993) (eds.), *New Dimensions in Regional Integration* (New York: Cambridge University Press).

Fernandez, R., and Portes, J. (1998), 'Returns to Regionalism: An Analysis of Non-Traditional Gains from Regional Trading Arrangements', *World Bank Economic Review*, 12/2: 197–220.

Finger, M., Ingco, M., and Reincke, U. (1996), *The Uruguay Round: Statistics on Tariff Concessions Given and Received* (Washington: World Bank).

Foroutan, F. (1993), 'Regional Integration in Sub-Saharan Africa: Past Experience and Future Prospects', in J. de Melo and A. Panagariya (eds.), *New Dimensions in Regional Integration* (New York: Cambridge University Press), 234–71.

Grilli, E. (1993), *The European Community and the Developing Countries* (Cambridge: Cambridge University Press).

Kennes, W. (1998), 'The European Union and Regionalism in Developing Countries', in *Regionalism and Development: Report of the European Commission and World Bank Seminar* (European Commission, Studies Series, No. 1, Brussels).

Michaely, M. (1996), 'Trade Preferential Agreements in Latin America: An Ex-Ante Assessment', Policy Research Working Paper, No. 1583, World Bank.

Olarreaga, M., and Soloaga, I. (1998), 'Endogenous Tariff Formation: The Case of the Mercosur', *World Bank Economic Review*, 12: 297–320.

Oyejide, T. A. (1996), *Regional Integration and Trade Liberalization in Sub-Saharan Africa: Summary Report*. (Special Report, No. 28; Nairobi: AERC).

Pritchett, L., and Sethi. G. (1994), 'Tariff Rates, Tariff Revenue, and Tariff Reform: Some New Facts', *World Bank Economic Review*, 8: 1–16.

Richardson, M. (1995), 'Tariff Revenue Competition in a Free Trade Area', *European Economic Review*, 39: 1429–37.

Rodrik, D. (1998), 'Why Is Trade Reform so Difficult in Africa?', *Journal of African Economics*, 7, suppl. 1: 10–36.

Sapir, A. (1998), 'The Political Economy of EC Regionalism', *European Economic Review*, 42: 717–32.

Schiff, M., and Winters, A. (1998), 'Regionalism as Diplomacy', *World Bank Economic Review*, 12/2: 260–85.

Solignac Lecomte, H.-B. (1999), 'Lomé V et le commerce ACP–UE: Quels enjeux pour les pays de la francophonie?', Report ECDPM, No. 9, Maastricht.

Stevens, C., McQueen, M., and Kennan, J. (1998), 'After Lomé IV: A Strategy for ACP–EU Relations in the 21st Century', Commonwealth Secretariat, London.

Wang, Z. K., and Winters, A. (1998), 'Africa's Role in Multilateral Trade Negotiations: Past and Future', *Journal of African Economics*, 7: 1–33.

Winters, A. (1993), 'Expanding EC Membership and Association Accords: Recent Experience and Future Prospects', in K. Anderson and R. Blackhurst (eds.), *Regional Integration and the World Trading System* (New York: Wheatsheaf).

—— (1997), 'What Can European Experience Teach Developing Countries about Integration?', *The World Economy*, 889–912.

—— (1998), 'Post-Lomé Trading Arrangements: The Multilateral Alternative', mimeo, World Bank.

World Bank (1999), 'Trade Blocs and Beyond: Cooperating to Increase Competition', Policy Research Report, World Bank.

Yeats, A. (1998a), 'What Can Be Expected from African Regional Trade Arrangements?', Policy Research Working Paper, No. 2004, World Bank.

—— (1998b), 'Revenue Raising Consequences of a Regional Trade Agreement among East African Countries', mimeo, World Bank.

Comment on 'Regional Integration Agreements' by Anthony J. Venables and 'Asymmetric Regionalism in Sub-Saharan Africa' by Olivier Cadot *et al.*

PIERRE JACQUEMOT

Topics that have been brought to the fore, in particular in the fields of economic development and environmental issues, require more than ever to be approached in a coherent geographical framework. This argument is also valid for food security, water management, the fight against drought, or the implementation of networks of transport and energy.

The interest for regionalism

A considerable number of institutions with a regional vocation have been implemented. Regional cooperation nevertheless has progressed slowly during the last twenty years in the developing countries, in spite of the formation of many regional unions (WAMU, CEMAC, SADC, ASEAN, MERCOSUR, and so on) and the progressive harmonization of rules (in the tax and customs fields, in business law, in insurance, and so on). Previous attempts failed both in their goals and in their accomplishments. Regionalism has advanced more in an increasingly pragmatic way around the food markets, the transportation systems, the electric interconnections, and telecommunications.

To integrate is not to add. It is to increase the compatibility as a whole of the plans of decision-making centers to reach a threshold of irreversibility in the control of problems. Quite obviously, where significant economies of scale are possible, when specializations are not fully exploited, regional approaches are still essential.

Until now, the actions of integration have often remained marked by an administrative, encompassing, and normative approach, associated with the idea of standardization. Only pragmatic thought processes based on the knowledge of economic and social realities and on the identification of the common interests of the members of viable subspaces are likely to succeed. This approach, which aims at building integration on actors having a real interest in cooperation, must proceed by stages, dealing with sectional activities and limited targets. Only this will make it possible to cause the true adherence of the partners, and to lead to the execution of the decisions and the strategies, as well as the application of rules and sanctions.

II. THE CASE OF SUB-SAHARAN AFRICA

The potential to expand regional exchanges could be better exploited, initially by good knowledge of the regional markets, then by better development, and an improvement in the competitiveness of the local product organization, and, finally, by rationalization of the administrative and tax barriers. Agriculture and breeding are, in this respect, key sectors. The liberalization of exchanges can contribute to food security only if the trans-regional cereals markets are first organized and if the initiatives of various stakeholders are not curbed by the administration. The importance of frontier exchanges makes the flow of knowledge necessary. A joint system of forecasts for harvests, or joint actions in the fight against cattle diseases, are also advantageous for all the countries concerned.

The economic policies recommended by the international institutions would benefit from adopting a deeper regional foundation. The reforms introduced by the adjustment programs give an opportunity to create trade relations on a reciprocal basis and to harmonize the tax and customs policies. A solution could consist in introducing 'a regional conditionality'—that is, using the resources of the macroeconomic and sectional programs to finance regional solutions; for example, financing transborder networks in exchange for the progressive reduction of trade barriers or the liberalization of the movement of capital. This idea is making progress today. The difficulty lies nevertheless in the complexity of conducting simultaneous negotiations with several countries.

As far as French and European cooperation is concerned, in particular within the framework of the agreements of the EU and ACP countries, support for the development of common regional policies will be continued. In Africa, it will be advisable to continue support in the fields where there has already been some progress, such as convergence on economic policies within the franc zone, social welfare systems, common statistics, banking management, public office management, technological training, medical research, food security in the Sahel, and so on.

III. INSTITUTIONAL DIMENSION

Regional organizations are numerous, with overlapping skills. Financial management is increasingly threatened by non-payment of national contributions. A rigorous selection of these organizations should follow the criteria of viability, effectiveness, a clearly defined mandate, and true decision-making powers. The most important criterion should be that of excellence, especially in all matters concerning information, communications, research, training, consultation, and technology.

It is also important that official initiatives should extend beyond the regional approach. There should also be interest in the formation of professional regional networks, in relations between agricultural trade unions, and in cooperation of organizations of the associative type.

17

Benefits and Costs of EU Enlargement: Theoretical and Practical Considerations on Trade Policy Issues

ANDRÁS INOTAI

I. REMARKS ON COST-BENEFIT ANALYSES

Any change in a given system generates a redistribution of previously fixed positions. Although, in a strategic framework, decisions on changes are taken deliberately and in the conviction that the new situation will increase the level of general welfare, nevertheless, even the most careful planning is unable to guarantee that all actors involved will immediately gain from the changes. While the exercise is rightly expected to be a positive-sum game, it is more difficult to create, from the very beginning, a clear win–win scenario.

Positive-sum games, in which the benefits generated are obviously higher than the costs incurred, characterize overall macroeconomics thinking. A positive macro-balance based on higher growth and increasing welfare, however, cannot hide the fact that the generally positive framework consists of a number of partial imbalances.

First, benefits and losses are not spread evenly in space: some actors (countries, sectors, entrepreneurs) will be beneficiaries of a certain change while others will be worse off. Secondly, benefits and losses also differ in time. Some actors may be beneficiaries from the very beginning, while other beneficiaries may emerge only after a certain time. Thirdly, direct and indirect impacts have to be distinguished. Some actors are immediately affected, either positively or negatively, by a given change, while others will feel the impacts only after a delay and in other, 'indirect' areas of their activities.

Fourthly, and more importantly, benefits and losses are never static. They are part of a constant change. Thus, short-term benefits may easily turn into long-term losses and short-term losses may become the basis of long-term benefits. Moreover, the map of potential winners and losers needs continuous observation, because, in a dynamic process, even the (relative) position of the strongest pressure groups is subject to modifications.

Fifthly, the picture becomes extremely complicated once elements enter into the system that cannot be quantified. In fact, gains and losses in an international community of nation states, such as the European Union (EU), cannot be measured by short-term and economic criteria only. Security, political, social, psychological, and other considerations may be at least as important as strictly economic factors. Therefore, the balance of costs and benefits needs an interdisciplinary approach.

There are two fundamental scenarios in which necessary changes cannot be supported by a direct, convincing, and positive argument according to which the larger part of those to be affected will be an immediate winner. The first case is the well-known 'negative approach', which argues that some painful changes are necessary in order to avoid an even worse situation. Interestingly, 'damage limitation', or identifying the cost of not taking a given decision, frequently creates much more support for progress and the implementation of policies than positive arguments used to.[1] The second case is more the result of a 'distorted perception', which, unfortunately, can easily increase the number of losers of a given change. Actors involved in a changing framework generally do not consider their situation as compared with their previous position, but rather as measured against those with whom they were on the same level before changes started. In such a case, even if they are relative winners of the process, they feel they are losers.[2]

II. SOME SPECIFIC FEATURES OF THE AEU'S NEXT ENLARGEMENT

In order to rightly assess costs and benefits, one has to be aware of the specificity's of the EU's coming enlargement.

First, more than in any other regional integration in the world economy, the widening of the EU involves not only economic but also security and political considerations. Without a more or less predictable security framework, the continent can hardly compete with other major global players. Resources to generate additional growth and competitiveness in the EU can be used adequately only if they do not have to be diverted to finance a fragile stability in Europe. However, one key element of the needed stability is predictable and sustainable growth in the associated countries. Without quick economic development, with sizable positive impacts on the dominant part of business and society, stability cannot be guaranteed.

Secondly, the applicant countries do not follow the way defined by traditional integration theories and practiced by some regional groupings, with rather disappointing consequences. In fact, in the aftermath of the collapse of the old system, some experts have suggested creating a special East and Central European economic community, something similar to the EU, instead of working for membership in the EU. It was thought that (sub)regional integration could pave the way towards the EU at a later stage (if ever), and produce the desired level of international competitiveness. Fortunately, Central and Eastern Europe has always considered accession to the EU as *the* priority. Since the EU is the largest trading bloc in the world, accession could guarantee not only

---

[1] The arguments in favor of creating the internal market in the European Community in the 1980s did not work. However, substantial support could be generated by the Cecchini Report using the approach of the 'costs of non-Europe'.

[2] This has been a widespread consequence of transformation in Central and Eastern Europe. If all those who felt they were losers had been *genuine* losers (in comparison with their previous position), social peace and political stability could hardly have been sustained in the region.

a large integrated market but also an entry into global markets. While, in regional integrations established by less developed countries, liberalization of (sub)regional trade was believed to represent a stepping stone towards global competitiveness, in the case of Central and Eastern Europe these two stages have never been separated.

Thirdly, and mainly for the more developed first-round Central European economies, the sequence of approaches to the EU differs from that followed by less-developed member states in the 1980s. Greece, Portugal, and Spain first became full members of the European Community, and, as a result of institutional integration, then started to develop strong (or less strong, in the case of Greece) microeconomic and intra-industry linkages with the developed core of the integration. In contrast, Hungary, the Czech Republic, and Slovenia, and increasingly also Poland, did establish such microeconomic links with the EU in recent years. Because of rapid economic and trade liberalization, quick (although differing from country to country) privatization, the inflow of foreign direct capital, and a skilled and mostly flexible labor, their integration into EU (and partly global) production networks is today deeper than that of the Mediterranean countries not only a few years before their accession to the AU, but even in comparison with their present position.

Fourthly, and again challenging traditional wisdom, the Central European candidate countries reveal a 'more developed' export pattern towards the EU than within the framework of (sub)regional cooperation (EFTA). According to trade theories on integration, less developed countries used to have higher value-added exports to other less developed countries and a material- and energy-intensive export pattern towards more developed ones. One of the overriding arguments of regional integration used to be that 'modern' sectors have to be developed on the basis of regional markets. The manifold Latin American experience supports this approach but also points to the weakness of such a development (machinery and other goods of higher technology content generally became prisoners of the regional market and, apart from a very few cases, could not become competitive on global markets). Central (and partly Eastern) Europe followed a different way. While almost 60 percent of Hungary's total exports to the EU consist of machinery, electronics, computers, and transport equipment, its exports to other EFTA countries are characterized by agricultural goods, semi-manufactured products, and chemicals.

Fifthly, integration of the candidate countries into EU structures is taking place in a period of unprecedented liberalization and globalization. In consequence, the different 'mobility' of various production factors becomes more manifest than in previous periods. Despite some (temporary) barriers, commodities and most services already move freely. Capital, literally, moves in the global framework. In contrast, labor markets are highly restricted. Central Europe has been a major beneficiary of this contradiction, because part of the capital inflow from Western Europe was due to inflexible and increasingly uncompetitive labor markets in Western Europe. Future member countries of the EU offer locational advantages.

Sixthly, and finally, none of the regional integrations established by less developed countries has the geographical advantage of Central (and Eastern) Europe of being very close to the market of a major global player.

III. FEARS AND BENEFITS OF THE EU IN AN ENLARGING COMMUNITY

The discussion about the costs and benefits of eastern enlargement started at the moment when the Copenhagen declaration of the European Council expressed the political will of the EU that 'those countries which want so' may become members of the integration at a later, not yet defined time. As new steps were made towards accession/enlargement, the discussion also started to be more and more concrete. Today, with negotiations on accession with five East Central European countries[3] well underway, enlargement has become a genuine, intrinsic part of the overall integration strategy.

Nevertheless, until recently, cost-benefit approach to eastern enlargement was characterized by three main factors not—or at least not to this extent—present during previous enlargements.

First, all approaches after the opening-up of Central and Eastern Europe were based on short-term business considerations. The fall of the Berlin wall was seen as the defeat of the old and hostile system in the eastern part of Europe, and as an obvious victory of Western Europe (including democracy, market economy, and European integration). While a collapse made transformation unavoidable, the (short-term?) winners got an extremely good argument why not to change their status quo. The rapid and partially unprepared liberalization of markets (trade, capital, privatization) offered unexpected and quick benefits to Western European companies, without any effort being made to extend the integration umbrella to this region.[4] If, rarely, a strategic idea emerged, it would be to enhance even more the unilateral benefits of Western Europe. The French proposal to create a political and security community in Europe, without any support for the economic modernization and catching-up of the transforming countries, is the most telling example in this context.

Secondly, and partly following on from the lack of strategic considerations, eastern enlargement was perceived by a large part of the West European community (business, politics, and civil societies) as a threat and not as an opportunity. Certainly, if change is unavoidable, it is always easier to define the threats and eventual losses, because they can be quantified without difficulty. In turn, benefits from changes are expected to mature in the longer term only and they remain potential until they materialize.

Threats and fears can be identified in four main areas:

- security;
- competitiveness;
- redistribution of resources;
- institutional changes in the EU decision-making process.

---

[3] The Czech Republic, Estonia, Hungary, Poland, and Slovenia, plus Cyprus (5 + 1 group).

[4] It has to be noted that Ireland, Greece, Portugal, and Spain, all less developed members of the EU, liberalized their domestic markets at the moment of entering the EU, and in many cases with temporary exceptions. The associated countries, on the other hand, have to open up their markets not only before membership but without any linkage between liberalization and membership.

It has to be stressed that these threats and fears, although associated with the enlarge-ment process, have more than one root, often rather different ones, and, in some cases, have nothing to do with the proper enlargement.

In general, the EU economy has been an evident beneficiary of the liberalization and adjustment process made by the candidate countries in recent years. Between 1992 and 1997, the EU generated an accumulated surplus of ECU 64 billion in trade with the ten associated countries of Central and Eastern Europe (of which ECU 60 billion was with CEFTA countries[5] only). While, on the average, this region had a share of less than 10 percent in the EU's total external exports, it generated 83 percent of the EU's global trade surplus (Inotai 1998). Unfortunately and incorrectly, this gain has not been considered as part of the cost-benefit approach to eastern enlargement. It is considered to be an auto-matic gain, and a sustainable situation for the future. If, however, the importing Central and Eastern European countries are not able to keep financing this deficit, Western Europe's exports may decline.[6] Unlike in the 1980s and the early 1990s, economic growth in the EU is increasingly dependent on its export performance in Central and Eastern Europe. In recent years, this region proved to be by far the most dynamic market for EU products (and services), and the only one keeping pace with the expansion of world trade. Between 1993 and 1998, total extra-regional exports of the EU grew by 57 percent or, on an average, about 10 percent a year, while exports to the candidate countries experienced a growth of 157 percent (or over 20 percent a year). In 1998, 13.5 percent of the EU's total external exports were marketed in Central and Eastern Europe. If we consider that about 10 percent of the EU's GDP is exported to third countries, exports to the associated coun-tries amount to 1.35 percent of the EU's GDP. Based on a yearly growth of 20 percent, 0.27 percentage points of EU growth can be attributed to the dynamism of the Central and East European markets. Provided the EU had a high growth rate of 4–5 percent, the contribution of export growth to Central and Eastern Europe would be small. At present, however, with 1.5 percent of EU growth, this region provides nearly 20 percent of the increment of the EU's GDP. Evidently, Central and Eastern Europe is much more 'dependent' on Western Europe. However, as a result of growing integration between the two parts of the continent, the EU has been reaching a 'sensitivity threshold', where any setback in its exports to the region would have serious repercussions, not only on some sectors or regions, but on the overall EU growth rate as well.[7]

Business interests in enlargement are, however, not limited to exports. Increasingly, large EU (and US) companies use some EU candidate countries as international produc-tion sites offering substantial cost advantages in the international competition. Such investors have already benefited from the opening-up of EU markets for the associated countries, and can export products produced in Hungary, Poland, and other countries of

[5] The Czech Republic, Hungary, Poland, Romania, Slovakia, and Slovenia.

[6] Big deficits for less developed countries arose also following the Spanish and Portuguese accession. However, in this case, trade liberalization was organically linked to access to EU transfers. Consequently, trans-fers covered part of the emerging trade deficit. This linkage, unfortunately, has not been created by the association agreements between the EU and the Central and East European countries.

[7] For countries with heavier reliance on Central and East European markets, such as Germany or Austria, the 'sensitivity threshold' is even more manifest.

the region free of duties, customs, and quotas. Most of them have made and are making heavy investments anticipating the eastern extension of the EU in the next few years. Without quick enlargement, their business forecasts could become uncertain and their global (and European) competitiveness may be threatened. Therefore, they are the most powerful supporters of rapid enlargement.[8]

IV. COSTS AND BENEFITS OF CANDIDATE COUNTRIES

It is interesting that Central and East European countries did not start a fundamental discussion about the costs and benefits of joining the EU for almost a decade. The general view was that membership in the EU does not have any reasonable alternative, and as such should not be dealt with in detail. All the time, the EU was considered the fundamental external anchor of economic and social modernization through the opening-up of markets, by making business environment more predictable, and by providing financial resources, mostly in the form of foreign direct investment and, to a much more modest extent, through the PHARE program. In sum, benefits were assumed to exceed costs substantially.

This general view was supported by the fact that the heavy costs of recent years, in both economic and social terms, were associated with the transformation process. In this situation, costs related to the preparation for membership in the EU would have been very difficult to calculate. In addition, the national budgets did not single out EU-related expenditures; they remained part of the 'big basket' and assigned to the ministries and other organizations in a package containing very different components. Moreover, until very recently, no fundamental assessment had been prepared on the economic benefits and costs of membership. Only with the start of negotiations and the emergence of clear and sometimes conflicting information was the need to calculate the costs of the adjustment raised in some sectors. Evidently, the costs of membership would require further calculation.

In the present, critical situation of preparation for membership, two basic statements can be made.

First, regarding the distribution of costs and benefits, there is an obvious asymmetry between the EU and the candidate countries. For the EU, most of the benefits due to the adjustment of the CEECs have already been enjoyed. Markets were (almost fully) opened up, and West European companies participated in the privatization process and became market leaders in many sectors. In addition, Western business has started to exploit the favorable factor endowment in various candidate countries. If the trade surplus of the EU is compared with the amount of resources transferred in the framework of the PHARE program, the net benefit for the EU can easily be measured. In turn, the candidate countries have to finance most of the adjustment process from their own, rather limited resources. They are doing so to become members of the EU, and, as such, have access to still closed markets (agriculture, partly labor), and to the financial

---

[8] There are only a handful of foreign companies opposing enlargement. In general, they fear higher environmental, safety, and health standards resulting from legal harmonization (e.g. the tobacco industry).

resources of the EU.[9] While, in a rather simplified approach, the sequence for the EU is that benefits come first and potential costs (in the form of more transfers to the new members) at a later stage, less developed Central and East European countries are expected to finance the costs first and enjoy the benefits following a successful adjustment. The longer this period lasts, the higher may be the gap between advantages, on the one side, and increasingly heavy costs, on the other.

Secondly, the candidate countries have to recognize that the distribution of costs and benefits, both in size and in time, depends on their own policies aimed at a successful adjustment to EU rules. On the one hand, a well-designed policy can reduce costs and enhance benefits even before membership. On the other hand, the quicker the adjustment process runs, the shorter may be the time gap between the present stage of preparation and the date of membership.

Policy-makers have to consider that the optimization of the cost–benefit balance on the macroeconomic level generally does not correspond to the cost–benefit balance on sectoral levels. Although none of the sector-level costs can be compared with the potential benefits on macro-level (both in quantitative terms, as financial transfers, and in qualitative terms, as higher level of business and general security), it will be difficult to convince cost-takers to give up their resistance to adverse developments. It is probably a key task of an accession-related strategy to minimize temporary derogation requests and to compensate potential losers in a way that is not erecting new barriers to accession and delaying membership.

Enlargement in various stages may modify the cost–benefit balance within Central and Eastern Europe. This, however, seems to have more in common with the different 'transformation capacities' of the individual countries, which will also become manifest in their different 'adjustment capacities' to membership requirements. It is, however, a common interest that enlargement does not establish new dividing lines within the continent. In this context, the Agenda-2000 has developed a fundamental approach that should be considered in the future as well.

First, the EU has to remain open to all candidate countries and should approach them in a flexible way.

Secondly, free trade as stipulated in bilateral Association Agreements has to be maintained and, if possible, extended to agricultural goods. Membership of some CEFTA countries will not divert trade flows,[10] since all CEFTA countries have free trade with the EU.

Thirdly, large European investments in physical infrastructure and environment should be designed, from the very beginning, in a broad context rather than just involving the first-wave new members.

---

[9] According to the recently adopted financial framework for the period 2000–6, new member countries will be entitled to make use of EU funds as of 2002. The amount of the available resources will depend on how many countries join in the first group. In any case, the money will be several times higher than that provided in the PHARE program. On the other hand, it will in no way reach the level of net transfers to the present beneficiary countries. In 1997, per capita net transfers amounted to DM 1,300 in Ireland, DM 850 in Greece, and DM 510 in Portugal, in sharp contrast to DM 16 in Hungary.

[10] Apart from agricultural trade, if serious restrictions remain on EU imports from associated countries joining at a later stage.

Such an approach is required not only for obvious business considerations but also for the longer-term stability of second- and third-wave members.

Finally, new members joining the EU first have to remain open to other associated countries, mostly with common borders, and intensify cross-border cooperation. First-wave new members have always to remember that membership is not only a historical chance for their sustainable modernization but also an unprecedented historical responsibility for European stability and integration covering the whole of the continent. Therefore, costs and benefits have to be assessed in this strategic framework.

REFERENCE

Inotai, A. (1998), *The Main Features and Current Trends in the European Union's Trade Relations with Hungary and the Ten Associated Countries, 1987–1997* (Budapest: Institute for World Economics and National Committee for Technological Development).

Environment

18

The Precautionary Principle: Different Cases and Viewpoints

OLIVIER GODARD, PIERRE-HENRI GOUYON, CLAUDE HENRY,
AND PATRICK LAGADEC

In the past, health and environmental protection policies, on the one hand, and competition and international trade rules, on the other, have always developed along largely separate lines, both nationally and internationally, even though certain more or less disparate interactions can be observed, such as the impact of environmental policies on trade restrictions, as in the case of endangered species; the EU directive on state aids, based on the principle that the polluter pays while avoiding distortion of competition that would trigger a public assistance bidding war; as well as apparent attempts at protectionist measures cloaked in environmental considerations, such as the selective obligation to use reusable packagings for beverages, a measure that can penalize imported drinks. In the last thirty years, two parallel developments have occurred: first, the emergence of global environmental problems, such as the hole in the ozone layer, deteriorating biodiversity and the risk of a major change of climate; and, secondly, the gradual liberalization of world trade and growing economic overlap of activities conducted in the various regions of the world. These two trends have been accompanied by new institutional developments, particularly on the international scene, including the Montreal Protocol, the Framework Treaty on Climate Change, the Biodiversity Convention, and Agenda 21, on the one hand; and the conclusions of the Uruguay Round, notably the Sanitary and Phytosanitary Agreement, and the creation of the World Trade Organization (WTO), together with the growing role of international courts, on the other.

While these parallel developments are both designed to build a system of international rules to frame and guide economic and business relations, they do not pursue the same long-term objectives. Today, they are in conflict on basic issues, not just in a few relatively minor concrete areas of friction. Which objective should then be senior and, consequently, which branch of international law should prevail? Or, put in less black-and-white terms, how should these two fundamental developments be joined in a coherent and balanced way?

EU law has already settled these questions: in the case of a genuine conflict, the need for environmental protection in an EU member state may justify measures designed to place restrictions on the principle of free circulation of goods and neutral competition, if the existing EU mechanisms are unable to maintain the desired environmental quality in a given country.

The situation is different at a broader international level. Should environmental protection and safety, food, and health considerations be subjected to the modern laws of commerce, primarily designed to foster trade and to dismantle every kind of national protection erected in the past? Or should we recognize the pre-eminence of sustainable development objectives, of which preservation of our global environment and satisfaction of the basic needs of populations (including food safety and health protection) are an integral part (together with educational and economic growth objectives)?

Although development of world trade is not intrinsically incompatible with health and environmental protection, expansion of trade under modern technological conditions undeniably modifies the conditions on which the latter can be provided. There are broad circumstances in which these objectives do not converge easily. Health protection objectives have traditionally prompted governments to impose restrictions on the circulation of animals, agricultural produce, and foods. Governments may therefore consider themselves justified in limiting importation of products that could affect the safety standards they believe necessary to maintain for local consumers and citizens. Such measures frequently trigger commercial tension, since exporters tend to consider them inappropriate actions to protect special commercial interests. This was recently seen in the conflict between the EU and the USA regarding hormone-fed beef, which is forbidden on European soil. It is also seen in the unsettled issue of genetically modified organisms (GMOs) and GM foods, including products whose processing involved GMOs.

The precautionary principle has brought about a new era for these problems, which straddle the fault between the two great ideas underlying contemporary international legal structures.

I. GROWING AWARENESS OF HEALTH AND ENVIRONMENTAL RISKS

Our era is marked by a sudden increase in awareness on the part of the public institutions of industrialized countries, especially in Europe, of the health and environmental risks attached to the growing output and consumption of various industrial and agricultural products, from fossil fuels (greenhouse effect) and tropical woods (tropical deforestation and impact on biodiversity) to chemicals (pesticides) and biogenetic products (GMOs, such as genetically modified corn and soya varieties). Consumers, governments, and non-governmental organizations (NGOs) charged with environmental protection have adapted themselves to this new situation in three ways. First, the risks taken into account are no longer limited to hazards confirmed by scientific and technical knowledge validated according to traditional methods, but include contingent risks whose very existence, nature, or scope are as yet vaguely understood but can nevertheless not be ignored because of their possible seriousness and the impossibility of undoing damage (Swiss Re 1997, 1998; Gollier *et al.* 2000). Secondly, these players intend to extend traditional methods for determining the quality of traded goods to risks and impacts on all links of their production chain, if such risks and impacts touch issues of common interest, whether directly or indirectly. Lastly, they want to introduce specific circulation and trade constraints and rules for different classes of goods with significant health or environmental risks.

As regards extension of methods to define the quality of goods, it could be imagined that it would be enough to add new parameters to the usual criteria applied to concrete use of goods, since these have already been standardized by public authorities and industry associations alike. According to this view, mere analysis of products offered for trade should be enough. This would make it unnecessary to overhaul the rules of trade. But there is more to it than that. The very nature of the risks for sustainable development makes it necessary to question the fundamental distinctions usually applied between products and processes within the framework of trade rules. Governments are currently authorized to subject imported products to the same rules (taxes, standards, restrictions, and interdictions) as locally manufactured products when such measures are rooted in scientific evidence, but not when the adopted or contemplated measures target production conditions (processes) and the possible impact of these conditions, which are considered a sovereign prerogative. However, analysis of products at the border is no longer enough to establish the quality expected of certain products by consumers and their governments, either because such consumers have an interest in knowing the environmental conditions under which such goods are produced or because technical analysis is unable to detect possible risks at a reasonable cost in the current state of the art (such analysis implies a capacity to trace the entire production chain). Information on production processes and conditions throughout the chain helps to form a more complete picture of product risks. This trend is accompanied by the growing use of life cycle studies.

This new approach to product quality, which factors in both production and consumption risks, can intrinsically be expected to multiply special regimes for international circulation of goods. With the need to control existing and potential risks, one of the measures taken by national authorities has been to regulate and even ban trade in certain goods. This practice normally goes against the objectives pursued by free trade policies, which have steadily dismantled or lowered protectionist tariff and non-tariff barriers for the last thirty years.

This is demonstrated by the regulation and subsequent interdiction of chlorofluoro-carbons (CFCs) in the industrialized world. It is also visible in the European waste management directives that, based on the principles of proximity and self-sufficiency, limit waste trade flows in European territory and subject their exportation outside the EU to stringent conditions, including the obligation to grade waste according to several classes of potential danger.

We must, therefore, analyse the economic impact of environmental policies in order to judge under which circumstances specific trade restrictions may be justified and to show what the precautionary principle may change. We will enter the subject by examining the frequently used concept of 'ecological dumping'.

II. ECOLOGICAL DUMPING

Ecological dumping is a frequently voiced fear. While it remains a vague expression, it seems to imply that only the adoption of uniform environmental constraints throughout the world would bring about a fair and sound international trade environment. On first analysis, this idea should be opposed from an economic viewpoint. Based on the maxim that it takes individually expressed preferences to maximize collective well-being, there is no good reason why all populations in the world should opt for the same relation between environmental quality and access to economically produced goods and services. Depending on income levels as well as cultural and political differences, priorities may legitimately be ranked differently. This said, it should be explored to which extent this can occur and where the limits of this legitimacy lie.

Traditionally, dumping refers to the practice of companies that sell their goods outside their borders on conditions that either differ from the conditions prevailing on the national market or do not cover the cost of the sold goods (depending on the chosen definition). The concept of ecological dumping refers to another state of affairs and concerns the conduct of governments rather than businesses. With Scott Barrett, we could say that 'environmental policy is used strategically' when considerations connected with trade and the competitiveness of certain national businesses prompt a government to adopt another policy for its domestic environment than would be necessary for optimum internalization of external environmental effects. Optimum internalization must express the authentic preferences of the populations of the country concerned, based on all singular parameters involved in the formation of such preferences. When strategic use of environmental policy lowers environmental protection criteria compared with the norms required for optimum internalization of external effects, whether *de jure* (lower standards) or *de facto* (standards not applied), it is legitimate to talk about 'ecological dumping' by the country concerned. In other words, ecological dumping does not consist in observable differences in the environmental constraints imposed by different countries but in the application of a more relaxed environmental policy than would be required by compliance with the preferences of a country's own population. This concept is obviously delicate to apply in practice. Nevertheless, it shows which area to target. To be more precise, it can be used handily to distinguish between local and global environmental problems, on the one hand, and problems connected with production activities (processes) and with the use or consumption of products, on the other (see further Godard (1999*b*).

III. THE NEED TO QUALIFY THE DISTINCTION BETWEEN PROBLEMS

However useful distinctions between global and local problems and between problems linked with products and with processes may be for analysis purposes, their practical scope needs to be qualified.

From the decision-maker's viewpoint, the distinction between local and global problems is not as clear as might at first appear. The two are mixed by two concomitant mechanisms. One of the principles underlying action by non-governmental organizations (NGOs) specializing in environmental protection is to give the largest possible scope to local crises and events by including them in issues with planetary significance, such as the preservation of biodiversity, the prevention of climate-related risks, and the fight against the encroachment of the desert. They also endeavour to give maximum worldwide publicity to certain local practices considered unacceptable compared with their own ideas of sustainable development or environmental protection. In response, experience and the influence of the media have shown multinationals—which need to maintain their reputation and legitimacy—the extra-local implications of accidents for which they are liable and of environmental carelessness at their production units. A few have begun to standardize environmental management rules at their industrial facilities throughout the world. As such NGOs and multinationals give global significance to local events. The political basis underlying the definition of preferences on which environmental policies are based tends to become broader and so to extend the sphere in which the question of common or harmonized international environmental rules is raised, thereby deviating from a strict normative economic representation of the impact of individual preferences.

Moreover, the growing concern expressed by consumers, NGOs, and major retailers, especially in Europe, about the health risks generated by the consumption of certain foods and the environmental impact of the production chain used to extract natural resources and produce goods imported by industrialized countries has resulted in a new approach to product quality, as explained above. For instance, suppliers must certify that the wood used in furnishings comes from forests managed according to sustainable rules, they must offer indirect guarantees that beef does not contain prions by certifying that the cattle were raised at a given farm in a given region where no such animal feed was used, must certify that certain peas did not grow in fields fertilized with liquid or urban manure over a period of at least five years, and so on. Here, the distinction between process and product is challenged because of the importance of quality, since certification of the quality of a product family depends on the capacity to certify the quality of the production chains.

This factor has the potential to upset the information required for trade relations, especially in international trade. Products exchanged in the current era of precaution must be supported by a complete series of analyses of life cycles, environmental management certificates, and traceability factors. In turn, these new information requirements will start affecting trade and distribution practices and channels. For products with a health risk or an environmentally sensitive manufacturing process, trade networks will have to align with the new information requirements and accept either of the following alternatives: either they will have to find ways to provide the information required to certify quality while preserving a mass manufacturing approach based on blending and lack of differentiation and focusing on long trade channels, or they will have to move towards production chains with precise specifications and adjust the size of trade channels to the guarantees they will be able to offer as regards the environmental and health quality of their production chains.

This analysis suggests that the future will bring a growing gap between standard goods traded according to liberal rules and other products—such as today's dangerous and toxic waste—subject to various restrictions designed to limit trade to a small area around their production site (principle of proximity) or to an area where their potential risks are accepted by common consent (the problem of GMOs). Moreover, without breaking with the need for a scientific approach, the precautionary principle definitely differs from the traditional positivistic approach to scientific proof. Its gradual inclusion in international law will necessarily modify the technical and political foundations of trade, since the various regions of the world will most likely have a different idea of acceptable risks or even the very nature of the scientific measures to be applied.

IV. TOWARDS A NEW SYSTEM?

Free trade reconsidered

Classical free trade theory is based on the idea that free trade in a competitive universe improves the well-being of all parties involved. Trade is not a zero-sum but a positive-sum game. The arguments for this view in international trade were originated by David Ricardo with his theory of comparative advantages as the basis of international economic specialization that is profitable for all nations: even a country that would be less competitive than certain other countries in every possible area of production would have a place in the international economic order by specializing in products where its disadvantage is smallest. According to this view, the use of various mechanisms to restrict international trade harms collective well-being and must therefore be opposed.

While the new theory of international trade, which notably factors in increasing returns and imperfect competition, identifies theoretical cases in which countries can improve their economic positions by helping national companies to break into markets dominated by foreign companies or by dissuading potential competitors from diversifying into certain existing production sectors, it does not question the general advantages of free circulation of goods and the resulting specialization.

The foregoing theories on the advantages of free trade were formulated in a framework that entirely sidesteps the issue of environmental protection, or, to put it differently, that axiomatically assumes that all components of the social cost of producing goods are internalized by the producers of external diseconomies. The theory of internalization gives birth to a profile of optimum corrections to reconcile free trade and environmental protection according to the origin of externalities (consumption of products or production processes) and the local or global character of the externalities concerned.

Distinctions based on this approach are themselves called into question by the challenges raised by the precautionary principle around the quality of the goods with which health and environmental risks are associated. By no longer postulating correct internalization of all social costs and by recognizing the essential critical role of the uncertain quality of goods to be traded in situations where their quality cannot be determined satisfactorily by the buyer (in the context of trade or by experience), the challenges of health and environmental protection introduce a new wedge in the fundamental equation that identifies free trade and well-being: free trade contributes to well-being only if adequate guarantees are offered in addition to health and environmental criteria, even if the available scientific and technical knowledge does not make it possible to offer such guarantees directly in contexts where the buyer legitimately wishes to apply the precautionary principle. The definition of specific circulation rules for goods accompanied by such risks, in view of the corresponding capacity to provide information, seems therefore the best way to serve collective well-being towards sustainable development.

Moreover, uncertainty of scientific knowledge and expertise makes it essential to review their nature and rules entirely, as certain great scientists have realized long since.[1]

A need for cultural change

The gap between risk treatment habits and the references necessary to make the precautionary principle an integral part of the equation creates a genuine need for cultural change. Experience shows that the following are essential factors in this process of change:

- development of a culture of questioning instead of the habit to look for answers presumed to exist in the available expertise (granted, questioning is part of pilots but experience shows that it tends to be replaced by a mere search for solutions when confronted with serious questions with a high degree of uncertainty and a strong crisis potential);
- development of a culture of anticipation, and no longer just action after materialization of risks that were previously deemed impossible to prove;
- similarly, development of a collective learning process based on simulations rather than materialized risks (with a prohibitive social, economic, and human cost);
- development of a culture open to issues outside the boundaries of existing organizations, especially problems without obvious technical solution and without diagnosis on which it will be easy to agree.

Experience gained in the area of crisis management can be a valuable source of information for the application of the precautionary principle (crises often arise because of uncertainties precisely requiring the application of the precautionary principle). The main lesson is this: regardless of demonstrations based on rational explanations, the deep-seated fears raised by crisis prospects are so strong that the absence of cultural preparation will be decisive and crippling. The theoretical (rational) aspect of these problems is probably not the most complex issue.

Fortunately, however, the economist and the political scientist—like the biologist, the chemist, and the physician (see n. 1)—have the conceptual weapons needed to face future rifts. While working on his thesis, F. Knight had already identified the rift between the concepts of risk and uncertainty, as had J. M. Keynes in his *Treatise on Probability*. And doesn't J. M. Keynes's famous preference for liquidity in his *General Theory* reflect the very precautionary principle itself?[2]

---

[1] Notably, see the reflections of W. Heisenberg (his ambiguous conduct *vis-à-vis* nazism does not affect the depth and relevance of his epistemological analyses), I. Prigogine, B. d'Espagnat, etc. See also Godard (1999a).

[2] For historical analyses of risk and uncertainty and their position in the evolution of economic thought, see M. Blaug (1978) and P. L. Bernstein (1996).

REFERENCES

Acache, G. (1996) (ed.), *La Prudence: Une morale du possible* (Paris: Collection Morales, Éditions Autrement).

Arrow, K. J. (1965), 'Aspects of the Theory of Risk Bearing', Yrjo Jahnson Lectures, Helsinki. Reprinted in *Essays in the Theory of Risk Bearing* (Chicago: Markham Publishing, Co., 1971).

Bernstein, P. L. (1996), *Against the Gods: The Remarkable Story of Risk* (New York: John Wiley & Sons).

Blaug, M. (1978), *Economic Theory in Retrospect*, 3rd edn. (Cambridge: Cambridge University Press).

Godard, O. (1999a), 'De l'usage du principe de précaution en univers controversé', *Futuribles*, 239: 37–60.

—— (1999b), *Politiques d'environnement et lois du commerce international: Le Principe de précaution sur la ligne de fracture* (Paris: Laboratoire d'Économétrie de l'École Polytechnique).

Gollier, C., Jullien, B., and Treich, N. (2000), 'Scientific Progress and Irreversibility: An Economic Interpretation of the "Precautionary Principle",' *Journal of Public Economics*, 75: 229–53.

Keynes, J. M. (1921), *A Treatise on Probability*, repr. in *Collected Writings*, viii (London: Macmillan).

—— (1936), *The General Theory of Employment, Interest and Money*, repr. in *Collected Writings*, vii (London: Macmillan).

Knight, F. (1921), *Risk, Uncertainty and Profit* (New York: Houghton Mifflin). Revised version from the 1916 dissertation presented to Cornell University under the title: *A Theory of Business Profit*.

Lagadec, P. (1990), *States of Emergency, Technological Failures and Social Destabilization* (London: Butterworth-Heinemann).

—— (1994), *La Gestion des crises: Outils de réflexion à l'usage des décideurs* (Paris: Ediscience International).

Swiss Re (1997), *Insuring Environmental Impairment Liability. L'Environnement, la responsabilité civile et l'assurance* (Zurich: Swiss Re Publishing).

—— (1998), *Global Warming: Element of Risk. Climat et risque* (Zurich: Swiss Re Publishing).

19

Energy Crisis versus Climate Change:
Is there a Lesson to be Learned?

OLLI TAHVONEN

The energy crisis that began in the early 1970s and ended around the mid-1980s was becoming nothing more than a bad dream when climatologists started the discussion on climate change. One major theme in the energy crisis was the threat of fast depletion of fossil energy resources, while the problem in climate change is that this material does not disappear after it is used in energy production. In spite of this difference, these two problems have many similarities. Both are related to global energy markets, natural resources, and economists' ability to take environmental problems seriously while focusing on empirically relevant issues. My aim is to offer a brief comparison of the energy crisis and climate change discussion from the point of view of environmental economics.

The energy crisis had two origins: one in actual energy markets and one in scientific predictions. In 1972, a group of scientists from MIT published an ambitious study for the Club of Rome titled *Limits to Growth*. Based on new digital computers, the study predicted that world population, food, and industrial production would first grow exponentially and then collapse during the next century as the world economy reached its physical limits. A number of vital minerals such as copper, gold, lead, oil, and natural gas could be exhausted even before the turn of this century.

The other origin of the energy crisis was the formation of OPEC, which, by using its market power, was able to double oil prices around 1973 and then increase prices fivefold at the beginning of the 1980s. As a consequence, all energy prices increased, causing inflation, unemployment, and regression in most Western countries.

In public discussion and also partly in economic science, these two causes were mixed and it was thought that economic growth necessarily causes the fast depletion of oil and other natural resources. Economists criticized *Limits to Growth* views and developed a vast literature of resource economic models analyzing the role of the market mechanism in respect of exhaustible resources.

From the present-day perspective one is forced to observe that not a single non-renewable resource has been depleted and that the reserves of most resources—for example, oil—are larger than ever. The increase in energy prices was due to a change of market form and had nothing to do with the physical depletion of fossil fuels. Higher oil prices and technical development have made it possible to utilize resources from locations that were earlier beyond imagination. From the intellectual point of view, one may note that *Limits to Growth* sold nine million copies in twenty-nine languages while another earlier and still relevant study showing that the real prices of most natural resources have been declining since 1880 was more or less forgotten (Barnett and Morse 1963).

It is, however, possible to question the orientation of economists studying the natural-resource issues during and after the energy crisis. A major part of research seems to find its inspiration from views based on *Limits to Growth* in which at some day non-renewable resources will be totally depleted. Geologists especially argue that such an event is phys-ically impossible. In addition, most models neglect technical development. Such an approach typically yields gloomy predictions that contradict virtually all empirical evidence (Tahvonen and Salo 2000). In comparison to this, the main cause of energy crisis, the change in the market structure in oil markets and its prevailing oligopolistic market form, still contains numerous open questions (Salo and Tahvonen 2000).

A recent study by Chakravorty *et al.* (1997) presents an interesting comparison between the energy crisis and climate change. They argue that, like the predictions of the Club of Rome, the Intergovernmental Panel of Climate Change (IPCC) neglects tech-nical development and substitution possibilities in energy production. As a consequence, the IPCC emission and climate change scenarios may be serious overestimates. Chakravorty *et al.* argue that using current predictions on the development of commer-cial solar energy leads to a scenario where, even without any climate change policy, market forces produce a drastic decline in emissions around the middle of the next century. When technical development is taken into account, a 1–2 degree temperature rise will require no or little policy intervention. Keeping in mind that the most irritating lapses of memory in the energy crisis discussion were perhaps technical change and market forces, this argument, although being somewhat provocative, is interesting and calls for discussion.

Any climate change scenario includes some prediction on the future development of carbon emissions, fossil fuels markets, and technical development. Historically, technical development and market forces have caused an expansion in economic reserves of fossil fuels. One main incentive for this has been the price increases during the energy crises. As a consequence, there has not occurred any real threat to the continuous increase in global fossil fuels consumption. This type of technical development may still have room to continue instead of remaining at its present level. In contrast, the technology needed to cut down fossil fuels consumption and carbon emissions is rather different, and it is unclear whether market forces yield enough incentives for the rapid development of solar energy, for example.

In the model of Chakravorty *et al.*, incentives to develop solar energy occur, since oil and natural gas are predicted to be totally used up during the next 50–70 years. This, however, raises the question of what will happen if technical development still increases the stock of economic reserves from those currently estimated. In the optimistic predic-tions of Chakravorty *et al.*, technical development decreases the costs of solar energy, but the costs of extracting the currently estimated fossil fuels reserves are postulated to remain constant or increasing. Thus the prediction may overestimate the role of market forces in developing commercial solar energy and underestimate the future carbon emissions.

To conclude, the energy crisis experience suggests that technical development and market forces are among the key issues also in the case of climate change. However, the economic incentives needed for developing suitable technology to cut down carbon emissions calls for well-designed market intervention in the form of emission permit markets, for example. Otherwise, market forces and technical development may evolve as in the past and then lead to new discoveries of resource deposits, for example, and then makes it possible to maintain the high level of fossil fuel consumption. Or should one believe Chakravorty *et al.* that the *Limits to Growth*-type of prediction finally works and that oil and gas will soon be depleted, which then solves the climate change problem.

REFERENCES

Barnett, H., and Morse, C. (1963), *Scarcity and Growth* (Baltimore: Resources for the Future).

Chakravorty, U., Roumasset, J., and Tse, K. (1997), 'Endogenous Substitution among Energy Resources and Global Warming', *Journal of Political Economy*, 105: 1201–34.

Meadows, D. H., Meadows, D. L., Randers, J., and Behrens, W. (1972), *The Limits to Growth: A Report for the Club of Rome's Project on the Predicament of Mankind* (New York: Signet).

Salo, S., and Tahvonen, O. (2000), 'Oligopoly Equilibria in Nonrenewable Resource Markets', *Journal of Economic Dynamics and Control.*

Tahvonen, O., and Salo, S. (2000), 'Economic Growth and Transitions between Renewable and Nonrenewable Resources', *European Economic Review.*

20

Global Governance for Environment: Equity and Efficiency

LAURENCE TUBIANA

The past decade shows that there has been major progress in governance related to global environmental problems. By the same token, however, the shortfalls, weaknesses, and inadequacy of institutional responses to these problems have proved particularly acute. The improvements have been reflected in the progress made in international negotiations on environmental issues, arising from a growing awareness of the risks involved and their widespread impact. Governments, together with the scientific community, the media, environmental organizations, and major corporations in a large number of industrialized countries, have taken part in the debate in order to assess the extent of the risks and to reflect on possible solutions and the required means for implementation. Networks of parties directly or indirectly involved in public decision-making and negotiations have been established in response to major issues regarding the global environment.

This awareness has also given rise to a wealth of economic research in order to define the most efficient means for providing international public goods in the form of environmental goods, while minimizing costs and avoiding wherever possible a free rider strategy.

Public environmental goods covered by international negotiations generally fall into the category of pure public goods—that is, consumption of them does not involve any rivalry or exclusion (the cost of exclusion is prohibitive), but also include public goods, defined, for example, by Ostrom as goods for which there is indeed rivalry (implying that the marginal cost of use of the goods is in fact above zero) but for which it is extremely difficult to deny consumer access.

Global environmental problems, whether they involve pure public goods or common goods, are subjected to extraneous factors that are clearly cross-border, even though these extraneous factors may be unevenly distributed between the countries and economic agents. These extraneous factors now have a major impact as they affect growth and economic development. They reflect a failure in the market or in public policies, thereby producing a failure not only in the domestic market but also in global markets as a result of economic globalization. However, the corrective measures applied in response to these market deficiencies lack the required infrastructure for implementation. There are, in fact, no international institutions or worldwide governments entrusted with the implementation of these corrective measures, involving, for example, economic incentive or the establishment of international rules and constraints.

The functioning of the market or of public policy at the national level can be corrected only by opening negotiations. If the outcome of these negotiations proves successful, policies can be coordinated in order to produce these goods. The international agenda shows that, while these negotiations are extremely slow, they are nonetheless partially successful, as mutually agreed targets have been set—as illustrated, for example, in the reduction of greenhouse gases within the convention on climatic change, or, in the case of chlorofluorocarbons (CFCs), the programme on the banning of gases that destroy the ozone layer.

The five following questions arise:

1. Do these negotiations provide an effective framework for establishing coordination between the countries, and if so on what terms?
2. Are market instruments the most efficient means of satisfying preferences for public goods or can they be replaced by procedures based on cooperation?
3. Is equity necessary in order to obtain international cooperation for global goods?
4. Who defines the collective preferences reflected in the positions taken by governments?
5. How is the choice of the public goods that will be negotiated determined, given the competition for available resources for the purposes of the negotiations? Furthermore, what is the nature of the problems in terms of norms and institutions arising from this competition?

I. NEGOTIATING FRAMEWORK

The coordination of public policies in order to obtain public international goods has been examined in order to understand how determined collective action could be implemented in the absence of directives from a supervisory body (cf. Olson 1965; Cooper 1985; Kindelberger 1986). Indeed, in the absence of collective action, the amount of public goods produced is insufficient. The main point is to determine on what terms those involved in the coordination will choose to adopt stringent rules in the public interest rather than revert to a strategy of non-cooperation or, worse still, a free rider strategy; there is no easy answer to this. In fact, according to the game theory as well as theories of international relations, particularly the neo-realist approach (Krasner 1983), non-cooperation seems to be the predominant pattern.

Under what terms can international agreements on the environment be effective in terms of environmental objectives?

Research has been published exploring the logic of coalitions in relation to both co-operative and non-cooperative games.

One of the most frequently cited examples of success in terms of environmental agreements is the Montreal protocol on the elimination of CFCs. This agreement is based on a quantified objective ('elimination') and commits the parties to major constraints—namely, trade sanctions if they conduct business on prohibited products with parties that have not signed the agreement. The obvious threat to the ozone layer does not account for the signatories' wish to undertake collective action: at the time of the agreement there was no scientific certainty on the state of the ozone layer nor on the impact of CFCs. Barrett (1999) explains that an agreement can only succeed in so far as compliance is self-enforced. Incentives and penalties enabling automatic enforcement of the treaty are difficult to implement: in the first instance they have to be credible and the countries that apply these penalties or incentives require clearly identified benefits in return. Montreal was a success because all the countries were required to participate using a combination of incentive and dissuasion; the incentives were defined in terms of compensation directed at developing countries and economies in a transition phase, while trade sanctions against non-signatory countries were used as a form of dissuasion. This agreement thus ensures almost full participation and there is a strong incentive to sign the Convention. A non-signatory country loses out as a result of the trade clause. It is easy to offer compensation to the developing countries, as the benefits expected from the protection of the ozone layer vastly outweigh the costs of compensation, which are in fact much lower than expected. In the case of Montreal, Russia's attempts to avoid applying the protocol, which would have destroyed the credibility of the constraints, failed: the terms for granting aid to Russia have been maintained and Russia has accepted the requirements of the protocol implementation committee. Furthermore, the developing countries acknowledged that it was in their interest to take part in the coalition: not only would they benefit in terms of the public good, but they would also enjoy the added benefit of an associated good—namely, technical cooperation and financial assistance. The Kyoto protocol as well as the biodiversity convention are being held up by the assessment of benefits; the benefits in terms of overall public goods (a decrease in greenhouse gases as well as the preservation of biodiversity), and associated goods aimed specifically at the developing countries through financial compensation (for example, a specific development framework or a share in the benefits derived from the application of biodiversity) or technical assistance, remain unquantified. The outcome of the negotiations will to a large extent determine the commitment of the developing countries to the Kyoto agreement as well as the biodiversity convention.

The second aspect of the success of a coalition is also dependent on the credibility of threats in the event of failure. According to the theory of rational choice, each country may be tempted to adopt a free rider strategy or to provide the exact amount of public good that enables it to offset the marginal cost of a decrease through the marginal benefit thereby obtained. In this case, even in the event of international agreement, the amount of public good provided will be too low (Murdoch and Sandler 1997; Carraro and Siniscalco 1998; Barrett 1999).

Full cooperation with respect to the greenhouse effect requires that each country reduces its emissions to a level where its marginal costs will equate to the overall marginal benefit calculated on the basis of the marginal benefit for all the countries.

Other situations may, however, arise in the event of major asymmetry between countries. In this case, some countries may choose to reduce their emissions of gas irrespectively of the choice made by other countries, as they may conclude that reductions by other countries may depend on their own decision. The manner in which the situation is stage set is of crucial importance for the successful outcome of the negotiations. While non-cooperative strategies and Nash equilibrium scenarios reflect one-shot negotiating situations, reality is very different. Whereas, according to theoretical models, the expected gains must be specified, this does not apply in the real world and the countries are not always able accurately to assess potential losses or benefits; this introduces an element of flexibility into the game. Disagreement over the consequences of potential action further to evaluation of the problems is among the considerations that influence the outcome of the negotiation, together with certain countries' capacity to dictate the negotiating agenda. In fact, the institutions should seek to strike a balance in relation to the level of threat: each country's incentive for non-cooperation is constrained by other countries' incentive to reject cooperation. The adoption of a free rider strategy creates the risk of a catastrophic situation and restricts the use of this strategy.

The structure of the negotiations also plays a role: negotiations are not necessarily conducted simultaneously by all of the countries involved. Negotiating techniques involving several rounds of talks between a limited number of countries may appear easier to handle, whereas in actual fact the size of the coalition lends a sufficient degree of credibility to the threat of a free rider strategy, thereby compelling all the countries to refrain from adopting this strategy.

Confirmation of the above approaches to rational choice is provided by political analysis.

The realistic theories expounded by political analysts stress the emphasis on national interest within each country, as well as each country's power in relation to others, given that this power appears to be the decisive factor in satisfying domestic interests. In international negotiations, one may consider that the dominant nation defines the system in order best to suit its own interests and thereafter compels the other nations to accept the rules while retaining the lion's share of the benefits. Furthermore, according to the theory of relative gains, a country will negotiate an international agreement only if the benefits derived in relation to the other participants—that is, relative benefits (including potential compensation)—are evenly distributed. Thus the prospect of major benefits in absolute terms is neither necessary nor sufficient in order to ensure policy coordination: the only important consideration is the relative distribution of these benefits between the relevant countries. A nation does not, therefore, seek to achieve the maximum level of benefit, but rather to slow down other countries' efforts to increase their capacity.

II. THE TOOLS OF COOPERATION

Which instruments are required in order to provide an effective, satisfactory response to the collective preference for global public goods? Two responses have been formulated in response to the problems posed by the lack of international governance in the environmental field: economists have rationalized deficiencies in environmental governance in terms of efficiency, environmental objectives have to be achieved at the lowest possible cost, and, in the absence of stringent rules, it is necessary to create instruments that enable objectives to be achieved as well as immediate compliance with the rules.

In the first instance, the reforms required in order to achieve efficiency should be aimed at the introduction of market or pseudo-market mechanisms through competitive factors or checks and balances, thereby countering capture strategies on the part of decision-makers. These mechanisms will reveal preferences. Two types of solutions should be contemplated: solutions advocated by Coase (involving the introduction of users' rights over common goods in order to encourage a competitive market in these rights), or solutions advocated by Lindahl (based on the readiness of the consumers of the public good to pay in order to express their preference), both of which represent major drawbacks in international affairs. They require a centralized authority that decides on the initial allocation of the rights or centralizes the formulation of citizens' willingness to pay. The problem in terms of international coordination is that there is no legitimate supranational body able to fulfil this role.

The most effective form of coordination should be provided by the market. If the agents find that they are not in possession of the full facts, the decentralized market framework may be supplemented with action on the part of an independent authority. In the case of the Kyoto protocol, the regulation of the market for rights of emission implies the resort to this type of body whose degree of centralization or decentralization remains to be defined.

An alternative approach involves improving the framework for consultation, which in turn implies offsetting the decentralization arising from market logic with a mechanism for social cooperation.

As international, public decisions on environmental issues are often taken in uncertain situations with asymmetry of information, the agents' capacity in terms of reasoning and formulating opinions is limited: proper coordination would therefore require an institutional framework. These mechanisms for social cooperation introduce a learning process into the game (Ostrom *et al.* 1993). Indeed, the logic underpinning collective action cannot always be restricted to the institutional model of a competitive market. Other types of social institution may achieve similar or better results, depending on the type of goods sought or the existing political system. Within this particular pattern of thought, the design of institutions aimed at improving cooperation is essential; it is dependent to a large extent on the quality and nature of the discussion process, the purpose of which is to reach a public decision. In the case of international negotiations, one realizes the importance of these processes in terms of reaching an agreement. One of the main reasons for this is that transparency in the negotiating process and fair procedures contribute to the establishment of a climate of confidence and bring about apprenticeship. In the case of the negotiations on biosafety, the consultation process played a major role in terms of building a base of shared concepts in an area where many points remain shrouded in uncertainty. The recent WTO trade talks provide the opposite example, as the lack of transparency in the decision-making process led the developing countries to withdraw from the game.

These processes also have an impact on reputation, thereby providing an incentive for countries to be cooperative in order to avoid shouldering responsibility in the event of failure. This aspect goes beyond the involvement of governments involved in the negotiations and has a bearing on internal political economic considerations related to their decision-making process.

III. POLITICAL ECONOMY OF NEGOTIATING CHOICES: STAKEHOLDERS' NETWORKS

The institutions and negotiating forums play a crucial role in the success or failure of cooperative strategies. Two dimensions require consideration. The first dimension involves pressure groups and national institutions. National institutions play a major role in supranational political decisions. Within this framework the degree of decentralization applied to political decision-making is also a consideration: as the system becomes increasingly decentralized, political mediation becomes more complex and the result becomes increasingly unpredictable; as the number of national agents involved in political decision-making grows, the political decision-makers encounter growing difficulty in establishing coordination beyond their own borders. An example of this was provided by the difficulties encountered by the US administration in maintaining a firm position during the negotiations over the climate, as it was finally compelled to fall back on a position in which it applied pressure on the developing countries.

National pressure groups pursue their objectives by influencing governmental decisions on both national and international issues. The gains and losses arising from the coordination of economic policies by national agents then have to be analysed: this particular approach requires not only that gains and losses at the national level be clearly identified, but also that the various pressure groups identify and recognize these gains (if they are capable of doing so) before stating their position. The opinion of these groups is of crucial importance as governments seek their support (Frey 1997).

Among the theoretical approaches on coordination, there is little material that draws together the three levels of coordination—that is, local, national, and international. Some studies are based on simultaneous negotiation, both at national and international level, using dual level games. However, none of these studies takes into account the local aspect, which is one of the key factors in national, and therefore international, negotiations: pressure groups within a particular country may well be sufficiently powerful to favour or hinder the successful outcome of top-level negotiations.

The acceptance of new ideas by several agents has led to the formation of new coalitions both at the national and international level (Goldstein and Keohane 1993; Thoyer and Tubiana 1998). Finally, the theory of international regimes is based on the role of international institutions in terms of organizing the mediation process, especially regarding the norms, principles, and rules for decision-making where agents' expectations coincide. Not only do international institutions limit the problems arising from defection and cheating, but their very existence reduces the costs of mediation. A similar theory takes into account the ideas and beliefs of political decision-makers (Haas 1997): in an uncertain environment, the latter seek expertise before taking a decision or launching a process of mediation. This particular system is based on expertise that determines the thought process of the decision-makers and gradually becomes established, thereby enabling the talks to converge. Changes in the prevailing ideas produce changes in the issues debated internationally. The international work group on climatic change that drew together scientists and government officials played a decisive role in identifying the risk of global warming and the recognition thereof by the international community.

IV. ECONOMIC AND ENVIRONMENTAL EFFICIENCY:
THE ROLE OF EQUITY

Developing countries have emphasized the problem of equity, both in terms of the consequences of environmental agreements and regarding negotiating procedures. In some cases their commitment to produce part of the required public goods has been conditional on due consideration for equity. India has demanded negotiation over the initial allocation of rights to the emission of greenhouse gases as a precondition for its contribution to limiting gaseous emissions.

In terms of rational choice, equity is not a requirement for achieving environmental objectives nor ensuring the success of the coalition. In actual fact, the largest countries should theoretically undertake the most significant measures, as they will be the main beneficiaries. In this case, the other countries will not play an active role, which in itself will have no great impact on actually providing the public good, except if the actual level of the latter is determined by the smallest contribution (as applies to the eradication of contagious disease). The need for cooperation is thus far smaller if the countries are asymmetrical.

In practice, unless there are clearly identified local benefits, the major countries may well not be ready to shoulder the greater part of the burden, especially if the efforts involved imply costs for specific segments of their economy, thereby giving rise to stiff resistance on the part of pressure groups. This is the reason why the USA is unwilling to impose constraints on the biotechnology industry or the automobile industry. The costs borne by these industries are fairly easy to identify: labelling compels the biotechnology industry to provide information on its products, thereby enabling it to anticipate potential losses. However, the attendant benefits—namely, the availability of information that enables consumers to make a choice—are diffuse and difficult to measure. In the absence of a body representing consumer interests, the government will find it more difficult to take a decision in their favour, despite the fact that the expected collective benefits vastly outweigh potential losses.

Finally, taking equity into consideration may well play a decisive role in the launch of a policy of cooperation between nations displaying a substantial degree of inequality. Given that in actual fact the countries are unable to assess the costs and benefits of the agreements under negotiation, negotiated objectives in terms of equity represent one of the means for reducing uncertainty. The inclusion of objectives in terms of equity in the international agenda therefore affords the least developed countries (which have the least influence) a guarantee (their negotiating stance will therefore seek to improve their position in terms of asymmetry or at the very least to prevent any further deterioration) and is thus an incentive to enter the agreements.

Applying the principle of equity, whatever the definition thereof, is thus one way of establishing a broader coalition, attracting membership amongst the developing countries at an earlier stage, and thereby launching the learning process. Assuming that information plays a major role in countering free rider strategies, and enables environmental objectives to be more clearly defined, equity may provide an effective means of generating information. Against this backdrop, particular attention should be paid to the equity of the procedures involved in the selection of the public good, together with its required level and the allocation of the costs involved.

V. THE STRUCTURE OF THE GOVERNANCE SYSTEM AND CONFLICTS OVER NORMS

By the same token, the overall issue of the environment has been broken down into several subissues handled in different negotiating venues. The subissues range from biosafety to the climate and also include nuclear and water supply issues. The growing number of issues included in the agenda of public environmental goods, together with the large number of parties involved, all of which seek to achieve diverse objectives, has reduced the visibility of international negotiations and is a threat to the coherence of the agreements that have been reached. International coordination requires coordination at both a national and a local level that is very difficult to implement.

Given that a growing number of domestic compromises involve international negotiation, a growing number of widely accepted international norms, requiring choices between collective national preferences, have emerged. This particular development raises a host of major issues: on the one hand, it requires a different set of negotiations—thereby giving rise to a growing number of forums and negotiating frameworks—and, on the other hand, it raises the closely related issue of the hierarchical relationship between these negotiating frameworks and the competition involved in order to define a coherent international agenda. This conclusion raises the issues surrounding the current restructuring of the international regulatory system. In some areas, the fact that institutional and negotiating logic is not guided by identical principles and objectives can become a source of conflict. This raises the issue of the hierarchical relationship between the negotiating bodies and the avowed objectives. For example, the objectives of the negotiations on the climate or on biodiversity differ from those pursued by the WTO or the various economic or monetary bodies. The Biodiversity Convention aims to provide a framework for trade in Genetically Modified Organisms (GMOs) and in some cases to block it. This Convention also raises the issues of national preferences, the precautionary principle and that of the state, representing the borderline with free market mechanisms. It may well be in direct contradiction with the liberalization policies pursued by the WTO and therefore require efforts to reconcile the different approaches to negotiation. The hierarchical relationship between public goods is thus defined as the simultaneous confrontation of divergent national preferences where the final decision will be reached through negotiation. One should not ignore the various power asymmetries involved in this process, as well as the agents' newly acquired capacity to involve other parties in the negotiations.

One of the widely used methods of arbitration involves calling on a judge; this method has been adopted by the WTO and confers a major role on the mechanism of settlement of disputes in terms of producing norms. For the time being this mechanism is unique in so far as international courts of law very rarely issue rulings on environmental disputes (with the exception of the European Court of Justice). This is, therefore, a powerful mechanism and enables the WTO trade agreements to supersede other agreements, most of which lack enforcement mechanisms. There are several possible approaches to improving global governance in relation to the environment: either greater recourse to a judge, implying wider jurisdiction, or, on the contrary, a broadening of negotiation procedures and the democratization thereof.

In any event, the failure of the Seattle conference illustrates the urgent need for reassessment of the structure of international regulation. The lack of a World Environment Organization –that is, a forum for producing and negotiating norms together with the means for enforcement thereof—provides a partial explanation for the failure at the WTO. The aim of opponents from the civil society to the launch of the millennium cycle was to remove issues of public interest such as health, education, and the environment from the WTO agenda. Their main objective was to ensure that commercial rules were not applied to areas involving public policy. The credibility of this approach is dependent on providing other institutions with the means of defining these objectives. The progress made in environmental negotiations, coupled with the fact that there are already several legally binding protocols, may facilitate the establishment of an organization based on the WTO—that is, a member-led organization empowered to settle disputes in order to ensure the enforcement of all the protocols. This would imply a bottom-up approach, involving a shared jurisdiction, underpinned by existing conventions defining the terms for implementation of some of the principles agreed at Rio (responsibility, precaution, polluter-pay principle, and so on).

VI. CONCLUSION

Taking into account common international goods shows that the market cannot in itself ensure the management of the system. In the absence of regulations and institutions providing a framework, this generates considerable costs as well as 'international public bads'. By the same token, national policies that disregard international implications may have a negative impact in terms of global goods.

What can be done in the absence of a global government empowered to enforce a set of laws, instigate legal proceedings in the event of failure to comply with the law, and guarantee sanctions? Until now, this role of international control has been assumed via the hegemony of the major powers. Hitherto this particular recourse has proved ineffective for a number of reasons.

Given this relative vacuum, the institutions arising from the many international agreements on issues that the international community regards as requiring urgent attention provide the only remaining resort. Both states and a host of other parties may not always have a clearly defined mutual agenda, yet they resolve conflicts of interest or shift them to other issues. These proceedings take place under various types of forums within which the agendas often diverge.

However the norms and rules produced by these various processes sometimes give rise to discrepancies. They are defined by specific bodies and recognized by institutions within the international system that do not have equal power or authority. The hierarchical relationship between these forums has become a crucial issue. In the absence of arbitration, the institutions that prevail over the others are those that are empowered to enforce their particular body of rules and principles. This establishes a hierarchical relationship between required public international goods that have not been covered by specific negotiations.

The international community must therefore specifically address the problem arising from the global structure of the institutions that oversee worldwide governance. Should there be an attempt to strike a balance between the institutions by establishing equilibrium in terms of their powers of enforcement? Or, on the contrary, should there be an institution acting as a guarantor and a final resort in order to enforce international standards agreed elsewhere? This issue should be addressed through a wide and open debate to respond to the growing number of questions surrounding globalization.

REFERENCES

Barrett, S. (1999), 'Environment as an International Public Good', in Kaul and N. Stern (eds.), *Global Public Goods* (New York: UNDP).

Carraro, C., and Siniscalo, D. (1998), 'International Environmental Agreements: Incentives and Political Economy', *European Economic Review*, 42: 561–72.

Cooper, R. N. (1985), 'Economic Interdependence and Coordination of Economic Policies', in R. W. Jones and P.B. Kenen (eds.), *Handbook of International Economies* (Amsterdam; Elsevier Science Publisher), ii. 1195–1234.

Ecchia, G., and Mariotti, M. (1998), 'Coalition Formation in International Environmental Agreements and the Role of Institutions', *European Economic Review*, 42/3–5: 573–82.

Frey, B. (1997), 'The Public Choice of International Organizations', in P. Mueller (ed.), *Perspectives on Public Choices: a Handbook* (Cambridge: Cambridge University Press).

Goldstein, J., and Keohane, R. (1993), *Ideas and Foreign Policy* (Ithaca, NY.: Cornell University Press).

Hass, P. M. (1997), *Knowledge and International Policy Coordination* (Columbia: University of South Carolina Press).

Kindelberger, C. P. (1986), 'International Public Goods without International Government', *American Economic Review*, 76/1: 1–13.

Krasner, S. (1983), *International Regimes* (Ithaca, NY.: Cornell University Press).

Murdoch, J. C., and Sandler, T. (1997), 'The Voluntary Provision of a Pure Public Good: The Case of Reduced CFC Emissions and the Montreal Protocol', *Journal of Public Economics*, 63: 331–49.

Olson, M. (1965), *The Logic of Collective Action, Public Goods and Theory of Group* (Cambridge, Mass.: Harvard University Press).

Ostrom, E., Gardner, R., and Walker, J. (1993), *Rules, Games and Common-Pool Resources* (Ann Arbor: University of Michigan Press).

Pellow, D. (1999), 'Negotiations and Confrontation: Environmental Policy Making through Consensus,' *Society and Natural Resources*, 12: 189–203.

Smouts, M.-C. (1998), *Les Nouvelles Relations internationales, pratiques et théories*. Pans: Presses de Sciences Politiques.

Thoyer, S., and Tubiana, L. (1998), 'Les Légitimités de la régulation internationale: États, acteurs et institutions dans l'économie politique des échanges', *Economies et Sociétés*, 4: 149–67.

21

Protecting the Global Environment: Towards Effective Governance and Equitable Solutions

RAJENDRA K. PACHAURI

Before this decade ends and human civilization enters the new millennium, these ten years will be remembered as a period that saw the emergence of several concerns on protecting the global environment. We see today a unique combination of scientific endeavour, economic decision-making, and the formulation of public policy that embraces various actions directed towards understanding and halting widespread damage to the global environment. However, while much has been achieved in this field, such as eliminating the production and use of ozone depleting substances (ODS), many other more serious problems threatening the global environment, specifically those related to climate change, loss of biodiversity, and large-scale deforestation, remain subjects of relative inaction and prolonged dispute. There is as yet no clarity both within international bodies and national as well as local governments on the means by which these problems will be addressed effectively. There is, therefore, considerable confusion among decision-makers on the governance structures that need to be activated or created for achieving results in these spheres. In other words, the architecture for creating solutions and human responses in the right direction remains very much an elusive development. Nor is there, as yet, any creative consensus on what might constitute effective and equitable actions for protecting the global environment.

Perhaps, the one area of global environmental concerns on which the greatest attention has been focused in recent years relates to the problem of climate change. This is also a sphere in which the greatest progress has perhaps taken place in articulating the problem, in identifying scientific and socio-economic solutions, and in structuring the evolution of institutions such as the Intergovernmental Panel on Climate Change (IPCC), the secretariat of the United Nations Framework Convention on Climate Change (UNFCCC), and several research groups and non-governmental organizations (NGOs) that are active in this field round the world. Despite these heartening developments, progress in action to reduce the emissions of greenhouse gases (GHGs) has been deeply disappointing. The high-level 1988 conference on climate change convened in Toronto by the then Prime Minister Brian Mulroney of Canada produced lofty rhetoric on the resolve of the developed nations to cut existing GHG emission levels by 20 per cent by the year 2000. Agreement on the provisions of the Fuel Framework Convention on Climate Change, reached during the 1992 Rio Summit, emphasized the 'common but differentiated responsibilities', which clearly require the developed nations to be the first to reduce GHG emissions. In acceptance of this principle, the member countries of the OECD set themselves voluntary targets to stabilize CO_2 emissions at 1990 levels by the year 2000.

Against this background, the actual performance of the OECD has been quite dismal in reducing GHG emissions. The Kyoto Protocol, which was negotiated in November 1997, requires an overall reduction of only around 5.2 per cent of 1990 GHG emissions by the period 2008–12. Yet even this modest target is in danger of being ignored, because the Kyoto Protocol faces the real prospect of not receiving ratification. If that were to happen, then almost a decade of effort in negotiating binding commitments for reducing GHG emissions would just simply vanish.

At the core of this unfortunate situation is a local disregard for principles of equity in taking action, on the one hand, and the lack of a suitable architecture for effective implementation of measures, on the other. The repeated demand for 'meaningful participation' of key developing countries as a prerequisite for ratification of the Kyoto Protocol is one symptom of the disregard for equity as a guiding principle. The complete absence of any strategy and methodology for implementing a GHG emissions reduction package in some of the richest nations, and more so the lack of public support for these measures in those societies, indicates the lack of a structure at the national level to protect the environment at the global level. Meanwhile, scientific evidence appears to be growing on the seriousness of the threat of climate change, which undoubtedly the IPCC will incorporate in its third assessment report (TAR). Perhaps, the release of the TAR will strengthen the basis and rationale for action by those responsible for the largest share of cumulative GHG emissions. Indeed, the release of the second assessment report (SAR) got high-level attention worldwide, resulting in a strong ministerial statement adopted at the third Conference of the Parties (COP) to the FCCC held in Geneva in 1996. But commitment to abide by the findings of the SAR withered away by the time of the Kyoto COP and beyond.

The challenge now is to develop a set of actions and initiatives by which the momentum of Rio can at least be partly restored. This would require understanding and statesmanship of the highest order in the developed countries and similar movement in the developing countries as well, consistent with the provisions of the FCCC and the Kyoto Protocol. The establishment of an appropriate governance structure and basic architecture would depend on:

- Creating a constituency for effective action through public awareness on the threat of climate change and principles of equity justifying urgent action by the developed countries. This would require political leadership imbued with unusual vision and conviction.
- Developing organizational mechanisms and processes that would ensure effective implementation of the FCCC and the Kyoto Protocol. In particular, there is a need for a structure that does not rest on a super-bureaucracy, such as, say, for monitoring and

verification of actions required by specific parties to the Convention. A decentralized approach is essential involving institutions with established credibility and competence round the world, who should be entrusted with the tasks to be performed, rather than through a centralized bureaucracy.

The political logic for action can be highlighted in the developed countries by clearly accepting and understanding what the developing countries are doing towards limiting GHG emissions in any case even without the imposition of any binding commitments. Evidence of such movement has been summarized in the War Resources Institute (WRI) publication by Reid and Goldemberg (1997), which has been quoted quite widely. There is much happening in the developing countries in spreading the use of renewable forms of energy, switching from high to low carbon fuels and in promoting higher levels of energy efficiency. It is also essential for developed country public opinion to understand not only the huge disparities in energy consumption per capita between developed and developing countries, but also the reality that poor societies will have to increase energy use if they are to develop. Pointing at aggregate increases in GHG emissions in China, India, and Brazil completely misses the point. What matters in the science of climate change is cumulative emissions or the stock of GHGs produced by a society. The developing countries will take up to a hundred years, on the basis of business as usual estimates, to rival the record of the developed nations in cumulative emissions per capita. But there is every reason to believe that even without coercion the developing countries would establish a far lower GHG emissions intensity path of development than projected.

Much attention is being directed in current discussions on the merit of the so-called flexibility mechanisms included in the Kyoto Protocol, and the need for the developing countries to become active participants in implementing the Clean Development Mechanism (CDM). Estimates on the range of possible financial transfers under the CDM range from between $3 billion to $17 billion in the year 2010. The financial attraction of the CDM is, therefore, not a major factor for the third world, but, as a signal of their willingness to be part of any global effort to reduce GHG emissions, it is significant. Early resolution of the disputes underlining the implementation of the CDM would, therefore, be a step in the right direction.

The most important means for engaging the developing world in reduction of GHG emissions, however, is through emphasis on solving local environmental problems in these countries. If one compares the path of development pursued by the industrialized countries and the corresponding trajectory being traversed by the developing nations, it is clear that, at equivalent levels of income, the latter face far more serious problems than did the former. Solving these problems would result in co-benefits that include the reduction of GHG emissions, such as in the case of pollution from transport, power generation, and even emissions from cooking stoves.

Arising out of imperfect institutions, high population densities, and very widespread poverty (which has disproportionately high pollution effects), the developing world is generally on a path of development with high levels of local pollution. There are enormous economic benefits in mitigating these local problems. A major exercise in hand at

Tata Energy Research Institute (TERI) called GREEN India 2047 (Growth with Resource Enhancement of Environment and Nature) quantifies the economic cost of pollution and natural resource degradation in India, which in the aggregate accounts for over 10 per cent of the GDP, and results in 2.5 million premature deaths from air pollution alone and high vulnerability to disease for the poorest sections of society. By 1997 India was generating 48 million tonnes of solid waste, which by 2047 could grow to 300 million tonnes. This would be a source of energy if collected and treated for conversion of organic matter to methane. There are several benefits from tackling local environmental problems, which in the aggregate would be significant. If a true win–win strategy is to be pursued, then the developed countries should act as partners with the developing world to solve local environmental problems, which would also have huge global co-benefits. Ignoring this imperative would only delay the establishment of a suitable architecture for managing the challenge of climate, and lead to costs that would be unbearable for future generations.

REFERENCES

Reid, W. V., and Goldemberg, J. (1997), 'Are Developing Countries Already Doing as much as Industrialized Countries to Slow Climate Change?', World Resources Institute Climate Notes (July).
TERI (1998): Tata Energy Research Institute, *GREEN India 2047: Looking Back to Think Ahead.*

Comment on 'Global Governance for Environment' by Laurence Tubiana and 'Protecting the Global Environment' by Rajendra K. Pachauri

CHARLES PERRINGS

I. INTRODUCTION

Tubiana and Pachauri identify a number of reasons for the poor performance of the global community in addressing one of the main global environmental problems. Amongst these are a local disregard for principles of equity and the lack of what they call a 'suitable architecture for effective implementation'. They argue that the establishment of an appropriate governance structure requires:

- the creation of a constituency for action by raising awareness of the threat of climate change;
- appeal to principles of equity to encourage action by developed countries;
- the creation of a decentralized agency for implementing the Fuel Framework Convention on Climate Change (FCCC).

I wish to consider just two issues raised by these arguments.

The first concerns the way we regard and respond to uncertainty about global environmental impacts that vary over space and time—that bear unevenly on members of this generation and on future generations. I want to ask the following. How is the 'constituency for action' affected by uncertainties about the incidence of the consequences of climate change, and what institutions are implied by those uncertainties?

The second concerns the governance of international common pool resources and the scope for decentralization. I want to ask how the characteristics of the public good provided by common pool resources affect international agreements and the 'architecture for their implementation'.

II. UNCERTAINTY ABOUT GLOBAL ENVIRONMENTAL
IMPACTS

The French have a saying that the only thing that is certain is uncertainty. Global environmental problems such as climate change or biodiversity loss are characterized by very high levels of uncertainty, and these levels of uncertainty increase the further into the future we look. But the nature of that uncertainty differs from one problem to the next. The risks associated with climate change or biodiversity loss have a number of features. They are imperfectly understood, frequently correlated, often irreversible, and potentially catastrophic.

The three responses to environmental risk that characterize most social behaviour are: (1) to ignore or discount the risks; (2) to mitigate or avoid them; and (3) to insure against them. Tubiana and Pachauri worry that the global response is too close to the first of these alternatives for the institutions established to deal with climate change to be effective. This is a legitimate concern—partly because the first response is also the default response. For any risk, if neither mitigation nor insurance is an option, there is no alternative but to live with the problem. We need to begin, therefore, with the scope for mitigation and insurance.

Take insurance first. Conventionally, economists think of the problem of market risk allocation in two rather different ways. The first is the Arrow–Debreu model of trade in state contingent commodities—commodities that are contingent on the state of nature. The state of nature in this case reflects the effects of sources of uncertainty, such as weather, earthquakes, pest outbreaks, and the like. We know that, if there is a complete set of markets for state contingent commodities, then the first theorem of welfare economics holds under uncertainty. But we also know that there cannot be a complete set of markets for state contingent commodities. Chichilnisky and Heal (1992) illustrated the problem quite nicely when they observed that in a population of 100 people experiencing individual risks (whose incidence varies from individual to individual within a population), each of whom faces two possible states, the number of markets needed is 2^{100}. The information requirements and transactions costs of state contingent commodity markets make this a particularly blunt tool. Markets for state contingent commodities may, however, provide an effective mechanism for allocating collective risks (the frequency distribution of effects within the population).

The second approach to risk allocation involves insurance by risk-pooling. This approach is very effective where the population is large, and risks are small, similar, and uncorrelated. This allows intermediaries to pool statistically independent risks to neutralize the risks faced by individual agents. Insurance has the advantage that it requires far fewer contracts than the state contingent commodity approach, and can deal with the problem of individual risks, but it fails when risks are highly correlated or when the relative frequencies of the states of nature are unknown. Both approaches fail where the risks are in the nature of public goods or bads. In practice, the institutions that currently exist to insure against agricultural risks contain elements of both approaches. Agricultural banks and cooperatives, for example, provide a degree of risk-pooling between members at any one point in time, and use buffer stocks to protect against risks over time.

The fact is, however, that many of the risks of climate change and other global environmental processes cannot be allocated through either state contingent commodity markets or insurance markets. These markets are incomplete and trade in them has external effects that bear on both present and future generations. The alternatives are the default—do nothing—or agreement over collective mitigation and avoidance measures. How countries regard the external effects of existing risk markets and their incidence over space and time, and how far they are willing to engage in collective mitigation, depend on their social preferences. In particular, they depend on: the concern they have for the well-being of members of the present generation (effectively the rate at which they discount across space); their concern for the well-being of future generations (the rate at which they discount over time); and their willingness to take risks (their degree of risk aversion). The greater reluctance of the USA relative to Europe to commit to collective mitigation measures, for example, may reflect both higher space and time discount rates, and a lower degree of risk aversion.

'Awareness' of the problem of climate change accordingly resolves itself into three rather different things: the rate at which countries discount or are averse to those risks, scientific uncertainty about the nature of the risks, and the effectiveness of institutions to allocate them. The fact that some countries may care more about risk, or about the intra- and intergenerational effects of climate change, than others is not by itself a reason why the market allocation of risks may fail. Indeed, it creates a basis for gains from trade. But if agents do not know the probability distribution of many of the risks of climate change, both market options are precluded. If the risks are known but are individual, state contingent markets are impracticable. If they are highly correlated and include irreversible, catastrophic effects, insurance markets will not work.

The problem addressed by the FCCC is the appropriate response to the failure of markets to allocate environmental risks. Tubiana's and Pachauri's concerns about awareness are mirrored in discussions about the principles governing collective action over environmental public goods. Environmentalists argue that, where the costs of current activities are uncertain, but are potentially both high and irreversible, society should take action before the uncertainty is resolved. This is the 'precautionary principle'. The rationale for the precautionary principle is that the conjectured discounted costs of not taking action may be greater than the conjectured discounted costs of preventative or anticipatory action (Taylor 1991).

The principle was defined in the Declaration of the Third Ministerial Conference on the North Sea as: 'action to avoid potentially damaging impacts of substances that are persistent, toxic and liable to bioaccumulate even where there is no scientific evidence to prove a causal link between effects and emissions' (Haigh 1993). This requires avoidance of potentially but uncertain damaging actions. A recent statement of principles for sustainable governance of the oceans (Costanza *et al.* 1998) provides a more succinct definition. It holds that, where there is uncertainty about potentially irreversible environmental impacts, decisions should 'err on the side of caution', and that the burden of proof should lie with those whose activities are the source of damage. The decision by the FCCC to reduce carbon emissions now in the absence of firm proof is a precautionary move. The decision to allow trade in emissions and sequestration capacity behind the targeted reductions under the Kyoto Protocol is designed to reduce the costs of the move. But what matters is the target. It is the target that reflects consensus on the importance of mitigation or avoidance.

III. INSTITUTIONS AND ENVIRONMENTAL PUBLIC GOODS

I now want to draw attention to a different aspect of the problem. If markets for the allocation of risks are failing, then it is reasonable to ask whether those markets may be able to work better. Chichilnisky (1998) argues that there is scope for developing Arrow–Debreu markets for securities to deal with the collective risks arising from scientific ignorance about the frequency distribution of impacts across the population. Such securities would pay if and only if there is a particular frequency distribution of impacts. Countries may then be able to spread the risks stemming from uncertainty about the distribution of impacts by trading in the securities. For example, suppose that Countries 1 and 2 face two states of the world, a and b, and that there are two probability distributions over these states, call them alpha and beta. The endowment of each country depends on the state, and Country 1 is relatively better off than Country 2 under State a and relatively worse off under State b. If there are two securities, one paying off only if the probability distribution is alpha and the other paying off only if the probability distribution is beta, the two countries can spread the cost of ignorance about the true distribution of states by trading in the securities.

While there may be scope for the development of securities markets that would enable countries to bet on which alternative future is the right one, there is another option that more directly addresses the issue of decentralization and governance raised by Tubiana and Pachauri. The correlation of risks poses a problem for insurance by risk-pooling. It is generally a function of the area over which they are evaluated. The European Union (EU) principle of subsidiarity holds that environmental resources should be managed at the appropriate level, where the appropriate level depends on the geographical and temporal spread of the environmental effects. This has implications for both institutions and structures of governance. In the case of environmental risk management by risk-pooling, the appropriate scale is that at which the law of large numbers and the statistical independence of risks hold. In the case of mutual insurance contracts of the type that have been operated by agricultural cooperatives for centuries, the appropriate scale is that at which risks are reasonably uncorrelated.

In the two-country example just cited, for example, the risks are assumed to be uncorrelated, implying that a mutual insurance contract would be a feasible option. It would specify a transfer from Country 1 to Country 2 if the state were a, and vice versa if the state were b. The expected transfer would be zero if the contract were actuarially fair. In the climate change case, however, the risks in neighbouring countries in a region tend to be correlated. Drought and floods will typically be experienced by a high proportion of farmers in one country, and often by a high proportion of the countries in a region. The right level of decentralization for a scheme of mutual insurance contracts for the impacts of climate change might therefore be the regional level.

The nature of environmental public goods

So what does this mean for institutional design? What makes global environmental protection difficult to achieve through the allocation of property rights is the fact that many of the resources involved are common pool resources. More importantly, many are subject to more or less open access common property. In these cases, the problem is to identify an institutional structure capable of sustaining cooperative behaviour on the exploitation of the common pool resources. Once again, since the sustainability of any cooperative regulatory regime depends on the incentives offered to the parties, an understanding of the incentive effects of the regime is critical to good institutional design.

The most effective means of insuring against the overexploitation of environmental public goods is to provide for some degree of exclusion. This has the effect of localizing the public good—creating a 'club good'. A considerable literature on the characteristics of institutions that have successfully regulated common pool resources suggests that the following are important (North 1990;Ostrom 1990): clearly defined membership and responsibilities; rules that are consistent with local conditions; membership; participation in decisions; effective monitoring; sanctions against the violation of rules; mechanisms for the resolution of conflicts; external recognition; repeated interaction between members; complete information about members' behaviour over time; and a small membership.

For an agreement to be worth negotiating, it must induce behaviour that yields greater benefits than the non-cooperative outcome. The non-cooperative outcome in many real world cases is in the nature of a prisoner's dilemma. In seeking to advance their separate interests countries behave in a way that is inconsistent with their joint interests. Studies of international agreements to limit atmospheric emissions have found that the number of signatories that can be sustained by an agreement depends critically on the costs and benefits of abatement. In fact, the only circumstances in which an agreement can sustain a large number of signatories are when the potential gains to cooperation are relatively small. The outcome in cases where the potential gains to cooperation are large is generally that the number of signatories will be smaller than the number that would deliver the greatest net benefits to society (Barrett 1997).

Where an international agreement has a large number of signatories, it will not be able to deliver much by way of benefits to society. In practice, the most effective international agreements appear to be those that involve a limited number of signatories; that have evolved through repeated renegotiation; and that include effective penalties or disincentives to defect from a precisely defined set of objectives. In any given case, the payoffs to individual nations under an agreement will depend on 'technology' of supply of the public good in question. Three cases are relevant (Sandler 1997).

First, there is a class of public goods where the most effective contribution determines the level of the public good enjoyed by all. An example is information on communicable diseases provided by the Atlanta Center for Disease Control. It is funded by the USA, but benefits all nations. Since this is a very effective method of public good supply, it is worth considering whether any given problem can be cast as such a 'strongest-link' problem.

Secondly, there is a class of public goods where the level of the public good enjoyed by all is the sum of the provisions by each nation. The conservation of stocks of air or water quality through harvest or emissions cuts is an example of this. The benefit enjoyed by all depends on the total reduction in harvest. Whereas free riding in the first case has no impact on the level of the public good, free riding in this case reduces the benefits to all. Most international environmental conservation involves a public good supply 'technology' of this sort.

Thirdly, there is a class of public goods where the level of the public good enjoyed by all nations is given by the least effective contribution. This is the so-called weakest link problem. For example, if control over a communicable disease involves eradication campaigns in all nations, that control will only be as good as the campaign run by the least effective nation. Weakest link problems are the least amenable to solution. Contracts need to be both stringent and binding on the behaviour of potential weak links in an agreement.

On the face of it, the climate change problem has aspects of both best-shot and additive technologies. The reduction in scientific uncertainty is a best-shot problem, while carbon emissions / sequestration are additive. The additive nature of the 'emissions' public good is what enables the development of a market in emissions. The best-shot nature of the 'knowledge' public good is what precludes the development of markets for that. Now any country considering the collective provision of a public good or avoiding a public bad must sequentially make at least two decisions. The first is whether or not to participate in an agreement to provide the public good at an agreed level. The second is to determine its actual commitment in terms of its endowments, opportunity costs, and the like. In the first stage the country will be concerned with the potential gains from cooperation, in the second with minimizing the cost of meeting a commitment (Murdoch *et al.* 1999). In the case of mixed technologies of this sort the incentives at each stage are different. For many signatories to the FCCC their incentive and capacity to commit resources to provision of the global additive public good is weak. This is because the local payoffs to the abatement of emissions are insignificant, or, put another way, because the local opportunity cost of abatement is high.

IV. CONCLUSIONS

Recall my questions:

- Is the 'constituency for action' affected by uncertainties about the incidence of the consequences of climate change, and what institutions are implied by those uncertainties?
- How do the characteristics of the public good provided by common pool resources affect international agreements and the 'architecture' for their implementation?

If we think of the problem of climate change as a problem in the allocation of risk, then the three concerns for any participating country are:

- the reduction in scientific uncertainty;

- the net benefits of the change in local individual risks owing to the targeted global reductions in emissions (mitigation);
- the effectiveness of mechanisms for neutralizing local individual risks (insurance).

The first—a best-shot public good—is well served by a centralized implementing agency. But the last two require decentralization of the mechanisms for implementing the FCCC. To address local individual risks requires institutions at the appropriate scale. To identify the frequency of individual risks and the scope for mutual insurance contracts requires an understanding of local conditions and the welfare implications of changes in local conditions. In this sense the problem of climate change is much more like the problem of biodiversity loss than is commonly assumed. Just as in the biodiversity problem the main costs and benefits of a global process are local. Like biodiversity conservation, emissions reduction is an impure public good. It yields privately appropriable as well as global benefits. More importantly, since it changes the distribution and severity of private risks to resource users, it changes the way in which those risks should be allocated. Beyond the collectively negotiated global reductions in emissions is a myriad of local problems of risk management, and the challenge for decentralization is to improve local markets for both insurance contracts and securities, and local institutions for mitigation.

REFERENCES

Barrett, S. (1997), 'Building Property Rights for Transboundary Resources', in S. Hanna, C. Folke and K.-G. Mäler (eds.), *Rights to Nature: Ecological, Economic, Cultural, and Political Principles of Institutions for the Environment* (Washington: Island Press), 265–84.

Chichilnisky, G. (1998), 'The Economics of Global Environmental Risks', in T. Tietenberg and H. Folmer (eds.), *The International Yearbook of Environmental and Resource Economics 1998/9* (Aldershot: Edward Elgar), 235–78.

—— and Heal, G. (1992), 'Global Environmental Risks', *Journal of Economic Perspectives*, 7/4: 65–86.

Costanza, R., Andrade, F., Antunes, P., van den Belt, M., Boersma, D., Boesch, D., Catarino, F., Hanna, S., Linburg, K., Low, B., Molitor, M., Pereira, J. G., Rayner, S., Santos, R., Wilson, J., and Young, M. (1998), 'Principles for Sustainable Governance of the Oceans', *Science*, 281: 198–9.

Haigh, N. (1993), *The Precautionary Principle in British Environmental Policy* (London: Institute for European Environmental Policy).

Murdoch, J. C., Sandler, T., and Vijverberg, M. (1999), 'Regional and Global Collective Action: The Participation Decision versus the Level of Participation', mimeo, Department of Economics, Iowa State University.

North, D. (1990), *Institutions, Institutional Change and Economic Performance* (Cambridge: Cambridge University Press).

Ostrom, E. (1990), *Governing the Commons: The Evolution of Institutions for Collective Action* (Cambridge: Cambridge University Press).

Sandler, T. (1997), *Global Challenges* (Cambridge: Cambridge University Press).

Taylor, P. (1991), 'The Precautionary Principle and the Prevention of Pollution', *Environmental Council of the States-British Association of Nature Conservationists*, 124: 41–6.

Knowledge and Development

22

R & D in Developing Countries: What should Governments Do?

PETER NEARY

In this paper I consider the implications of recent research for R & D policy in developing countries. Typical new growth models, which assume free entry and no strategic behaviour by R & D producers, are less appropriate for policy guidance than strategic oligopoly models. But the latter have ambiguous implications for targeted R & D subsidies, and caution against the anti-competitive effects of research joint ventures. A better policy is to raise the economy-wide level of research expertise. This avoids the need for governments to pick winners, is less prone to capture, and dilutes the strategic disincentive to undertake R & D with unappropriable spillovers.

Differences in technological knowledge, broadly defined, are clearly one of the principal explanations of the enormous variation in living standards between countries. Hence policies to encourage research and development might be expected to play a central role in programs designed to combat underdevelopment. Yet, notwithstanding the huge amount of research done on R & D, the complexity of the topic means that the issues are far from fully understood and the challenge to design appropriate policies remains considerable. It is commonplace to label the Solow residual, the portion of output growth not explained by factor accumulation, as 'total factor productivity', but the label itself suggests some understanding of the concept. An older label, the 'coefficient of ignorance', may be more appropriate given our present state of knowledge.

One field that considers R & D in detail is the theory of endogenous growth (see e.g. Aghion and Howitt 1998; Grossman and Helpman 1991). However, the assumptions made about industrial structure and firm behaviour in that literature seem unattractive in the context of discussions of policy design. R & D is typically assumed to be carried out by different firms from those engaged in production. Moreover, notwithstanding the complexities of the models in other respects, equilibrium is typically assumed to be monopolistically competitive, so firms do not engage in strategic behaviour and entry into the industry is free. For many purposes, these assumptions are not a drawback. For designing optimal policies towards R & D, they seem less appropriate.

For helpful comments I am grateful to Philippe Aghion, Tara Vishwanath, and, especially, Sarah Parlane. This research forms part of the International Economic Performance Programme of the Centre for Economic Performance, London School of Economics, supported by the UK SSRC, and was undertaken with support from the European Union Phare ACE Programme, contract no. P96–6092–R.

In this paper I review some of the results in an emerging literature that examines the determinants of R & D in a different framework, one in which barriers to entry, multi-stage competition, and strategic behaviour are central features. This literature draws on the theories of international trade and industrial organization, and in particular on the theory of strategic trade policy that developed in the 1980s. I begin by considering its implications for R & D subsidies.

I. STRATEGIC R & D SUBSIDIES

What does the theory of strategic trade policy imply for R & D subsidies? Recall first the basic result of the theory for optimal export subsidies in the simple static case with no R & D (see Brander 1995 for a detailed survey and extensive references). There are two firms, one domestic and one foreign, producing goods that are close substitutes. The home government does not care about consumers (perhaps because all home output is exported). Then it can use its superior commitment power (or 'first-mover advantage') to move the foreign firm along its reaction function by subsidizing or taxing the home firm's output. There is an unambiguous welfare gain (where welfare is just home profits before tax or subsidy payments). But the actual policy prescription is highly ambiguous, depending on the nature of competition between the firms. If they choose quantities, so that competition is of the Cournot type, then the optimal policy is an export subsidy; whereas if they choose prices, so that competition is of the Bertrand type, then the optimal policy is an export tax.[1]

Now add prior investments in R & D to this model. There is some level of R & D (in general a function of outputs or prices) that equates its marginal cost to its marginal return. Call this the 'efficient' level of R & D. In the absence of policy, each firm has an incentive to diverge from this efficient level, in a manner vividly described by the 'animal spirits' taxonomy of Fudenberg and Tirole (1984); and once again the nature of competition between the firms is crucial since it determines the direction of divergence. If competition is Cournot, then each firm has an incentive to behave like a 'top dog', over-investing relative to the efficient level in order to push its rival *down* its output reaction function and enjoy higher output and profits at its expense. If competition is Bertrand, then each firm has an incentive to behave like a 'puppy dog', *under*investing relative to the efficient level in order to push its rival *up* its price reaction function, so that both firms enjoy higher prices and profits.[2]

---

[1] To be more specific, the optimal subsidy is positive if the foreign firm's action is a 'strategic substitute' for the home firm's, meaning that an increase in the foreign firm's action lowers the marginal profitability of the home firm's. This is equivalent to downward-sloping reaction functions, the normal case in Cournot competition, just as upward-sloping reaction functions (or strategic complementarity) is the normal case in Bertrand competition.

[2] In behaving like this, the firms are essentially behaving just like the government in the static games of the previous paragraph: exercising their ability to precommit in order to influence in their favour the outcome of the output or price game. There is one crucial difference, however. Strategic investments by firms consume real resources, whereas government intervention does not (unless there are deadweight losses from financing subsidies, as in Neary 1994). That is why it is welfare-improving for the home government to take over the precommitment role from the home firm.

What is the optimal policy package in this case? It turns out that there is a natural division of labour between the optimal R & D subsidy and the optimal export subsidy. Essentially, R & D policy should be targeted towards restoring R & D efficiency, whereas trade policy should be targeted towards manipulating the foreign firm. The latter implies a policy identical to the static model: an export subsidy if competition is Cournot, an export tax if it is Bertrand. The former leads to an 'animal training' taxonomy. If competition is Cournot, then R & D should be taxed: the top dog should be 'restrained' from socially wasteful overinvestment. Conversely, if competition is Bertrand, then R & D should be subsidized: the puppy dog should be 'encouraged' to desist from underinvestment. To sum up, adding prior investments in R & D to this model compounds rather than reduces the ambiguity about the sign of policy that we found in the static case.[3]

One possible resolution to this ambiguity has been proposed by Brander (1995). This focuses on the case where export subsidies and taxes cannot be imposed, perhaps (realistically) because they are outlawed by international agreements. Brander notes that for this case a number of different authors have found that the optimal investment subsidy is positive irrespective of whether competition is Cournot or Bertrand, and he conjectures from this that R & D subsidies may be more robust than export subsidies as strategic policy tools.[4] However, Neary and Leahy (2000) point out that this is only a second-best argument. With trade policy ruled out, the R & D subsidy has to perform two distinct roles: both to offset inefficient investment and to act as a surrogate for the unavailable export subsidy or tax. As with all second-best results, the optimal policy is likely to be sensitive to the assumptions made about functional forms. Under a benchmark linear-quadratic specification, the optimal R & D subsidy is always positive, but simulations suggest that the welfare gain from intervention is extremely small (much less than in the case where both R & D and export subsidies can be offered, which itself yields only modest welfare gains relative to non-intervention).

So far, the lessons of this literature for practical policy-making seem to be limited. However, the last point suggests a more positive final observation. There is considerable evidence, from both theoretical simulations and empirical calibration exercises, that the gains from optimal strategic policies are small. On the other hand, much recent work suggests that the losses from suboptimal policies may be large if governments cannot commit in advance to future policies.[5] The problem that arises is that firms exploit the government's inability to commit by engaging in inefficient investment in order to influence the export subsidy that they anticipate in later periods.[6] All this shows clearly the

---

[3] These results for the Cournot case were first obtained by Spencer and Brander (1983). The general case is considered in Neary (1998: sec. IV) and Neary and Leahy (2000).

[4] The findings of Maggi (1996) give further support for this result. Building on Kreps and Scheinkman (1983), he considers only Bertrand competition, but uses a particular specification of costs such that the outcome of the two-stage game mimics that of a one-stage game, either Cournot or Bertrand depending on parameter values. He also finds that an investment subsidy is always optimal when export subsidies are unavailable.

[5] See e.g. Goldberg (1995), Karp and Perloff (1995), Leahy and Neary (1996), Grossman and Maggi (1998), and Neary and O'Sullivan (1999). Leahy and Neary (1999b) show how these losses can be minimized by adjusting policies at early stages to compensate for the inability to precommit to policies at later stages.

[6] Note that the issue is not a simple choice between rules and discretion: it is precisely because the export subsidy rate is determined by a rule that firms are able to influence it by prior decisions on R & D. Either

advantages of a stable policy environment. By analogy with arguments well known in the macroeconomic context, commitment to future subsidy programmes (even if the precise policies themselves are suboptimal) yields higher welfare than allowing subsidy programmes to be manipulated by firms.

II. R & D SPILLOVERS AND RESEARCH JOINT VENTURES

Until now I have assumed that R & D is a purely private good, so all its benefits are appropriable by the firm that undertakes it. Obviously this ignores one of the primary features of R & D, so suppose instead that R & D generates spillovers for other firms. A standard way of modelling this, in both theoretical and empirical work, is to assume that the marginal cost of production of each firm in a given industry depends negatively on both its own and its rivals' R & D, denoted by x and X respectively:[7]

$$c = c(x + \beta X), \quad c' < 0, \quad 0 \leq \beta \leq 1. \tag{1}$$

Here, β is the spillover parameter, which for the moment I take to be exogenous. A key result, which goes back at least to Arrow (1971), is that higher values of β reduce the incentive to engage in R & D. As with any public good, the inability to appropriate all the benefits of R & D leads private firms to underprovide it from a social point of view and, in principle, justifies subsidizing it.

However, the issues discussed in Section I remain relevant even when we allow for R & D spillovers. The desire to encourage spillovers coincides with the strategic motive for intervention when competition is Bertrand, but conflicts with it in Cournot competition, although for sufficiently high spillovers the optimal subsidy is positive.[8] A further consideration is that the case for subsidization is independent of whether the spillovers are national or international. As Leahy and Neary (1999a) note, this can lead to some surprising results. High spillovers mandate R & D subsidies even if the beneficiaries are foreign, not because the home government cares about foreign profits but because it wishes to offset the negative disincentives to investment arising from non-appropriability.

Two other practical difficulties arise with direct assistance to R & D. First, it is extremely hard to identify what kinds of spending should be classified as spending on R & D, except in the unrealistic case mentioned in the introduction where R & D and production activities are carried out by different firms. R & D subsidies give firms incentives to categorize as R & D all types of spending on fixed costs, and so they risk becoming merely generalized capital subsidies. Secondly, because of the fear of capture, the desire to minimize discretion, or budgetary constraints, it is often thought preferable to encourage R &

---

discretion or commitment to a long-term rule (i.e. one set before R & D decisions are taken) would be preferable, though of course the former would be more vulnerable to lobbying.

[7] By contrast, Muniagurria and Singh (1997) assume that rival R & D lowers the direct costs of own R & D rather than lowering marginal production costs for a given level of own R & D.

[8] Aspremont and Jacquemin (1988) showed that the threshold value of β equals ½ when competition is Cournot and demands are linear. Leahy and Neary (1997: propositions 1 and 7) show that in general the threshold value is positive if and only if rival firms' actions are strategic substitutes for each other, and must lie between zero and 1 in Cournot competition with homogeneous products.

D through tax concessions rather than direct subsidies. Paradoxically, this implies that *high-tax* rather than low-tax countries are at an advantage in competing for the location of R & D facilities. However, this conflicts with the fact that, in order to acquire a reputation for being well disposed to private enterprise, a developing country will typically want to aim for a low overall level of business taxes. Of course, this is just a reflection of the general point that poorer countries have a comparative advantage in production and assembly rather than in 'headquarters services' such as R & D.

An alternative route to combating the negative effects of R & D spillovers is to encourage firms to cooperate in R & D rather than to compete, through the formation of research joint ventures (RJVs). In principle, these internalize the R & D externality without the negative effects on product-market competition of a full merger. Since the work of Aspremont and Jacquemin (1988), an extensive literature has shown that RJVs raise welfare, especially if spillovers are high. They can also encourage information-sharing, raising endogenously the value of β, an aspect stressed by Kamien, Muller, and Zang (1992).

However, RJVs are not without difficulties. As Leahy and Neary (1997) point out, they can act as a surrogate for anti-competitive behaviour. Even though firms do not explicitly collude at the output stage, coordinating their R & D decisions gives them an opportunity to behave strategically in a manner that leads to suboptimal levels of output. As a result, the payoff from encouraging RJVs is likely to be low and the welfare cost of lax competition policy is likely to be high, even when spillovers are high. A further point made by Leahy and Neary (1997) is that industry profits are *always* higher when firms choose their R & D cooperatively, the more so the higher are spillovers. So, intervention to encourage cooperation (or to facilitate it by relaxing anti trust legislation) is likely to be least needed when cooperation itself is socially desirable. Of course, these results are not relevant to RJVs (whether exclusively domestic or between domestic firms and foreign multinationals) if the resulting output is to be exported. However, they are extremely relevant to the case of production for the home market.

III. ABSORPTIVE CAPACITY

In addition to raising productivity directly, R & D also improves a firm's 'absorptive capacity', its ability to benefit from spillovers both from rival firms and from outside the industry. This view was first put forward by Cohen and Levinthal (1989), and in this section I consider some of its implications for public policy, drawing on work in progress by Dermot Leahy and myself (Leahy and Neary 1999c; see also Kamien and Zang 1997).

A simple but general way to model absorptive capacity is to replace 1 by:

$$c = \tilde{c}(x + \tilde{\beta}y) \quad \text{where:} \quad y = y(\underset{+}{\chi}, \underset{+}{X}). \tag{2}$$

As before, marginal cost is decreasing in the total R & D available to the firm. The novel feature is that a firm's ability to access the results of other firms' R & D depends on its own investment. Once again, X is the *actual* level of R & D carried out by other firms in the industry, but now it differs from y, the level of *usable* rival R & D. It is only usable

R & D which gives rise to spillovers, and y is less than X. Usable R & D is increasing in both arguments, though it rises less than one-for-one with rival R & D: i.e. $y_x \geq 0$ and $0 \leq y_x \leq 1$.

To see the implications of this approach, combine the two parts of equation 2 into a reduced-form marginal cost function:

$$c(x, X) \equiv \tilde{c}[x + \tilde{\beta}y(x, X)]. \tag{3}$$

Now, we can define an *effective* spillover parameter, which gives the ratio of the marginal returns to rival and own R & D:

$$\beta \equiv \frac{c_X}{c_x} = \frac{\tilde{\beta}y_X}{1 + \tilde{\beta}y_x}.$$

The key result is that β is *less* than the direct spillover parameter.[9] Expenditure on R & D has an added payoff because it is needed to avail of spillovers from rivals' R & D. This in turn has crucial implications for the arguments given in the previous section. Absorptive capacity dilutes the strategic disincentive to engage in R & D that generates spillovers that benefit rival firms. Hence it *reduces* the case for subsidizing R & D.

A final implication of the absorptive capacity perspective concerns the role of knowledge from outside the industry. It seems plausible that in this case too the firm must engage in R & D before it can benefit from such knowledge. This suggests replacing equation 2 by:

$$c = \tilde{c}(x + \tilde{\beta}y, k) \quad \text{where:} \quad k = \underset{+\ +}{k(\chi, K).}$$

Here, K and k denote the levels of *actual* and *usable* extra-industry knowledge respectively. It can be checked that the effective spillover parameter β is now further reduced. Increasing external knowledge has an extra strategic effect, which dilutes the disincentive to refrain from investment that will benefit competitors. The policy message is clear. Measures to raise the general level of research expertise in the economy are in any case likely to be superior to direct subsidies to the extent that they avoid the need for governments to pick winners and are less prone to capture. Our result shows that they have the additional advantage of diluting the strategic disincentive to engage in research with unappropriable spillovers.

IV. CONCLUSION

In this short paper I have had space only to review some of the results in the emerging literature on strategic trade and industrial policy. I have not had time to discuss specific institutional features of developing countries, nor to discuss empirical evidence for any of the models mentioned.[10] (It is, however, worth mentioning that many of the lessons I

---

[9] To be precise, β cannot be *more* than the direct parameter: $\beta \leq$, with a strict inequality for either $y_x < 1$ or $y_x > 0$.

10 Though I should mention Griliches's (1992) summary of the empirical work on spillovers, which typically finds values of β between 0.2 and 0.4; and, from among a great deal of circumstantial evidence confirming

have suggested have been identified as playing a role in the successful growth performance of the Irish economy over the past forty years (see Barry 1999 for a recent assessment).) Among the policy lessons I would highlight are: the importance of a political consensus, to ensure a stable long-run policy environment (resisting both political pressures and academic proposals to tinker with it); generalized rather than firm-specific policies to encourage R & D, with a cautious attitude towards research joint ventures except when they are export oriented; and an emphasis on raising the general level of research expertise in the economy rather than providing targeted R & D subsidies.

REFERENCES

Aghion, P., and Howitt, P. (1998), *Endogenous Growth Theory* (Cambridge, Mass.: MIT Press).

Arrow, K. J. (1971), 'Economic Welfare and the Allocation of Resources for Invention', in K. J. Arrow (ed.), *Essays in the Theory of Risk Bearing* (Chicago: Markham).

Aspremont, C. d', and Jacquemin, A. (1988), 'Cooperative and Noncooperative R & D in Duopoly with Spillovers', *American Economic Review*, 78: 1133–7.

Barry, F. (1999) (ed.), *Understanding Ireland's Economic Growth* (London: Macmillan).

Blomström, M., and Sjöholm, F. (1999), 'Technology Transfer and Spillovers: Does Local Participation with Multinationals Matter?', *European Economic Review*, 43: 915–23.

Brander, J. A. (1995), 'Strategic Trade Policy', in G. Grossman and K. Rogoff (eds.), *Handbook of International Economics*, iii. (Amsterdam: North Holland), 1395–455.

Cohen, W. M., and Levinthal, D. A. (1989), 'Innovation and Learning: The Two Faces of R & D', *Economic Journal*, 94: 569–96.

Fudenberg, D., and Tirole, J. (1984), 'The Fat-Cat Effect, the Puppy-Dog Ploy, and the Lean and Hungry Look', *American Economic Review, Papers and Proceedings*, 74: 361–6.

Goldberg, P. (1995), 'Strategic Export Promotion in the Absence of Government Commitment', *International Economic Review*, 36: 407–26.

Griliches, Z. (1992), 'The Search for R & D Spillovers', *Scandinavian Journal of Economics*, 94: S29–S47.

Grossman, G.M., and Helpman, E. (1991), *Innovation and Growth in the World Economy* (Cambridge, Mass.: MIT Press).

—— and Maggi, G. (1998), 'Free Trade vs. Strategic Trade: A Peek into Pandora's Box', in R. Sato, R. V. Ramachandran, and K. Mino (eds.), *Global Competition and Integration* (Dordrecht: Kluwer Academic Publishers), 9–32.

Kamien, M.I., and Zang, I. (1997), 'Meet Me Halfway: Research Joint Ventures and Absorptive Capacity', mimeo, J. L. Kellogg, Graduate School of Management, Northwestern University.

—— Muller, E., and Zang, I. (1992), 'Research Joint Ventures and R & D Cartels', *American Economic Review*, 82: 1293–306.

Karp, L. S., and Perloff, J. M. (1995), 'The Failure of Strategic Industrial Policies due to Manipulation by Firms', *International Review of Economics and Finance*, 4: 1–16.

Kreps, D. M., and Scheinkman, J. A. (1983), 'Quantity Precommitment and Bertrand Competition Yield Cournot Outcomes', *Bell Journal of Economics*, 14: 326–37.

the importance of absorptive capacity, the findings of Blomström and Sjöholm (1999) and Navaretti and Carraro (1997) that spillovers are higher and RJVs more likely to form between firms with *similar* levels of technological expertise.

Leahy, D., and Neary, J. P. (1996), 'International R & D Rivalry and Industrial Strategy without Government Commitment', *Review of International Economics*, 4: 322–38.

—— —— (1997), 'Public Policy towards R & D in Oligopolistic Industries', *American Economic Review*, 87: 642–62.

—— —— (1999a), 'R & D Spillovers and the Case for Industrial Policy in an Open Economy', *Oxford Economic Papers*, 51: 40–59.

—— —— (1999b), 'Learning by Doing, Precommitment and Infant Industry Promotion', *Review of Economic Studies*, 66: 447–74.

—— —— (1999c), 'Absorptive Capacity, R & D Spillovers, and Public Policy,' mimeo, École Polytechnique, Paris.

Maggi, G. (1996), 'Strategic Trade Policies with Endogenous Mode of Competition', *American Economic Review*, 86: 237–58.

Muniagurria, M.E., and Singh, N. (1997), 'Foreign Technology, Spillovers, and R & D Policy', *International Economic Review*, 38: 405–30.

Navaretti, G. B., and Carraro, C. (1997), 'From Learning to Partnership: Multinational R & D Cooperation in Developing Countries', Discussion Paper No. 1579, CEPR, London.

Neary, J. P. (1994), 'Cost Asymmetries in International Subsidy Games: Should Governments Help Winners or Losers?', *Journal of International Economics*, 37: 197–218.

—— (1998), 'Pitfalls in the Theory of International Trade Policy: Concertina Reforms of Tariffs, and Subsidies to High-Technology Industries', *Scandinavian Journal of Economics*, 100: 187–206.

—— and Leahy, D. (2000), 'Strategic Trade and Industrial Policy towards Dynamic Oligopolies', *Economic Journal*, 110: 484–508.

—— and O'Sullivan, P. (1999), 'Beat 'Em or Join 'Em?: Export Subsidies versus International Research Joint Ventures in Oligopolistic Markets', *Scandinavian Journal of Economics*, 101: 577–96.

Spencer, B. J. and Brander, J. A. (1983), 'International R & D Rivalry and Industrial Strategy', *Review of Economic Studies*, 50: 707–22.

Gender Economics

23

Gender Economics:
Just Another Dummy Variable?

DIANE ELSON

I. INTRODUCTION

The aim of this short paper is to provoke a discussion about the position of 'gender economics' in the development economics agenda. Is it a new subspecialism that simply entails adding a male/female dummy variable in standard forms of applied micro-economics? Or should we go beyond this to rethink development paradigms from a new perspective with more wide-ranging implications for development economics?

The opportunity to discuss these issues is very timely, as the World Bank is engaged in the production of a Policy Research Report on Gender and Development, while the OECD Development Assistance Committee Working Party on Gender Equality is supporting the publication of a paper on gender-aware economic policy analysis for development cooperation. (I am engaged in the first venture as an adviser and the second venture as an author).

II. ADDING A DUMMY VARIABLE

Let me first introduce the approach to gender economics that entails adding a dummy variable, using as an example the analysis of agricultural productivity in developing countries. As a recent survey of the literature (Quisumbing 1996) indicates, a number of studies have attempted to estimate differences in technical efficiency between men and women farmers by including a male/female dummy variable in the estimation of the agricultural production function. This method aims to estimate the parameters of the production function of farmer i in household and community j, assuming that

$$Y_{ij} = f(V_i, X_i, Z_j)$$

where Y_{ij} is quantity produced

V_i is a vector of inputs used by the farmer
X_i is a vector of farmer attributes, including whether the farmer is male or female
X_j are household and community level variables.

There are a number of methodological problems with such studies (see Quisumbing 1996). Here I want to focus on the extent to which such an approach can fully capture the gender dimensions of systems of agricultural production and address policy relevant issues.

The first issue is the question of what the male/female dummy variable captures. Usually, the aim is to capture differences in the economic behavior of men and women farmers, irrespective of their acquired attributes, such as their human and social capital, and of the inputs they use, and the communities in which they live. It is a residual variable, picking up what has not been explicitly specified elsewhere, and is sometimes discussed in relation to ideas of innately different comparative advantages of men and women.

In so far as there is a full specification for each farmer of their acquired attributes and the inputs they use, what the male/female dummy variable represents is 'sex' (that is, the male or female biological endowments with which people are born) rather than 'gender' (that is, the system of social relations that constructs male and female 'norms' and provides incentives for individual men and women to conform to these norms).

Gender will be reflected in many of the acquired attributes of farmers. Their possession of human and social capital will be shaped by their positioning in the system of gender relations. The amount and type of knowledge a farmer has is typically a gendered variable. The amount and type of cooperation a farmer can secure from others is typically a gendered variable.

If the male/female dummy variable is found not to be significant while educational differences are significant (as is the case for many of the available studies), this does not mean that gender does not matter in the determination of productivity differences between men and women farmers. What it means is that a person's capacity to farm does not appear to be determined by his or her sex. This is an important finding insofar as it helps to counteract views that there is no point in policies to reduce women's systematic disadvantage in the possession of farming knowledge because they are not as talented as men in agricultural production. But what the introduction of a male/female dummy variable in the X_i vector cannot do is throw light on the operation of the processes that result in a systematic bias against women farmers in the acquisition of human and social capital.

The second issue is that gender is relevant not just to the determination of the vector of farmer characteristics, but also to the input vector and the vector of household and community characteristics.

Gender is relevant to the input vector in two ways: the gendered attributes of farmers, such as their knowledge, are likely to affect the way they select inputs; and the choice sets facing farmers are likely to be systematically structured by the gender system—for instance, female farmers often require a male guarantor in order to get loans, but the reverse is not true.

The gender dimensions of the input vector are not properly captured by the interaction of the male/female dummy variable with the input variables. Insofar as the dummy variable represents the sex of the farmer, the interaction may tell us something about whether men and women farmers have different preferences for inputs, irrespective of their acquired, gendered, attributes, such as their human and social capital. But it does not capture the way in which gender inequality in knowledge restricts women's choice of inputs—to do this one needs both the male/female dummy variable and the human capital variables. Nor does it capture the ways in which even very knowledgeable women farmers can face systematic barriers in access to inputs of a type that do not face comparable men farmers. For instance, it does not make much sense to model the decisions of farmers to adopt tea as a crop by incorporating a dummy variable to represent whether the farmer is male or female, in circumstances in which only male farmers are licensed as tea producers by a state-marketing board (as has been the case in Kenya) (see Ongile 1998).

The vector of household and community characteristics may include geographic and demographic data and information on the provision of public services to farmers (extension services, for instance). These sorts of variables have different implications for men and women because of their different positioning in the system of gender relations. Of particular importance is the way in which there are strong male and female 'norms' about who undertakes the work of nurturing other people in families and communities—provisioning the household on a daily basis, caring for children and old people, sustaining neighborhood networks that share the work of nurturing. Typically, the norm is that more of this work of 'social reproduction' is assigned to women than to men, through institutional structures that constitute this work as a female obligation rather than a female option. This division of labor means that the same household and community context has different implications for men and women. For instance, the location of a household with respect to sources of water and fuel for the provisioning of daily life has different implications for female farmers and for male farmers. If the sources are distant, then female farmers face a time constraint that does not apply to the same extent to male farmers. Similarly, household size has different implications for men and women. The provision of public services also has gendered implications—men and women farmers typically require a different mix of services, and face different constraints in accessing these services.

The point I wish to emphasize from this discussion is that the gender dimensions of a system of agricultural production are not captured by simply adding a dummy variable specifying whether the farmer is male or female. All of the variables are likely to be gendered, in the sense of being shaped by the system of gender relations. This does not mean that there is no point in the use of dummy variables indicating whether an economic agent is male or female. But it does mean that a great deal of care has to be exercised in their interpretation, so as not to confuse sex and gender.

If such dummy variables are not significant (as is the case in the majority of the studies reviewed by Quisumbing 1996), this means there are no significant male/female differences in the productive use of farm inputs, everything else being equal. It implies that, given the same assets and inputs, men and women behave the same way. This does not mean that gender is not relevant—gender is the reason why everything else is not equal. What it does mean is that sex is not relevant.

Thus the main limitation of the male/female 'dummy variable' approach to gender economics is that it places most emphasis on the characteristics of individuals (the comparative behavior of men and women) and does not bring to the fore the institutional dimension of gender.

III. ANALYZING ECONOMIC INSTITUTIONS AS GENDERED STRUCTURES

An alternative approach to gender economics takes economic systems and their structural characteristics as the entry point, rather than the comparative behavior of men and women; and argues for broadening the scope of thinking about how economies work to include the unpaid work of nurturing families and communities (often described in the literature as 'social reproduction') (see e.g. Picchio 1992; Folbre 1994).

Here I will briefly illustrate this approach through a discussion of agricultural product markets as gendered institutions drawing upon Harriss-White (1998) and Baden (1996), who review empirical research in sub-Saharan Africa and South India. This approach charts the ways in which the structure of agricultural market institutions intersects with the structure of social reproduction to segment markets, constraining women to more localized, small-scale, lower-risk, less remunerative forms of trade than men. Some of these constraints derive from state policy, in the way that trade is licensed and taxed; some from the legal system, especially different property rights of men and women; some from harassment of women traders by officials; some from strong social norms about what is an appropriate activity for women to undertake, which may bar women's access to some market places. A very important source is the ways in which market transactions are themselves organized—the incompleteness of market contracts puts a premium on maintaining shared systems of information, shared norms about how deals are done, shared systems for creating trust, shared systems for extending and receiving credit. These shared systems are systems of exclusion of outsiders, as well as inclusion of insiders—and the patterns of exclusion and inclusion are frequently constructed along gender lines.

Deregulation of markets tackles only the first of these constraints. Moreover, agricultural market liberalization may intensify rather than weaken women's disadvantages, as the competitive advantage of traders with greater access to capital and greater capacity to trade long-distance increases. A policy of gender-aware market development is required to create marketing systems that do not incorporate systematic disadvantages for women—requiring public policy interventions in the development of equitable systems for dissemination of information; provision of storage facilities, marketplaces, and transportation; credit facilities; and capacity building for compliance with quality standards. Such systems cannot be equitable as between men and women unless they are designed and operated in ways that take into account non-market-based processes of social reproduction as well as market-based processes of production and trade. Cross-sectional policies that tackle women's legal disadvantages and their extra time burdens (stemming from the way in which social reproduction is typically organized) are required, as well as policies that directly focus on agricultural marketing systems. Reducing the entry barriers for women is, of course, not only equitable—it also facilitates competition.

It may be objected that a focus on gender as a systemic aspect of economic institutions casts women and men as mere puppets acting out predetermined roles and occludes the scope for change in gender relations. This can be guarded against by allowing for ambiguities and contradictions in the way that institutions operate, in the norms and incentives they provide—a disequilibrium, rather than an equilibrium approach to the functioning of institutions leaves more space for processes of individual and collective agency.

IV. MAINSTREAMING GENDER ECONOMICS? INFILTRATING EXISTING PARADIGMS OR CREATING NEW ONES?

Much of the emphasis in introducing gender economics into the mainstream of development economics has focused upon efficiency arguments. For instance, it has been argued that families underinvest in the education of girls, because they do not capture many of the benefits of education of girls and that public investment in girls' education will promote development by reducing fertility, improving children's health, and raising productivity. Moreover, there is empirical research that suggests that gender inequality is associated with lower rates of growth (e.g. World Bank 1999).

In considering these efficiency arguments, I would suggest two notes of caution. The first is that there are also research results that associate gender inequality with higher rates of growth (e.g. Seguino 2000). This may suggest that there are multiple equilibria in the relationship between gender inequality and growth: lose–lose situations when there is gender inequality and low growth, win–win situations when there is gender equality and high growth, but also lose–win and win–lose situations. Moreover, the causation may run in different directions for different trajectories of development, and different dimensions of gender equality.

The second note of caution concerns the way in which efficiency is conceptualized and measured. Too often it is conceptualized and measured in ways that focus only market-oriented production and ignore unpaid processes of social reproduction. This may be conducive to processes of economic restructuring that shift costs from the paid economy of the public and private sectors to the unpaid economy of the household and community, rather than result in genuine increases in efficiency.

An alternative approach to mainstreaming gender economics is to engage with those development economists who have been arguing the need for new paradigms (whether of the human development variety or the post-Washington consensus variety) to ensure that these new paradigms do not repeat the oversights of the old ones by ignoring social reproduction (Elson 1997). For instance, in comparing economic systems, we need to consider how they organize the day-to-day and inter-generation reproduction of people and communities. Do governments support and value the unpaid work that this requires through appropriate public expenditure, taxation, labor standards, and other policies? Do business corporations recognize that skills developed and sustained in nurturing can enhance the workplace effectiveness of employees—or do they regard time spent by employers in provision of care for family and neighbors as a liability? What mechanisms are there for dealing with the public good aspects of caring for families and friends, the spillover effects that are not fully captured by the recipients of the care, but also benefit taxpayers, shareholders, employers, and others, as well? What mechanisms are there for ensuring that those who disproportionately provide the public good of unpaid care are not thereby penalized in their terms of participation in paid work? What policy coordination processes link (or fail to link) policy on competition and privatization with policy on social welfare and social security? Does competition policy give any consideration to the ways in which different forms of competition have different implications for ways in which children and old people are cared for? For instance, policy that supports forms of competition based on twenty-four hours' instant availability and disposability of the labor force is not likely to be consistent with the objective of promoting stable, caring, and inclusive communities.

The key issue for new paradigms of development is not achieving narrowly defined improvements in efficiency judged according to market-based criteria. It is devising better ways of coordinating market and non-market processes; of integrating economic policy with social policy, and promoting more dialogue about the formulation and implementation of economic and social policy. A gender economics that focuses on economic institutions can make a helpful contribution to this project (for an example, see Elson and Cagatay 1999).

REFERENCES

Baden, S. (1996),'Gender Issues in Agricultural Market Liberalization', paper prepared for Directorate General for Development, European Commission, Brussels.

Elson, D. (1997), 'Economic Paradigms Old and New: The Case of Human Development', in R. Culpepper, A. Berry, and F. Stewart (eds.), *Global Development Fifty Years after Bretton Woods* (London: Macmillan).

—— and Cagatay, N. (1999), 'Engendering Macroeconomic Policy and Budgets for Sustainable Human Development', paper presented to Global Forum on Human Development, New York.

Folbre, N. (1994), *Who Pays for the Kids? Gender and the Structures of Constraint* (London: Routledge).

Harriss-White, B. (1998), 'Female and Male Grain Marketing Systems: Analytical and Policy Issues for West Africa and India', in C. Jackson, and R. Pearson (eds.), *Feminist Visions of Development* (London: Routledge).

Ongile, G. (1998), 'Gender and Agricultural Supply Responses to Structural Adjustment Programmes—A Case Study of Small Holder Tea Producers in Kericho, Kenya', Ph.D. thesis, University of Manchester.

Picchio, A. (1992), *Social Reproduction: The Political Economy of the Labour Market* (Cambridge: Cambridge University Press).

Quisumbing, A. (1996), 'Male-Female Differences in Agricultural Productivity: Methodological Issues and Empirical Evidence', *World Development*, 24/10: 1579–95.

Seguino, S. (2000), 'Gender Inequality and Economic Growth: A Cross-Country Analysis', *World Development*, 28/7: 1211–30.

World Bank (1999), *SPA Report on Poverty on Sub-Saharan Africa* (Washington: World Bank).

Comment on 'Gender Economics: Just Another Dummy Variable?' by Diane Elson

The aim of Diana Elson's paper was to stimulate mainstreaming of gender economics in the main agenda and to my mind the aim has been reached. Her presentation stimulates thought, interest and discussion.

Quite a few issues have been raised:

- the necessity to extend gender-oriented analysis beyond microeconomics looking at structural characteristics of economies;
- the extension of macroeconomic analysis by incorporating the process of social reproduction with women's unpaid work as the key unit;
- the interrelationship between gender inequality and the process of development, the equilibrium between gender equality and economic efficiency;
- the implications of the ways families are organized for the way that the market works;
- the ways that gender economics can contribute to the creation of equitable global markets.

All these issues are most interesting.

The presentation shows us that gender economic studies make gender studies less political and more academic; gender economics widens horizons of research and suggests new directions.

As the title of Diane Elson's paper shows, the very concept of gender economics is discussed. Any new science has more questions than answers. I'd like to put some more for the discussion that are definitely under-researched.

1. One of the basic directions of gender economic research is women's unpaid work within households. Unpaid female labour in the households is widely discussed. What about male unpaid labour at home: repairing a chair or a tape recorder, fixing a socket, moving heavy objects? Some men do participate in everyday cleaning and washing, some take a big part in raising children. I understand that an easy answer can be about breast-feeding, and so on, but that is not what I mean. What do we do with unpaid male labour at home? I have not met such research. Is it due to my limited access to information?

Still another perspective—if you are doing hairdressing yourself, is it unpaid labour? And what about shaving? And so on.

There is another question here. Civilization has substituted a lot of unpaid home labour for that of machines. Whose functions has civilization primarily transferred to the machines, male or female? Whose unpaid home labour is substituted for paid services and in what countries?

Being academic, we have to research both.

2. Another issue connected to the first one. Let us consider a hypothetical set of functions people (both men and women) perform in their everyday life.

Under socialism the number of these functions performed by men has been dramatically reducing, while the number of functions performed by women during this century has been growing. Has that made men weaker and women stronger? What has been happening in the West in this respect? What is good and what is bad here? Women under socialism became very 'efficient', as problems stimulated imagination and creation of time- and resource-saving technologies. They can easily make a dinner out of nothing, a dress with no visible means, and so on. But what about the impact on their health of such a difficult life, or the consequences on the quality and quantity of time they could devote to their children—that is, the quality of subsequent generations?

'Patience limit' methodology is very appropriate here, but it has to be comparative to understand global change and modern trends.

3. Still another issue. I want to draw your attention to gender aspects of global-information society formation. It is a big issue and a lot can be said here. I just want to draw your attention to the fact that we have lived through the era of male technology. Modern information and communication technologies are no longer male oriented; they are woman friendly. There are still no (or few) gendered stereotypes in an information society. More to it, there is sociological evidence that men tend to be fanatic with this technology while women are very functional. The majority of teleworkers are women. The economic efficiency of many types of information activities has not yet become gendered. Cultural norms and values are being destabilized. Deconstruction of the former norms and values is taking place now. That leaves women no excuse to say it is a male culture and provides a lot of opportunities for catching up.

4. It has often been said that gender problems are not only economic, but are also cultural, and I think we should not separate them. Very often it is even difficult to do so.

The cultural factor of economic development has been introduced by the head of French sociology, Pierre Bourdieu. I would like to stress that the role of this factor is growing for developing and transitional economies, giving different perspectives to well-known things. We are discussing development economics here and the very concept of development may be different in different cultures.

According to the neoclassical theory of development, development is achieved if government policy is directed by two basic principles:

1. the maintenance of a stable macroeconomic and political environment;
2. the strict following of market principles, and non-interference of the state.

Such a concept of development is considered as cultural violence against socially vulnerable groups of population in eastern and south-eastern Asia. The experience of the 4 Tigers shows that they followed the first principle but reformulated the second: cooperation of the state and market, state decisions on big private investments, and social infrastructure development. Their approach was sociological and not purely economical.

The division of labour by gender is not universal. For instance, feminized branches of economy are different in Eastern and Western countries.

Still another to a great extent cultural problem is that of the motives for economic activity. Personal benefit is not the only drive for the economic activity. The Bible says there are three motives of human activity: retribution, fright, and love. God help us! We have almost forgotten that fright is a powerful driving force. But altruism as a form of love is a strong and not-accounted-for motive of economic development.

5. The fifth question I'd like to raise is not so much a question as a proposition—to use the 'wave' of sustainable development movement to promote gender-oriented reconsideration of the concept of economic efficiency.

We know that the position of women has been acknowledged as a problem within the discourse of sustainable development, to my knowledge rather theoretically .

Though one of the latest programme books on sustainable development, *Financing Change*, issued by the World Business Council for Sustainable Development (Stephan Schmidheiny and Federico Zoraaquin) with a foreword by James Wolfensohn, does not raise this issue, the authors do brilliantly raise the necessity to reconsider the concept of efficiency when long-term instead of short-term effects will be socially awarded. And they plan to launch a worldwide campaign to that purpose. Preservation resources for the future cannot ignore social reproduction issues. Joint efforts can be taken.

A lot of gender-oriented research is being conducted, but a lot has still to be done. Quite a few problems need further consideration. Science is seeking universal global trends and only comparative research can give them to us.

The Global Financial Crisis

24

Financial Fragility, Crises, and the Stakes of Prudential Control

MICHEL AGLIETTA

I. THE CAUSES OF FINANCIAL FRAGILITY ARE NOT ONLY FOUND IN THE EMERGING MARKETS

During the last two decades, most countries progressing towards financial liberalization have been faced with a combination of banking crises and declining asset prices (property, equity, foreign currency). This phenomenon is so widespread that it can be assumed not to be circumstantial or transitional but to be tied to the intrinsic operation of the financial systems themselves. Crises seem to be part of the dynamism of finance when capital markets emerge. This assumption tends to be borne out by history, with its long list of known international financial crises.

The stakes are high given the efforts required to cope with the disruptions triggered by such crises. Assuming that they are inherent in the operation of liberalized financial systems, it is pointless to attempt their elimination except by restoring restrictions on capital movements, reintroducing strict separations between financial activities and credit restraints by commercial banks. The only reason crises can continue to erupt unexpectedly in the liberalized financial world and that no learning process exists to predict them is that they are rooted in the typical microeconomic behaviour occurring in such a financial environment, leaving nothing to predict.

Financial crises are due to the uncertainty on the macroeconomic impact of the inter-dependencies between capital markets participants. This makes it pointless to attempt their elimination by developing indicators designed to predict their occurrence, since no such indicators can predict the timing of a crisis. Faced with financial crises, the prudential focus should be on precaution instead of prevision.

This outlook is supported by an overall view of financial globalization—that is, the combination of liberalization of financial systems and their integration, which can be considered a systemic innovation.

Financial globalization is a systemic innovation

Financial globalization modifies the behaviour of all economic agents, whether financial professionals or not. It weakens previously regulated financial systems.

In order to understand the meaning of this innovation, it is necessary to accept the idea that this is nothing less than a change in the concept of finance. The major financing problem is the tension between the need of economic agents to have the liquidity necessary for payments and the need for long-term capital in order to create value. Financial systems are organized to overcome this tension. But they can do so only by applying two fundamental principles.

The first is the *principle of intermediation*. Liquid investments are converted into fixed assets by financial institutions—that is, either banks or institutions connected with banks. According to this principle, investors are rewarded with a low but stable yield. In return for low interest, savings are protected. This is achieved by insuring deposits and providing banks with privileged access to the lender of last resort according to the principle of 'too big to fail'. Low interest on savings ensures low cost of capital despite intermediation margins charged by banks. Since such intermediaries carry loans to maturity, there are no secondary markets. Assets are valued according to traditional accounting standards. Banks manage their credit risk at a microeconomic level by monitoring debtors individually within the framework of close customer relations. Macroeconomic tensions are triggered by the inflationary impact of an uncontrolled increase in bank loans on the property market. In this financial rationale, the symptom of malfunctioning is the inflationary risk, not financial fragility. The central bank uses different methods to limit credit and counter this risk.

The second is the *principle of the secondary markets*. The secondary markets are used to increase the liquidity of property rights tied to fixed assets or claims on debt instruments issued on the primary markets. Whether the tension is felt, therefore, depends on the depth of these secondary markets and the size of the diversified portfolios held by institutional investors. These factors determine the liquidity of the markets. Financial systems geared to the second principle value assets and manage risk in an entirely different way from systems governed by the first principle.

In the second case, assets are marked-to-market. This means that their valuation changes continually, which leads to interdependence between credit risk and market risk stemming from the volatility of the asset values on the secondary markets. Debt contracts underpinned by negotiable securities are transaction based, effectively eliminating customer relations between lenders and borrowers. Lenders hold diversified portfolios of negotiable debt instruments. Evaluation of the market risk therefore becomes statistical, in line with the theory of optimum portfolio diversification. A new tool emerges to measure risk: value at Risk or VAR. The derivatives markets enjoy spectacular growth and become vitally important to manage risk and generate liquidity. They establish ties between capital markets with different maturities and risk classes (swaps); they modify risk profiles (options) and they foster very high leverage (OTC futures market). Market intermediaries (investment banks, large commercial banks, securities brokers) become important for regulation of liquidity on OTC derivatives markets. The derivatives markets carry the greatest weight in this structure, which grants high importance to off-balance-sheet positions, whose amounts and risks are frequently little known.

This form of market financing is rooted in a very different rationale from intermediation-based financing. The market is controlled by institutional investors who collect contractual savings. They seek optimum return/risk ratios for their portfolios. They engage in active asset/liability management strategies. They put strong pressure on borrowers to deliver the promised returns.

This change in logic brings about financial fragility

First of all, it is evidently difficult to learn the ropes of the new organizational structure. The systemic innovation reflected in the change in financial rationale creates serious disruptions in the financial community. The impact of these disruptions is proportional to the efficacy of the financial systems organized according to the old principle, based on intermediation by banks. This has happened not only on the emerging markets in Asia, but also in Japan, the Nordic countries, Southern Europe, and so on. All have gone through banking crises in the search for financial liberalization.

Deregulation is a discretionary government act. However, it takes a long time to modify the organization of financial institutions, governance of borrowers, risk control systems, performance criteria, and employee incentives and skills. But, while this behavioural transition has definitely aggravated the uncertainty surrounding the structural changes, it is not the key to the problem. The key lies in the financial fragility brought about by the liquidity supplied by the secondary markets. It is nourished by several factors.

The search for very high returns on savings brings about high interdependence between changes in the prices of financial assets and the leverage created by credit. The dynamic of asset prices itself is highly speculative, owing to competition between the fund managers and banks that regulate the derivatives markets. As more users buy contracts on these markets in order to model their risk profiles, market-makers tend to concentrate their risks. Such risks go out of control when unforeseen price movements on the underlying markets trigger transactions in the same direction as the derivatives markets.

In the presence of speculative forces, the liquidity of the secondary markets depends on the confidence of investors in their ability to liquidate their positions without loss and therefore on the ability of market-makers to act as counterparties for selling orders and their own capacity to find counterparties who wish to buy the risk of volatile asset prices. Their confidence is therefore part of the coordination of anticipation by market participants. It changes abruptly when doubt arises about the previously shared opinion. Because the market is liquid only if not all participants want to test it at the same time and because everyone will want to test it if they think the others will, liquidity evaporates as soon as everyone wants to convert their belief into reality. This is why the secondary markets are subject to an alternation of euphoric phases, during which the risk that liquidity may dry up is underestimated, and recession phases, during which traders want to withdraw at all costs from markets that they do not believe to be liquid.

When this change occurs, it triggers speculative attacks on markets where confidence has deteriorated. A sharp and unexpected decline in prices results in losses, as everyone wants to sell. As portfolios are diversified, losses on asset sales on a given market cross over to other markets, setting off chain sales. The correlation of risks rises rapidly between the attacked markets. Moreover, the flight to sufficiently deep markets brings about sudden withdrawals of capital and reallocations, in turn leading to concentration of previously diversified portfolios.

Financial fragility can, therefore, be defined as a combination of three crucial factors: underestimation of interdependent and endogenous risks, concern about liquidity precipitated by leverage, and the correlation of risks underlying contagion. Systemic risk lies in the latent interdependence of these three factors. The realization of the systemic risk as deterioration of confidence leads to a rush on cash in a given secondary market as a systemic event usually referred to as a financial crisis.

II. FINANCIAL CRISES HAVE DIFFERENT ORIGINS BUT ALL DESTROY LIQUIDITY

A financial crisis is always a cash crunch and always triggers a shift among multiple equilibria. Which aspect of the underlying fragility is involved and which markets are vulnerable differ from one crisis to the next. However, the processes set in motion by the response to lack of liquidity tend to be the same.

Crises as breakdowns of equilibrium

Crises spark changes in the prices of financial assets and in capital flows that are disproportional to previous changes in macroeconomic magnitudes (known as 'fundamentals'). Far from being a moving equilibrium or the downward turning point in a business cycle, a crisis is a leap between two discontinuous equilibria. Multiple equilibria must be able to exist before a financial crisis can take place. A crisis is a shift from a 'good' equilibrium supported by optimistic forecasts of financial asset prices to a 'bad' equilibrium where at least certain markets default and certain economies are depressed.

Contemporary financial crises can be divided into generations, depending on the financial system concerned, the nature of debtors, and foreign exchange regimes. These generations reflect the models proposed to demonstrate the existence of multiple equilibria as well as the determinants of vulnerability to deteriorating confidence.

In first-generation crises, debtors are sovereign and carry debt in foreign currency. The quality of debt depends on a country's ability to earn foreign currency, itself dependent on changes in identifiable macroeconomic variables known to all lenders: announced and expected public deficits, the growth rate of the money supply, inflation forecasts, deficits in the current account, and real exchange rate overvaluations. Vulnerability is *inter alia* brought about by the existence of a fixed or rigid foreign exchange system set up to attract foreign capital and the commitment of the authorities to this system. The potential existence of multiple equilibria is rooted in the tie between the foreign exchange system and debt in foreign currency. The robustness of the existing foreign exchange regime depends on the shadow flexible exchange rate, which makes the foreign debt sustainable in the long run. When this implicit exchange rate depreciates more than the rate supported by the government, the country becomes vulnerable to a balance of payments crisis. Concern about liquidity depends on the foreign exchange reserves available to pay short-term commitments in foreign currency. When speculators are convinced that reserves are almost exhausted and the exchange rate is therefore about to slump, the rush on the remaining currency reserves occurs early enough to dodge incurring losses. The sovereign debt crises of the 1980s have nevertheless clearly shown that this reasoning on the part of creditors is deceptive. For instance, banks were caught off foot when Mexico defaulted in August 1982. This kind of situation occurs because there is often uncertainty about the sovereign borrower's capacity to obtain new loans in order to restore reserves with the guarantee of the IMF or the policy loans of the G7.

Second-generation crises are referred to as self-fulfilling crises since the multiple equilibria are not determined by anticipation of a country's insolvency based on a common observation of deteriorating 'fundamental' variables. Equilibria are conjectural—that is, conditional upon the way in which expectations are coordinated. Examples are the French franc crisis in 1992 and 1993, and the HK dollar crisis in October 1997 and the spring of 1998. Participants on the foreign exchange market establish scenarios regarding conjectural multiple equilibria. Their raw material is the way speculators value the cost of defending the exchange rate against a speculative attack. Speculators may come to the conclusion that a speculative attack is plausible once they manage to convince each other that the cost of defending the exchange rate regime will be prohibitive in the case of an attack and that the authorities will prefer to go along with the change in the foreign exchange rate. In this type of crisis, the date and outcome of the attack are completely unknown. The crucial question in the advent of this type of crisis is how much liquidity the authorities whose currency is under attack will be able to amass. In this case, insolvency of the financial system is entirely due to the collapse of the exchange rate when speculation triumphs. There is no pre-existing insolvency.

History shows that third-generation crises are most frequent. Vulnerability to a liquidity crisis is a form of financial fragility connected with private debt. As we have seen, this fragility is more likely when the systemic innovation embodied by the emergence of market financing occurs before financial players have learned how to deal with the new organization. However, such crises are far from being limited to transition periods. They can be found throughout the entire forty years of the gold standard before the First World War. This is because this form of financial fragility cannot be detected by means of definite macroeconomic variables known to all. Taking the three determinants of financial fragility, the following can be said: underestimation of risk is due to the inability of counterparties to factor in externalities (moral hazard) linked to the credit risk fostered by the anonymous character of market debt. It is impossible to define excessive leverage beforehand. Correlations between risks are not visible before the crisis erupts. This leaves space for multiple conjectural equilibria, depending on the degree of financial fragility. In the case of international debt in foreign currency, an attack causing exchange rates to collapse makes debtors in foreign currency insolvent and confirms the expectation of financial fragility. Here, too, the liquidity crisis is unforeseeable and contagion is caused by deteriorating confidence in financial systems considered similar.

Contagion in the midst of crises

When a breakdown occurs on a secondary financial assets market (foreign exchange, stock market, property, government, or private-sector bonds) in any segment of a series of integrated markets, the liquidity crisis spreads through all markets. Shared by all participants, statistical risk evaluation methods give only one signal, 'Sell!'. This signal results from dynamic hedging when the potential decline in the net value of the portfolio exposed to the risk increases sharply as the volatility of certain asset classes soars. In this case, it will be necessary to sell assets that have become very risky and to focus on quality assets—that is, those that are least sensitive to the price restructuring resulting from the change in equilibrium. In other words, portfolios lose much of their diversity during crises. The extent to which the crisis spreads from the market where it started to other markets that have become similar depends on the rise of correlation between risks sparked by the shared increase in volatility. This means that an environment of distress sales will spread from one market to the next. The chain of panic sales and the downward spiral of prices combine to create a vicious circle. This can be called a *valuation crisis* in that speculators who are likely to buy assets at discount prices will be confused about the nature of the price decline, as they do not know whether the movement is temporary or a sudden shift to a new equilibrium. Hence they refuse to expose themselves in a buying rally. As a result, prices are driven down by a one-way selling pressure. This clearly indicates a lack of coordination in the markets.

The reason for such a market failure is the sudden and massive increase in the liquidity needs of traders with positions on markets where prices are declining and the inability of these markets to provide such liquidity. Liquidity needs are caused by margin calls on the derivatives markets and the withdrawal or non-renewal of credit lines granted by banks to investors wishing to trade in highly leveraged assets. Restricted credit combined with the declining value of collateral forms a vicious circle that makes it necessary to sell distressed assets on other markets, in turn aggravating the contagion. This may lead to the collapse of confidence in all asset markets except for the deepest government securities markets in the major Western countries, as occurred in September 1998 when the Russian government and banks defaulted on their debts. The extreme danger of an all-out flight to liquidity is sparked by risk premiums that spread like wildfire to all types of private debt. Without exception, economic agents with short-term debts or debts at variable rates who need to renew their loans are faced with the risk of bankruptcy because of the prohibitive cost of debt. If liabilities exceed assets, as happened in 1932 and 1933, they will need to sell everything that can be liquidated. In this case, deflation spreads to the property markets because of a surplus of second-hand goods (real property, industrial equipment). Because of the meltdown, money becomes an end in itself and sets off an economic depression.

III. WAYS AND MEANS TO REDUCE THE FRAGILITY OF THE FINANCIAL SYSTEMS

As we have seen, financial crises are unforeseeable and their social cost is very high if the monetary authorities adopt a passive attitude and allow contagion to spread. The systemic risk justifies public intervention in the financial systems as a precaution rather than in anticipation. Redundancy of measures is the best way to keep the destructive processes from spreading over the financial markets. This expedient needs to be of international scope and needs to be deployed in two directions. The first need is to reduce vulnerability to crises by subjecting the major market participants to much stricter prudential supervision than in the past. The second is to stifle nascent liquidity crises by obtaining assistance from the lender of last resort (LLR).

Reducing vulnerability to crises

Redundancy of measures is essential and must have a visible impact on the exposure of financial agents to market risk and on market operation in order to diminish financial fragility.

An effective long-term measure would be to make prudential supervision an integral part of the financial systems of the emerging markets, where it is almost non-existent, as has become abundantly obvious, or in any case highly insufficient compared with the needs created by growing financial liberalization. However, this type of measure should not be imposed by the IMF. This would first of all amount to intolerable interference with national sovereignty. Secondly, the IMF has no powers in the area of banking risks and no mandate to deal with private agents. The only conceivable method is to invite emerging market supervisors to participate in the work of the Basle Committee, which develops international prudential standards in continuous dialogue with the financial community. This solution would also make it necessary to grant membership in the Bank for International Settlements (BIS) to the central banks of interested emerging countries and to train the banking supervisors of these countries within this framework.

The most destructive financial fragility during the 1990s has been the tie between short-term debt in foreign currency and rigid foreign exchange regimes. This brings about excessive capital inflows attracted by temporarily high yield. This is the most fruitful soil for multiple equilibria and therefore a latent systemic risk. Exposure to risk can be reduced only by establishing controls on the inflow of foreign capital. Such controls may be flexible and modular, depending on the financial situation. They may take the form of mandatory reserves for foreign currency deposits at local banks and caps on business financing in foreign currency.

Rigid foreign exchange rates were clearly responsible for most of the recent crises (ERM, Mexico, Asia, Russia, Brazil). It has become necessary to develop more flexible exchange rate regimes—that is, flexible but managed by the government. An unannounced benchmark exchange rate that can change over time to preserve competitiveness and intervention methods negotiated with international banks in the form of contingent credit lines attached to debt in foreign currency. Such credit lines could be made mandatory by the governments of debtor countries as a prerequisite for the foreign currency loans wanted by local private borrowers. The advantage of such credit lines would be that they would implicitly tax capital inflows, since they would be expensive. As such credits would be used by solvent but illiquid borrowers, they would erect a first bulwark against the emergence of liquidity crises.

The most important—but least proposed—measure is to boost supervision of inter-national banks. These organizations have had overwhelming responsibility for the Asian crisis, even though this is never mentioned, since it is more convenient to assign the blame entirely to the borrowers. It has nevertheless become obvious that these banks (especially from Europe) committed themselves massively, often in the hidden form of off balance sheet derivatives and short-term loans and that their risk control systems entirely failed to predict the crisis. Tighter supervision is therefore amply justified. This applies to the club of supervisors of major Western countries who are supposed to coop-erate in the Basle Committee. The necessary measures are well known. Their adoption is merely a matter of shared political will. It is necessary to bolster capital reserves for portfolios with volatile positions. It is necessary to boost information for supervisors on exposure to derivatives risks. It is necessary to make sure that internal risk management officers at banks systematically apply stress tests to extreme scenarios and factor in the results of such tests in risk pricing and credit limits. Lastly, it is above all necessary to apply early corrective measures to banks when supervisors detect abnormal risk expo-sure. This means that the supervisors themselves must have adequate expertise and be subject to performance obligations.

Reviewing the function of international lender of last resort

Financial globalization has highlighted the problem of the international lender of last resort, since it strengthens the role of the financial markets and increases debt in foreign currency. International credit is the preserve of private creditors and private debtors. This type of market financing is vulnerable to second- and third-generation crises, which are triggered by liquidity problems.

The official solution to improve crisis management, which turned out to be disastrous in Asia, is to continue extending the mechanism implemented in the 1980s to combat sovereign debt crises tied to traditional bank loans to public borrowers or secured by the government, as the private sector was subject to capital controls at the time. In the wake of these first-generation crises, where the financial fragility of private debtors was not in issue, the G7 governments assigned the IMF the task to defend the interests of creditor banks. The IMF helped solve the macroeconomic adjustment problems of debtor countries in order to ensure that bank loans remained performing loans. Not only was the problem of lender of last resort ignored; steadily rising IMF funding maximized the moral hazard of banks.

These sovereign debt crises did not raise problems with the LLR and were discon-nected from the fragility of financial globalization, which has to do with market dynamics. Globalization requires an LLR to restore confidence on the secondary markets. The LLR is an agent with the capacity to provide the market immediately with an amount of cash to ward off systemic risk. This amount is not predetermined but depends on the diagnosis of the likelihood of a systemic event, which is conceivable only if the LLR is at all times involved with the markets, as reflected in banking supervision and monetary policies. The LLR's aim is to contain the moral hazard. It does so in two ways. The first is to maintain constructive ambiguity about the occurrence of intervention in last resort. The other is to organize banking clubs in order to ensure that banks positioned on the crisis market contribute cash so as to involve participants in the rescue of their market. This line of defence is made possible by the authority of central banks over the commercial banks in their jurisdiction.

The principles of lending in last resort have been known for the last two centuries. They nevertheless had to be highlighted again, since they lead to the inescapable conclusion that *the IMF cannot be the lender of last resort on globalized markets.* Its Articles of Association and assignments, the political conditionality of its financings, its inability to create money instantly—indeed the very reason for its existence is to correct macroeconomic imbalances, not to preserve market liquidity.

This said, the international LLR cannot be an international institution since the LLR is a monetary function. Although the financial markets are integrated by foreign exchange, currencies remain separated. *It follows that the international LLR can be a contingent cooperation network only between central banks.* The BIS can provide this network with information about the consolidated positions of international banks and analysis of systemic risk to help establish diagnoses in emergencies. Moreover, the zones of influence of the dollar and soon the euro make the Federal Reserve and the ECB the foremost LLR in many market situations. These networks are highly centralized in each area of influence in the form of bilateral relations between the peripheral central banks and the central bank of the key currency in the area. Cooperation between the two major central banks will be the foremost tool to help combat crises with a global impact.

Comment on 'Financial Fragility, Crises, and the Stakes of Prudential Control' by Michel Aglietta

URI DADUSH

Michel Aglietta provides a *tour de force* of analysis and policy prescription relating to financial crises, all in a few pages. This is a 'big-picture' paper: stylized facts, broad analytical sweep, followed by a grand synopsis of the policy implications. It makes the argument while relying only on logical exposition, and assumes that the reader knows the facts, and the literature.

Aglietta begins with the observation that financial integration with world markets completely transforms a previously closed financial system. While closed financial systems are dominated by bank intermediaries and are characterized by underdeveloped secondary markets for assets, global markets are dominated by large institutional investors operating primarily on well-developed secondary and derivatives markets. As a result, credit risks come to depend closely on the price of assets traded in secondary markets. For various other reasons well set out in the paper, this greatly increases volatility, and, since the volatility occurs within the context of a severely undeveloped institutional framework, the risk of systemic distress increases manifold. Hence, financial crises are endemic in these recently liberalized financial systems.

Some central policy messages emerge. The market imperfections that account for the high incidence of crises are very serious, creating a broad scope for public interventions. The scope of these interventions is likely to be international—that is, to require cross-country coordination. For example, regulation of financial institutions needs to be much tighter, especially in the emerging markets, but also in creditor countries. The function of international lender of last resort (ILLR) becomes even more critical. However, Aglietta argues, the IMF as currently configured is ill suited to play such a role. In particular, its command on resources is inadequate for the task.

I agree with the thrust of the paper. In recent reports on the crisis (World Bank 1998, 1999a, b), we struck a similar note. At the World Bank we have inadvertently tended to underplay the risks but hail the benefits of developing countries' international financial integration. Like many others, we failed to see the crisis in Asia coming, and we were unprepared to deal with it.

Let me now highlight some differences in emphasis on some of the major issues raised in the paper. These differences have policy implications.

I. WHAT MAKES DEVELOPING COUNTRIES DIFFERENT?

Aglietta describes three generations of crisis: sovereign debt crises, traditional currency crises, and financial crises originating in the private sector, but draws no distinction in the way that they affect developing and industrial countries. In fact, one can think of many examples of second- and third-generation crises that occurred in industrial countries. Yet, it is striking how much more severe and frequent these episodes have been in developing countries, even though both industrial and developing countries have been engaged in financial and capital account liberalization in the post-war period. To be sure, a major financial crisis rages in Japan—a country where the rise to developed country status has been achieved at a record pace, while its financial system remained retrograde in many respects. But, even after seven years of low growth and rising share of bad loans throughout the banking system, Japan's prime credit rating remains virtually untouched, its policy interest rates have come down to be the lowest in the world, and its currency remains strong.

In contrast, financial crises in developing countries have been devastating. In the developing countries in crisis, 1998 saw current account swings of 8 percent of GDP or more; in Korea and Thailand, the swing was more than 15 percent of GDP, implying a dramatic contraction in domestic demand. Real interest rates exceeded 20 percent of cases for extended periods. In those two countries, GDP growth swung from positive 6–7 percent to negative 8–10 percent between 1997 and 1998.[1] While financial contagion affected nearly all developing countries, the industrial countries, with the possible exception of Japan, have suffered only limited spillover effects. In part, this reflects the fact that this crisis was (as happened in the early 1980s) accompanied by a shift of the terms of trade in favor of the industrial countries, as well as a redirection of the flow of capital to them. One result was the fall in long-term interest rates at the core while they soared in the developing periphery.

The crucial question—not adequately addressed in the paper—is: 'What sets developing countries apart?' The author mentions their weak financial regulation. Yet the problems inherent in managing financial integration in developing countries run much deeper. I would underline three. First, developing countries have low credit ratings, and historically exhibit much higher volatility of capital flows and spreads than do industrial countries. The status of developing countries as marginal borrowers implies that adverse shocks lead to a perceived increase in the probability that they will default, inducing capital to flow out at precisely the time they need it most. Now, one doesn't just 'snap out' of low credit ratings by passing laws on financial regulation. Credit ratings are

---

[1] During the first two years of the Great Depression of the 1930s, the USA and Germany saw declines in output comparable to those of the Asian crisis countries in 1998. But their per capita incomes then compared with those of modern-day Korea, and were only about 50% higher than those of the middle-income developing countries today (Brazil). In some ways, today's Korea and Brazil parallel the USA and Germany of the 1930s. In the latter countries, the Great Depression provided the impetus for the institution of banking regulations, the set-up of the Federal Reserve System and the Federal Deposit Insurance Corporation, the introduction of unemployment and national retirement benefits, as well as the adoption of counter-cyclical macroeconomic policies, including infrastructure projects (and rearmament!). These policies and institutions provide protection against financial crises in industrial countries. Some of these reforms are being introduced or more widely extended in Asian countries in the wake of the recent crisis.

statistically associated with per capita incomes, sound macroeconomic policies, institutional quality, and the stability of macroeconomic aggregates. Rich countries have AAA or AA ratings, while very few poor countries achieve investment grade (BBB–). Secondly, in the event of an adverse shock, most developing countries find it impossible to engage in counter-cyclical fiscal and monetary policies. The cyclicality of their revenues, initial high debt levels, and the fear of capital flight deter them. Thirdly, even in the richer developing regions, such as Latin America, over 36 percent of the population lives on less than $2 a day. Such widespread poverty implies that the room to absorb shocks is limited, and social safety nets are absent to a large extent because they are unaffordable.

These basic differences in the extent to which industrial and developing countries are subject to volatility, and in their ability to alleviate adverse shocks, imply that measures to forestall crises take on great importance in developing countries, and they entail more than Aglietta's prescription of better financial regulation and a stronger lender of last resort. A broad effort is required to strengthen the fiscal position, to bring down the debt burden to manageable levels, to make exchange rate and macroeconomic policies consistent, to strengthen financial and legal institutions, including corporate governance, bankruptcy codes, and practices, and to create adequate safety nets. This long list is, unfortunately, not too different from a checklist for successful development, and development takes time. No wonder then that the consensus in favor of rapid capital account liberalization has been turned on its head since the crisis began. And no wonder that many are skeptical about the likely effects of reform of the international financial architecture on reducing volatility except in the very long term.

II. THE TYPE OF CAPITAL FLOW MATTERS

In Aglietta's paper, three elements are said to combine to cause financial fragility: underestimation of risks that are interdependent, high leverage, and the tendency towards contagion. But are all capital flows alike in their potential to cause instability according to these criteria? The answer is clearly no, yet the paper is largely silent on this question that is so crucial for policy.

Our own analysis of what happened in the most recent crisis has led us to identify short-term bank debt in foreign currency as the central cause of financial fragility in Asia. For example, the turnaround in this type of flow in Thailand in the twelve months following the devaluation represented about 20 percent of GDP. Using Aglietta's three criteria, foreign banks systematically underestimated the risk, in part encouraged by high interest rates combined with a perceived currency guarantee; they were by their nature very highly leveraged; and, since they operated in similar fashion throughout much of Asia, the contagion effects were enormous.

Foreign direct investment, on the other hand, was resilient in all the crisis countries except Indonesia, as it had been in Mexico in 1995. Indeed it rose in Thailand and Korea in the wake of the crisis, as companies sought to take advantage of lower production costs and the opportunity to make strategic investments at a favorable price. Applying

Aglietta's three criteria, to a large extent corporations risk the money of their share-holders, and their leverage is much lower than that of banks. Perhaps for that reason they appear to be more careful in evaluating investments than banks in Asia evaluating loans. These corporations operate in highly differentiated markets where they take a long-term view, so contagion is less likely to affect their decisions

In general, discussion of policies designed to derive the benefits of financial integration while minimizing the risks must differentiate between types of flows. FDI constituted the largest source of capital flows to developing countries even before the outbreak of the crisis, and significant FDI flows (expressed as a share of GDP) reach a very wide set of developing countries, including some very poor ones. Recent research suggests that FDI is statistically much more closely associated with an increase in domestic investment than is financial capital inflow (Bosworth and Collins 1999).

III. RETHINKING THE INTERNATIONAL LENDER OF LAST RESORT

Before concluding, I would also like to comment on Aglietta's discussion of the lender of last resort (LLR). I think a prerequisite for that role to be carried out effectively is clarity of objectives, which in this case should give overwhelming weight to limiting systemic risk at the global level. Yet the international financial institutions, including the IMF, are increasingly engaged in an enormous range of activities, from macroeconomic stabilization to poverty reduction.

There is an inevitable trade-off inherent in financial rescue—that is, that between increased systemic risk and, on the other hand, paying out taxpayer money and inducing moral hazard. When neither the markets nor the IFIs themselves can tell whether a particular program is a loan to strengthen the financial system, or to fight poverty, or to forestall a crisis in international relations, or a precaution, or an outright rescue, the moral hazard and the potential for conflict of interest increase exponentially. One result is excessive lending, combined with added confusion, and ultimately volatility in the markets.

I doubt whether Aglietta's suggestion that the Federal Reserve and the ECB should work in tandem to conduct international rescue provides a better alternative than the current unsatisfactory arrangements, since each of these institutions has other, and less than 'global systemic' objectives. Everyone can agree, however, that major change is needed, even if there is no agreement yet on the blueprint.

Despite these differences in emphasis, Aglietta's thrust is correct. His paper contains many insights that should stimulate further research in a vital field.

REFERENCES

Bosworth, B. P., and Collins, S. M. (1999), 'Capital Flows to Developing Economies: Implications for Savings and Investment', *Brookings Papers on Economic Activity*, 1: 143–69.

World Bank (1998), *Global Development Finance 1998* (Washington: World Bank).
—— (1999a), *Global Development Finance 1999* (Washington: World Bank).
—— (1999b), *Global Economic Prospects and the Developing Countries 1998/99: Beyond Financial Crisis* (Washington: World Bank).

Capital Flows and Development

25

Growth and External Debt: A New Perspective on the African and Latin American Tragedies

DANIEL COHEN

This paper addresses two puzzles of the growth literature—namely, the failure of standard growth equation to account for Latin American and African slow growth; and the surprising failure of trade to explain growth whereas 'trade liberalization' appears to play a significant role. The paper shows (1) that African growth is readily explained by macro-economic mismanagement and low investment; (2) that 'trade liberalization' should be taken as a proxy of such 'macroeconomic' good management rather than a genuine measure of the effect of trade upon growth, and (3) that Latin American poor growth (which does not appear to be accounted by any of the preceding feature) is well explained by a variable (constructed in the text) that represents the likelihood of debt crisis.

I. INTRODUCTION

Growth specialists have long had difficulties pinning down the causes of two mysteries, two 'tragedies' in the words of Easterly and Levine (1997): the poor growth of Africa and Latin America. According to early estimates such as those performed by Barro (1991), each of these continents is growing—*ceteris paribus*—at a lower yearly rate of about 1.3–1.5 percent. Recent endeavors to analyze the origin of these discrepancies had some success in explaining African tragedy. Easterly and Levine make use of the 'ethnic' diversity of Africa as an argument for understanding why the nations of this continent could not agree upon an efficient set of institutions fostering growth. Sachs and Warner (1996) construct a variable measuring the degree of 'trade liberalization' explaining the reasons why African economies failed to build upon the wealth of the world for catching up the other nations.

As I will review in this paper, the problem with these interpretations is that they leave intact the Latin American tragedy. Accounting for ethnic dimensions or trade liber-

The paper was written while the author was visiting the Debt Division of the World Bank. He thanks Fred Kilby for comments, Bill Easterly for his help with the data, and Karine Jacques–Antoine and Thomas Jung for great research assistance. The views expressed in this paper do not necessarily represent those of the World Bank.

alization always leaves Latin America's growth rate 1.5 percent behind the performance of other countries. Another difficulty arises when dealing with 'trade liberalization'. When controlling directly for the degree of openness itself, conventionally measured by trade over GDP, one finds that such ratio appears to play no role in explaining growth (when account is taken of investment). One answer to this puzzle may be that openness is a poor indicator of what it is supposed to measure—namely, the ability of a given country to import the goods that it needs. Typically, a large country will always appear to be less open than a small one. The surprising feature that we shall document in the paper is the following: when openness is corrected by size, the corresponding measure appears to be *negatively* correlated with growth. Splitting the sample in two (those that liberalized trade and the others), we find that trade *hurts* the countries that did not liberalize, but does nothing to those that did. 'Trade liberalization' appears to be a means to dampen the harmful effects of trade upon protected countries, rather than a means to raise growth in the open economies. The question then becomes: through which channel is it that trade hurts the protected economies, rather than: through which channel is it that trade fosters growth opportunity?

The answer that I will offer is twofold. For one thing, exchange rate mismanagement is one key avenue through which trade hurts protected economies. When the exchange rate is overvalued, the more open the economy, the worse is its growth performance. The second dimension has to do with the debt crisis. Being subject to the risk of a debt crisis has been a long-time feature of Latin American economies. Surely, a closed economy should not risk much by threatening to default. But, along with exchange rate mismanagement, external debt mismanagement hurts countries that are open to trade.

Such is the avenue that, we shall argue, helps explain the two underlying mysteries that we outlined: the Latin American and the trade puzzle. When the risk of a debt crisis, and the exchange rate mismanagement (weighted by trade), are taken into account, these two puzzles are settled.

II. GROWTH AND MISMANAGEMENT

We take as a starting point the analysis that has been performed by Easterly and Levine for understanding what they call the 'African tragedy'. First consider a framework, *à la* Barro, in which growth is written as a function of the log of initial income, LRGDP, squared of Log of initial income, LRGDPSQ, schooling (LSCHOOL measured by *Log* (1 + number of years of schooling of the population)), population growth (measured by LPOP = *Log* (0.05 + n) as in Mankiw, Romer and Weil (1990), where n *is* population growth) and two continental dummies for Africa and Latin America and the Caribbean. This produces the results that are displayed in Equation 1.1 (see Table 1), in which we focus on the 1970s and the 1980s (similar results are obtained when including the 1960s). All variables are highly significant (except LPOP, which is only significant at the 10 percent confidence level). In particular, one sees that both continental dummies are significant and that their point estimate is large. According to Equation 1.1, Africa experiences a 1.3 percent growth discrepancy to the other countries, while Latin America and the Caribbean experience an even larger shortfall of 1.6 percent.

One variable that is missing from the Easterly–Levine framework is the investment ratio, while it is critical to the analysis in Mankiw, Romer, and Weil, which reinterprets growth equation as a linearized version of the Solow model. When account is taken of the *Log* of investment (variable *LINV*), the African dummy is marginally reduced to 1.1 percent (and remains significant) while the Latin American dummy is increased to 1.9 percent.

By taking account of terms of trade fluctuation (TOT), one manages to reduce further the African dummy to a point estimate of 0.9 percent, and to have its significance fall below the 5 percent degree of confidence. These results are maintained when instrumenting investment (by openness, relative price of investment, and income) (see Equation 1.5, in which LINV2 is the instrumented value), which shows that the endogeneity of investment does not seem to be a problem here.

A number of other variables are added to the regression, which encompass various channels through which the economy might be either distorted or perturbed. These variables are:

Table 1. *Determinants of growth*

Variables	Equation 1.1	Equation 1.2	Equation 1.3	Equation 1.4	Equation 1.5
C	0.080	−0.28	−0.34	−0.43	−0.38
	(2.26)	(−2.43)	(−2.80)	(−3.39)	(−2.94)
DUM80	−0.015	−0.015	−0.013	−0.017	−0.013
	(4.71)	(−4.65)	(4.08)	(−5.26)	(−3.97)
AFRICA	−0.012	−0.011	$-0.87.10^{-2}$	−0.013	$-0.87.10^{-2}$
	(−2.59)	(−2.24)	(−1.68)	(−2.62)	(−1.51)
LATINCA	−0.015	−0.019	−0.019	−0.023	−0021
	−3.85)	(−4.72)	(−4.62)	(−5.55)	(−4.97)
LRGDP	$-0.40.10^{-2}$	0.083	$0.093.10^{-2}$	0.10	0.11
	(−1.25)	(3.09)	(3.37)	(3.78)	(3.72)
LRGDPSQ		$-0.57.10^{-2}$	$-0.64.10^{-2}$	$-0.74.-10^{-2}$	$-0.75.10^{-2}$
		(−3.26)	(−3.57)	(−3.89)	(−4.02)
LSCHOOL	$-0.33.10^{-3}$	$0.29.10^{-2}$	$0.56.10^{-2}$	0.015	0.010
	(−0.062)	(0.58)	(1.03)	(2.81)	(1.85)
LPOP	$-0.62.10^{-2}$	−0.019	−0.023	−0.016	−0.019
	(−0.44)	(−1.33)	(−1.59)	(−1.01)	(−1.28)
LINV	0.017	0.017	0.016		
	(5.05)	(4.93)	(4.51)		
LINV2					0.016
					(2.54)
TOT			0.10	0.12	0.11
			(2.48)	(2.81)	(2.60)
Adj.R²	0.39	0.48	0.44	0.37	0.40

Note: t statistic in parentheses.

Daniel Cohen

- the financial deepness of the economy, LLY (total domestic debt to GDP);
- the black market discount, BLCK;
- the government surplus, SURP.

As one can read from Table 2, these three variables add power to the regression, either when investment is not introduced (Equation 2.1) or introduced (Equation 2.2) or instrumented (Equation 2.3). When investment is introduced in the regression or instrumented, the African dummy falls to –0.5 percent, and loses significance even to the

Table 2.

Variables	Equation 2.1	Equation 2.2	Equation 2.3	Equation 2.4	Equation 2.5	Equation 2.6
C	−0.35	−0.32	−0.3	−0.22	−0.24	−018
	(−2.48)	(−2.43)	(−2.13)	(−1.57)	(−1.77)	(−1.23)
DUM80	−0.014	−0.010	−0.012	−0.014	−0.010	−0.012
	(−4.14)	(−3.17)	(−3.42)	(−4.07)	(−3.21)	(−3.45)
AFRICA	−0.011	$-0.53.10^{-2}$	$-0.52.10^{-2}$	$-0.9.10^{-2}$	$-0.21.10^{-2}$	$-0.3.10^{-2}$
	(−2.10)	(0.97)	(−0.84)	(−1.59)	(−0.34)	(−0.46)
LATINCA	−0.016	−0.013	−0.014	−0.019	−0.015	−0.017
	(−3.52)	(−3.03)	(−3.13)	(−4.23)	(−3.41)	(−3.84)
LRGDP	0.098	0.093	0.098	0.076	0.080	0.075
	(3.06)	(3.10)	(3.06)	(2.37)	(2.63)	(2.33)
LRGDPSQ	$-0.69.10^{-2}$	$-0.67.10^{-2}$	$-0.72.10^{-2}$	$-0.58.10^{-2}$	$-0.60.10^{-2}$	$-0.59.10^{-2}$
	(−3.34)	(−3.44)	(−3.47)	(−2.77)	(−3.04)	(−2.85)
LSCHOOL	$0.96.10^{-2}$	$0.81.10^{-2}$	$0.90.10^{-2}$	0.011	$0.35.10^{-2}$	0.011
	(1.68)	(1.42)	(1.50)	(2.02)	(6.16)	(1.96)
LPOP	−0.011	−0.025	−0.010	$-0.37.10^{-2}$	−0.017	$0.28.10^{-2}$
	(−0.71)	(−1.62)	(−0.67)	(−0.23)	(−1.11)	(−0.17)
LINV		0.016			0.015	
		(4.40)			(3.79)	
LINV2			0.016			0.013
			(2.18)			(2.02)
TOT	0.063	0.045	0.058	0.056	0.043	0.051
	(1.43)	(1.12)	(1.34)	(1.31)	(1.06)	(1.22)
LLY	0.024	0.016	0.016	0.020	0.014	0.012
	(3.31)	(2.29)	(2.08)	(2.83)	(2.05)	(1.64)
SURP	0.14	0.14	0.11	0.13	0.13	0.10
	(3.88)	(4.20)	(3.11)	(3.77)	(3.88)	(2.88)
BLCK	−0.018	−0.015	−0.020	−0.019	−0.016	−0.021
	(−3.30)	(−2.93)	(−3.55)	(−3.56)	(−3.26)	(−3.74)
ETHNIC				−0.021	−0.017	−0.023
				(−2.77)	(−2.31)	(−2.96)
Adj.R^2	0.49	0.56	0.51	0.53	0.58	0.54

Note: t statistic in parentheses.

10 percent confidence level. In all instances, however, the Latin American dummy is unchanged to about –1.4 percent, and remains highly significant.

In order to account for the ' African tragedy', Easterly and Levine have introduced a new variable, ETHNIC, which measures the ethnic diversity of any given country. The idea behind this variable is that ethnically diverse countries find it more difficult to agree upon an efficient government and the means to foster growth. Adding the ETHNIC variable to the other regressors raises further the quality of the fit and lowers the value of the African dummy. Even when investment is not taken into account, the African dummy falls to 1 percent and is significant only at the 10 percent degree of confidence. When investment is taken into account (or instrumented), the African dummy becomes negligible at –0.2 percent and loses all significance.

At this stage, one then sees that the 'African tragedy' can be explained by taking account of the low African investment rate, its mismanagement of the economy and its ethnic diversity (which proxies other channels through which the economy might be distorted). More work is needed to understand Africa's low investment, but we certainly gained something in understanding that this is one of the critical variables through which low growth is explained.

As already pointed out in Fischer (1993), domestic macroeconomic mismanagement stands as the other key variable that explains the poor performance of African countries. In none of these exercises, however, do we explain the 'Latin American tragedy'. When all the variables suggested by Easterly and Levine are taken into account, as well as the investment ratio, the Latin American dummy remains at –1.5 percent.

III. GROWTH AND OPENNESS

Sachs and Warner have suggested another avenue through which growth might be affected: the degree of trade liberalization of a country. They construct a new variable, which we call OPEN, which takes 1 if the country has 'liberalized' trade in 1970 and zero otherwise. Table 3 reports the results that are obtained when this variable is introduced on top of the key Mankiw *et al.* variables. As one sees from Equation 3.2, it is highly significant. It does some good to the Latin American dummy, which falls to –1.2 percent, although the variable remains highly significant. When all previous variables drawn from the 'African tragedy' paper are included (see Equation 3.3), the African dummy falls to zero, but the Latin American dummy gets back to the 1.5 percent value that it reached in Table 2. Meanwhile, however, schooling becomes insignificant and wrongly signed. When insignificant variables are dropped out (see Equation 3.4), the African dummy is worth –0.8 percent and the Latin American dummy is at –1.5 percent so that, at the end, not much is gained with respect to the previous section.

Let us comment further on the significance of the OPEN variable. One surprising feature of the result that is achieved by accounting for this variable is the corresponding failure to obtain significant results for the degree of openness itself. One potential reason for this discrepancy may be due to the fact that the degree of openness conventionally measured (through ½(import + export)/GDP)) does not appropriately measure what it

Table 3.

Variables	Equation 3.1	Equation 3.2	Equation 3.3	Equation 3.4	Equation 3.5
C	-0.34	-0.23	-0.18	-0.025	-0.016
	(-2.80)	(-1.93)	(1.27)	(-0.27)	(-1.06)
DUM80	-0.013	-0.012	-0.010	-0.011	-0.013
	(-2.91)	(-3.89)	(-2.98)	(-3.69)	(-3.93)
AFRICA	$-0.87.10^{-2}$	$-0.67.10^{-2}$	$-0.13.10^{-2}$	$-0.81.10^{-2}$	$-0.79.10^{-2}$
	(-1.68)	(-1.35)	(0.22)	(-1.62)	(-1.35)
LATINCA	-0.019	-0.012	-0.013	-0.013	-0.015
	(-4.62)	(-3.05)	(-2.84)	(3.17)	(-3.43)
LRGDP	0.092	0.081	0.069	0.0364	0.065
	(3.37)	(3.03)	(2.22)	(1.54)	(2.01)
LRGDPSQ	$-0.64.10^{-2}$	$-0.56.10^{-2}$	$-0.50.10^{-2}$	$-0.32.10^{-2}$	$-0.48.10^{-2}$
	(-3.57)	(-3.17)	(-2.50)	(-2.11)	(-2.28)
LSCHOOL	$-0.56.10^{-2}$	$-0.52.10^{-3}$	$-0.25.10^{-2}$		$-0.42.10^{-2}$
	(1.03)	(0.098)	(-0.43)		(0.70)
LPOP	-0.23	$0.44.10^{-2}$	$-0.80.10^{-2}$		$0.80.10^{-2}$
	(-1.59)	(0.28)	(-0.47)		(0.46)
LINV	0.016	0.014	0.015	0.12	
	(4.51)	(3.87)	(3.64)	(3.4)	
TOT	0.10	0.08	0.027	0.52	0.035
	(2.5)	(2.1)	(0.68)	(1.57)	(0.84)
OPEN		0.018	0.012	0.015	0.015
		(4.16)	(2.64)	(3.65)	(3.17)
LLY			$-0.22.10^{-2}$		
			(0.26)		
SURP			0.096	0.065	0.10
			(2.84)	(-2.14)	(2.82)
BLCK			-0.017	-0.019	-0.018
			(-3.33)	(-4.02)	(-3.49)
ETHNIC			-0.014	-0.020	-0.017
			(-1.89)	(-3.43)	(-2.31)
Adj.R^2	0.44	0.49	0.63	0.56	0.59

Note: t statistic in parentheses.

is intended to capture—namely, the ability of a country to freely import those goods that it does not efficiently supply domestically. Typically, a large country will always appear to be less open than a small country, simply because it is able to supply domestically more of the goods that it needs.

In order to take account of such problem, we have regressed the degree of openness upon the inverse of the square root of population (the idea being that traders are on the borders of a circle of size πR^2 and of periphery $2\pi R$). The variable is highly significant (t statistic $+$ 10.6). We then extract from openness the correction brought by size, and take this new variable, called DOPN, as a proxy for the degree of 'true' openness of a country. The result is shown in Table 4, Equation 4.1. We find that our new variable DOPN is wrongly signed: being more open, *ceteris paribus*, lowers growth! How do we reconcile this finding with the role of the Sachs–Warner variable?

In order to shed light on this issue, let us interact these two variables DOPN and OPEN by constructing:

$$DOPSWO = DOPN * (1—OPEN)$$

$$DOPSW1 = DOPN * OPEN$$

The result is shown in Equation 4.2. It turns out that the significant variable that remains is DOPSWO, *with a negative sign.* In words: *it is those countries that have not liberalized their trade that suffer from trade openness.* The Sachs–Warner variable therefore appears to capture the harmful effects of distortion upon trade rather than the benefits of trade openness *per se.*

IV. THE RESCHEDULING VARIABLE

As a preliminary step towards explaining the effect of the debt crisis upon growth, we shall review in this section the indicators of the debt crisis. We started from the rescheduling data that have been produced by the World Debt Tables publication of the World Bank, and which exist for the 1970s and 1980s.

We constructed a variable RES, which is zero if the country never rescheduled and 1 if the country did reschedule (for each of the two subperiods the 1970s and the 1980s). From such variable, and as a manner of instrumenting it, we estimated a probit model in which the RES variable is regressed upon the beginning of period Debt-to-GDP Ratio (DEBT), the liquidity of the Economy (LLY), the Latin American dummy, and the Sachs–Warner variable OPEN. (Interestingly, the African dummy is not significant.) We took one model for the 1970s, and one for the 1980s. We call PRES the probability of a rescheduling, which has been computed through a probit model based upon the rescheduling that took place during the 1970s and the 1980s.

The results come as follows:

In the 1970s

$$PRES = c + 0.37 \, Latin \, America + 0.034 \, DEBT - 0.85 \, OPEN - 1.43 \, LLY$$

$$(1.0) \qquad\qquad (3.3) \qquad (-1.44) \qquad (-0.84)$$

Percentage of correct predictions: 0.81 (t statistic in parentheses).

In the 1980s

$$PRES = c + 1.83 \, Latin \, America + 0.04 \, DEBT - 2.06 \, OPEN - 4.22 \, LLY$$

$$(3.20) \qquad\qquad (3.2) \qquad (-2.54) \qquad (-3.0)$$

Percentage of correct predictions: 0.90 (t statistic in parentheses).

One sees, as should be expected, that the debt variable is highly significant, and—interestingly—that the point estimate of the coefficient is not significantly changed in the 1980s compared to the 1970s.

Table 4.

Variables	Equation 4.1	Equation 4.2	Equation 4.3
C	−0.16	−0.17	−0.15
	(−1.27)	(−1.35)	(−1.19)
DUM80	−0.012	−0.011	−0.012
	(−4.04)	(−3.65)	(−3.79)
AFRICA	$0.13.10^{-2}$	$0.43.10^{-2}$	$0.38.10^{-2}$
	(0.21)	(0.74)	(0.66)
LATINCA	−0.016	−0.017	−0.015
	(−3.57)	(−4.04)	(−3.58)
LRGDP	0.068	0.074	0.070
	(2.4)	(2.66)	(2.49)
LRGDPSQ	$-0.49.10^{-2}$	$-0.53.10^{-2}$	$-0.50.10^{-2}$
	(−2.61)	(−2.92)	(−2.74)
LSCHOOL	$0.66.10^{-2}$	$0.88.10^{-2}$	$0.77.10^{-2}$
	(1.21)	(1.68)	(1.42)
LPOP	$0.82.10^{-2}$	$0.86.10^{-2}$	0.013
	(0.52)	(0.57)	(0.81)
LINV	0.014	0.018	0.016
	(3.50)	(4.73)	(4.15)
TOT	0.099	0.12	0.11
	(2.51)	(3.13)	(2.87)
ETHNIC	−0.02	−0.019	−0.018
	(−2.92)	(−2.62)	(−2.64)
OPEN	0.017		$0.73.10^{-2}$
	(3.93)		(1.33)
DOPN	−0.012		
	(−1.60)		
DOPSWO		−0.062	−0.051
		(−4.70)	(−3.39)
DOPSW1		$0.12.10^{-2}$	$0.23.10^{-2}$
		(0.16)	(−0.28)
Adj.R²	0.55	0.57	0.57

Note: t statistic in parentheses.

   On the other hand, the other explanatory variables are only highly significant in the 1980s. The Latin American dummy is very significant in the 1980s, pointing to a regional factor that is well documented in the debt literature. Interestingly, the Sachs–Warner variable is also highly significant: those countries that have liberalized trade are also less likely to reschedule their debt (in the 1980s). It is not totally obvious to understand the channels for which this correlation stands, and to some extent it takes us back to the ambiguous status of this variable. It can be taken either as an indicator of 'good management' in general, or as an implicit measure of the signaling effects of trade liberalization upon the credit rating of a country.

V. BACK TO THE GROWTH EQUATION

Beyond the risk of a debt crisis, there is another avenue through which openness may hurt a country: the mismanagement of the exchange rate. The more distorted is the exchange rate, the more likely it is that import competition will hurt domestic producers. We shall then define an additional variable, OPB, the product of openness with black market premium. When interacted with the degree of openness, we find that the black market premium OPB is highly significant and dominates the standard black market premium. Furthermore, when splitting the sample of countries in two, those for which the Sachs–Warner variable is zero from those for which it is 1, one finds that it is only in the subgroup of countries that did not open to trade that the variable appears to play a role.

Putting all such variables together, we then get results that are displayed in Table 5. Both variables OPB (black market × openness) and PRES (probability of rescheduling) are highly significant variables. Conditioning upon these variables, the Sachs–Warner variable OPEN loses significance at the 5 percent degree of confidence (but it appears through its effect on rescheduling), and ETHNIC survives. When all these variables are taken into account, neither the Africa dummy (which is now positive and significant at the 10 percent degree of confidence!) nor the Latin American dummy (which is exactly nil) remains a problem. Interestingly, one also sees that the LLY variable becomes insignificant, which is an indication that its role in explaining growth also originates from its interaction with the debt crisis. The results are robust to instrumenting investment (Equation 5.4). The role of the debt crisis on growth comes on top of the role of debt on investment that I described in Cohen (1993).

As a test of the robustness of our variable PRES, we have proceeded to two exercises. First, we have split the sample of countries in two: those that did reschedule their debt and those that did not. We then tested in which of these two samples our PRES variable was significant. If PRES was a proxy for 'something else' such as mismanagement 'in general', we should expect it to be significant in both subsamples. If PRES was collinear to the rescheduling variable itself, so that a problem of reverse causality would really arise, we should expect it to be non-significant in the sample that did not reschedule. If, instead, we believe that PRES is really a proxy for the risk of debt crisis, then it should be significant only in the sample of countries that did not reschedule, because those are the ones for which the risk of a forthcoming crisis is still there. On the other hand, it should not be significant for the subgroup of countries that did reschedule and for which it has no more predictive power (the role of the debt crisis being encompassed in the constant). And this is indeed what we observe: the PRES variable comes out significant (with a t of 2.5) only in the subsample that did not reschedule.

As another test of the robustness of the PRES variable, we have discretized its value by constructing a variable DPRES50 that is worth 1 if the country experiences a probability larger than 50 percent to reschedule its debt, and zero otherwise. The result is shown in Equation 5.5, in which one sees that the Latin American dummy remains negligible (while the OPEN variable regains significance). Interestingly, one also sees that the introduction of the risk of a rescheduling into the equations also make the time dummy 1980

Table 5.

Variables	Equation 5.1	Equation 5.2	Equation 5.3	Equation 5.4	Equation 5.5
C	−0.24	−0.24	−0.19	−0.15	−0.21
	(−1.84)	(−1.87)	(−1.40)	(−1.04)	(−1.7)
DUM80	$-0.14.10^{-2}$	$-0.17.10^{-2}$	$-0.25.10^{-2}$	$-0.29.10^{-2}$	$-0.36.10^{-2}$
	(−0.36)	(−0.44)	(−0.64)	(−0.72)	(−1.06)
AFRICA	$0.85.10^{-2}$	$0.85.10^{-2}$	$0.73.10^{-2}$	$0.48.10^{-2}$	$0.01.10^{-2}$
	(1.44)	(1.45)	(1.23)	(0.77)	(1.6)
LATINCA	$0.11.10^{-3}$	$0.20.10^{-3}$	$0.13.10^{-4}$	$-0.48.10^{-2}$	$0.76.10^{-2}$
	(0.022)	(0.040)	$(0.26.10-2)$	(−0.93)	(0.17)
LRGDP	0.082	0.083	0.073	0.073	0.074
	(2.80)	(2.85)	(2.47)	(2.34)	(2.74)
LRGDPSQ	$-0.62.10^{-2}$	$-0.63.10^{-2}$	$-0.56.10^{-2}$	$-0.59.10^{-2}$	$-0.56.10^{-2}$
	(−3.25)	(−3.32)	(−2.87)	(−2.93)	(−3.11)
LSCHOOL	$-0.16.10^{-2}$	$-0.19.10^{-2}$	$0.29.10^{-4}$	$-0.64.10^{-2}$	$-0.13.10^{-2}$
	(0.27)	(0.33)	$(0.47.10-2)$	(1.05)	(−0.25)
LPOP	−0.020	−0.020	−0.012	$-0.69.10^{-2}$	$-0.11.10-2$
	(−1.33)	(−1.32)	(−0.72)	(−0.42)	(−0.72)
LINV	0.019	0.019	0.018		0.018
	(5.04)	(5.15)	(4.56)		(4.85)
TOT	0.045	0.046	0.037	0.051	0.026
	(1.21)	(1.23)	(0.97)	(1.28)	(0.74)
LLY	$0.2.10^{-2}$		−0.035		
	(−0.23)		(−0.41)		
SURP	0.052	0.055	0.043	0.069	0.030
	(1.37)	(1.48)	(1.13)	(1.75)	(0.94)
ETHNIC	−0.013	−0.013	−0.014	−0.018	$-0.98.10^{-2}$
	(−1.89)	(−1.89)	(−2.00)	(−2.47)	(−1.50)
OPB	−0.047	−0.047	−0.046	−0.041	−0.061
	(−2.72)	(−2.79)	(−2.70)	(−2.29)	(−4.64)
PRESS	−0.032	−0.031	−0.030	−0.031	
	(−4.44)	(−4.62)	(−4.01)	(−4.29)	
DPRES50					−0.02
					(−4.97)
OPEN			$-0.65.10^{-2}$		$-0.89.10^{-2}$
			(1.38)		(2.21)
LINV2				0.021	
				(3.40)	
Adj.R^2	0.64	0.64	0.64	0.58	0.70

Note: t statistic in parentheses.

insignificant, which is then an indication of the role of the debt crisis in explaining the poor performance of the 1980s.

Clearly, one needs to rely on further explanations to understand why it is that Latin America appears to be so highly vulnerable to a debt crisis. Other works exist (such as

Ozler 1993) that point to the role of history, and many others that describe the way a financial crisis is spread out to neighboring countries. But to repeat what we said on Africa's low investment: to the extent that we can rule out reverse causality (by taking the beginning of period variable for explaining PRES, and through the in-sample test of its predictive power among the countries that did not reschedule), we believe to have gained insights in identifying the channel through which the poor Latin American growth has to be explained.

VI. CONCLUSION

The literature on growth had, for a long time, some trouble understanding the reasons why Africa and Latin America were performing so poorly. Building upon two recent contributions by Easterly and Levine, and Sachs and Warner, our paper has attempted to shed some additional light on these issues.

Regarding Africa, first, we have shown that low investment, policy distortions, and terms of trade fluctuations turned out to be the key factors behind the slow growth of the continent. Both the Easterly–Levine and Sachs–Warner variables add significance to the equations but do not change much the point estimate of the African dummy. None of these variables, however, appears to be able to resolve the Latin American tragedy. Furthermore, the Sachs–Warner variable appears to contradict a surprising result according to which trade itself appears to be negatively correlated to growth.

We progressed in analyzing these questions by introducing two additional variables: black market premium interacted with degree of openness and probability of a debt crisis. When this is done, the negative effect of trade upon growth loses significance and so does the Latin American dummy. Economic mismanagements are the channels that appear to matter.

Appendix. A Framework of Analysis for Estimating Growth Equations

As an alternative way of evaluating the relative strength of domestic and external constraints, we have run an econometric evaluation of the impact of each of these constraints upon the growth of the developing nations.

We borrow here our framework from the analysis from Mankiw, Romer, and Weil (MRW) (see Cohen 1996, for further insights).

MRW writes output as:

(1) $Q = K^{\alpha}H^{\beta}(AL)^{\gamma}, \alpha + \beta + \gamma = 1$

in which K is physical capital, H is human capital, L is raw labor and A is worldwide technological progress. The law of motion of human and physical capital is then written:

$$\dot{K}_t = -dK_t + s_k Q_t$$

$$\dot{H}_t = -dH_t + s_h Q_t$$

so that, by log linearization, income per capita can be written:

$$y_T = a_T - a_0 + [1 - e^{-\lambda T}]\hat{y} + +e^{\lambda T} \cdot y_0$$

in which small letters are the logarithm of capital letters and in which

$$\lambda = (d + n + \mu)(1 - a - \beta)$$

and

$$\hat{y} = \frac{\alpha}{1 - \alpha - \beta} \operatorname{Log} s_k + \frac{\beta}{1 - \alpha - \beta} \operatorname{Log} s_h \frac{\alpha + \beta}{1 - \alpha - \beta} \operatorname{Log} (d + n + \mu).$$

In the sequel s_k is simply the investment-to-GDP ratio and s_h is the secondary school enrollment of children.

In the steady state, income per capita is then driven, up to a constant that is determined by world technology, to $\hat{y}$.

As an econometric strategy, we shall then rely upon the following specification:

$$g = a + b \operatorname{Log} (d + n + \mu) + c \operatorname{Log} s_k + d \operatorname{Log} s_h + ey_0 + time\ dummies + others$$

in which we take n to be population growth and let $d + \mu = 0.05$; $\operatorname{Log} s_k$ is the log of the investment rate; $\operatorname{Log} s_h$ is the log of the secondary school of enrollment of children, and y_0 is the beginning of period of the log of income per capita.

REFERENCES

Barro, R. (1991), 'Economic Growth in a Cross-Section of Countries', *Quarterly Journal of Economics*, 106/2: 407–43.

Cohen, D. (1991), *Private Lending to Sovereign States: A Theoretical Autopsy* (Cambridge, Mass.: MIT Press).

—— (1993), 'Low Investment and Large LDC Debt in the 1980s', *American Economic Review*, 8/3.

—— (1995), 'Large External Debt and Slow Domestic Growth', *Journal of Economic Dynamics and Control*, 19: 1141–63.

—— (1996), 'Tests of the Convergence Hypothesis: Some Further Results', *Journal of Economic Growth* (Sept.).

Easterly, W., and Levine, R. (1997), 'African Growth Tragedy: Policies and Ethnic Divisions', *Quarterly Journal of Economics*, 112/4 (Nov.).

Fischer, S. (1993), 'The Role of Macroeconomic Factors in Growth', *Journal of Monetary Economics*, 32: 485–512.

Husain, M., and Diwan, I. (1989), 'Dealing with the Debt Crisis' (Washington: World Bank).

Mankiw, G., Romer, D., and Weil, D. (1990), 'A Contribution to the Empirics of Economic Growth', *Quarterly Journal of Economics*.

Ozler, S. (1993), 'Have Commercial Banks Ignored History?', *American Economic Review*, 83/3: 608–20.

Sachs, J., and Warner, A. (1996), 'Economic Reform and the Process of Global Integration', *Brookings Papers on Economic Activity*, 1: 1–118.

World Debt Tables. 'External Debt of Developing Countries' (Washington: World Bank).

Comment on 'Growth and External Debt: A New Perspective on the African and Latin American Tragedies' by Daniel Cohen

TCHÉTCHÉ N'GUESSAN

Professor Cohen's paper is essential because of its scope and depth. In several respects, it enriches our understanding of the reasons for weak economic growth in Africa and Latin America. It offers a new approach to predict the risk of a debt crisis, which is one of the variables explaining the tragedies of Africa and Latin America. It shows that the debt/tax revenue ratio complements the debt/export sales and debt/GDP ratios, since it can be used to predict the risk of a debt crisis.

The author also demonstrates that the indicator used traditionally to measure liberalization of trade is inappropriate. The import + export/GDP ratio does not genuinely measure a country's economic liberalization, which is its free capacity to import needed goods that are not produced efficiently by local agents. To solve this problem, the author suggests a substitute indicator that takes into account the country's size.

Another important conclusion of this paper, written at a time of economic globalization, is that the variable of commercial liberalization does not offer a genuine explanation of economic growth.

I have decided not to discuss these aspects—which have helped in the advance of economic research—but to use the limited space and time at my disposal to focus on what I consider the central thesis of Professor Cohen's paper.

Like Easterly and Levine (1997), Professor Cohen maintains that the African tragedy—that is, weak economic growth—is due to ethnic diversity, bad management, and low investment.

This assumption covers three major issues of development economics that deserve to be discussed or to be examined at greater length:

- the reliability of economic growth indicators in Africa;
- ethnic diversity as an explanation of weak economic growth in Africa;
- bad management.

I. THE RELIABILITY OF ECONOMIC GROWTH INDICATORS IN AFRICA

Since the central thesis of Professor Cohen's paper is backed by econometric analysis, it is important to verify whether the explained variable is reliable (Devoize 1982; Hugon 1993). The aim is not to question the fact that average economic growth is weaker in Africa and Latin America than elsewhere, but to stress that the informal sector plays a significant role in Africa. In other words, such economic statistics as gross domestic product (GDP) and gross national product (GNP) do not always reflect actual economic growth. Unrecorded flows could, therefore, double the GDP of certain countries, as was the case with the Democratic Republic of Congo in 1990 (Hugon 1993).

II. ETHNIC DIVERSITY

The second theme to be reviewed is the issue of ethnic diversity and its role in slow economic growth in Africa.

Since Taylor and Hudson's research (1972), ethnic diversity has been considered the key variable underlying Africa's position at the bottom of the economic growth league tables.

Granted, ethnic problems exist in Africa. But I would be inclined to say that ethnic polarization is more likely to lead to ethnic problems than ethnic diversity.

In my opinion, ethnic diversity may even help a country without dominant ethnic group. This is why I believe that Easterly and Levine's thesis (1997), to which Professor Cohen's paper refers, is debatable.

Indeed, their thesis is refuted by the research conducted by D. Rodrik (1998), and by J. L. Arcand, P. Guillaumont, and S. Guillaumont (2000). D. Rodrik's research results show that ethnic diversity has a positive impact on economic growth.

The error—considering ethnic diversity as the variable behind weak economic growth in Africa—is no doubt due to the way the causal relation between ethnic diversity and bad economic management is envisaged.

Granted, a systemic relation can be contemplated, but, in my opinion, bad economic management is the main factor behind the conflicts resulting from ethnic diversity and even ethnic polarization, instead of the other way round.

Professor Cohen's insistence that ethnic diversity does not explain weak economic growth in Latin America is therefore not surprising.

III. BAD MANAGEMENT

Before looking at bad management in Africa and Latin America, we need to verify that it is an endogenous factor and that such exogenous factors as worsening terms of trade are not ignored. This said, bad management seems to me the key factor underlying the tragedies of Africa and Latin America.

All the same, bad management must first be defined. Does it refer to the nature of economic policy? Or both economic policy and the institutional framework?

These questions reflect general agreement on the existence of bad governance.

The key question is, therefore, to know how to achieve good governance in Africa and Latin America.

This question can be dealt with by reference to the proposals found in economic literature on good state governance and good corporate governance. State governance applies to the way in which a country's resources are managed for development purposes (N'Guessan 1996). Corporate governance concerns the 'organisation of power and its supervision in a corporation' (Duplat and Carton de Tournai 1998).

Bad governance explains low investment and especially bad investment, due mainly to the nature of the financial systems and corruption. The prevention of moral hazard, considered the key to the current international financial crisis, is also applicable to the African financial systems.

Another indicator of bad economic management chosen by Professor Cohen is misuse of exchange rates as an economic policy instrument. This remains a vital issue for the African countries in the franc zone, which have pegged their currencies to the euro. O. Davanne (1998) points out that there is a tendency to assume that, 'without the monetary union mechanism, a fixed exchange rate between two currencies is actually only desirable in the extreme case of hyperinflation in order to restore the credibility of a national currency rapidly'.

This is not the case with the African countries in the franc zone, showing that Professor Cohen was right to stress the importance of using the exchange rate judiciously as an economic growth instrument.

Lastly, Professor Cohen's paper focuses on the 1970s and the 1980s. It may therefore well be asked whether the international financial crisis dating from 1997, which differs from earlier crises, does not offer lessons capable of changing or enriching the interpretation of his results.

REFERENCES

Arcand, J. L. Guillaumont, P., and Guillaumont, S. (1999), 'How to Make a Tragedy: on the Alleged Effect of Ethnicity on Growth', *Journal of International Development*.

Davanne, O. (1998), 'Instabilité du système financier international' (Instability of the International Financial System). Documentation française.

Devoize, S. (1982), 'Des économies dualistes: Le Secteur informel' (Dual Economies: The Informal Sector), in *Comprendre l'économie africaine* (Paris: L'Harmattan).

Duplat, J. L., and Carton de Tournai, G. (1998), 'La Commission bancaire et financière et le corporate governance,' (The French Banking Commission and Corporate Governance), in *Corporate Governance* (De Boeck Université).

Easterly, W., and Levine, R. (1997), 'Africa's Growth Tragedy: Policies and Ethnic Division,' *Quarterly Journal of Economics*, 112/4 (Nov.).

Hugon, P. 1993, *L'Économie de l'Afrique* (The Economy of Africa) (La Découverte).

N'Guessan, T. (1996), *Gouvernance et politique monétaire* (Governance and Monetary Policy) (Paris: L'Harmattan).

Rodrik, D. (1998), 'Trade Policy and Economic Performance in Sub-Saharan Africa', NBER Working Paper, No. 6562.

Taylor, C., and Hudson, M. (1972), *World Handbook of Political and Social Indicators,* 2nd edn. (New Haven: Yale University Press).